# A GUIDE TO
# THE HISTORY OF
# ILLINOIS

**Recent Titles in**
**Reference Guides to State History and Research**
*Light T. Cummins and Glen Jeansonne, series editors*

A Guide to the History of Louisiana
*Light Townsend Cummins and Glen Jeansonne, editors*

A Guide to the History of Massachusetts
*Martin Kaufman, John W. Ifkovic, and Joseph Carvalho III, editors*

A Guide to the History of Texas
*Light Townsend Cummins and Alvin R. Bailey, Jr., editors*

A Guide to the History of California
*Doyce B. Nunis, Jr., and Gloria Ricci Lothrop, editors*

A Guide to the History of Florida
*Paul S. George, editor*

# A GUIDE TO THE HISTORY OF ILLINOIS

*Edited by* John Hoffmann

Reference Guides to State History and Research

Greenwood Press
New York • Westport, Connecticut • London

**Library of Congress Cataloging-in-Publication Data**

A Guide to the history of Illinois / edited by John Hoffmann.
     p.   cm.   —   (Reference guides to state history and research)
   ISBN 0–313–24110–4 (alk. paper)
   1. Illinois—History—Bibliography.      I. Hoffmann, John.
II. Series.
Z1277.G86 1991
[F541]
016.9773—dc20        90–36776

British Library Cataloguing in Publication Data is available.

Library of Congress Catalog Card Number: 90–36776
ISBN: 0–313–24110–4

First published in 1991

Greenwood Press, 88 Post Road West, Westport, CT 06881
An imprint of Greenwood Publishing Group, Inc.

Printed in the United States of America

The paper used in this book complies with the
Permanent Paper Standard issued by the National
Information Standards Organization (Z39.48–1984).

10 9 8 7 6 5 4 3 2 1

# CONTENTS

**Part Two: Archival and Manuscript Collections**

## PART ONE

---

# BIBLIOGRAPHICAL ESSAYS

# INTRODUCTION

IN *THE LITERATURE of American Local History: A Bibliographical Essay* (New York, 1846), Hermann E. Ludewig took only three pages to list the sources for Illinois. The Antiquarian and Historical Society of Illinois had foundered soon after its formation in 1827, and the first book-length history of the state had appeared only in 1844. Illinoisans, unlike New Englanders, were not a "documentary people."

During the second half of the nineteenth century, however, old settlers' associations, war veteran groups, and county historical societies proliferated, while county histories and atlases came into vogue. In 1889, the Illinois State Historical Library was established as a state-funded agency, independent from the state museum, and a decade later the Illinois State Historical Society was formed, becoming a department of the Historical Library in 1903. By 1905, the collection of Illinois materials in the library's rooms at the state capitol in Springfield was sufficient to support an eighty-page list of references, published in Jessie Palmer Weber, *An Outline for the Study of Illinois State History*. Although the early writings on Illinois history are yet to be assessed in a general account of the development of the field, the record of organizational activity is ably discussed in Robert W. Johannsen, "History on the Illinois Frontier: Early Efforts to Preserve the State's Past," *Journal of the Illinois State Historical Society*, 68 (Apr. 1975), and Roger D. Bridges, "The Origins and Early Years of the Illinois State Historical Society," ibid.

The only annotated bibliography for Illinois history as a whole began as a pamphlet compiled by Paul M. Angle, *Suggested Readings in Illinois History, with a Selected List of Historical Fiction*, issued by the Illinois State Historical Society in 1935. Angle and Richard L. Beyer expanded this work into "A Handbook of Illinois History," in the society's *Papers in Illinois History and Transactions for the Year 1941*, reprinted as *A Handbook of Illinois History: A Topical Survey with References for Teachers and Students* (Springfield, 1943). The *Handbook*, a useful but now dated guide to the field, is in a sense the precursor of the present work.

The following paragraphs cover in some measure both general works in Illinois history and specialized materials that cannot be accommodated in the historiographical chapters of this guide. The first category includes surveys, reference books, and periodicals, while the second ranges from local histories to studies of the medical and legal professions, to publications relating to maps and newspapers of Illinois. Here, as throughout the book, the coverage is selective and intended only to orient the reader to the vast bibliographical accumulation that is Illinois history.

Robert P. Howard, *Illinois: A History of the Prairie State* (Grand Rapids, 1972) is the most widely used introduction to the field. Satisfactory as a textbook, it also serves for reference and review purposes. Howard was the Springfield correspondent of the *Chicago Tribune*, covering state politics, and this background is reflected in the traditional framework of the book and its emphasis on political history. Drawn from secondary sources and unaffected by recent currents in American historiography, his work became the standard one-volume history of the state both on its own merits and because it lacks competitors.

Theodore Calvin Pease, *The Story of Illinois* (Chicago, 1925), although revised and expanded by the author in 1949 and by Marguerite Jenison Pease in 1965, provided a summary view for an earlier generation. The book's enduring interest may now lie in the elegant writing of its opening chapters. Richard J. Jensen, *Illinois: A Bicentennial History* (New York, 1978) briefly recasts the subject to fit the idea of modernization, a popular theory among recent American historians. For *Illinois: Its History and Legacy* (St. Louis, 1984), Roger D. Bridges and Rodney O. Davis obtained eighteen short articles on selected topics in the field. A number of these essays reappraise old subjects or explore new ones, but the book as a whole is only a supplement, not an alternative, to Howard's *Illinois*. Another essay, encapsulating the history of the state, is Cullom Davis, "Illinois: Crossroads and Cross Section," in James H. Madison, ed., *Heartland: Comparative Histories of the Midwestern States* (Bloomington, Ind., 1988).

Illinois historians have long been indebted to a multivolume history of the state, the Centennial History of Illinois. Issued by the Illinois Centennial Commission (Springfield, 1917–20) and reprinted commercially as a set (Chicago, 1922), this series includes an "Introductory Volume" by Solon Justus Buck, *Illinois in 1818*, and five chronological volumes: Clarence Walworth Alvord, *The*

*Illinois Country, 1673–1818*; Theodore Calvin Pease, *The Frontier State, 1818–1848*; Arthur Charles Cole, *The Era of the Civil War, 1848–1870*; Ernest Ludlow Bogart and Charles Manfred Thompson, *The Industrial State, 1870–1893*; and Bogart and John Mabry Mathews, *The Modern Commonwealth, 1893–1918*. The authors were associated with the University of Illinois, at least when the project began, and Alvord served as editor of the series. Although Bogart and his coauthors taught economics and political science, those responsible for the period to 1870 were professional historians, and it is their work especially that made the series a bellwether in the field. As late as 1987, the Illinois State Historical Society, using funds from the Illinois Sesquicentennial Commission, arranged for another printing, with new introductions, of the Alvord, Pease, and Cole volumes. However, the Sesquicentennial Commission did attempt to supersede the Centennial History for the period since 1865, sponsoring two important but very different volumes: John H. Keiser, *Building for the Centuries: Illinois, 1865 to 1898* (Urbana, 1977) and Donald F. Tingley, *The Structuring of a State: Illinois, 1899 to 1928* (Urbana, 1980).

Other publications of the sesquicentennial readily found a place among the reference books for Illinois history. John Clayton compiled *The Illinois Fact Book and Historical Almanac, 1673–1968* (Carbondale, 1970), a compendium of retrospective data and current information as of the 1960s. Densely packed with statistical tables, biographical notices, and chronologies of different subjects, and open to nongovernmental topics such as transportation and sports in the state, the *Illinois Fact Book* resembles the *Blue Book of the State of Illinois* in its attention to governmental agencies and its listings of public officials. The *Blue Book*, a responsibility of the Secretary of State since 1899, became a biennial publication in 1903. It followed a variety of private and public directories dating from the 1860s, a checklist of which appears in the *Blue Book* for 1943–44. The new series, known as the *Illinois Blue Book* since the 1951–52 edition, combines encyclopedic entries for state government, including the courts, General Assembly, and executive departments, with articles of current and historical interest on such matters as state parks, education, and the press in Illinois. Unfortunately, the 1931–32 *Blue Book* was the last edition to provide a cumulative index to the series.

The Sesquicentennial Commission sponsored not only the *Illinois Fact Book* but also *Illinois: Guide and Gazetteer*, written mainly by Hal Foust and Percy Wood and edited by Paul M. Angle (Chicago, 1969). The bulk of this reference book is devoted to descriptions of more than six hundred cities and towns, from Abingdon to Zion, with the coverage of Chicago divided into more than fifty topics. This gazetteer is preceded by a brief introduction and followed by a set of itineraries for fourteen tours around the state, making a three-part book not unlike its model in the American Guide Series, *Illinois: A Descriptive and Historical Guide*, compiled by the Federal Writers' Project of the Work Projects Administration (Chicago, 1939). That volume, in which the background and tour sections are no less important than entries for cities and towns, went through two revisions, edited by Harold L. Hitchins (Chicago, 1947) and Harry Hansen (New York, 1974), before it was reissued in its original form as *The WPA Guide to Illinois: The Federal Writers' Project Guide to 1930s Illinois* (New York, 1983). The new introduction to this last edition, by Neil Harris and Michael Conzen, is a splendid commentary on the book, an Illinois classic. Another important reference work, containing historical as well as statistical data, is the *Local Community Fact Book, Chicago Metropolitan Area, Based on the 1970 and 1980 Censuses* (Chicago, 1984), part of a series since the 1930 census.

Finally, the sesquicentennial of statehood was the occasion for a selection of writings about Illinois, *Prairie State: Impressions of Illinois, 1673–1967, by Travelers and Other Observers*, compiled by Paul M. Angle (Chicago, 1968). Another anthology, including both primary and secondary sources and illustrating the variety of topics in the field, is Robert P. Sutton, ed., *The Prairie State: A Documentary History of Illinois* . . . (2 vols., Grand Rapids, 1976). More than half of Sutton's extracts duplicate Angle's or come from the serial publications of the Illinois State Historical Society and Library.

The leading periodical in the field of Illinois history is the *Illinois Historical Journal*, formerly the *Journal of the Illinois State Historical Society*. First issued in April 1908, the *Journal* changed its name with the Autumn 1984 issue, midway through Volume 77. Although the *Journal* became established as a quarterly, four volumes (1, 17, 25–26) include only three numbers and another four volumes (14–16, 19) include only two numbers, each due to double issues, while two volumes (67–68) contain five numbers each. In order to bring the numbers of a volume within the calendar year, the date of the first quarterly issue became March rather than April in 1938. The publication has been dated by seasons, not months, from 1950 through 1973, and since 1980.

The *Journal* was at first edited by the head of the Illinois State Historical Library and Society (whose titles changed from librarian to state historian in 1945 and from secretary to executive director in 1958): Jessie Palmer Weber, 1908–26; Georgia L. Osborne, 1927–32; Paul M. Angle, 1932–45; Jay Monaghan, 1945–50; Harry E. Pratt, 1951–55; Marion D. Pratt, 1956; and Clyde C. Walton, 1956–67. Later, a member of the library staff was designated editor (or, for a time under Walton, managing editor): Howard F. Rissler, 1957–70; Ellen M. Whitney, 1970–78; and Mary Ellen McElligott, since 1979. The editors have usually worked in close proximity to the collections of the Historical Library, which moved to the Centennial Building in 1923 and to the Old State Capitol in 1970.

Although the format and emphases of the *Journal* have changed over the years, and its pages have reflected different editorial standards, the publication has amply fulfilled the "modest salutatory" of the prospectus: to include in each issue "at least one paper or address of real historical value and interest." The fiftieth anniversary of the Lincoln-Douglas debates was the occasion of the first issue of the *Journal*, and articles and notes about Lincoln have been a staple ever since. More generally, the *Journal* has mirrored at a distance the changing interests and expectations of American historiography. The editors have included book reviews and notes in most issues, but the coverage of publications relating to Illinois history has been less than comprehensive. The *Journal* also served as a newsletter for the Illinois State Historical Library and Society, and for local historical societies, until two other publications carried notices of their activities. Specifically, the *Dispatch from the Illinois State Historical Society* has appeared since May 1958, usually as a quarterly or bimonthly newsletter for society members, while *Congress News*, the predecessors of which began in 1968, is now issued quarterly for the Congress of Illinois Historical Societies and Museums.

Indispensable in mining the *Journal's* riches are the indexes published by the Historical Library. James N. Adams compiled the *General Index* . . . (1949) to Volumes 1–25, which covered issues through January 1933, and the *Cumulative Index* . . . (1968) to Volumes 26–50, which ended with the Winter 1957 issue, while Cynthia H. Smith compiled the *Cumulative Index* . . . (1971) to Volumes 51–60, for the decade from 1958 to 1967. More recent issues are accessible only through separately printed annual indexes.

A cluster of Illinois State Historical Library and Society publications, issued generally on an annual basis, was initiated before the *Journal*. The longest series in this group, the *Transactions of the Illinois State Historical Society* . . . , ran from 1900 through 1942. In a numbered sequence of Historical Library publications, it was preceded by three particular studies (1–3; 1899–1901) and interrupted by three catalogs of the library's holdings (5, 18, 25; 1900–19). The series appeared as *Illinois State Historical Society Transactions* . . . for 1932–36 and as *Papers in Illinois History and Transactions* . . . for 1937–42, the last title being used for six unnumbered volumes which, however, were numbered 44–49 when James N. Adams compiled the *Index to the Transactions of the Illinois State Historical Society and Other Publications of the Illinois State Historical Library* (2 vols., 1953). Volumes in the *Transactions* typically combined the proceedings of the society's annual meeting with separately prepared articles, most of which are similar to but longer than contributions to the *Journal*. The society's organization of an annual Illinois History Symposium in 1980 led to a new series including six issues for the first eight years. These publications (1982–89) are *Selected Papers in Illinois History, 1980* . . . ; additional issues with the same title but different dates: *1981, 1982,* and *1983*; and double issues for 1984–85 and 1986–87, retitled *Transactions of the Illinois State Historical Society* . . . . The publication for 1984–85 contains a cumulative index.

Sets of these quarterly and annual series should be checked at an early point for information relevant to most topics in the field of Illinois history. In *An Illinois Reader* (DeKalb, 1970), Clyde C. Walton provided a sampling of twenty-five articles from the *Journal* and the *Transactions*, all but two of which predate his appointment in 1956 as general editor of the *Journal*.

The Illinois State Historical Society has also issued irregularly other serial publications, the most substantial of which appeared as Collections of the Illinois

State Historical Library (38 vols., 1903–78). As a rule, a volume in this series attempted to incorporate all the sources relevant to a particular topic or period and is thus cited as appropriate in the following pages. The Illinois Historical Collections exemplified some of the best work in Illinois history in the early twentieth century, and the set retains its value, for documentary volumes of this kind never become so dated as secondary studies of the same period.

*Chicago History*, the magazine of the Chicago Historical Society, became in 1970 the principal historical forum for Chicago topics. In issues from Fall 1945 to Summer 1969, *Chicago History* had been a small, informal quarterly, ably written by Paul M. Angle, the society's director, but concerned mainly with its collections and activities. The new series, after seven semiannual issues, became a quarterly, although Volumes 11, 16, and 17 included double issues, and an exhibit catalog was substituted for the last two issues of Volume 13. Edited by David Lasswell, 1970–72; Isabel S. Grossner, 1972–77; Fannia Weingartner, 1977–82; Timothy C. Jacobson, 1982–85; and Russell Lewis, since 1985, *Chicago History* has succeeded in presenting articles of substance in a popular, heavily illustrated format. Each volume of Angle's *Chicago History* covered three years and was indexed separately, as were the first two volumes of the new series. There is a cumulative *Index* for Volumes 3–7 (1981) and 8–16 (1989), and indexes in the concluding issues of Volumes 17 and 18.

Several publications of the Chicago Historical Society predate the organization of the Illinois State Historical Library, and pertain to the history of the state as a whole, not to Chicago in particular. Fergus' Historical Series (35 booklets, 1876–1914) included many papers read before the society, some on early Illinois. Another series, the Chicago Historical Society's Collection (12 vols., 1882-1928), combined primary and secondary work of local, state, and even national importance. Numerous items in the society's *Proceedings* (5 vols., 1884–1911) were issued as separate publications for a statewide audience. Even the later *Bulletin* of the Chicago Historical Society, which appeared in two series (30 issues, 1922–26; 8 issues, 1934–39), gave as much attention to Illinois as to Chicago history.

Another scholarly periodical, similar to the *Illinois Historical Journal* and *Chicago History* in its concern with aspects of the state's history, is *Western Illinois Regional Studies*, published by Western Illinois University. Identified with the area between the Illinois and Mississippi rivers known in the time of settlement as the Military Tract, this journal has appeared semiannually since the Spring 1978 issue. Three years earlier, in March 1975, Miami University (Oxford, Ohio) began the *Old Northwest*, a journal dedicated to the culture, early and recent, of the area included in the Northwest Territory, from which the states of Ohio, Indiana, Illinois, Michigan, and Wisconsin evolved. A quarterly (except for two double issues in Volume 11 and one in Volume 13), the *Old Northwest* contains an assortment of articles and reviews pertaining to Illinois. A few articles in *Origins*, a quarterly newsletter of the Newberry Library since September 1984, point to research in the field. The journals of neighboring states, such as the *Indiana Magazine of History*, the *Wisconsin Magazine of History*, and *Gateway Heritage* (a publication of the Missouri Historical Society, in St. Louis), from time to time publish studies directly relevant to Illinois history, as do periodicals in different fields of American history as a whole.

A number of periodicals have endeavored to tap the nonacademic market for Illinois history, presenting bits of local and state lore without scholarly accouterments such as footnotes. The leading example of this genre began publication in March 1962 as *Outdoor Illinois*, changing its name to *Illinois Magazine* with the August-September 1977 issue. Edited until 1980 by Dan Malkovich, a champion of historic preservation as well as environmental protection, especially in southern Illinois, the magazine in recent years became statewide in its coverage and more conventionally historical. It appeared ten times a year through 1979, before adopting a bimonthly schedule. While *Illinois Magazine* carries an array of short, illustrated articles, mainly by free-lance writers, other efforts to create a popular forum for Illinois history have depended upon contributions by the editors, including Will L. Griffith in *Illinois Quest* (7 issues, 1937–40) and *Egyptian Key* (16 issues, 1943–51) and Richard M. Phillips in *Iliniwĕk* (65 issues, 1963–76). Occasionally, a serial publication of a local historical society or museum has become a vehicle for substantial articles on topics of statewide interest.

A few professional historians have written regularly on Illinois themes for newspapers and magazines of general circulation, and some of these columns have appeared in book form. A weekly series by John H. Keiser, who taught at Sangamon State University, led to *Illinois Vignettes* (Springfield, 1977), and columns by John E. Hallwas of Western Illinois University became *Western Illinois Heritage* (Macomb, 1983). Historians with a knack for opening up new topics are represented in two other series that are not yet collected: Perry R. Duis and Glen E. Holt, sometime colleagues at the University of Illinois at Chicago, wrote "Chicago as It Was" for the monthly magazine *Chicago* (May 1977-Aug. 1985), and Natalia M. Belting of the University of Illinois at Urbana-Champaign prepared "Illinois Past" each week for newspapers including the *Champaign-Urbana News-Gazette* (Sept. 17, 1978-June 29, 1986). The most successful venture of this kind was the column of regional pieces written by John W. Allen, a museum curator at Southern Illinois University, and collected in *Legends and Lore of Southern Illinois* (Carbondale, 1963) and *It Happened in Southern Illinois* (Carbondale, 1968).

Regardless of academic interest in Illinois topics of state or even national significance, no category of historical writing has matched the popularity of narrowly defined local histories and biographical compendia. In the late nineteenth and early twentieth centuries, most of this literature related to particular counties, but histories of cities and towns have become more common in recent years. The typical county history of the Gilded Age was assembled by a big-city publisher whose agents canvassed a county for subscribers, gathered biographical data for sketches of the "leading citizens," and collected information regarding the first settlements, local schools and churches, notable events in the area, and so on. Compilations of this sort were also combined with state histories such as Newton Bateman and Paul Selby, eds., *Historical Encyclopedia of Illinois* . . . (Chicago, 1899), later editions of which appeared with at least forty-four county histories, usually in a two-volume format, although a single volume entitled *Illinois, Historical* . . . was sufficient for six counties. Another popular format of the early twentieth century was the multivolume set, containing in different volumes first a state or regional history and then a collection of biographical sketches. Thus, biographies fill the last three volumes of George W. Smith, *A History of Illinois and Her People* (6 vols., Chicago, 1927) and Edward F. Dunne, *Illinois: Heart of the Nation* (5 vols., Chicago, 1933) and the last two volumes of Royal Brunson Way, ed., *The Rock River Valley* . . . (3 vols., Chicago, 1926) and John Leonard Conger, ed., *History of the Illinois River Valley* (3 vols., Chicago, 1932).

Meanwhile, a tradition of local historical writing was fostered in communities throughout the state by a host of privately printed reminiscences, picture books, club and church annals, and other encapsulations of the past. Although professional historians often refer condescendingly to this literature as written by local antiquarians who lack an understanding of the historical context of their work, such compilations can be usefully studied in relation to Illinois history as a whole. Local histories as a rule have reflected the initiative of individuals, sponsored on occasion by organizations but usually free to define each project as they choose. An interesting exception to this pattern was the extension of the American Guide Series to Illinois communities, but the printed legacy of this part of the WPA Federal Writers' Project was limited to a few relatively modest volumes (all issued locally): *Delavan, 1837–1937* . . . (1937), *Galena Guide* (1937), *Cairo Guide* (1938), *Nauvoo Guide* (1939), *Princeton Guide* (1939), *Hillsboro Guide* (1940), *Rockford* (1941), and a final, delayed publication, *Du Page County: A Descriptive and Historical Guide, 1831–1939* (Elmhurst, Ill., 1948). Certain commercial series of the period were nominally related to American rivers, lakes, and trails but were in fact histories of entire regions. The Rivers of America series, for instance, included three readable excursions into the state's past: James Gray, *The Illinois* (New York, 1940; new ed., Urbana, 1989); Harry Hansen, *The Chicago* (New York, 1942); and Edgar Lee Masters, *The Sangamon* (New York, 1942; new ed., Urbana, 1988).

The production of local histories since the 1950s has been stimulated by community centennials and sesquicentennials and by state and national anniversaries. Enterprising individuals have rewritten earlier accounts of their community and its institutions. County historical and genealogical societies, often in league with commercial publishers, have adapted old forms to new circumstances, issuing local histories laden with family sketches. They also have updated illustrated formats with an array of picture books, as if to imitate on the local level such publications for a wider audience as Jay Monaghan, *This*

*Is Illinois: A Pictorial History* (Chicago, 1949) and C. William Horrell et al., *Land between the Rivers: The Southern Illinois Country* (Carbondale, 1973). Finally, they have augmented the stock of new publications by a plethora of reprints. A modern-day copy may reduce the size of the original, abridge its coverage, or combine two or three works into a single volume, but it also may include a new or more complete index, at least for names. Many early county histories and similar works for which no reprint edition is available are included in the microform series of University Microfilms, Research Publications, and Americana Unlimited.

Lists of local historical writing are less than complete. The early years are covered best, especially in Solon Justus Buck, *Travel and Description, 1765–1865, together with a List of County Histories, Atlases, and Biographical Collections, and a List of Territorial and State Laws*, Collections of the Illinois State Historical Library, 9 (1914). Buck wrote ably on "The Historiography of Illinois Counties" and examined most of the titles himself. P. William Filby compiled *A Bibliography of American County Histories* (Baltimore, 1985) from secondary sources and missed a number of Illinois books in the period since Buck's list. Two inventories are useful: Richard H. Kaige and Evelyn L. Vaughan, "Illinois County Histories: A Checklist of Illinois County Histories in the Illinois State Library," *Illinois Libraries*, 50 (Sept. 1968), and the Illinois pages of Marion J. Kaminkow, ed., *United States Local Histories in the Library of Congress: A Bibliography* (5 vols., Baltimore, 1975).

The proliferation of local histories is such that an adequate inventory may be dependent on a network of researchers willing to compile county and city lists. A team of four bibliographers laid the basis for Michael P. Conzen and Kay J. Carr, eds., *The Illinois and Michigan Canal National Heritage Corridor: A Guide to Its History and Sources* (DeKalb, 1988), a specialized but uneven bibliography. Introduced by four essays regarding the canal and focused on communities between Chicago and LaSalle-Peru, this topical listing of local and relevant statewide materials unfortunately lacks an author index. In a project directed by Patsy-Rose Hoshiko, another region of the state was surveyed for the Shawnee Library System's *Southern Illinois History Inventory* (Carterville, Ill., 1983), a listing of printed and manuscript sources held by libraries and other institutions in a sixteen-county area. Other libraries and library systems have issued similar bibliographies. For Chicago, an indispensable but imperfect guide is Frank Jewell, *Annotated Bibliography of Chicago History* (Chicago, 1979), which gave some order to a mass of relevant materials. Loretto Dennis Szucs, *Chicago and Cook County Sources: A Genealogical and Historical Guide* (Salt Lake City, 1986) was compiled for genealogists, not historians, and was carelessly produced. Parts of Cook and Will counties are inventoried in Larry A. McClellan, comp., *Local History South of Chicago: A Guide for Research in the Southern Suburbs* (Chicago, 1987). Solid work on particular counties includes Alexander Summers, *The Literature of Coles County, Illinois: A Survey and Bibliography* (Mattoon, 1968); James Krohe, Jr., *Sangamon Sources: A*

*Research Guide to Local History, 1865–1970* (Springfield, 1975); and Gordana Rezab's bibliographies for eleven western Illinois counties, published in the Spring issue, 1981–88, of *Western Illinois Regional Studies*.

A burgeoning historic preservation movement, supported by the National Historic Preservation Act of 1966 and subsequent legislation, gave a new dimension to historical research at the local level. Programs such as the National Register of Historic Places have led to studies of particular sites and structures. The Illinois Department of Conservation at first administered these programs in Illinois, just as it managed a group of state-owned historic sites, but in 1985 the Illinois Historic Preservation Agency was created to oversee both matters as well as the Illinois State Historical Library. Fortunately, the new agency has continued several earlier publications, including *Historic Illinois*, a bimonthly magazine which features informative articles on buildings and sites of architectural and historical importance. Dating from June 1978, with most issues edited by Evelyn R. Taylor, *Historic Illinois* is indexed only by a typed subject listing for the first seven years. An issue of the Illinois Preservation Series has appeared annually since 1980. The agency's *Map Guide to Historic Illinois Places* (1989) lists by county some 925 sites and districts on the National Register as of August 1987 and locates as many sites as possible in a well-crafted sequence of maps drawn by Melissa A. Records. Additional data is contained in the *National Register of Historic Places, 1966–1988* (Washington, D.C., 1989), while *The National Register of Historic Places* (Part 1, through 1982; Part 2, through 1988) is Chadwyck-Healey's microfiche compilation, state by state, of the descriptions and photographs of historic properties contained in applications to the National Register.

As early as 1934, the Illinois State Historical Society began a program to erect historical markers in cooperation with local organizations and highway officials. Two publications have collected the texts of these markers: Lina S. Plucker and Kaye L. Roehrick, eds., *Brevet's Illinois Historical Markers and Sites* (Sioux Falls, S.Dak., 1976) and Nancy Hochstetter, ed., *Guide to Illinois' Historical Markers* (Verona, Wis., 1986). Neither book is well organized and neither identifies local historical sites as clearly as many travel books, an excellent example of which is Margaret Beattie Bogue, *Around the Shores of Lake Michigan: A Guide to Historic Sites* (Madison, 1985). An earlier generation erected monuments, not markers, mainly to commemorate the Civil War. Monuments within the state are most fully listed in the 1903 *Blue Book*, while Don Russell inventoried "Illinois Monuments on Civil War Battlefields" in Illinois State Historical Society, *Papers in Illinois History and Transactions for the Year 1941*.

Reference librarians, if not state historians as well, are familiar with recurring questions about Illinois, some of which have been answered since 1970 in the Secretary of State's *Handbook of Illinois Government*. This abridgment of the *Blue Book* includes data on the state flag, state song, and similar matters previously available in *The Great Seal and Other Official State Symbols* and updates the fullest coverage of these symbols, which appeared in the 1937–38 *Blue Book*. In the early 1940s, Margaret A. Flint began "A Chronology of Illinois History" and of Chicago history for the *Blue Book*, and the popularity of the former list led to several revisions and separate printings. For the years 1937–47 and 1954–57, the *Journal of the Illinois State Historical Society* carried a chronology of events in the state, the lists for each year appearing in the first issue of the subsequent year. A dozen single events are depicted by Robert A. Thom and others, and discussed by Robert M. Sutton, in a sesquicentennial series, *A History of Illinois in Paintings* (Urbana, 1968).

The market for primers in the field dates back at least to Arthur C. Dresbach, *Young People's History of Illinois . . . Written to Interest Both Old and Young* (Chicago, 1886). As publishing ventures, the most successful recent text may be [John] Allan Carpenter, *Illinois: Land of Lincoln* (Chicago, 1968), while the most economical may be *The Heartland: Pages from Illinois History* (Lake Forest, Ill., 1982), first compiled by Robert M. Sutton in 1975. Gerald A. Danzer and Lawrence W. McBride, *People, Space, and Time: The Chicago Neighborhood History Project . . .* (Lanham, Md., 1984) provides an innovative approach to urban history on the high school level. In 1947, the Illinois State Historical Society initiated the *Illinois Junior Historian*, which in 1957 became *Illinois History: A Magazine for Young People*. Issued on a monthly basis from October to May, *Illinois History* is chiefly written by and for junior and senior high school students. For many years it has used a thematic approach, occasionally treating topics that are scarcely represented in the academic literature. There is a *Cumulative Index . . .* for Volumes 1–25 (1947–72), but only annual indexes for subsequent issues.

Popular accounts for a school or general audience seem to outnumber academic studies in many fields of Illinois history, including, for instance, the development of transportation in the state. One such publication is Carlton J. Corliss, *Trails to Rails: A Story of Transportation Progress in Illinois* (Chicago, 1934), reprinted most recently with Eileen Smith Cunningham, *Rural Railroads: Greene County* (Carrollton, Ill., 1976). Milo M. Quaife, *Chicago's Highways, Old and New: From Indian Trail to Motor Road* (Chicago, 1923) connects the city with the hinterland and is complemented by Josephine Boylan, "Illinois Highways, 1700–1848: Roads, Rivers, Ferries, Canals," *Journal of the Illinois State Historical Society*, 26 (Apr.-July 1933), which emphasizes the southern part of the state, and Judson Fiske Lee, "Transportation: A Factor in the Development of Northern Illinois Previous to 1860," ibid., 10 (Apr. 1917). Other topics of popular interest are treated in Paton Yoder, *Taverns and Travelers: Inns of the Early Midwest* (Bloomington, Ind., 1969) and Thelma Eaton, *The Covered Bridges of Illinois* (Ann Arbor, 1968).

Waterways were important in the development of the state, and the U.S. Army Corps of Engineers has sponsored numerous studies for the general reader, placing its activities in a larger historical context. These works include John W. Larson, *Those Army Engineers: A History of the Chicago District . . .*

(Washington, D.C., 1980); Leland R. Johnson, *The Falls City Engineers: A History of the Louisville District* . . . (Louisville, Ky., 1975); Fredrick J. Dobney, *River Engineers on the Middle Mississippi: A History of the St. Louis District* . . . (Washington, D.C., 1978); and Roald Tweet, *A History of the Rock Island District* . . . *1866–1983* (Rock Island, 1984). Tweet also wrote *History of Transportation on the Upper Mississippi and Illinois Rivers* (Washington, D.C., 1983). Philip V. Scarpino, *Great River: An Environmental History of the Upper Mississippi, 1890–1950* (Columbia, Mo., 1985) provides a fresh perspective.

Although histories of the Illinois and Michigan Canal and of railroads such as the Illinois Central are noted at later points, the literature as a whole is inventoried in Conzen and Carr's *Guide*, already cited, and in Helen R. Richardson, comp., *Illinois Central Railroad Company: A Centennial Bibliography, 1851–1951* (Washington, D.C., 1950). The history of other modes of transportation such as interurban railroads seems engulfed by picture books for buffs, with little but Thomas R. Bullard, *Illinois Rail Transit: A Basic History* (Oak Park, Ill., 1986) to lead the way, but the formative period of aviation in the state is well covered in Howard L. Scamehorn, *Balloons to Jets* (Chicago, 1957) and David Young and Neal Callahan, *Fill the Heavens with Commerce: Chicago Aviation, 1855–1926* (Chicago, 1981).

Other topics, less popular than transportation, include the medical and legal professions. Historians could well give more attention to medical practice in the state. The available studies, largely by doctors, are adequate but either too biographical or too compartmentalized to make an appropriate contribution to Illinois history. The leading compendium in the field is the two-volume *History of Medical Practice in Illinois*, sponsored by the Illinois State Medical Society and edited in turn by Lucius H. Zeuch and David J. Davis (Chicago, 1927–55). The volumes are subtitled by date, *Preceding 1850* and *1850–1900*, but these dates are not rigid (thus Paul M. Angle's chapter on the "hardy pioneer" appears in Volume 2). A similar compilation is the Chicago Medical Society's *History of Medicine and Surgery and Physicians and Surgeons of Chicago* (Chicago, 1922), in which biographies encase a historical section.

Because these standard histories serve mainly as reference works, two more recent studies may provide a better introduction to the field: John K. Crellin, *Medical Care in Pioneer Illinois* (Springfield, 1982), a slim volume focused on central Illinois and relating to the entire nineteenth century, and Thomas Neville Bonner, *Medicine in Chicago, 1850–1950: A Chapter in the Social and Scientific Development of a City* (Madison, 1957), a more substantial history. Regional treatments include Madge E. Pickard and R. Carlyle Buley, *The Midwest Pioneer: His Ills, Cures, and Doctors* (Crawfordsville, Ind., 1945), a readable account of frontier medical practices, and Erwin H. Ackerknecht, *Malaria in the Upper Mississippi Valley, 1760–1900*, Supplements to the *Bulletin of the History of Medicine*, 4 (Baltimore, 1945), an excellent study. Illustrative of thematic work on the local level are articles by Emmet F. Pearson, "First Hospital in the Illinois Country," at Fort de Chartres, and "The Historic

Hospitals of Cairo," in the Civil War era, in *Journal of the Illinois State Historical Society*, 70 (Nov. 1977) and 77 (Spring 1984). For aspects of a Coles County medical practice and vignettes of pioneer life, see Willene Hendrick and George Hendrick, eds., *On the Illinois Frontier: Dr. Hiram Rutherford, 1840–1848* (Carbondale, 1981). Janet Kinney, *Saga of a Surgeon: The Life of David Brainard, M.D. . . .* (Springfield, 1987) records the contributions of the founder of Rush Medical College in Chicago.

Despite the widening definition of medical history in recent years, the literature for Illinois is weighted with institutional studies of medical schools and hospitals. An early example is George H. Weaver, *Beginnings of Medical Education in and near Chicago: The Institutions and the Men* (Chicago, 1925). Weaver's schools predate by a decade the institution chronicled in Leslie B. Arey, *Northwestern University Medical School, 1859–1979: A Pioneer in Educational Reform* (Evanston, 1979), which revises and extends a book published in 1959. A school dating from 1881 is sketched in Patricia Spain Ward, "An Experiment in Medical Education, or How the College of Physicians and Surgeons of Chicago Became the University of Illinois College of Medicine," in Edward P. Cohen, ed., *Medicine in Transition: The Centennial of the University of Illinois College of Medicine* (Urbana, 1981). For the Illinois dimension of the Flexner report of 1910, a landmark in the reform of medical education, see the same author's study, "The Other Abraham: Flexner in Illinois," in *Caduceus: A Museum Quarterly for the Health Sciences*, 2 (Spring 1986). A post-Flexner foundation is celebrated in C[ornelius] W. Vermeulen, *For the Greatest Good to the Largest Number: A History of the Medical Center, the University of Chicago, 1927–1977* (Chicago, 1977). A host of hospitals, not only in Chicago but also Downstate, have sponsored similar accounts, usually to mark an anniversary.

At the same time, a few publications testify to the divided and fragmented nature of the medical profession in Illinois history. Frederick Karst, "Homeopathy in Illinois," *Caduceus*, 4 (Summer 1988), indicates the importance of a nineteenth-century alternative to regular medicine. For an account of a twentieth-century development, see Theodore A. Berchtold, *To Teach, to Heal, to Serve! The Story of the Chicago College of Osteopathic Medicine; The First 75 Years, 1900–1975* (Chicago, 1975). H. Wayne Morgan, " 'No Thank You. I've Been to Dwight': Reflections on the Keeley Cure for Alcoholism," *Illinois Historical Journal*, 82 (Autumn 1989), describes Leslie E. Keeley's controversial formula and institutes for alcoholics, a flourishing treatment of the 1890s. For the disputes surrounding an unorthodox cancer treatment in the 1950s, see Patricia Spain Ward, " 'Who Will Bell the Cat?' Andrew C. Ivy and Krebiozen," *Bulletin of the History of Medicine*, 58 (Spring 1984). Vermilion County, especially Danville, becomes a case study of social attitudes toward death in James J. Farrell, *Inventing the American Way of Death, 1830–1920* (Philadelphia, 1980).

Aspects of public health in Illinois are studied in Constance Bell Webb's monograph, *A History of Contagious Disease Care in Chicago before the Great Fire* (Chicago, 1940), and F. Garvin Davenport's articles, "The Sanitation

Revolution in Illinois, 1870–1900," *Journal of the Illinois State Historical Society*, 66 (Autumn 1973), mainly on Chicago, and "John Henry Rauch and Public Health in Illinois, 1877–1891," ibid., 50 (Autumn 1957), on the State Board of Health. The history of the board and its successor is chronicled in Isaac D. Rawlings, *The Rise and Fall of Disease in Illinois* (2 vols., Springfield, 1927–28); B[axter] K. Richardson, *A History of the Illinois Department of Public Health, 1927–1962* (Springfield, 1963); and Eugene L. Wittenborn, . . . *1962–1977* (Springfield, 1983).

As for other fields of medical practice, including nursing, pharmacy, dentistry, and veterinary medicine, only dentistry has been studied to any extent. Julian Jackson and Eleanor Jackson, *Dentists to the World: Illinois's Influence on the Growth of the Profession* (Chicago, 1964) provides an introduction, while biographies of a leading figure in the field include B. W. Gilbert, *Greene Vardiman Black* . . . , Pearson Museum Monograph Series, 82:3 (Springfield, 1982), and Carl Ellsworth Black and Bessie McLaughlin Black, *From Pioneer to Scientist: The Life Story of Greene Vardiman Black, "Father of Modern Dentistry," and His Son, Arthur Davenport Black, Late Dean of Northwestern University Dental School* (St. Paul, Minn., 1940).

Illinois legal history is not a well-developed field. David F. Rolewick, *A Short History of the Illinois Judicial Systems* (Springfield, 1968; revised ed., Springfield, 1971) provides a skeletal outline of the courts under successive state constitutions. George Fiedler, *The Illinois Law Courts in Three Centuries, 1673–1973: A Documentary History* (Berwyn, Ill., 1973) is mainly concerned with the courts in the territorial period and under the Judicial Article of 1964 and the Constitution of 1970. Frederic B. Crossley offers a more connected account in the first volume of *Courts and Lawyers of Illinois* (Chicago, 1916). Volumes 2 and 3 of this work are set aside for biographical sketches.

The literature is largely written by lawyers, not historians. Much of it is listed under "Illinois" in Kermit L. Hall, *A Comprehensive Bibliography of American Constitutional and Legal History, 1896–1979* (5 vols., Millwood, N.Y., 1984). This inventory is fullest for Abraham Lincoln and his contemporaries, but its bias toward legal rather than historical journals may be illustrated by the fact that it fails to cite more than half of the selections in Mark Johnson et al., comps., *Lincoln in the State and Federal Courts: A Book of Readings* (Springfield, 1986).

Several dissertations consider facets of Illinois legal history in the mid-nineteenth century. The extension of judicial authority in the period is assessed in Keith Robert Schlesinger, "In Search of the Power That Governs: The Growth of Judicial Influence over Public Policy in Illinois, with Special Reference to Railroad Regulation, 1840–1890" (Ph.D. diss., Northwestern Univ., 1985). The records of a law practice in Clinton are examined in Maurice Graham Porter, "Portrait of a Prairie Lawyer, Clifton H. Moore, 1851–1861 and 1870–1880: A Comparative Study" (J.S.D. diss., Univ. of Illinois, 1960). The contrasting fortunes of antebellum lawyers and doctors are studied in Deborah L. Haines,

"City Doctor, City Lawyer: The Learned Professions in Frontier Chicago, 1833–1860" (Ph.D. diss., Univ. of Chicago, 1986).

A number of law offices trace their history to the nineteenth century and have commissioned commemorative volumes. One of the oldest firms, Brown, Hay & Stephens, is sketched in Paul M. Angle and Robert P. Howard, *One Hundred Fifty Years of Law: An Account of the Law Office Which John T. Stuart Formed in Springfield, Illinois a Century and a Half Ago* (Springfield, 1978). A typical house history in Chicago is Herman Kogan, *Traditions and Challenges: The Story of Sidley & Austin* (Chicago, 1983), a firm dating from 1866. These works are heavily biographical, as are such compendia as "The Bench and Bar," Volume 6 of *Industrial Chicago* (Chicago, 1896). Bar associations, alert to anniversaries, have issued celebratory publications, including Herman Kogan, *The First Century: The Chicago Bar Association, 1874–1974* (Chicago, 1974) and *Brief Histories of Some County Bars and Other Legal Organizations in Illinois and a Brief History of the Illinois State Bar Association, 1877–1977* (Springfield, 1977).

Certain academic studies suggest the potential for more substantial work. In history, for instance, there is Lawrence Edmund Sommers, "Lawyers and Progressive Reform: A Study of Attitudes and Activities in Illinois, 1890 to 1920" (Ph.D. diss., Northwestern Univ., 1967) and, for a similar time span, Andrew J. King, "Law and Land Use in Chicago: A Prehistory of Modern Zoning" (Ph.D. diss., Univ. of Wisconsin, 1967). Historically oriented studies of the judiciary, based on dissertations in political science, include Edward M. Martin, *The Rôle of the Bar in Electing the Bench in Chicago* (Chicago, 1936) and James A. Gazell and Howard M. Rieger, *The Politics of Judicial Reform* (Berkeley, Calif., 1969). The former work reviews the record since the Constitution of 1870, while the latter charts the campaign for the Judicial Article of 1964. Sociological profiles of the legal profession since World War II may be read as contemporary history. Illustrative of this literature are Joel F. Handler, *The Lawyer and His Community: The Practicing Bar in a Middle-Sized City* (Madison, 1967), a study of Decatur; John P. Heinz and Edward O. Laumann, *Chicago Lawyers: The Social Structure of the Bar* (Chicago, 1982); and such focused work as Jerome E. Carlin, *Lawyers on Their Own: A Study of Individual Practitioners in Chicago* (New Brunswick, N.J., 1962) and Marion S. Goldman, *A Portrait of the Black Attorney in Chicago* (Chicago, 1972).

In the field of legal education, Chicago's leading institutions are covered in James A. Rahl and Kurt Schwerin, *Northwestern University School of Law . . . 1859–1959* (Chicago, 1960) and Frank L. Ellsworth, *Law on the Midway: The Founding of the University of Chicago Law School* (Chicago, 1977). The history of a local and more traditional institution, dating from 1874 to 1927, is outlined in Michael H. Hoeflich, "The Bloomington Law School," in Peter Hay and Hoeflich, eds., *Property Law and Legal Education: Essays in Honor of John E. Cribbet* (Urbana, 1988).

Illinoisans became nationally important in two well-studied developments affecting women and children. See Nancy T. Gilliam, "A Professional Pioneer: Myra Bradwell's Fight to Practice Law," *Law and History Review*, 5 (Spring 1987), and Graham Parker, "The Juvenile Court Movement: The Illinois Experience," *University of Toronto Law Journal*, 26 (Summer 1976). The latter subject may also be approached through Paul Gerard Anderson, "The Good to be Done: A History of Juvenile Protective Association of Chicago, 1898–1976" (Ph.D. diss., Univ. of Chicago, 1988). Joan Gittens skillfully surveys three interrelated topics in *The Children of the State . . . in Illinois, 1818–1980s*, the ellipsis standing for the changing subtitles: *Delinquent Children, Dependent Children*, and *Child Labor Reform and Education* (Chicago, 1986).

The chronological scope of subsequent chapters does not encompass a range of studies relating to Illinois political and constitutional history. One such synthesis is Janet Cornelius, *A History of Constitution Making in Illinois* (Urbana, 1969; revised ed., *Constitution Making in Illinois, 1818–1970*, Urbana, 1972). Preparations for the constitutional conventions in 1920–22 and 1969–70 included such commentaries on earlier texts of the state constitution as Emil Joseph Verlie, ed., *Illinois Constitutions*, Collections of the Illinois State Historical Library, 13 (1919), and George D. Braden and Rubin G. Cohn, *The Illinois Constitution: An Annotated and Comparative Analysis* (Urbana, 1969). These and similar publications are listed in Charlotte B. Stillwell and Stanley E. Adams, comps., *The Constitution of Illinois: A Selective Bibliography* (Springfield, 1970).

Since the 1880s, the Secretary of State or the State Board of Elections has published voting data for major offices in either the *Blue Book* or a separate pamphlet, usually entitled *Official Vote of the State of Illinois . . . .* These and additional sources are used in Samuel K. Gove, ed., *Illinois Votes, 1900-1958: A Compilation of Illinois Election Statistics* (Urbana, 1959). Such data for every state are merged in certain machine-readable files collected by the Inter-University Consortium for Political and Social Research, in Ann Arbor, Michigan. The archival holdings of this consortium, described in its periodic *Guide to Resources and Services*, include U.S. census data, congressional roll call votes, and such local files as that used in Wesley G. Skogan, *Chicago since 1840: A Time-Series Data Handbook* (Urbana, 1976). Kenneth C. Martis assembled a wealth of information in two cartographic works, *The Historical Atlas of Political Parties in the United States, 1789–1989* (New York, 1989) and *The Historical Atlas of United States Congressional Districts, 1789–1983* (New York, 1982), while similar data are presented in Stanley B. Parsons et al., *United States Congressional Districts, 1788–1841* and *United States Congressional Districts and Data, 1843–1883* (Westport, Conn., 1978–86).

A few publications have focused on particular offices. The most readable, and most opinionated, is Robert P. Howard, *Mostly Good and Competent Men: Illinois Governors, 1818–1988* (Springfield, 1988). See also Daniel J. Elazar, *The Office of Governor in Illinois, 1818–1933: A Study of Gubernatorial Roles and Styles* (Philadelphia, 1976), which extends Elazar's essay in *The Office of*

*Governor* . . . (Urbana, 1963). Michael J. Howlett wrote about himself and his predecessors in *History of 23 Illinois Auditors of Public Accounts* (Springfield, 1968) and *Keepers of the Seal: A History of the Secretaries of State of Illinois and How Their Office Grew* (Springfield, 1977). Collective biography in capsule form is also exemplified by Mary Redmond, *Mr. Speaker: Presiding Officers of the Illinois House of Representatives, 1818–1980* (Springfield, 1980). Lewis Ethan Ellis, "A History of the Chicago Delegation in Congress, 1843–1925," *Transactions of the Illinois State Historical Society for the Year 1930*, 37, is more substantial. The development of the Illinois State Natural History Survey, Water Survey, and Geological Survey is traced in Robert G. Hays, *State Science in Illinois: The Scientific Surveys, 1850–1978* (Carbondale, 1980).

Historical geographers have explored many topics of interest to Illinois historians. For instance, the period of settlement is studied in Douglas R. McManis, *The Initial Evaluation and Utilization of the Illinois Prairies, 1815–1840*, University of Chicago Department of Geography, Research Paper 94 (Chicago, 1964), and B[rian] P. Birch, "The Environment and Settlement of the Prairie-Woodland Transition Belt: A Case Study of Edwards County, Illinois," *Southampton Research Studies in Geography* (Southampton Univ.), 6 (June 1971). From a historical perspective, much of this literature seems either suggestive or opaque, and much of it is scattered in the journals, but a sampling of relevant work may be found in the *Bulletin of the Illinois Geographical Society*. A well-indexed list of graduate studies at nine departments in the state is contained in John Thompson, "The Geography of Illinois in Theses and Dissertations Submitted at Universities in Illinois," ibid., 28 (Spring 1986).

Maps are a major source of historical as well as geographical information. An important tool for identifying early maps of the region is Robert W. Karrow, Jr., ed., *Checklist of Printed Maps of the Middle West to 1900* (13 vols. in 11, Boston, 1981), compiled at the Newberry Library, the sponsoring institution. Arranged in chronological order, this catalog is also accessible through a subject, author, and title index (Chicago, 1983), Volume 14 of the set. Volume 4, *Illinois*, was compiled by David A. Cobb and includes maps of Chicago, compiled by Marsha L. Selmer. It contains nearly three thousand entries for city, county, and state maps in a single alphabetical sequence. Other maps, for instance those depicting several states, the Great Lakes, or the Mississippi River, are represented in Volume 1, *North Central States Region*, compiled by Patricia A. Moore.

The *Checklist* is relatively comprehensive, encompassing maps in books as well as separately published maps and including state, county, and city atlases, bird's eye views and fire insurance maps of cities and towns, and other cartographic productions. Yet it may be supplemented, and also extended beyond 1900, by numerous national and specialized bibliographies. Clara Egli LeGear compiled the fullest inventories of maps in books, in *A List of Geographical Atlases in the Library of Congress* . . . (4 vols., Washington, D.C., 1958–74), which continues Philip Lee Phillips's earlier four-volume work of the same title,

and in *United States Atlases* . . . (2 vols., Washington, D.C., 1950–53), which
lists national, state, county, city, and regional atlases, first in the Library of
Congress and then also in a host of cooperating libraries. A leading collection
of maps as well as atlases of the pre–Civil War period is listed in Douglas W.
Marshall, ed., *Research Catalog of Maps of America to 1860 in the William
L. Clements Library, University of Michigan, Ann Arbor, Michigan* (4 vols.,
Boston, 1972).

Illinois is well represented in the land ownership maps and atlases that
became popular in the second half of the nineteenth century. These commercially
produced county and township maps located and identified individual farms,
depicted towns and cities, and indicated such features of the cultural landscape
as roads, railroads, schools, churches, and cemeteries. Richard W. Stephenson,
comp., *Land Ownership Maps: A Checklist of Nineteenth Century United States
County Maps in the Library of Congress* (Washington, D.C., 1967) includes
thirty-eight sheet maps for Illinois counties, mainly in the northern part of
the state, but the coverage of county atlases was more complete, as the
list in Buck's *Travel and Description* indicates. Many of these atlases were
embellished with local histories, biographies of subscribers, and views of their
farms and businesses. After World War I, however, another kind of publication,
the simpler, less expensive plat book, became standard for every county of the
state. Both cartographic types are enumerated in Clara LeGear's lists.

In recent years, most of these maps and atlases have been republished in one
form or another. For instance, Research Publications microfilmed atlases as well
as histories for many counties in its Illinois series (Woodbridge, Conn., 1976),
a publication included in Arlyn Sherwood's list of the "Illinois State Library's
Complete Holding of Illinois County Land Ownership Maps and Atlases," in
*Illinois Libraries*, 66 (Sept. 1984). Also, many local societies have sponsored a
combined edition of their county atlases, often in a reduced format and without
the color of the original but with a more complete index. The *Atlas of the State
of Illinois* . . . (Chicago, 1876), which went through four earlier editions, is
a compendium of county maps, like other state atlases of the late nineteenth
century. Those who paid to have their names on the plates are indexed in Jeanne
Robey Felldin and Charlotte Magee Tucker, comps., *Landowners of Illinois,
1876* (Tomball, Tex., 1978), which is keyed to the *Atlas* as rearranged and
abridged in *Maps of Illinois Counties in 1876* . . . (Knightstown, Ind., 1972).

Illinois is conspicuous in historical accounts of land ownership maps, including
Norman J. W. Thrower, "The County Atlas of the United States," *Surveying and
Mapping*, 21 (Sept. 1961), and chapters on county and state atlases in Walter
W. Ristow, *American Maps and Mapmakers: Commercial Cartography in the
Nineteenth Century* (Detroit, 1985). Chicago's role in these developments is the
subject of an entire issue of *Chicago History*, 13 (Sept. 1984), reprinted in
Michael P. Conzen, ed., *Chicago Mapmakers: Essays on the Rise of the City's
Map Trade* (Chicago, 1984). Some of these studies pertain to the period before
the advent of land ownership maps, as does John V. Bergen, "Maps and Their

Makers in Early Illinois: The Burr Map and the Peck-Messinger Map," *Western Illinois Regional Studies*, 10 (Spring 1987), a somewhat pedantic analysis of cartographic coverage of western Illinois in the late 1830s.

A surprising number of panoramic views and fire insurance maps, two specialized cartographic forms, document Illinois towns and cities in the late nineteenth and early twentieth centuries. Communities in a panoramic or bird's eye view are pictured as if seen from above, at an oblique angle. Not only street patterns but individual buildings are shown in such maps, which were often colored and accompanied by illustrations of particular structures in town. Views of Illinois communities are inventoried in a Library of Congress checklist, *Panoramic Maps of Anglo-American Cities* . . . , compiled by John R. Hébert (Washington, D.C., 1974; 2nd ed., revised by Patrick E. Dempsey and retitled *Panoramic Maps of Cities in the United States and Canada* . . . , Washington, D.C., 1984), and in Part 3 of John W. Reps, *Views and Viewmakers of Urban America: Lithographs of Towns and Cities in the United States and Canada, Notes on the Artists and Publishers, and a Union Catalog of Their Work, 1825–1925* (Columbia, Mo., 1984), a compendious study of the genre.

A different kind of map developed in mid-nineteenth-century America to assist insurance agents in estimating the potential fire risk for particular urban structures. These large-scale maps depict the size, shape, and construction material of homes, businesses, and factories in hundreds of towns across the land. They also show street names, house numbers, and lot lines, although they do not give the names of property owners. Because fire insurance maps were published for nearly a century, files of successive editions and updates of particular areas provide an invaluable record of urban development. For example, the Rascher Map Company issued a series for Chicago in the late nineteenth century. The Sanborn Map Company, founded in 1867, monopolized the field by 1900, and a checklist for the largest Sanborn collection, *Fire Insurance Maps in the Library of Congress* . . . (Washington, D.C., 1981), is the basis for Chadwyck-Healey's microfilm edition of these maps. Unfortunately, the originals were rendered in colors that are lost in microfilming. Another inventory is R. Philip Hoehn et al., *Union List of Sanborn Fire Insurance Maps Held by Institutions in the United States and Canada* (2 vols., Santa Cruz, Calif., 1976–77).

Certain reference works are useful for cartographic questions pertaining to state and county boundaries. One such publication is a pamphlet, *Counties of Illinois: Their Origin and Evolution, with Twenty-three Maps Showing the Original and the Present Boundary Lines of Each County of the State* (Springfield, 1906). Reprinted from the 1905 *Blue Book*, it has been reissued by secretaries of state ever since and is now entitled *Origin and Evolution of Illinois Counties*. A Newberry Library project has so far led to John H. Long, ed., *Historical Atlas and Chronology of County Boundaries, 1788–1980* (5 vols., Boston, 1984). Volume 2 of this set, compiled by Stephen L. Hansen, covers Illinois, Indiana, and Ohio and includes computer-drawn state outline maps, a chronology of all changes in boundaries and county seats, references to the laws, and a detailed map of each county. Impressive as a whole, the work is flawed in certain particulars. A publication such as John L. Andriot, comp., *Township Atlas of the United States: Named Townships* (McLean, Va., 1977) may be consulted for the location of a township in Illinois when the county is not known, while township and section lines in each county are satisfactorily pictured in the *Atlas of Illinois*, issued in the 1930s by W. W. Hixson and Company of Rockford together with its series of county plat books. More recent books published by Andriot and by Rockford Map Publishers contain such small-scale maps as to limit their value for research purposes.

The early editions of many contemporary maps have historical uses. For example, topographic maps of Illinois quadrangles compiled by the U.S. Geological Survey date from 1888, while the comparable series of aerial photographs issued by the U.S. Agricultural Stabilization and Conservation Service began in 1936. The potential for tracking local changes cartographically, through a sequence of maps and aerial photographs, is suggested by David Buisseret and Gerald Danzer, *Skokie: A Community History Using Old Maps* (Chicago, 1985). For a bibliographical review of Chicago maps, see "Past Cityscapes: Uses of Cartography in Urban History," a chapter in Thomas J. Schlereth, *Artifacts and the American Past* (Nashville, Tenn., 1980).

Many historical questions find answers in the early gazetteers of the state, most of which were incorporated into business directories after the mid-nineteenth century. By the late 1870s, Illinoisans could expect a Polk directory and a Rand McNally atlas every year or two. But none of the gazetteers in these publications is as complete as the U.S. Geological Survey's listing of present-day Illinois place names that appear on its large-scale quadrangle maps. This computerized inventory of *Illinois Geographic Names* (2 vols., Reston, Va., 1981) is a preliminary component of the Geological Survey's Professional Paper 1200, *The National Gazetteer of the United States of America*.

*Illinois Place Names* (Springfield, 1969), compiled by James N. Adams in 1961 and before, edited by William E. Keller, and first published in *Illinois Libraries*, 50 (Apr.–June 1968), is the principal list of both current and historical places in the state. Based on county histories, atlases, newspapers, and especially post office records, the work contains nearly fourteen thousand place names, over half of which have disappeared from recent maps. Additional data is contained in a new edition (Springfield, 1989) and in the Illinois Postal History Society's *Listing of Illinois Post Offices by County* (Buffalo Grove, Ill., 1983), a revision of information in its *Bulletin* in the late 1950s. The society's new serial, the *Illinois Postal Historian*, began in 1980, became a quarterly with the second issue, and was edited until 1990 by Jack Hilbing. David S. Zubatsky compiled in five parts "A Tentative Bibliography for the Study of Illinois Postal History," ibid., 1–2 (Nov. 1980–Nov. 1981). The society's publications, including postal histories of Carroll, Coles, and Jo Daviess counties, relate to interests of local historians as well as philatelists. Another work in the field, focused on Chicago's first half century, is Harvey M. Karlen, ed., *Chicago Postal History . . .* (Chicago, 1971).

Because Adams emphasized postal data, not the origin of place names, his compilation did not wholly supersede William D. Barge and Norman W. Caldwell, "Illinois Place-Names," *Journal of the Illinois State Historical Society*, 29 (Oct. 1936). More particularly, Virgil J. Vogel studied places named by or for Indians, in a four-part series, "Indian Place Names in Illinois," ibid., 55 (1962), reprinted with minor changes in a book with the same title (Springfield, 1963). Don Hayner and Tom McNamee, *Streetwise Chicago: A History of Chicago Street Names* (Chicago, 1988) is an entertaining compilation. Although the Papers of the North Central Names Institute, retitled the Publications of the North Central Name Society (8 issues, 1980–89), include some work on Illinois, the state is not a well-tilled toponymic field. As Richard B. Sealock et al., *Bibliography of Place-Name Literature: United States and Canada* (3rd ed., Chicago, 1982) indicates, only "Chicago" and "Egypt" have really exercised place-name scholars.

Place names are correlated with the linguistic geography of the state in Timothy C. Frazer, "Cultural Geography in Illinois: Regional Speech and Place Name Sources," *Great Lakes Review*, 4 (Winter 1978). This study is part of a larger realm of scholarship, the national outlines of which are charted in Craig M. Carver, *American Regional Dialects: A Word Geography* (Ann Arbor, 1987). Folklore is another complex field of research, one approach to which is contained in "Illinois Egyptians," the longest section of Richard M. Dorson, *Buying the Wind: Regional Folklore in the United States* (Chicago, 1964).

Historians have long recognized that newspapers form a vast reservoir of fact and opinion for study, a more comprehensive source for historical data than maps and gazetteers. As Edmund J. James wrote in the first research publication of the Illinois State Historical Library, *A Bibliography of Newspapers Published in Illinois Prior to 1860* (1899), "The newspapers of a community form one of the most valuable sources of its history, and if we could only get complete files of Illinois newspapers, it would be possible to write a fair history of the State from these alone." James's checklist was revised and enlarged in Franklin William Scott, *Newspapers and Periodicals of Illinois, 1814–1879*, Collections of the Illinois State Historical Library, 6 (1910). Scott's work, while of course dated by the discovery of additional files, is still useful. The most extensive listing of newspapers published in Illinois is the catalog of papers on microfilm in the Historical Library, the most recent edition of which is "Newspapers in the Illinois State Historical Library," *Illinois Libraries*, 70 (Mar.–Apr. 1988). Appearing triennially in *Illinois Libraries* since 1964, and compiled in turn by James N. Adams, William E. Keller, and Sandra M. Stark, this catalog makes available on microfilm more than thirty-eight hundred newspapers from nearly eight hundred communities in the state.

The holdings of other libraries may be traced in several national lists, including the Library of Congress catalog, *Newspapers in Microform: United States, 1948–1983* (2 vols., Washington, D.C., 1984), a recent edition of a well-established series. A more comprehensive effort to identify and locate American newspapers, both in their original format and in microform, is the United States Newspaper Program. Through this program, funded mainly by the National Endowment for the Humanities, a cluster of national repositories and a growing number of state projects have input newspaper data into the union catalog of the Online Computer Library Center. From this database has come OCLC's *United States Newspaper Program National Union List* (8 vols., Dublin, Ohio, 1985; 3rd ed. on microfiche, 1989), a massive compilation of bibliographic and holdings information, arranged alphabetically by title, with indexes for newspaper dates, intended audience and language, and place of publication or printing. As this list expands, it will quite supersede Winifred Gregory, ed., *American Newspapers, 1821–1936: A Union List of Files Available in the United States and Canada* (New York, 1937).

Histories of Illinois newspapers are scattered and uneven, but some of the relevant studies not cited in later chapters should be noted here. Relatively few accounts pertain to the state as a whole. Scott prefaced his bibliography with a history of the Illinois press before 1880. Frederic Arthur Russell covered the next generation in "The Newspaper and Periodical Publishing Industry in Illinois from 1880 to 1915" (Ph.D. diss., Univ. of Illinois, 1916). Russell based his work on the national newspaper catalogs of the period, especially N. W. Ayer's, the current successor of which is Donald P. Boyden and John Krol, eds., *Gale Directory of Publications* . . . (3 vols., Detroit, 1990). An Illinois compilation and Hiram L. Williamson's annals of the state's newspaper organization, founded in 1865, is in *Illinois Newspaper Directory: History of Illinois Press Association* . . . (Springfield, 1934).

Graduate students have often examined segments of the state's newspaper history. Leonard John Hooper, Jr., "Decade of Debate: The Polemical, Political Press in Illinois, 1814–1824" (Ph.D. diss., Southern Illinois Univ., 1964) documents the early controversy over slavery. David Roger Wrone, "Prairie Press in Transition: The East Central Illinois Newspaper Scene, 1830–1870" (Ph.D. diss., Univ. of Illinois, 1964) relates to a ten-county area encompassing the eastern half of the judicial circuit that Abraham Lincoln rode. The record of one of these counties is extended in Wrone's "Newspapers of DeWitt County, 1854–1960: A Bibliography and Checklist," *Illinois Libraries*, 46 (May 1964). James V. Gill reviewed "Rural Northern Illinois Newspapers and Newspapermen before 1851" (M.A. thesis, Northern Illinois Univ., 1982). A single paper is traced for more than a century in Merwin G. Fairbanks, "A History of Newspaper Journalism in Alton, Illinois, from 1836 to 1962, as Represented by the Alton *Evening Telegraph* and Its Predecessors" (Ph.D. diss., Southern Illinois Univ., Carbondale, 1973), while thirty-eight papers are analyzed for a single year in David R. Cassady, "The Content of the Rural Weekly Press in Illinois in 1882" (Ph.D. diss., Univ. of Iowa, 1980).

Published studies of Chicago's papers are equally specialized. Edward L. Sheppard, *The Radical and Labor Periodical Press in Chicago: Its Origin and*

*Development to 1890* (Urbana, 1949) is sketchy. An important news-gathering agency for Chicago's papers since the late nineteenth century is covered in A[rnold] A. Dornfeld, *Behind the Front Page: The Story of the City News Bureau of Chicago* (Chicago, 1983). A Chicago-based enterprise is reconstructed in Lawrence D. Hogan, *A Black National News Service: The Associated Negro Press and Claude Barnett, 1919–1945* (Rutherford, N.J., 1984). Albert Lee Kreiling, "The Making of Racial Identities in the Black Press: A Cultural Analysis of Race Journalism in Chicago, 1878–1929" (Ph.D. diss., Univ. of Illinois, Urbana-Champaign, 1973) is a richly informative interpretation of the topic.

Numerous bibliographical projects have opened the way for historians of Illinois newspapers. An early inventory of the ethnic press, including publications in thirty-four languages, is the *Bibliography of Foreign Language Newspapers and Periodicals Published in Chicago*, compiled by the Chicago Public Library Omnibus Project of the Work Projects Administration of Illinois (Chicago, 1942). Dirk Hoerder, ed., *The Immigrant Labor Press in North America, 1840s–1970s: An Annotated Bibliography* (3 vols., Westport, Conn., 1987) provides another approach to foreign language newspapers in Illinois through its place index for each linguistic group. Among the listings for specific foreign language papers are the Illinois pages of Lilly Setterdahl, comp., *Swedish-American Newspapers: A Guide to the Microfilms Held by Swenson Swedish Immigration Research Center, Augustana College . . .* , Augustana Library Publications, 35 (Rock Island, 1981), and of Karl J. R. Arndt and May E. Olson, *German-American Newspapers and Periodicals, 1732–1955: History and Bibliography* (Heidelberg, 1961), with addenda in later editions, the third being the first volume of Arndt and Olson, *The German Language Press of the Americas* (3 vols., Munich, 1973–80).

Other specialized inventories are also available. A. Gilbert Belles, "The Black Press in Illinois," *Journal of the Illinois State Historical Society*, 68 (Sept. 1975), provides a checklist and bibliography. The Illinois volume of Eugene P. Willging and Herta Hatzfeld, *Catholic Serials of the Nineteenth Century in the United States: A Descriptive Bibliography and Union List*, Series 2, Part 3 (Washington, D.C., 1961), includes newspapers as well as periodicals that were Catholic by purpose, attitude, or national tradition. Earle Lutz, "The *Stars and Stripes* of Illinois Boys in Blue," *Journal of the Illinois State Historical Society*, 46 (Summer 1953), identifies a scattering of Civil War regimental and camp newspapers. Wayne Stewart Yenawine, "Civilian Conservation Corps Camp Papers: A Checklist of Papers Published before July 1, 1937, with Bibliographical and Other Notes" (M.A. thesis, Univ. of Illinois, 1938) is still useful.

Illinois historians may use to advantage not only newspaper bibliographies but also collections of newspaper extracts. The newspaper research for the Centennial History of Illinois included some thirty thousand excerpts from nineteenth-century newspapers, typed on five-by-eight-inch cards which the Illinois Historical Survey retains. In *The Annals of Labor and Industry in Illinois . . .* (3 vols., Chicago, 1939–41), the WPA Writers' Project published extracts from a group of thirty newspapers issued during the first nine months of 1890. The library of the Chicago Historical Society fell heir to the project's unpublished extracts for other periods, mainly 1870–1940. The Writers' Project collection at the Illinois State Historical Library contains similar files on other topics, including agriculture, sports, and theater in Illinois.

A more successful undertaking of this kind was the Chicago Foreign Language Press Survey, a separate WPA program, sponsored in the end by the Chicago Public Library Omnibus Project. In this effort, workers translated articles and editorials from newspapers of twenty-two Chicago foreign language groups, from Albanian to Ukrainian. The newspapers dated from 1861 to 1938, but varied with each language. Each group of translations was arranged by a subject classification system that is outlined in *The Chicago Foreign Language Press Survey: A General Description of Its Contents* (Chicago, 1942). Typed on some 120,000 five-by-eight-inch sheets, the translations were then microfilmed (67 reels), making available to researchers ever since a selection of the ethnic press far beyond the reach of each scholar alone. The project lived up to the buoyant expectations of its first director, James [Jay] Monaghan, in "A New Source of Information for Historians," *Journal of the Illinois State Historical Society*, 30 (July 1937).

The WPA also undertook to make the ephemeral output of the press accessible through retrospective indexing. The Chicago Public Library Omnibus Project planned an index for at least one Chicago paper for each year since 1833 but was able to complete only "The Chicago Daily Democratic Press Index for the Year 1855" (1940), a three-volume typescript at the Chicago Historical Society, also available on microfilm (1 reel). *Chicago in Periodical Literature: A Summary of Articles*, 1 (Chicago, 1940), is a Writers' Program list of material about the city before the Fire of 1871.

Downstate, the WPA prepared a number of indexes, some of which have been microfilmed by the Illinois State Historical Library, including the *Alton Telegraph*, 1836–1933 (5 reels); six Belleville papers, 1840–1940 (11 reels); and nine East St. Louis papers, 1865–1938 (4 reels). The Peoria Historical Society collection at Bradley University contains indexes to fifteen local papers, 1834–64, while the McLean County Historical Society and Bloomington Public Library hold indexes to six Bloomington-Normal papers, 1849–1986, reflecting in the case of the *Pantagraph* a supplement to the work of the WPA. None of these indexes has been microfilmed. At the Historical Library, James N. Adams opened a window on affairs in Springfield by indexing the *Illinois State Journal* and its predecessors from 1831 to 1860, in four volumes now microfilmed (2 reels), a project continued through 1865 by an incomplete card index. The Historical Records Survey culled some eighteen Illinois newspapers of the same period for references to Abraham Lincoln, leaving copies of this unpublished index in the Historical Library and the Illinois Historical Survey. More recently, the Historical Library initiated a project to index by regiment Civil War letters written by Illinois soldiers to hometown editors.

Turning to twentieth-century sources, researchers gain the benefit of several contemporary indexes. The annual *Index to the Chicago Record-Herald . . .* , 1904–12, filled some sixteen hundred double-column pages which have been microfilmed (2 reels). In 1972, Bell and Howell (Wooster, Ohio) began a continuing index to the *Chicago Tribune*; since 1983, this publication has been distributed by University Microfilms (Ann Arbor). Bell and Howell also published an index to the *Chicago Sun-Times*, 1979–82, which the newspaper continued on microfiche until 1985. In 1977, Bell and Howell began the *Index to Black Newspapers*, including the *Chicago Defender*. Another set of indexes is useful for that part of Illinois within the St. Louis metropolitan area. The St. Louis Public Library's annual *Index to St. Louis Newspapers* covered four papers when it began in 1975, and was followed in 1980 by Bell and Howell's ongoing index to the *St. Louis Post-Dispatch*. The exact title of these indexes varies from year to year. In 1977, the Illinois Information Service, a division of the Illinois Department of Central Management Services, instituted a weekday *Press Summary*, a collection of articles of statewide importance or about state government, photocopied from about thirty newspapers in the state. These articles are indexed only by a subject listing on the cover of each issue. Beyond this assortment of published indexes is an array of unpublished and usually specialized indexes kept by newspaper offices, public libraries, and local societies around the state.

The leading study of printing in early Illinois is Cecil K. Byrd, *A Bibliography of Illinois Imprints, 1814–58* (Chicago, 1966). Listing books, pamphlets, and broadsides but not newspapers of the period, Byrd annotated many entries with historical and biographical data that often cannot be found in any other secondary account. A multitude of topics, not only political and economic but also educational and religious, came within his ken. Although addenda to his bibliography can be expected, Byrd more than doubled the number of items previously recorded and largely superseded Douglas C. McMurtrie's lists of early Chicago and Peoria imprints. However, two master's theses at the University of Illinois in 1938 went beyond Byrd's period and touched on aspects of printing history that he bypassed: Elizabeth Arnold Windsor, "Illinois Imprints, 1851 through 1860 (Exclusive of Chicago)" and Reva Nearhood, "Illinois Imprints, 1861–1871: A Checklist and Study," also excluding Chicago. Another supplement to Byrd is the *Check List of Chicago Ante-Fire Imprints, 1851–1871*, American Imprints Inventory, 4 (Chicago, 1938), part of a larger WPA project initiated by McMurtrie and carried forth by the Historical Records Survey.

Two national bibliographies come into play for the vast number of books relating to Illinois history but printed in other states. The first is an inventory of American imprints after 1800, one volume per year, with additional volumes for author, title, and other indexes. Based on the book slips left by the WPA and published since 1958 by Scarecrow Press in New York and Metuchen, New Jersey, the series includes Ralph R. Shaw and Richard H. Shoemaker, comps., *American Bibliography: A Preliminary Checklist for 1801* [–1819]; Shoemaker,

*A Checklist of American Imprints for 1820* [–1829]; and Gayle Cooper et al., *A Checklist of American Imprints for 1830*, now reaching through 1839. The second and more inclusive work, an incomparable bibliographical tool, is *The National Union Catalog: Pre-1956 Imprints* (754 vols., London, 1968–81). The *NUC*, primarily a catalog of main entries, is continued for the period since 1953 both in quinquennial and annual volumes and on microfiche.

Several lists bring some order to the intractable field of government publications. Margaret C. Norton, "Illinois Documents: A Checklist, 1812–50," published serially in *Illinois Libraries*, 32–33 (Oct. 1950-June 1951), is a record of legislative directions for printing, not of extant materials. Adelaide R. Hasse, *Index of Economic Material in Documents of the States of the United States: Illinois, 1809–1904* (Washington, D.C., 1909) is a little-known bibliographical gem. Using the term "economic" in the broadest sense, the work analyzes the printed reports of administrative officials, legislative committees, and special commissions as well as governors' messages for nearly a century, omitting only items accessible through Carroll D. Wright, U.S. Department of Labor, *Index of All Reports Issued by Bureaus of Labor Statistics in the United States . . .* (Washington, D.C., 1902).

More recent listings include Dorothy G. Bailey, comp., "Illinois State Documents," appearing irregularly in *Illinois Libraries*, 21–42 (Oct. 1939–Apr. 1960), and a series initiated by the Secretary of State in 1959, *Illinois State Publications*, retitled *Publications of the State of Illinois* in 1961 and issued annually since 1983. An early effort to inventory governmental and organizational materials in Chicago led to *Chicago and Cook County: A Union List of Their Official Publications . . .* (Chicago, 1934) and *Private Civic and Social Service Organizations of Chicago: A Union List of Their Reports and Publications* (Chicago, 1936).

A compendium, useful both for Illinois citations and as an outline for potential research, is G[eorge] Thomas Tanselle, *Guide to the Study of United States Imprints* (2 vols., Cambridge, Mass., 1971). Tanselle includes, for example, not only regional, genre, and author lists but also references to individual printers and publishers, such as Stone and Kimball and the Lakeside Press of Chicago. Those firms were part of an expansive industry that is surveyed in George Eugene Sereiko, "Chicago and Its Book Trade, 1871–1893" (Ph.D. diss., Case Western Reserve Univ., 1973). Studies of publishers that have appeared since Tanselle's *Guide* include Ralph E. McCoy, comp., *Open Court: A Centennial Bibliography, 1887–1987* (LaSalle, Ill., 1987) and Joe W. Kraus, *A History of Way & Williams . . . 1895–1898* (Philadelphia, 1984).

The best index to library history in the state is Doris Cruger Dale, comp., *Bibliography of Illinois Library History*, in *Journal of Library History* Bibliography, 14 (Tallahassee, 1976). Usually written by librarians, not historians, this literature tends to be narrowly institutional, not unlike the histories of public and school libraries in *Illinois Libraries*, 50 (Sept. and Nov. 1968). A detailed study of an early proprietary library in the state is Milton C. Moore,

*The Edwardsville Library of 1819: Its Founders, Catalog, Subsequent History, and Importance* (Edwardsville, 1981).

Researchers can expect to find in most academic libraries and many public libraries an array of reference works relevant to Illinois history. The leading biographical set remains the *Dictionary of American Biography*, edited by Allen Johnson and Dumas Malone (20 vols., New York, 1928–36). The *Index* (1937) contains a list of subjects by birthplace, while the *Supplement* (8 vols., New York, 1944–88) should be checked for those dying in recent years, through 1970, including such prominent Illinoisans as Mayor William H. Thompson of Chicago and Gov. Henry Horner, each sketched by Paul M. Angle. Many conspicuous figures in colonial Illinois appear both in the *DAB* and in George W. Brown et al., eds., *Dictionary of Canadian Biography* (4 vols. and an index for subjects through 1800, Toronto, 1966–81). Nineteenth-century Illinoisans are scattered through the *American Biographical Archive*, a microfiche cumulation of entries in pre-1910 biographical volumes, published by K. G. Saur since 1986. In the proliferation of topically defined biographical works, the most useful is Edward T. James, ed., *Notable American Women, 1607–1950: A Biographical Directory* (3 vols., Cambridge, Mass., 1971), which is extended by Barbara Sicherman and Carol Hurd Green, eds., *Notable American Women: The Modern Period . . .* (Cambridge, Mass., 1980).

Research in Illinois history can often be facilitated by reference to two national bibliographies, *Writings on American History* and *America: History and Life*. The *Writings* series, published or sponsored by the American Historical Association, includes annual volumes for 1902–61 (except for 1904–5 and 1941–47); *A Subject Bibliography of Books and Monographs* and *A Subject Bibliography of Articles* for 1962–73, in ten- and four-volume sets, respectively; and annual listings of articles since 1973–74. *America: History and Life*, introduced in 1964 by the American Bibliographical Center, Clio Press, has evolved into an annual four-part bibliography that provides article abstracts and a book review index. Although dissertations are now incorporated into both series, a useful listing for Illinois history is Roger D. Bridges, comp., "A Bibliography of Dissertations Relating to Illinois History, 1884–1976," *Journal of the Illinois State Historical Society*, 70 (Aug. 1977). Since 1938, University Microfilms has made this mass of scholarship accessible through *Dissertation Abstracts International* and its predecessors. An excellent starting point for Illinois historians wishing to tap the increasingly specialized literature of American history is Francis Paul Prucha, *Handbook for Research in American History: A Guide to Bibliographies and Other Reference Works* (Lincoln, Nebr., 1987).

# 1

---

# THE ILLINOIS COUNTRY
# BEFORE 1765

---

## MARGARET KIMBALL BROWN

THE "ILLINOIS COUNTRY"—that is, the land inhabited by the Illinois Indians—became known to Europeans through French and French Canadian efforts to trade with the Indians and to Christianize them. Illinois history is generally said to date from the Jolliet and Marquette expedition of 1673, the first to enter the Illinois Country. The French established trading posts and missions and developed several small villages, forming a distinctive French colonial society that lasted until British troops occupied the Illinois Country in 1765.

Although the French period of Illinois history has long been the subject of historical scholarship, the field clearly needs new and fresh attention. Indeed, the lack of substantial modern research in the period is a great gap in Illinois studies. Perhaps symbolic of the early but now dated scholarship in the field is the fact that the best introduction is still Clarence Walworth Alvord, *The Illinois Country, 1673–1818* (Springfield, 1920). Fortunately, the lack of a satisfactory modern synthesis of the period is to some extent overcome by more particular studies that concern, in turn, the Indians after contact with European civilization, the early explorers of the seventeenth century, and the colonial settlers of the eighteenth century.

The complex and often misunderstood history of the Indians in the Illinois Country is reliably surveyed in Bruce G. Trigger, ed., *Northeast*, Volume 15 of the Smithsonian Institution's *Handbook of North American Indians* (Washington,

D.C., 1978). This excellent introduction to Algonquian and Iroquoian studies includes appropriate chapters by many specialists. For example, Charles Callender's "Great Lakes–Riverine Sociopolitical Organization" is based in part on his monograph, *Social Organization of the Central Algonkian Indians*, Milwaukee Public Museum, Publications in Archaeology, 7 (Milwaukee, 1962), and James A. Clifton's "Potawatomi" reflects his book, *The Prairie People: Continuity and Change in Potawatomi Indian Culture, 1665–1965* (Lawrence, Kans., 1977). Another account that summarizes the history of particular tribes is Wayne C. Temple, *Indian Villages of the Illinois Country: Historic Tribes*, Illinois State Museum, Scientific Papers, Vol. 2, Part 2 (Springfield, 1958; revised ed., Springfield, 1966).

The people from whom the state received its name are described in several studies, including Emily J. Blasingham's two-part article, "The Depopulation of the Illinois Indians," *Ethnohistory*, 3 (Summer and Fall 1956); two articles by Raymond E. Hauser, "The Illinois Indian Tribe: From Autonomy and Self-Sufficiency to Dependency and Depopulation," *Journal of the Illinois State Historical Society*, 69 (May 1976), and "Warfare and the Illinois Indian Tribe during the Seventeenth Century: An Exercise in Ethnohistory," *Old Northwest*, 10 (Winter 1984–85); and Margaret Kimball Brown, *Cultural Transformations among the Illinois: An Application of a Systems Model*, Michigan State University, Publications of the Museum, Anthropological Series, Vol. 1, No. 3 (East Lansing, 1979).

Archaeological investigations of Indian sites in the historic period have not been extensive but have illuminated tribal life in both northern and southern Illinois. The Kaskaskia can be studied in James A. Brown, ed., *The Zimmerman Site: A Report on Excavations at the Grand Village of Kaskaskia, LaSalle County, Illinois*, Illinois State Museum, Reports of Investigations, 9 (Springfield, 1961); Margaret Kimball Brown, *The Zimmerman Site: Further Excavations at the Grand Village of Kaskaskia*, ibid., 32 (Springfield, 1975); and, for a surface collection, Mary Elizabeth Good, *Guebert Site: An 18th Century, Historic Kaskaskia Indian Village in Randolph County, Illinois*, Central States Archaeological Societies, Memoir, 2 (Wood River, Ill., 1972). The Michigamea in southwestern Illinois are discussed in Margaret Kimball Brown, "The Search for the Michigamea Village," *Outdoor Illinois*, 11 (Mar. 1972), and Charles Edward Orser, Jr., "The Kolmer Site: An Eighteenth Century Michigamea Village" (M.A. thesis, Wayne State Univ., 1975).

The evidence regarding the celebrated Indian pictographs on the bluffs near the mouth of the Illinois River is considered in Wayne C. Temple, "The Piasa Bird: Fact or Fiction?" *Journal of the Illinois State Historical Society*, 49 (Autumn 1956), and Natalia Maree Belting, "The Piasa—It Isn't a Bird!" ibid., 66 (Autumn 1973).

The preeminent collection of sources relating to the Indians is Reuben Gold Thwaites, ed., *The Jesuit Relations and Allied Documents: Travels and Explorations of the Jesuit Missionaries in New France, 1610–1791* . . . (73 vols.,

Cleveland, 1896–1901). Thwaites and his assistants set forth on facing pages the original texts, mainly in French, and the English translations, and also supplied extensive notes. A list of documents published in the series appears in Volume 71, and a general index is in Volumes 72–73. These sources document native life in detail but are heavily colored by the missionaries' prejudices about Indian morals and mores. However, the best contemporary account of the Illinois provides a near ethnographic viewpoint: known as the De Gannes memoir although written by Pierre Deliette, it appears in Theodore Calvin Pease and Raymond C. Werner, eds., *The French Foundations, 1680–1693*, Collections of the Illinois State Historical Library, 23 (1934). A contemporary report of a visit of Indians to Paris and Versailles is translated in Richard N. Ellis and Charlie R. Steen, "An Indian Delegation in France, 1725," *Journal of the Illinois State Historical Society*, 67 (Sept. 1974). See also Frank Norall, *Bourgmont, Explorer of the Missouri, 1698–1725* (Lincoln, Nebr., 1988). A series of articles by Joseph L. Peyser, including "The Fate of the Fox Survivors: A Dark Chapter in the History of the French in the Upper Country, 1726–1737," *Wisconsin Magazine of History*, 73 (Winter 1989–90), uses newly identified maps and reports to reinterpret the Fox Wars. Some later sidelights on the Indians are provided in Seymour Feiler, ed., *Jean-Bernard Bossu's Travels in the Interior of North America, 1751–1762* (Norman, Okla., 1962).

Europeans became aware of the Illinois Country as the French extended their explorations westward up the St. Lawrence River and through the Great Lakes. In 1673, the Jesuit missionary Jacques Marquette and the Canadian trader Louis Jolliet reached the Mississippi by way of the Fox and Wisconsin rivers, descended to the mouth of the Arkansas, and returned by way of the Illinois River and the Chicago portage to Lake Michigan. The records pertaining to their expedition have created an intricate scholarly puzzle for biographers. In particular, Jean Delanglez, *Life and Voyages of Louis Jolliet, 1645–1700* (Chicago, 1948) and Raphael N. Hamilton, *Marquette's Explorations: The Narratives Reexamined* (Madison, 1970) confronted in detail the issues presented by Francis Borgia Steck in *The Jolliet-Marquette Expedition, 1673* (Washington, D.C., 1927; revised eds., Quincy, Ill. and Glendale, Calif., 1928) and in *Marquette Legends* (New York, 1960). Less complicated biographies are Hamilton's *Father Marquette* (Grand Rapids, 1970) and Joseph P. Donnelly, *Jacques Marquette, S. J., 1637–1675* (Chicago, 1968).

In 1680, Robert Cavelier, sieur de La Salle, and Henry de Tonty opened a second and equally dramatic chapter in the history of French Illinois. Entering the region by way of the St. Joseph and Kankakee rivers, they built Fort Crèvecoeur at the site of Peoria, an outpost that their men soon destroyed. In 1682, after an expedition to the mouth of the Mississippi, they constructed Fort St. Louis on the promontory later known as Starved Rock, a trading center that declined when Tonty built a second fort at Peoria in 1691. La Salle, like Marquette, has attracted many biographers, and again certain points in dispute were resolved by Jean Delanglez, in *Some La Salle Journeys* (Chicago, 1938). Edmund Robert

Murphy, *Henry de Tonty: Fur Trader of the Mississippi* (Baltimore, 1941) is a satisfactory biography of La Salle's lieutenant. Carl A. Brasseaux considers "The Image of La Salle in North American Historiography" and Patricia K. Galloway discusses "Sources for the La Salle Expedition of 1682" in Galloway, ed., *La Salle and His Legacy: Frenchmen and Indians in the Lower Mississippi Valley* (Jackson, Miss., 1982).

The principal accounts of the early explorers are still most easily consulted in Louise Phelps Kellogg, ed., *Early Narratives of the Northwest, 1634–1699* (New York, 1917). Hiram W. Beckwith made an earlier selection of these sources in Volume 1 of the Collections of the Illinois State Historical Library (1903). In the same series, Pease and Werner edited not only the De Gannes memoir but considerable material on La Salle. Although Thwaites' monumental collection remains basic to the period, many documents have been separately translated and published. This literature is partly tabulated in Robert R. Hubach, *Early Midwestern Travel Narratives: An Annotated Bibliography, 1634–1850* (Detroit, 1961). In *A Jean Delanglez, S. J., Anthology . . .* (New York, 1985), Mildred Mott Wedel reprints from *Mid-America* a dozen articles, especially textual studies of documents of the period of exploration, which supplement Delanglez's books on Jolliet and La Salle.

The first permanent settlements in French Illinois began as missions in the Mississippi Valley. In 1699, the Seminarians of Quebec founded a mission to the Tamaroa and Cahokia Indians at Cahokia, opposite the future site of St. Louis. In 1703, the Jesuits accompanied the Kaskaskia Indians to a site about sixty miles to the south which became the village of Kaskaskia. Cahokia remained small in the French period, but Kaskaskia became the principal settlement and fur-trading entrepôt in the West. A third community formed about sixteen miles above Kaskaskia at Fort de Chartres, built in 1720 as the center of governmental power in the Illinois Country. Nearby, Prairie du Rocher and St. Philippe soon came into being. By 1750, Ste. Genevieve had also begun to take shape; located on the west bank of the Mississippi, opposite Kaskaskia, it was part of the Province of Illinois in the French period.

Demographic information for the five settlements in present-day Illinois is included in Marthe Faribault-Beauregard, *La population des forts français d'Amérique, XVIIIe siècle: Répertoire des baptêmes, mariages et sépultures célébrés dans les forts et les établissements français en Amérique du Nord . . .* (2 vols., Montreal, 1982–84). Norman Ward Caldwell, *The French in the Mississippi Valley, 1740–1750*, University of Illinois Studies in the Social Sciences, 26 (Urbana, 1941), describes the administration and economy of the region, and is a suggestive work for the entire period, not just the decade specified in its title. Winstanley Briggs, "Le Pays des Illinois," *William and Mary Quarterly*, 47 (Jan. 1990), discerns the rapid development of a self-governing society in the villages of French Illinois. Carl J. Ekberg, "Black Slavery in Illinois, 1720–1765," *Western Illinois Regional Studies*, 12 (Spring 1989), introduces an important topic.

The earliest continuous settlement is closely studied in Gilbert J. Garraghan, "New Light on Old Cahokia," *Illinois Catholic Historical Review*, 11 (Oct. 1928); Charles E. Peterson, "Notes on Old Cahokia," *Journal of the Illinois State Historical Society*, 42 (Mar.–Sept. 1949); and John Francis McDermott, "Cahokia and Its People," in McDermott, ed., *Old Cahokia: A Narrative and Documents Illustrating the First Century of Its History* (St. Louis, 1949). An important work for French colonial culture is Natalia Maree Belting, *Kaskaskia under the French Regime*, University of Illinois Studies in the Social Sciences, 29 (Urbana, 1948). Another community is studied at length in Carl J. Ekberg, *Colonial Ste. Genevieve: An Adventure on the Mississippi Frontier* (Gerald, Mo., 1985). The literature on Fort de Chartres is less than comprehensive but includes, for example, Jane F. Babson, "The Architecture of Early Illinois Forts," *Journal of the Illinois State Historical Society*, 61 (Spring 1968). Misinformation perpetuated in Clyde C. Walton, ed., *John Francis Snyder: Selected Writings* (Springfield, 1962) is corrected in Walter J. Saucier and Kathrine Wagner Seineke, "François Saucier, Engineer of Fort de Chartres, Illinois," in John Francis McDermott, ed., *Frenchmen and French Ways in the Mississippi Valley* (Urbana, 1969). For biographical sketches of the commandants at Fort de Chartres, see Helen W. Mumford, *The French Governors of Illinois* (Evanston, 1963) and, for the 1750s, William P. McCarthy, "The Chevalier Macarty Mactigue," *Journal of the Illinois State Historical Society*, 61 (Spring 1968).

Several articles probe certain aspects of the early French colonial economy. Trading operations of Tonty and François de la Forest are discussed in Floyd Mulkey, "Fort St. Louis at Peoria," *Journal of the Illinois State Historical Society*, 37 (Dec. 1944). An early eighteenth-century monopolistic venture on the Ohio River, not far from the Mississippi, is considered in John Fortier and Donald Chaput, "A Historical Reexamination of Juchereau's Illinois Tannery," ibid., 62 (Winter 1969). Interest in mineral wealth is documented in Stanley Faye, ed., "A Search for Copper on the Illinois River: The Journal of Legardeur Delisle, 1722," ibid., 38 (Mar. 1945). And a cattle drive from Fort de Chartres to the Arkansas River in 1739 is described in Margaret Kimball Brown, "Allons, Cowboys!" ibid., 76 (Winter 1983). An early but important study of the entire jurisdiction is N[ancy] M. Miller Surrey, *The Commerce of Louisiana during the French Regime, 1699–1763* (New York, 1916).

The sources for the French period are more scattered than the secondary literature. No student, however, should miss the excellent portfolio of contemporary maps compiled by Sara Jones Tucker, *Indian Villages of the Illinois Country: Atlas*, to which Wayne C. Temple added a *Supplement*, Illinois State Museum, Scientific Papers, Vol. 2, Part 1 (Springfield, 1942–75). The history of the communities near Fort de Chartres is illuminated by church and land records published in Margaret Kimball Brown and Lawrie Cena Dean, eds., *The Village of Chartres in Colonial Illinois, 1720–1765* (New Orleans, 1977). This volume, despite its size, includes only a sampling of the notarial archives from the several French villages that came to rest in the Randolph County Courthouse at Chester, Illinois. Brown's "The Kaskaskia Manuscripts," *Illinois Libraries*, 62 (Apr. 1980), provides a history of this collection, a heterogeneous group of over six thousand documents including marriage contracts, work agreements, wills, inventories, deeds, and the like. This collection is placed in strict chronological order, microfilmed on eleven reels, and accessible through Dean and Brown, *The Kaskaskia Manuscripts, 1714–1816: A Calendar of Civil Documents in Colonial Illinois* (Introduction and English summaries on two reels, with a name index on one reel, Chester, Ill., 1981).

Records pertaining to political, military, and diplomatic affairs in the mid-eighteenth century are set forth in Theodore Calvin Pease, ed., *Anglo-French Boundary Disputes in the West, 1749–1763* and in Pease and Ernestine Jenison, eds., *Illinois on the Eve of the Seven Years' War, 1747–1755*, Collections of the Illinois State Historical Library, 27 and 29 (1936–40). These volumes draw on many sources, including the papers of the Marquis de Vaudreuil in the Huntington Library, for which see Bill Barron, *The Vaudreuil Papers: A Calendar and Index of the Personal and Private Records of Pierre de Rigaud de Vaudreuil, Royal Governor of the French Province of Louisiana, 1743–1753* (New Orleans, 1975). The larger governmental context for French Illinois is also apparent in collections located in Louisiana, some of which are described in John R. Kemp and Edward F. Haas, "Louisiana State Museum: Louisiana Historical Center," in Light Townsend Cummins and Glen Jeansonne, eds., *A Guide to the History of Louisiana* (Westport, Conn., 1982) and, for holdings at the University of Southwestern Louisiana, in Carl A. Brasseaux, "The Colonial Records Collection of the Center for Louisiana Studies," *Louisiana History*, 25 (Spring 1984). The archives of the Superior Council of Louisiana in particular are partly calendared in Heloise H. Cruzat et al., *Louisiana Historical Quarterly*, 1–26 (Jan. 1917–Jan. 1943). John Francis McDermott, ed., *The French in the Mississippi Valley* (Urbana, 1965) includes chapters on other North American collections relating to Illinois; see, for example, Noël Baillargeon, "The Seminary of Quebec: Resources for the History of the French in the Mississippi Valley." An early but still useful tool for identifying sources in the French capital is N[ancy] M. Miller Surrey, *Calendar of Manuscripts in Paris Archives and Libraries Relating to the History of the Mississippi Valley to 1803* (2 vols., Washington, D.C., 1926–28). More recently, the Archives Nationales issued an inventory of Series C13, an important part of its colonial archives: Marie-Antoinette Menier et al., *Correspondance à l'arrivée en provenance de la Louisiane* (2 vols., Paris, 1976–83). Some materials from French depositories that relate to Illinois are included in Dunbar Rowland and A. G. Sanders, eds., *Mississippi Provincial Archives: French Dominion* . . . (5 vols., Jackson, Miss. and Baton Rouge, La., 1927–84).

Historical efforts to comprehend the sources are described in three studies by Henry Putney Beers: *The French in North America: A Bibliographical Guide to French Archives, Reproductions, and Research Missions* (Baton Rouge, 1957), *The French and British in the Old Northwest: A Bibliographical Guide to Archive and Manuscript Sources* (Detroit, 1964), and *French and Spanish Records of Louisiana: A Bibliographical Guide to Archive and Manuscript Sources* (Baton Rouge, 1989). A chapter in the first book, for example, concerns "Historians of the French Regime in America," such as John Dawson Gilmary Shea, Pierre Margry, Francis Parkman, and Reuben Gold Thwaites, who in the nineteenth century opened the field of French colonial studies. Their successors were most active in the early twentieth century, but the subject has not been entirely neglected in recent years, partly because scholarly interest in it has extended from traditional historians to specialists in historical anthropology and the new social history.

It seems inevitable that American historians will study the English colonies on the East Coast more intensively than the French settlements in the Mississippi Valley, but Illinois historians, at least, should recognize the potential for renewed attention to the state's colonial past. Not only is the exploration of the French period from new orientations needed, but it promises at last an adequate understanding of a little-known period in Illinois history.

# 2

# BRITISH RULE AND AMERICAN SETTLEMENT, 1765–1818

## RAND BURNETTE

THE HISTORY OF Illinois between the French period and the time of statehood may be divided into three major phases: Illinois as a British possession, as part of Virginia, and as a territory of the United States. The "Illinois Country" was at first subjected to a measure of British sovereignty, extending formally from the Treaty of Paris of 1763 to the Treaty of Paris of 1783, but lasting in effect only from the arrival of British troops in 1765 to the conquests of George Rogers Clark in 1778–79. The State of Virginia, having sponsored Clark's expedition, then claimed the area by creating the County of Illinois. This arrangement lasted from 1778 to 1784, at which point Virginia ceded the land to the United States as organized under the Articles of Confederation. Finally, this cession, and the treaty of 1783, enabled the Confederation Congress, through the Northwest Ordinance of 1787, to chart steps toward the admission of Illinois into the Union in 1818.

The population of Illinois in the late colonial and early territorial periods was quite small. Estimated at 2,500 in 1752, not counting the Indians, it was no larger a half century later. Only at the end of the territorial period, especially after 1809, did the population grow substantially, exceeding 35,000 by 1818. Moreover, these Illinoisans were mostly clustered in a few villages along the Mississippi River. Yet they played a role in the larger imperial and national history of the period.

The colonial and territorial years were surveyed by several nineteenth-century writers, including, for example, John Reynolds, *The Pioneer History of Illi-*

*nois* . . . (Belleville, Ill., 1852; reprinted Chicago, 1887). But the first comprehensive account to be produced by a trained historian was Clarence Walworth Alvord, *The Illinois Country, 1673–1818* (Springfield, 1920), and this book is still a useful guide to the period. In a related work, *The Mississippi Valley in British Politics: A Study of the Trade, Land Speculation, and Experiments in Imperialism Culminating in the American Revolution* (2 vols., Cleveland, 1917), Alvord helped to shape the broad perspectives of the "imperial school" of American colonial historiography. This larger context for early Illinois was in time most fully developed by Lawrence Henry Gipson, *The British Empire before the American Revolution* . . . (15 vols., Caldwell, Idaho and New York, 1936–70).

As an introduction to the period, Alvord's *Illinois Country* may to some extent be supplemented and updated by John D. Barnhart and Dorothy L. Riker, *Indiana to 1816: The Colonial Period* (Indianapolis, 1971). Illinois and Indiana share a common history at many points, especially when both were included in the Northwest Territory and when Illinois was part of Indiana Territory. As it happens, historians connected with universities in the two states have also set the pace for research in the period. At first, Alvord and his associates at the University of Illinois, especially Clarence E. Carter and Theodore C. Pease, made important contributions. More recently, Barnhart and his students at Indiana University, including Jack M. Sosin and Reginald Horsman, have revised and extended the Illinois legacy.

Several writers have prepared well-written overviews of the period, or parts of it. Theodore Calvin Pease and Marguerite Jenison Pease, *George Rogers Clark and the Revolution in Illinois, 1763–1787: A Sesquicentennial Memorial* (Springfield, 1929) is brief but insightful. Illinois' place in the larger history of westward expansion is apparent in Jack M. Sosin, *The Revolutionary Frontier, 1763–1783* (New York, 1967) and Reginald Horsman, *The Frontier in the Formative Years, 1783–1851* (New York, 1970). Illinois also figures in two more popular series. One is by Dale Van Every, who wrote *Forth to the Wilderness: The First American Frontier, 1754–1774*; *A Company of Heroes: The American Frontier, 1775–1783*; *Ark of Empire: The American Frontier, 1784–1803*; and *The Final Challenge: The American Frontier, 1804–1845* (New York, 1961–64). The other by Allan W. Eckert, who invents conversations to enliven the story, includes two books that relate to Illinois before statehood, *The Frontiersmen: A Narrative* and *Gateway to Empire* (Boston, 1967–83).

Maps are often helpful in studying the period. The atlases cited in the previous chapter are again relevant, as is W. Raymond Wood, comp., *An Atlas of Early Maps of the American Midwest*, Illinois State Museum, Scientific Papers, 18 (Springfield, 1983), and Lester J. Cappon et al., eds., *Atlas of Early American History: The Revolutionary Era, 1760–1790* (Princeton, 1976). James Truslow Adams, ed., *Atlas of American History* (New York, 1943; revised ed., New York, 1984) includes a number of plates clearly depicting Illinois and the West. Helen Hornbeck Tanner, ed., *The Atlas of Great Lakes Indian History* (Norman,

Okla., 1987) pertains to both the colonial and the early national periods and is especially useful for its coverage of military affairs.

The most important sources for the decade of British rule in Illinois are published in Clarence Walworth Alvord and Clarence Edwin Carter, eds., *The Critical Period, 1763–1765*; *The New Régime, 1765–1767*; and *Trade and Politics, 1767–1769*, Collections of the Illinois State Historical Library, 10, 11, and 16 (1915–21). Carter also edited *The Correspondence of General Thomas Gage . . . 1763–1775* (2 vols., New Haven, 1931–33) and "Documents Relating to the Occupation of the Illinois Country by the British," *Transactions of the Illinois State Historical Society for the Year 1907*, 12. Carter's *Great Britain and the Illinois Country, 1763–1774* (Washington, D.C., 1910) is still the best introduction to the subject. Another study, taking issue with Alvord's work, is Jack M. Sosin, *Whitehall and the Wilderness: The Middle West in British Colonial Policy, 1760–1775* (Lincoln, Nebr., 1961).

Indian problems in the West delayed Britain's occupation of the Illinois Country. Francis Parkman's classic account, *History of the Conspiracy of Pontiac . . .* (Boston, 1851; later eds., *The Conspiracy of Pontiac . . .* ), though eminently readable, has been superseded by several studies, including Howard H. Peckham, *Pontiac and the Indian Uprising* (Princeton, 1947) and Wilbur R. Jacobs, *Dispossessing the American Indian: Indians and Whites on the Colonial Frontier* (New York, 1972). For the British representative who played an important role in the Illinois Country at this time, see Nicholas B. Wainwright, *George Croghan, Wilderness Diplomat* (Chapel Hill, 1959). John Wilkins, a commandant at Fort de Chartres, is sketched in Colton Storm, "The Notorious Colonel Wilkins," *Journal of the Illinois State Historical Society*, 40 (Mar. 1947). An engineer at the fort, and a distinguished cartographer of the period, is traced in Anna Margaret Quattrocchi, "Thomas Hutchins, 1730–1789" (Ph.D. diss., Univ. of Pittsburgh, 1944).

Trade and politics were closely linked in the Illinois Country, a point that is well illustrated by the activities of a Philadelphia firm, sources for which are microfilmed (10 reels) and inventoried in Donald H. Kent et al., *Guide to the Microfilm of the Baynton, Wharton, and Morgan Papers in the Pennsylvania State Archives . . .* (Harrisburg, Pa., 1967). Max Savelle, *George Morgan, Colony Builder* (New York, 1932) is an outstanding study of the partner most in touch with Illinois affairs. See also Robert M. Sutton, "George Morgan, Early Illinois Businessman: A Case of Premature Enterprise," *Journal of the Illinois State Historical Society*, 69 (Aug. 1976), and Peter Marshall, "Lord Hillsborough, Samuel Wharton, and the Ohio Grant, 1769–1775," *English Historical Review*, 80 (Oct. 1965). Another trader's career is followed in Anna Edith Marks, "William Murray, Trader and Land Speculator in the Illinois Country," *Transactions of the Illinois State Historical Society for the Year 1919*, 26.

Spain became more interested in the Illinois Country after the treaty of 1763 gave it Louisiana west of the Mississippi River. John Francis Bannon introduces this subject in "The Spaniards and the Illinois Country, 1762–1800," *Journal of the Illinois State Historical Society*, 69 (May 1976), and in the first chapter of John Francis McDermott, ed., *The Spanish in the Mississippi Valley, 1762–1804* (Urbana, 1974). For a fuller view, see Abraham Phineas Nasatir, "Indian Trade and Diplomacy in the Spanish Illinois, 1763–1792" (Ph.D. diss., Univ. of California, Berkeley, 1926) and Carl J. Ekberg, *Colonial Ste. Genevieve: An Adventure on the Mississippi Frontier* (Gerald, Mo., 1985). For a translation of materials from the Spanish archives, see Lawrence Kinnaird, "Spain in the Mississippi Valley," *Annual Report of the American Historical Association for the Year 1945*, 2–4 (Washington, D.C., 1946–49). Aspects of the American Revolution in particular are considered in Nasatir's "The Anglo-Spanish Frontier in the Illinois Country during the American Revolution, 1779–1783," *Journal of the Illinois State Historical Society*, 21 (Oct. 1928), and in William Collins, "The Spanish Attack on Fort St. Joseph," in Robert J. Holden, ed., *Selected Papers from the 1983 and 1984 George Rogers Clark Trans-Appalachian Frontier History Conferences* (Vincennes, Ind., 1985).

Historians have studied Illinois during the American Revolution somewhat more intensively than Illinois under the British. Overviews of the subject include George M. Waller, *The American Revolution in the West* (Chicago, 1976) and Reginald Horsman, "Great Britain and the Illinois Country in the Era of the American Revolution," *Journal of the Illinois State Historical Society*, 69 (May 1976). The importance of land companies during and even after the Revolution is apparent in Thomas Perkins Abernethy, *Western Lands and the American Revolution* (New York, 1937) and George E. Lewis, *The Indiana Company, 1763–1798: A Study of Eighteenth Century Frontier Land Speculation and Business Venture* (Glendale, Calif., 1941). Another topic is well treated in Randolph C. Downes, *Council Fires on the Upper Ohio: A Narrative of Indian Affairs in the Upper Ohio Valley until 1795* (Pittsburgh, 1940).

But the center of attention for most scholars of the period has been George Rogers Clark, leader of an expedition that captured the British outposts in the Mississippi Valley and at Vincennes in 1778–79. Of the many biographies, the best include James Alton James, *The Life of George Rogers Clark* (Chicago, 1928) and John Bakeless, *Background to Glory: The Life of George Rogers Clark* (Philadelphia, 1957). James also edited the *George Rogers Clark Papers, 1771–1781* and . . . *1781–1784*, Collections of the Illinois State Historical Library, 8 and 19 (1912–26). Another, less skillful compilation is Kathrine Wagner Seineke, *The George Rogers Clark Adventure in the Illinois and Selected Documents of the American Revolution at the Frontier Posts* (New Orleans, 1981). See also Robert M. Sutton, "George Rogers Clark and the Campaign in the West: The Five Major Documents," *Indiana Magazine of History*, 76 (Dec. 1980).

The reputation of Clark's opponent at Vincennes is rehabilitated in John D. Barnhart, "A New Evaluation of Henry Hamilton and George Rogers Clark," *Mississippi Valley Historical Review*, 37 (Mar. 1951); in Barnhart's edition of Hamilton's journal, *Henry Hamilton and George Rogers Clark in the American Revolution with the Unpublished Journal of Lieut. Gov. Henry Hamilton* (Crawfordsville, Ind., 1951); and in the work of one of Barnhart's students, Orville John Jaebker, "Henry Hamilton, British Soldier and Colonial Governor" (Ph.D. diss., Indiana Univ., 1954). An important additional source is William A. Evans, ed., *Detroit to Fort Sackville, 1778–1779: The Journal of Normand MacLeod* (Detroit, 1978).

George C. Chalou considers "George Rogers Clark and Indian America, 1778–1780" in *The French, the Indians, and George Rogers Clark in the Illinois Country* . . . (Indianapolis, 1977), and Bernard W. Sheehan probes the psychological ambiguities in the situation in " 'The Famous Hair Buyer General': Henry Hamilton, George Rogers Clark, and the American Indian," *Indiana Magazine of History*, 79 (Mar. 1983). Two of Clark's contemporaries are studied in Joseph P. Donnelly, *Pierre Gibault, Missionary, 1737–1802* (Chicago, 1971) and James Alton James, *Oliver Pollock: Life and Times of an Unknown Patriot* (New York, 1937).

The period immediately after Clark's conquest of Illinois is discussed in Theodore Calvin Pease, "1780: The Revolution at Crisis in the West," *Journal of the Illinois State Historical Society*, 23 (Jan. 1931), and in John H. Hauberg, "Hard Times in Illinois in 1780," ibid., 44 (Autumn 1951). Clarence Walworth Alvord's initial studies in the field included *The County of Illinois* (Springfield, 1907), which served as the introduction to his edition of *Cahokia Records, 1778–1790*, Collections of the Illinois State Historical Library, 2 (1907), followed by a similar volume, *Kaskaskia Records, 1778–1790*, ibid., 5 (1909), and an article, "Virginia and the West: An Interpretation," *Mississippi Valley Historical Review*, 3 (June 1916). The work of one of Alvord's students, Paul Chrisler Phillips, *The West in the Diplomacy of the American Revolution* (Urbana, 1913), should be supplemented by Norman A. Graebner, "The Illinois Country and the Treaty of Paris of 1783," *Illinois Historical Journal*, 78 (Spring 1985).

Although Great Britain recognized the United States by the treaty of 1783, ceding to the new government its lands east of the Mississippi, the formation of the national domain was complicated by the claims of several states. Virginia in particular controlled Illinois, at least nominally, and did not fully sign away its interests northwest of the Ohio River until 1784. The situation is concisely described in Merrill Jensen, "The Cession of the Old Northwest," *Mississippi Valley Historical Review*, 23 (June 1936), and is more extensively, if repetitively, considered in Peter S. Onuf, *The Origins of the Federal Republic: Jurisdictional Controversies in the United States, 1775–1787* (Philadelphia, 1983). The emergence of a central, nationalizing government, formally established by the Articles of Confederation, is skillfully traced in Jack N. Rakove, *The Beginnings of National Politics: An Interpretive History of the Continental Congress* (New York, 1979).

The Confederation Congress established the principles for surveying the national domain in the Land Ordinance of 1785. The impact of this legislation is studied in several works, including Hildegard Binder Johnson, *Order upon the Land: The U.S. Rectangular Land Survey and the Upper Mississippi Country* (New York, 1976) and C. Albert White, *A History of the Rectangular Survey System* (Washington, D.C., 1983). For Illinois alone, see Raymond H. Hammes, "Land Transactions in Illinois Prior to the Sale of Public Domain," *Journal of the Illinois State Historical Society*, 77 (Summer 1984); Ladislav Matousek, "The Beginnings of Illinois Surveys," *Illinois Libraries*, 53 (Jan. 1971); and Joe D. Webber, *Early Public Land Surveys in the Northwest Territory and Procedures for the Retracement of Original Government Surveys in Illinois* (Rochester, Ill., 1981).

Congress addressed the question of government in the Northwest Territory first in the Ordinance of 1784 and then in the Ordinance of 1787. The recent bicentennial celebrations have produced a number of important studies. Peter S. Onuf, *Statehood and Union: A History of the Northwest Ordinance* (Bloomington, Ind., 1987) is the most significant and also the most comprehensive since it reviews the land ordinance as well as the two governmental enactments. Although Onuf did not fully integrate his earlier articles into the book, his work contains some brilliant insights. A more sweeping account is Jack Ericson Eblen, *The First and Second United States Empires: Governors and Territorial Government, 1784–1912* (Pittsburgh, 1968), a standard but now somewhat dated book.

Important articles concerning the 1784 enactment include Merrill Jensen, "The Creation of the National Domain, 1781–1784," *Mississippi Valley Historical Review*, 26 (Dec. 1939); Robert F. Berkhofer, Jr., "Jefferson, the Ordinance of 1784, and the Origins of the American Territorial System," *William and Mary Quarterly*, 29 (Apr. 1972); and Reginald Horsman, "Thomas Jefferson and the Ordinance of 1784," *Illinois Historical Journal*, 79 (Summer 1986). A useful compilation regarding the legislation of 1787 is Robert M. Taylor, Jr., ed., *The Northwest Ordinance, 1787: A Bicentennial Handbook* (Indianapolis, 1987). Several interpretations are outlined in Ray A. Billington, "The Historians of the Northwest Ordinance," *Journal of the Illinois State Historical Society*, 40 (Dec. 1947), and Phillip R. Shriver, "America's Other Bicentennial," *Old Northwest*, 9 (Fall 1983). Papers from conferences commemorating the Northwest Ordinance appear in *Pathways to the Old Northwest: An Observance of the Bicentennial of the Northwest Ordinance* (Indianapolis, 1988); Frederick D. Williams, ed., *The Northwest Ordinance: Essays on Its Formulation, Provisions, and Legacy* (East Lansing, 1989); and a special issue of the *Indiana Magazine of History*, 84 (Mar. 1988). The last publication includes, for example, David Brion Davis, "The Significance of Excluding Slavery from the Old Northwest in 1787," which should be read together with Paul Finkelman's articles, "Slavery and the Northwest Ordinance: A Study in Ambiguity," *Journal of the Early Republic*, 6 (Winter 1986), and "Evading the Ordinance: The Persistence of Bondage in Indiana and Illinois," ibid., 9 (Spring 1989).

The process of settlement and state making in the West is examined in a major work by John D. Barnhart, *Valley of Democracy: The Frontier versus the Plantation in the Ohio Valley, 1775–1818* (Bloomington, Ind., 1953). The topic is studied in quantitative terms in James E. Davis, *Frontier America, 1800–1840: A Comparative Demographic Analysis of the Settlement Process* (Glendale, Calif., 1977). The emerging culture north of the Ohio River is considered in Beverley W. Bond, Jr., *The Civilization of the Old Northwest: A Study of Political, Social, and Economic Development, 1788–1812* (New York, 1934). Regarding Illinois in particular, see Arthur Clinton Boggess, *The Settlement of Illinois, 1778–1830*, Chicago Historical Society's Collection, 5 (Chicago, 1908), and Margaret Cross Norton, ed., *Illinois Census Returns, 1810, 1818* and *Illinois Census Returns, 1820*, Collections of the Illinois State Historical Library, 24 and 26 (1934–35).

Documentary sources for Illinois history in the territorial period are provided in two series, the Territorial Papers of the United States and the Collections of the Illinois State Historical Library. In the former, Clarence Edwin Carter edited *The Territory Northwest of the River Ohio, 1787–1803* (2 vols.); *The Territory of Indiana, 1800–1810*; and *The Territory of Illinois, 1809–1814* and . . . *1814–1818*, Volumes 2–3, 7, and 16–17 of the series (Washington, D.C., 1934–50). In the latter, Theodore Calvin Pease edited *The Laws of the Northwest Territory, 1788–1800*, and Francis S. Philbrick edited *The Laws of Indiana Territory, 1801–1809* and *The Laws of Illinois Territory, 1809–1818*, Volumes 17, 21, and 25 of the series (1925–50). Philbrick's introductions to these volumes are unusually long and detailed, and extend to related documents such as the proceedings of the executive council and the territorial legislature. Philbrick also edited *Pope's Digest, 1815*, ibid., 28 and 30 (1938–40). On the judiciary, see Robert Paul Fogerty, "An Institutional Study of the Territorial Courts in the Old Northwest, 1788–1848" (Ph.D. diss., Univ. of Minnesota, 1942).

Only three men were territorial governors of Illinois: Arthur St. Clair when it was part of the Northwest Territory, William Henry Harrison when it was part of Indiana Territory from 1800 to 1809, and Ninian Edwards when it was a separate jurisdiction. See, in turn, Gordon L. Wilson, "Arthur St. Clair and the Administration of the Old Northwest, 1788–1802" (Ph.D. diss., Univ. of Southern California, 1957); Dorothy Burne Goebel, *William Henry Harrison: A Political Biography*, Indiana Historical Collections, 16 (Indianapolis, 1926); and Michael J. Bakalis, "Ninian Edwards and Territorial Politics in Illinois, 1775–1818" (Ph.D. diss., Northwestern Univ., 1966). Jo Tice Bloom examines "The Congressional Delegates from the Northwest Territory, 1799–1803" and "The Delegates from Illinois Territory, 1809–1818" in *Old Northwest*, 3 (Mar. 1977) and 6 (Fall 1980). Studies of conspicuous political figures in territorial Illinois include Paul M. Angle, "Nathaniel Pope, 1784–1850: A Memoir," *Illinois State Historical Society Transactions for the Year 1936*, 43; Charles E. Burgess, "John Rice Jones, Citizen of Many Territories," *Journal of the Illinois State Historical Society*, 61 (Spring 1968); and Joseph E. Suppiger, "Amity to

Enmity: Ninian Edwards and Jesse B. Thomas," ibid., 67 (Apr. 1974).

Relations with the Indians posed an intractable problem for American settlers. For a general perspective, see Reginald Horsman, *Expansion and American Indian Policy, 1783–1812* (East Lansing, 1967). More particular works include Dwight L. Smith, "Indian Land Cessions in the Old Northwest, 1795–1809" (Ph.D. diss., Indiana Univ., 1949); Otis Louis Miller, "Indian-White Relations in the Illinois Country, 1789 to 1818" (Ph.D. diss., St. Louis Univ., 1972); and Grant Foreman, "Illinois and Her Indians," in Illinois State Historical Society, *Papers in Illinois History and Transactions for the Year 1939*. Two important tribes are traced in A[rrell] M. Gibson, *The Kickapoos, Lords of the Middle Border* (Norman, Okla., 1963) and R[ussell] David Edmunds, *The Potawatomis, Keepers of the Fire* (Norman, Okla., 1978).

Relations with Great Britain were strained in the period between the Revolution and the War of 1812. J[ames] Leitch Wright, Jr., *Britain and the American Frontier, 1783–1815* (Athens, Ga., 1975) is the best survey of Britain's influence in the West. Not until Gen. Anthony Wayne's victory over the Indians at Fallen Timbers in Ohio in 1794 did the British vacate certain western posts and did their former Indian allies, in the Treaty of Greenville of 1795, cede strategic areas in the Northwest Territory. Wayne's plan to establish control over the southern part of the territory is described in Leland R. Johnson, "The Doyle Mission to Massac, 1794," *Journal of the Illinois State Historical Society*, 73 (Spring 1980).

The United States, caught as a neutral nation in the struggles between Great Britain and France, encountered persistent difficulties with both countries and eventually declared war on Britain in 1812. These developments have been covered in several first-rate studies, including two that focus on the Old Northwest: Harrison Bird, *War for the West, 1790–1813* (New York, 1971) and Alec R. Gilpin, *The War of 1812 in the Old Northwest* (East Lansing, 1958). An unusually full account of Illinois in particular is Frank E. Stevens, "Illinois in the War of 1812–1814," *Transactions of the Illinois State Historical Society for the Year 1904*, 9. See also Robert J. Holden, "Governor Ninian Edwards and the War of 1812: The Military Role of a Territorial Governor," in Illinois State Historical Society, *Selected Papers in Illinois History, 1980*. The massacre at Fort Dearborn on August 15, 1812, is ably discussed in Milo Milton Quaife, *Chicago and the Old Northwest, 1673–1835: A Study of the Evolution of the Northwestern Frontier, together with a History of Fort Dearborn* (Chicago, 1913) and H. A. Musham, "Where Did the Battle of Chicago Take Place?" *Journal of the Illinois State Historical Society*, 36 (Mar. 1943). Important documents related to this event include Mentor L. Williams, "John Kinzie's Narrative of the Fort Dearborn Massacre," ibid., 46 (Winter 1953), and John D. Barnhart, ed., "A New Letter about the Massacre of Fort Dearborn," *Indiana Magazine of History*, 41 (June 1945), which reviews previous accounts.

After the War of 1812, Illinois developed rapidly toward statehood. The best description of these formative years and of the entry into the Union is still Solon

Justus Buck, *Illinois in 1818* (Springfield, 1917). Another substantial work, R[oscoe] Carlyle Buley, *The Old Northwest: Pioneer Period, 1815–1840* (2 vols., Indianapolis, 1950), provides a wider perspective. An important aspect of economic development is examined in Donald Zochert, "Illinois Water Mills, 1790–1818," *Journal of the Illinois State Historical Society*, 65 (Summer 1972). Two specialized studies are Keith Linus Miller, "Building Towns on the Southeastern Illinois Frontier, 1810–1830" (Ph.D. diss., Miami Univ., Oxford, Ohio, 1976) and John Leslie Tevebaugh, "Merchant on the Western Frontier: William Morrison of Kaskaskia, 1790–1837" (Ph.D. diss., Univ. of Illinois, 1962). Nicolas de Finiels, *An Account of Upper Louisiana* (Columbia, Mo., 1989) is a newly translated source for life in the Illinois Country at the turn of the nineteenth century.

While Buck's *Illinois in 1818* covers the state's first constitution, the journal of the convention is in Richard V. Carpenter, "The Illinois Constitutional Convention of 1818," *Journal of the Illinois State Historical Society*, 6 (Oct. 1913). Studies of important participants include Henry Barrett Chamberlin, "Elias Kent Kane," *Transactions of the Illinois State Historical Society for the Year 1908*, 13, and Robert P. Howard, "Myths after Shadrach Bond," in the *Transactions* for 1986–87.

Although this bibliographical review points to only part of the literature on the period of British rule and American settlement, it is clear that practically every aspect of Illinois history from 1765 to 1818 is open for research. Contemporary scholars tend to pay the colonial and territorial periods much less attention than did scholars in Alvord's day. Thus, the field not only offers many opportunities for particular investigations but also calls for a major synthesis, now long overdue.

# 3

# THE FRONTIER STATE, 1818–48

## RODNEY O. DAVIS

PIONEER ILLINOIS WAS both a place of escape and a land of hope for its earliest American settlers. In its latter capacity, it began to attract the attention of publicists and literary tourists as early as the years just after the War of 1812. The resulting promotional and travel literature, followed later by contemporary indigenous descriptions and reminiscent accounts by pioneers and political figures, ensured that much source material for historians would come to exist for this formative period in the state's history. Indeed, to a large extent the pioneer history of Illinois *was* the history of Illinois until the Civil War era, and a heavily studied portion of that history for the rest of the nineteenth century. Throughout the twentieth century, the preeminence of Abraham Lincoln also encouraged research on frontier Illinois, although admittedly much of it evinces a bias toward the biographical. The end result for the period has been an unusual richness of conventional sources as well as a considerable output of what might be called traditional "impressionistic" historical work.

Probably the best introduction to pioneer Illinois is still Theodore Calvin Pease, *The Frontier State, 1818–1848* (Springfield, 1918). Although it lacks a quality of conceptual precision, Pease's book is full of information, and his insights and evaluations for the most part continue to be sound. A more recent survey is R[oscoe] Carlyle Buley, *The Old Northwest: Pioneer Period, 1815–1840* (2 vols., Indianapolis, 1950), which affords the advantage of placing Illinois in a comparative context with the other emerging states of the Great Lakes region. Ray A. Billington's Turnerian essay, "The Frontier in Illinois History," *Journal of the Illinois State Historical Society*, 43 (Spring 1958), is still worth reading.

Nineteenth-century introductions to the frontier period include Alexander Davidson and Bernard Stuvé, *A Complete History of Illinois from 1673 to 1873* . . . (Springfield, 1874), which treats the era as a kind of heroic age; heavy on the Black Hawk War, it stints on economic and social matters. Henry Brown, *The History of Illinois* . . . (New York, 1844) was written by a Chicago lawyer only in the state since 1836 and is not insightful. Thomas Ford, *A History of Illinois from Its Commencement as a State in 1818 to 1847* . . . (Chicago, 1854; best ed., 2 vols., Chicago, 1945–46) is the outstanding early survey. Indeed, it may still be the basic text for the period, although it is limited by its time of publication and the strong biases of its author. Ford was cynical, defensive, and self-serving, but he had an unrivaled sensitivity to the dynamics of frontier life, the peculiarities of developing democratic institutions in the West, and the presence of cultural conflict among the immigrants to Illinois.

Almost in a separate category are the state's county histories, published in two distinct phases, in celebration of the nation's centennial in the 1870s and 1880s, and again around the turn of the century. Frequently inaccurate and unreliable, they must nonetheless be reckoned with by students of Illinois' frontier history. The volumes of the centennial era are the more valuable because of the strong presence within them of pioneers' perspectives. Much of the information in these older books was taken from the memories of surviving old settlers, which information was irretrievable by the end of the century. The biographical sketches found in the older county histories can also be useful to political and social historians or to students of community development. Generally of better quality are those county histories published by the Charles C. Chapman, H. F. Kett, and William LeBaron companies, all of Chicago, and by the Continental Historical Company of Springfield. Of lesser quality are histories published by Brink, McDonough and Company of Philadelphia, and by O. L. Baskin and Company of Chicago. A still helpful bibliography of Illinois county histories is Solon Justus Buck, *Travel and Description, 1765–1865, together with a List of County Histories, Atlases, and Biographical Collections* . . . , Collections of the Illinois State Historical Library, 9 (1914). Rodney O. Davis, "Coming to Terms with County Histories," *Western Illinois Regional Studies*, 2 (Fall 1979), undertakes a contemporary appraisal.

Among the earliest promotional descriptions of Illinois were those from the English Settlement in Edwards County, founded by Morris Birkbeck and George Flower. Writing both to advertise for colonists and in response to criticism of the venture by William Cobbett, Birkbeck published *Letters from Illinois* (Philadelphia, 1818; best ed., New York, 1970) and *An Address to the Farmers of Great Britain* . . . (London, 1822). If judiciously used, each can be taken as indicative of pioneer life and the character and availability of land in Illinois.

The prairie was early Illinois' most striking physical feature and frequently suspect among Southern-born or European immigrants. Birkbeck's *Address* contains an essay on the prairie that is one of the earliest to regard it positively. Richard Flower, *Letters from the Illinois* . . . (London, 1822) is in the same promotional category. Two Britishers wrote widely read accounts of their life in the English Settlement: W[illiam] Faux, *Memorable Days in America* . . . (London, 1823) is gossipy and rather sour, but John Woods, *Two Years' Residence in the Settlement on the English Prairie* . . . (London, 1822; best ed., Chicago, 1968) is straightforward. The Flower, Faux, and Woods accounts are reprinted in Reuben Gold Thwaites, ed., *Early Western Travels, 1748–1846* . . . , 10–12 (32 vols., Cleveland, 1904–7). A German observer who was attracted to the English Settlement but who traveled farther in the state was Ferdinand Ernst. See "Travels in Illinois in 1819," *Transactions of the Illinois State Historical Society for the Year 1903*, 8.

Also useful for the earliest years of statehood, but for an entirely different part of the state, are two guides designed for land seekers in the Illinois Military Tract. They are Nicholas Biddle Van Zandt, *A Full Description of the Soil, Water, Timber, and Prairies of Each Lot or Quarter Section of the Military Lands between the Mississippi and Illinois Rivers* (Washington, D.C., 1818) and E[dmund] Dana, *A Description of the Bounty Lands in the State of Illinois* . . . (Cincinnati, 1819). Each contains a section-by-section description of the bounty lands, taken from surveyor's notes. Less promotional but equally laudatory is Barbara Lawrence and Nedra Branz, eds., *The Flagg Correspondence: Selected Letters, 1816–1854* (Carbondale, 1986), which is revealing about economic and social conditions in early Madison County.

The trans-Appalachian boom of the 1830s was also productive of promotional literature about Illinois, one of the most indefatigable authors of which was John Mason Peck. An early model for Peck was Lewis C. Beck, *A Gazetteer of the States of Illinois and Missouri* . . . (Albany, N.Y., 1823), which is as interesting for its misrepresentations as for its descriptions. Improving on Beck, Peck wrote two types of books, each issued in several editions. *A Guide for Emigrants Containing Sketches of Illinois, Missouri, and the Adjacent Parts* . . . (Boston, 1831) deals heavily with Illinois, but its descriptions are general. It was intended to attract Yankee immigrants to a state that Peck considered too much under the influence of a Southern-born element and of uneducated Hoosiers. *A Gazetteer of Illinois* . . . (Jacksonville, Ill., 1834) is a comprehensive county-by-county inventory of Illinois' environmental, social, and economic assets. Samuel Augustus Mitchell published a similar volume, *Illinois in 1837* . . . (Philadelphia, 1837), which Peck rightly insisted was cribbed from his own.

Among the works of travelers of the 1830s and 1840s who went to look at Illinois or actually lived in the state awhile, some of the most important are A[bner] D. Jones, *Illinois and the West* . . . (Boston, 1838); [Edmund Flagg], *The Far West, or a Tour beyond the Mountains* . . . (2 vols., New York,

1838; reprinted in Thwaites, *Early Western Travels*, 26–27); William Oliver, *Eight Months in Illinois* . . . (Newcastle-upon-Tyne, 1843); S[arah] M[argaret] Fuller, *Summer on the Lakes in 1843* (Boston, 1844); Eliza W. Farnham, *Life in Prairie Land* (New York, 1846); and Rebecca Burlend, *A True Picture of Emigration* . . . (London, 1848; best ed., Chicago, 1936). Jones and Farnham were especially conscious of the anomaly of the prairies to Anglo-Saxons and Europeans; unable to find adequate descriptive language, Jones referred to them as "immense sea fields" (p. 92).

The prairie also attracted the attention of James Hall, who tried for two years to publish a literary magazine in Vandalia before retreating to Cincinnati. His "Notes on Illinois," *Illinois Monthly Magazine*, 1–2 (1830–32), include realistic assessments of the grassland's potential and sensitive descriptions of Illinois' pioneer society. Never intended for publication was John Goodell, ed., *Diary of William Sewall, 1797–1846* . . . (Lincoln, Ill., 1930), which contains a slaveholding New Englander's reflections on agriculture and politics in Cass County at about the same time. For a bibliography of travel literature and emigrants' guides, see Buck's *Travel and Description*.

Published reminiscences of frontier-era Illinois figures can be valuable if used with care. Among those descriptive of pioneer economic and social conditions are Christiana Holmes Tillson, *Reminiscences of Early Life in Illinois* . . . , apparently printed in Amherst, Massachusetts in 1872 (reprinted as *A Woman's Story of Pioneer Illinois*, Chicago, 1919); James Haines, "Social Life and Scenes in the Early Settlement of Central Illinois," *Transactions of the Illinois State Historical Society for the Year 1905*, 10; and Charles H. Rammelkamp, ed., "The Memoirs of John Henry, a Pioneer of Morgan County," *Journal of the Illinois State Historical Society*, 18 (Apr. 1925).

Book-length reminiscences more focused on politics and law than on social and economic matters are Usher F. Linder, *Reminiscences of the Early Bench and Bar of Illinois* (Chicago, 1879), which is colorful but unreliable; John Dean Caton, *Early Bench and Bar of Illinois* (Chicago, 1893), which unlike Linder's book deals with the author's own experience and only a little hearsay; John M. Palmer, ed., *The Bench and Bar of Illinois* . . . (2 vols., Chicago, 1899); and Thomas J. McCormack, ed., *Memoirs of Gustave Koerner, 1809–1896* . . . (2 vols., Cedar Rapids, Iowa, 1909), which is very good on Jacksonian politics in the state and on the German-born element in the American Bottom. A valuable work that defies classification is John Reynolds, *My Own Times, Embracing Also the History of My Life* (Belleville, Ill., 1855; reprinted Chicago, 1879). Although discursive and chaotically organized, it spans the frontier period, and its author's involvement in early state politics was constant.

In the late 1870s, the Fergus Printing Company of Chicago began to gather the recollections of surviving Illinois and Chicago legal and political figures. Among the most valuable are John Wentworth, *Early Chicago* . . . , Fergus' *Historical Series*, 7 (1876), and his *Fort Dearborn*, ibid., 16 (1881); Joseph Gillespie, *Recollections of Early Illinois and Her Noted Men*, ibid., 13 (1880);

Isaac N. Arnold, *Reminiscences of the Illinois Bar Forty Years Ago* . . . , ibid., 14 (1881), and his *Recollections of the Early Chicago and Illinois Bar*, ibid., 22 (1882); James C. Conkling, *Recollections of the Bench and Bar of Central Illinois*, ibid.; and Thomas Hoyne, *The Lawyer as a Pioneer*, ibid.

Political history is central to the treatments by Ford, Pease, and Buley; they are limited by the source materials their authors consulted and by the questions they asked of them. Ford's major source, of course, was his memory; Pease and Buley relied on such traditional evidence as newspapers and manuscript collections. Their books are therefore full of rather old-fashioned political history, including election campaigns and the rivalries of factional leaders. They generally overlook such matters as legislative or electoral behavior that are more difficult to document. Another work that is basic to an understanding of the politics of the era is John Francis Snyder, *Adam W. Snyder and His Period in Illinois History, 1817–1842* (Springfield, 1903; revised ed., Virginia, Ill., 1906). Although opinionated, and part biography, part reminiscence, and part history, it contains information not found elsewhere.

It should therefore not be surprising that much of the writing about Illinois' early political history has been either heavily biographical in nature or concerned with gubernatorial administrations. An example is Ninian W. Edwards, *History of Illinois from 1778 to 1833, and Life and Times of Ninian Edwards* (Springfield, 1870), which is a son's stilted and filiopietistic study of Illinois' territorial governor, its third state governor, and one of its first U.S. senators. It has been updated by Richard Lance Wixon, "Ninian Edwards, a Founding Father of Illinois" (Ph.D. diss., Southern Illinois Univ., Carbondale, 1983). Revealing of the difficult balancing act required of a politician such as Edwards in a new commonwealth is E[lihu] B. Washburne, ed., *The Edwards Papers* . . . , Chicago Historical Society's Collection, 3 (Chicago, 1884). The state's other first senator is the subject of Joseph Edward Suppiger, "Jesse Burgess Thomas, Illinois' Pro-Slavery Advocate" (Ph.D. diss., Univ. of Tennessee, 1970).

Edward Coles, an outsider who came to Illinois rather quickly to become its second governor, and then to aid immeasurably in defeating an effort to introduce slavery, deserves a full biography. Until recently the literature was limited to E[lihu] B. Washburne, *Sketch of Edward Coles* . . . (Chicago, 1882; best ed., *Governor Edward Coles*, Collections of the Illinois State Historical Library, 15 [1920]); Eudora Ramsey Richardson, "The Virginian Who Made Illinois a Free State," *Journal of the Illinois State Historical Society*, 45 (Spring 1952); and Donald S. Spencer, "Edward Coles: Virginia Gentleman in Frontier Politics," ibid., 61 (Summer 1968). Now Kurt E. Leichtle, in "Edward Coles, an Agrarian on the Frontier" (Ph.D. diss., Univ. of Illinois, Chicago, 1982), has moved toward a fuller scholarly treatment.

Josephine Louise Harper, "John Reynolds, 'The Old Ranger' of Illinois, 1788–1865" (Ph.D. diss., Univ. of Illinois, 1949) takes her subject more seriously than many authors do but falls short of making total sense of that fascinating frontier figure. Elizabeth Duncan Putnam, "The Life and Services of

Joseph Duncan, Governor of Illinois, 1834–1838," *Transactions of the Illinois State Historical Society for the Year 1919*, 26, is adulatory and incomplete. Evarts Boutell Greene and Clarence Walworth Alvord, eds., *The Governors' Letter-Books, 1818–1834*, Collections of the Illinois State Historical Library, 4 (1909), and Greene and Charles Manfred Thompson, eds., *The Governors' Letter-Books, 1840–1853*, ibid., 7 (1911), provide some additional documentation for the administration of early chief executives. The latter volume includes Thompson's "A Study of the Administration of Governor Thomas Ford," which is still authoritative on that topic. For lesser figures, see William Coffin, *Life and Times of Hon. Samuel D. Lockwood* (Chicago, 1889) and nine articles published under the rubric "Forgotten Statesmen of Illinois" in *Transactions of the Illinois State Historical Society for the Year 1903* through . . . *1908*, 8–13. About the only recent institutional study of the early Illinois governor's office is Daniel J. Elazar, "Gubernatorial Power and the Illinois and Michigan Canal: A Study of Political Development in the Nineteenth Century," *Journal of the Illinois State Historical Society*, 58 (Winter 1965).

Many Illinois political careers of the 1830s and 1840s developed out of the Black Hawk War of 1832, an affair that was probably more important to the state's political and economic development than as a notable military achievement. But work proceeds on its military aspects. The massive collection of documents edited by Ellen M. Whitney, *The Black Hawk War, 1831–1832*, Collections of the Illinois State Historical Library, 35–38 (1970–78), is a mine for researchers, and its introductory essay, also separately printed, is the standard secondary source on the coming of the war: Anthony F. C. Wallace, *Prelude to Disaster* . . . (Springfield, 1970). Other accounts of the war abound. John A. Wakefield, *History of the War between the United States and the Sac and Fox Nations of Indians* . . . (Jacksonville, 1834; best ed., *Wakefield's History of the Black Hawk War*, Chicago, 1908) is a participant's record. The most comprehensive edition of the *Life of Ma-ka-tai-me-she-kia-kiak or Black Hawk* . . . (Cincinnati, 1833) is Donald Jackson's, retitled *An Autobiography* (Urbana, 1955). Joseph B. Herring, *Kenekuk, the Kickapoo Prophet* (Lawrence, Kans., 1988) deals with a band of Indians who left Illinois peacefully in 1832–33.

An early effort to deal with group behavior in early Illinois politics is Charles Manfred Thompson, *The Illinois Whigs before 1846*, University of Illinois Studies in the Social Sciences, 4 (Urbana, 1915). Thompson details the coalescence of a two-party system in the state out of the highly personalized factions of the 1820s. His work is complemented by Theodore Calvin Pease, *Illinois Election Returns, 1818–1848*, Collections of the Illinois State Historical Library, 18 (1923), which contains a wealth of valuable county-level data on candidates for state and federal offices. Pease's introductory essay in this volume is more satisfactory than are his political chapters in *The Frontier State*. The first author to study the Illinois General Assembly as an arena of meaningful political activity was Albert J. Beveridge, whose own legislative experience made him sensitive to the subject. In *Abraham Lincoln, 1809–1858* (2 vols., Boston, 1928), he deals knowledgeably with Illinois legislative politics, albeit as it involved Lincoln during his four terms in the House. Paul Simon ably expands that subject in *Lincoln's Preparation for Greatness: The Illinois Legislative Years* (Norman, Okla., 1965).

A few recent students have attempted to measure the intensity of political partisanship in frontier Illinois and to discover its sources, particularly after recognizable parties began to function in the legislature and the electorate in the early 1830s. Using legislative roll-call analysis techniques, Rodney Owen Davis, "Illinois Legislators and Jacksonian Democracy, 1834–1841" (Ph.D. diss., Univ. of Iowa, 1966) argues that legislative partisanship was stronger over moral issues, and issues involving political power or office holding, than over matters of economic development, such as banks or internal improvements. Davis summarizes and augments some of his findings in "Partisanship in Jacksonian State Politics: Party Divisions in the Illinois Legislature, 1834–1841," in Robert P. Swierenga, ed., *Quantification in American History: Theory and Research* (New York, 1970). William Gerald Shade covers a longer time period than does Davis and studies all the states of the Old Northwest in *Banks or No Banks: The Money Issue in Western Politics, 1832–1865* (Detroit, 1972). He finds the conflict over money and banking to be strong and persistent, and most evident among the immigrant subcultures of the area, not merely between haves and have-nots.

In a pioneering use of surviving pollbooks for the study of politics before the Illinois Constitution of 1848, John Michael Rozett relates electoral behavior both to wealth and to ethnocultural origins. See "The Social Bases of Party Conflict in the Age of Jackson: Individual Voting Behavior in Greene County, Illinois, 1838–1848" (Ph.D. diss., Univ. of Michigan, 1974). His findings are very impressive, but other authors, most notably Richard J. Jensen in *Illinois: A Bicentennial History* (New York, 1978), probably generalize too much from his study of a single county.

The conditions of state politics in Illinois from 1818 to 1848 were set by the faulty first state constitution. Thomas Ford in his *History* acerbically commented on some of its weaknesses, and Arnold Shankman more temperately points out some others in "Partisan Conflicts, 1839–1841, and the Illinois Constitution," *Journal of the Illinois State Historical Society*, 63 (Winter 1970). Arthur Charles Cole, ed., *The Constitutional Debates of 1847*, Collections of the Illinois State Historical Library, 14 (1919), details the proceedings of the convention that jettisoned that instrument.

Considering the frequency of vigilantism across the state in the 1830s and 1840s, there are surprisingly few studies of violence, law enforcement, and the judiciary in frontier Illinois. On the courts in general, John Wesley McNulty's work on Sidney Breese is helpful. His Ph.D. dissertation, "Chief Justice Sidney Breese and the Illinois Supreme Court: A Study of Law and Politics in the Old West" (Harvard Univ., 1962), was followed by two articles, "Sidney Breese:

His Early Career in Law and Politics in Illinois," *Journal of the Illinois State Historical Society*, 61 (Summer 1968), and "Sidney Breese, the Illinois Circuit Judge, 1835–1841," ibid., 62 (Summer 1969), both of which, unfortunately, are somewhat skeletal.

Hancock County's anti-Mormon violence has been the inspiration of much of the literature concerning violence and peace keeping. The subject of Dallin H. Oaks and Marvin S. Hill, *Carthage Conspiracy: The Trial of the Accused Assassins of Joseph Smith* (Urbana, 1975) is obvious from the title, but the book is also a critique of frontier Illinois' circuit court system. See in addition Annette P. Hampshire's articles, "Thomas Sharp and Anti-Mormon Sentiment in Illinois, 1842–1845," *Journal of the Illinois State Historical Society*, 72 (May 1979), and "The Triumph of Mobocracy in Hancock County, 1844–1846," *Western Illinois Regional Studies*, 5 (Spring 1982). Rodney O. Davis notes Thomas Ford's sympathy, if not connivance, with the northern Illinois vigilantes in "Judge Ford and the Regulators, 1841–1842," in Illinois State Historical Society, *Selected Papers in Illinois History, 1981*. The Ogle County vigilante episode is also covered in Robert Huhn Jones, "Three Days of Violence: The Regulators of the Rock River Valley," *Journal of the Illinois State Historical Society*, 59 (Summer 1966). The only study of the Ohio Valley's vigilante activity is antiquated: James A. Rose, "The Regulators and Flatheads in Southern Illinois," *Transactions of the Illinois State Historical Society for the Year 1906*, 11.

Any agenda for further research on frontier Illinois politics should include additional analysis of existing pollbooks for such key counties as Sangamon, to expand on John Rozett's work. Also needed is a study of the development of the General Assembly, both structurally and in terms of its output; very little is generally known about state legislatures in the nineteenth century, although Rodney O. Davis, " 'The People in Miniature': The Illinois General Assembly, 1818–1848," *Illinois Historical Journal*, 81 (Summer 1988), is a start for Illinois. The pioneer judiciary of Illinois would reward systematic investigation, for this is a field that is yet basically pristine. Equally undone is any consideration of the federal influence in the state's early political system, through the agencies of land office personnel, judges, and U.S. marshals. And in spite of the past emphasis on biography, there are still important full political biographies to be written and published. Ninian Edwards, Edward Coles, John Reynolds, and Thomas Ford all continue to rate scholarly attention.

Early in statehood, Illinois' major economic links with the rest of the nation were through such extractive enterprises as the trade in furs and lead. The important production and sale of salt was undertaken mainly for local consumption. All of these activities deserve more research than they have attracted. The standard source for Illinois' waning early nineteenth-century fur trade is still Henry E. Hamilton, ed., *Incidents and Events in the Life of Gurdon Saltonstall Hubbard* (Chicago, 1888; reprinted in large part in *The Autobiography of Gurdon Saltonstall Hubbard*, Chicago, 1911). A differently focused view is John D. Haeger, "The American Fur Company and the Chicago of 1812–1835,"

*Journal of the Illinois State Historical Society*, 61 (Summer 1968).

The economic history of the Galena lead trade may be beyond documentation; hence most studies of the Lead Region have dwelt on its settlement, or on the difficulty of implementing federal regulations on the leasing of mineral lands. B. H. Schockel, "Settlement and Development of the Lead and Zinc Mining Region of the Driftless Area with Special Emphasis upon Jo Daviess County, Illinois," *Mississippi Valley Historical Review*, 4 (Sept. 1917), needs updating. James E. Wright, *The Galena Lead District: Federal Policy and Practice, 1824–1847* (Madison, 1966) and Duane K. Everhart, "The Leasing of Mineral Lands in Illinois and Wisconsin," *Journal of the Illinois State Historical Society*, 60 (Summer 1967), both cover well the failure of the federal leasing policy. Of Illinois' once-important salines the least of all is known. George W. Smith, "The Salines of Southern Illinois," *Transactions of the Illinois State Historical Society for the Year 1904*, 9, and Clint Clay Tilton, "John W. Vance and the Vermilion Salines," ibid., *1931*, 38, are both anecdotal and unsatisfactory. Theirs is a topic worth further pursuing.

Agriculture, of course, has been the mainstay of Illinois' economic life since early statehood, and for the study of pioneer Illinois farming, Allen G. Bogue, *From Prairie to Corn Belt: Farming on the Illinois and Iowa Prairies in the Nineteenth Century* (Chicago, 1963) is without peer. Bogue uses both traditional and innovative sources and techniques, and covers the farm-making process from land acquisition through the development of equipment and the adaptation of crops and livestock appropriate to the needs of prairie farmers. Bogue's approach to agricultural history builds on Paul W. Gates's work, especially *Landlords and Tenants on the Prairie Frontier: Studies in American Land Policy* (Ithaca, 1973), a collection of articles including three published in the 1940s that relate to Illinois: "Land Policy and Tenancy in the Prairie States," "Frontier Landlords and Pioneer Tenants," and "Cattle Kings in the Prairies." These studies tend to emphasize the apparently anomalous development of large landholdings in early Illinois in spite of a land policy supposedly intended to benefit small farmers.

Other aspects of early Illinois agriculture are developed in Richard Bardolph, *Agricultural Literature and the Early Illinois Farmer*, University of Illinois Studies in the Social Sciences, 29 (Urbana, 1948), and "Illinois Agriculture in Transition, 1820–1870," *Journal of the Illinois State Historical Society*, 41 (Sept. and Dec. 1948), and in Robert Eugene Ankli, *Gross Farm Revenue in Pre-Civil War Illinois* (New York, 1977). Helen M. Cavanagh, *Funk of Funk's Grove . . .* (Bloomington, Ill., 1952) is a case study of early prairie farming and cattle raising. John G. Clark, *The Grain Trade in the Old Northwest* (Urbana, 1966) gives careful attention to the evolution of agricultural marketing in Illinois and neighboring states. David E. Schob, *Hired Hands and Plowboys: Farm Labor in the Midwest, 1815–60* (Urbana, 1975) is an equally important look at a previously neglected topic. Hard times on the agricultural frontier is the subject of George L. Priest, "Law and Economic Distress: Sangamon County, Illinois, 1837–1844," *Journal of Legal Studies*, 2 (June 1973). For a compelling literary view of the back-breaking farm-making process in early Illinois, see Joseph Kirkland's novel, *Zury, the Meanest Man in Spring County* (Boston, 1887).

The conveyance of public lands into private hands is a process that has long fascinated frontier historians. Although it has not been dealt with comprehensively for the state as a whole, perhaps it now can be, through use of the federal land office records as computerized by the Illinois State Archives. Land disposal is, of course, a subject of attention in Bogue's *Prairie to Corn Belt*, and the administrative details of the public land system are carefully laid out in Malcolm J. Rohrbough, *The Land Office Business: The Settlement and Administration of American Public Lands, 1789–1837* (New York, 1968). Existing studies pertaining to Illinois exclusively apply to quite specific localities. One such is Theodore L. Carlson, *The Illinois Military Tract: A Study of Land Occupation, Utilization, and Tenure*, University of Illinois Studies in the Social Sciences, 32 (Urbana, 1951). Two more specialized articles are Siyoung Park, "Land Speculation in Western Illinois: Pike County, 1821–1835," *Journal of the Illinois State Historical Society*, 77 (Summer 1984), and Gordana Rezab, "Land Speculation in Fulton County, 1817–1832," *Western Illinois Regional Studies*, 3 (Spring 1980). John D. Haeger investigates townsite speculation in the upper Illinois River valley in "The Abandoned Townsite on the Midwestern Frontier: A Case Study of Rockwell, Illinois," *Journal of the Early Republic*, 3 (Summer 1983).

Business and the means of expediting it were in their infancy in pioneer Illinois. John W. Eilert, "Illinois Business Incorporations, 1816–1869," *Business History Review*, 37 (Autumn 1963), details some efforts to marshal development capital. The state's rather pathetic attempts at banking are covered by George William Dowrie, *The Development of Banking in Illinois, 1817–1863*, University of Illinois Studies in the Social Sciences, 2 (Urbana, 1913), and Fred R. Marckhoff, "Currency and Banking in Illinois before 1865," *Journal of the Illinois State Historical Society*, 52 (Autumn 1959). John H. Krenkel, *Illinois Internal Improvements, 1818–1848* (Cedar Rapids, Iowa, 1958) partly supersedes James William Putnam, *The Illinois and Michigan Canal . . .* , Chicago Historical Society's Collection, 10 (Chicago, 1918), the standard history of the canal. That project is also the focus of Catherine Tobin, "The Lowly Muscular Digger: Irish Canal Workers in Nineteenth Century America" (Ph.D. diss., Univ. of Notre Dame, 1987). There are few studies of land transport of goods or passengers in Illinois before the railroads. Thomas L. Hardin, "The National Road in Illinois," *Journal of the Illinois State Historical Society*, 60 (Spring 1967), was a start. Edwin Daniel Karn, "Pre-Railroad Transportation in the Upper Mississippi Valley" (Ph.D. diss., Univ. of Wisconsin, Madison, 1986) makes a special contribution here. The state's primitive initial moves to finance its own activities are among the subjects of Robert Murray Haig, *A History of the General Property Tax in Illinois*, University of Illinois Studies in the Social Sciences, 3 (Urbana, 1914).

Anyone studying the historic peopling of Illinois must still begin with Arthur Clinton Boggess, *The Settlement of Illinois, 1778–1830*, Chicago Historical Society's Collection, 5 (Chicago, 1908), and William V. Pooley, *The Settlement of Illinois from 1830 to 1850*, Bulletin of the University of Wisconsin, History Series, 1 (Madison, 1908). Pioneer studies of the chronology and sources of immigration into Illinois, they are unsystematic by today's standards but are not yet superseded. In effect, Richard Lyle Power builds on the work of Boggess and Pooley in *Planting Corn Belt Culture: The Impress of the Upland Southerner and Yankee in the Old Northwest*, Indiana Historical Society Publications, 17 (Indianapolis, 1953), a reflection of the cultural mix that resulted from the sometimes abrasive association of different immigrant strains.

Indeed, in the historiography of community building in Illinois, at either the state or the local level, the tension between conflict and consensus has frequently been close to the surface. Jensen's *Illinois*, in an overstated but stimulating way, depicts conflict between "Traditionalists" and "Modernizers" as the central explanatory element in the development of the state. Don Harrison Doyle, *The Social Order of a Frontier Community: Jacksonville, Illinois, 1825–70* (Urbana, 1978) finds a kind of interpretive middle ground. He professes to discover important local contentions based on sectional, developmental, and sumptuary issues in early Jacksonville, the destructive impact of which was mitigated by the cohesive influence of boosterism, voluntary associations, and national politics. Doyle is seconded by John Mack Faragher, *Sugar Creek: Life on the Illinois Prairie* (New Haven, 1986). In the rural Sangamon County community that he studied, Faragher finds that traditional ties of kinship, neighborhood, and church held fast in the face of modernizing change.

Other significant Illinois community studies, albeit with a variety of focuses, include Richard S. Alcorn, "Leadership and Stability in Mid-Nineteenth-Century America: A Case Study of an Illinois Town," *Journal of American History*, 61 (Dec. 1974), on the development of a stabilizing local power structure in Paris, in Edgar County; Carl Abbott, *Boosters and Businessmen: Popular Economic Thought and Urban Growth in the Antebellum Middle West* (Westport, Conn., 1981), which examines reasons for urban "success" or "failure" in four cities, including Chicago and Galena; and Timothy R. Mahoney, "Urban History in a Regional Context: River Towns on the Upper Mississippi, 1840–1860," *Journal of American History*, 72 (Sept. 1985), which is heavily concerned with Illinois towns. Juliet E. K. Walker investigates the rise and fall of New Philadelphia in Pike County and the career of its remarkable promoter in *Free Frank: A Black Pioneer on the Antebellum Frontier* (Lexington, Ky., 1983). She considers the economic and demographic development of neighboring communities in "Entrepreneurial Ventures in the Origin of Nineteenth-Century Agricultural Towns: Pike County, 1823–1880," *Illinois Historical Journal*, 78 (Spring 1985). Finally, a recent study of scattered rural settlement is Robert W. McCluggage, "The Pioneer Squatter," *Illinois Historical Journal*, 82 (Spring 1989).

Certainly the most broadly disruptive social issues in frontier Illinois were those having to do with slavery. An anomaly in the first constitution ensured that slaves would live and work in Illinois until the mid-1840s. This fact only further exacerbated what was basically a Hoosier-Yankee cultural conflict over the general antislavery movement. The most comprehensive introduction to these topics is still N[orman] Dwight Harris, *The History of Negro Servitude in Illinois and of the Slavery Agitation in That State, 1719–1864* (Chicago, 1904), although this study is updated by Paul Finkelman, "Slavery, the 'More Perfect Union,' and the Prairie State," *Illinois Historical Journal*, 80 (Winter 1987). There is a large primary and secondary literature on Elijah Lovejoy and his abolitionist career; aside from Thomas Ford's critical account of the martyr's activities, it is overwhelmingly pro-Lovejoy. Nineteenth-century sources include Edward Beecher, *Narrative of Riots at Alton* . . . (Alton, 1838; best ed., New York, 1965); Joseph C. Lovejoy and Owen Lovejoy, *Memoir of the Rev. Elijah P. Lovejoy* . . . (New York, 1838); and [Henry Tanner], *The Martyrdom of Lovejoy* . . . (Chicago, 1881). The best modern biography of Lovejoy is still Merton L. Dillon, *Elijah P. Lovejoy, Abolitionist Editor* (Urbana, 1961).

Other sources on antislavery in Illinois include Fred Landon, "Benjamin Lundy in Illinois," *Journal of the Illinois State Historical Society*, 33 (Mar. 1940); Larry Gara's very reasonable "The Underground Railroad in Illinois," ibid., 56 (Autumn 1963); Hermann R. Muelder, *Fighters for Freedom: The History of Anti-Slavery Activities of Men and Women Associated with Knox College* (New York, 1959), which is instructive not only about cultural conflict in Illinois but also about sectarianism in the antislavery movement; and Donald Martin Bluestone's ingenious " 'Steamboats, Sewing Machines, and Bibles': The Roots of Antislaveryism in Illinois and the Old Northwest, 1818–1860" (Ph.D. diss., Univ. of Wisconsin, Madison, 1973). C. C. Tisler, "Prudence Crandall, Abolitionist," *Journal of the Illinois State Historical Society*, 33 (July 1940), does not begin to do justice to its subject; her forty years of activism in Illinois entitle her to further attention.

The majority of prospective settlers came to Illinois as individuals or in kinship groups, but an important contrasting settlement mode was that of people who came together united by similar ethnicity or religious or ideological persuasions. The earliest such colony was the English Settlement, already noticed as productive of literature publicizing Illinois to the rest of the world. The first history of that community was written by one of its founders, George Flower, *History of the English Settlement in Edwards County, Illinois* . . . , Chicago Historical Society's Collection, 1 (Chicago, 1882; reprinted Chicago, 1909). A modern treatment is still needed, for neither of two subsequent volumes qualifies. Both Gladys Scott Thomson, *A Pioneer Family: The Birkbecks in Illinois, 1818–1827* (London, 1953) and Charles E. Boewe, *Prairie Albion: An English Settlement in Pioneer Illinois* (Carbondale, 1962) are narratives contrived from lengthy selections from the sources. The best current historical scholarship on the English Settlement is by Mary Ann Salter, including "George Flower

Comes to the Illinois Country: A New Look at Motivations," *Journal of the Illinois State Historical Society*, 69 (Aug. 1976), and "Quarreling in the English Settlement: The Flowers in Court," ibid., 75 (Summer 1982). For a lesser-known and shorter-lived ethnic community, see Paul E. Stroble, Jr., "Ferdinand Ernst and the German Colony at Vandalia," *Illinois Historical Journal*, 80 (Summer 1987), and for an enduring one, the Highland Settlement in Madison County, see Joseph Suppiger et al., *Journey to New Switzerland . . .* (Carbondale, 1987).

The best known of Illinois' early communitarian settlements was that of the Latter Day Saints at Nauvoo, and the literature on Mormonism is enormous. The best coverage of its Illinois phase is Robert Bruce Flanders, *Nauvoo: Kingdom on the Mississippi* (Urbana, 1965), which emphasizes the secular side of the Saints' effort to establish their Illinois New Jerusalem. Entire issues of the *Journal of the Illinois State Historical Society*, 64 (Spring 1971), and *Western Illinois Regional Studies*, 11 (Fall 1988), are given over to Mormonism in Illinois. There are two scholarly biographies of Joseph Smith: Fawn M. Brodie, *No Man Knows My History: The Life of Joseph Smith, the Mormon Prophet* (New York, 1945; revised ed., New York, 1971) and Donna Hill, *Joseph Smith, the First Mormon* (New York, 1977). Hill had access to Mormon archival sources not available to Brodie, and her book is the more acceptable to Mormon readers, but it is not as well written as Brodie's. Joseph Smith's wife, who remained in Illinois, is the subject of Linda King Newell and Valeen Tippetts Avery, *Mormon Enigma: Emma Hale Smith . . .* (Garden City, N.Y., 1984).

Still needed is a full-scale social history of the Bishop Hill colony of Swedish immigrants, comparable to what Flanders did for Nauvoo, for the available treatments are either superannuated or somewhat skimpy. They include Michael A. Mikkelsen, *The Bishop Hill Colony: A Religious Communistic Settlement in Henry County, Illinois*, Johns Hopkins University Studies in Historical and Political Science, 10 (Baltimore, 1882); Sivert Erdahl, "Eric Janson and the Bishop Hill Colony," *Journal of the Illinois State Historical Society*, 18 (Oct. 1925); and Olov Isaksson, *Bishop Hill, Ill.: A Utopia on the Prairie* (Stockholm, 1969). Paul Elmen, *Wheat Flour Messiah: Eric Jansson of Bishop Hill* (Carbondale, 1976) is much fuller on the Swedish phase of the leader's career than on Bishop Hill itself.

Étienne Cabet's Icarian commune, which succeeded the Mormons at Nauvoo, is the subject of Albert Shaw, *Icaria: A Chapter in the History of Communism* (New York, 1884); Janice Clark Fotion, "Cabet and Icarian Communism" (Ph.D. diss., Univ. of Iowa, 1966); Robert D. Bush, "Communism, Community, and Charisma: The Crisis in Icaria at Nauvoo," *Old Northwest*, 3 (Dec. 1977); and Jacques C. Chicoineau, "Étienne Cabet and the Icarians," *Western Illinois Regional Studies*, 2 (Spring 1979). The fullest study of Illinois' short-lived Fourierist phalanxes is George E. Dawson, "The Integral Phalanx," *Transactions of the Illinois State Historical Society for the Year 1907*, 12.

Several years ago, Donald Zochert admonished the state's historians to recognize that "the task of illuminating the past may be accomplished with candles as well as floodlights," as he proposed a number of rather modest "Research Projects in Illinois History," *Journal of the Illinois State Historical Society*, 66 (Winter 1973). It is refreshing to acknowledge that as long and as well as the frontier period in Illinois history has been studied, there remain within its compass subjects to be illuminated with both candles and floodlights. The availability of new kinds of sources and of new techniques to work with them, and the development of new subject matter interests, all ensure that the frontier period will remain a field of great research potential.

# 4

# THE ERA OF THE CIVIL WAR, 1848–70

JOHN Y. SIMON

THE CIVIL WAR era brought Illinois to the height of its importance in the nation. Between 1850 and 1860, the population of Illinois increased from 851,470 to 1,711,951, and its ranking among the states advanced from eleventh to fourth. Four successive presidential elections beginning in 1860 placed an Illinois resident in the White House. A few miles of unprofitable railroad at the beginning of 1848 expanded to a comprehensive network by 1870. Chicago grew from a town to the capital of the Midwest.

Arthur Charles Cole, *The Era of the Civil War, 1848–1870* (Springfield, 1919) stands as the work that defines the period and still provides the best comprehensive survey. Prodigious research included use of nearly every extant Illinois newspaper. As Cole's work suggests, the Civil War generation cared passionately about politics, and later generations cared passionately about Abraham Lincoln. Much of Illinois history in this period is most easily accessible through the Lincoln literature, which is discussed in a later chapter.

Prominent Illinois Democrats of Lincoln's day have usually received inadequate treatment. The magnificent exception is Robert W. Johannsen, *Stephen A. Douglas* (New York, 1973), which supplants all other Douglas biographies. Johannsen also edited *The Letters of Stephen A. Douglas* (Urbana, 1961). Potential biographers might profitably look to other Democrats for a subject, despite the fact that Democrats are underrepresented in manuscript collections.

A Democratic convert to the Republican party fares better. Horace White, *The Life of Lyman Trumbull* (Boston, 1913) was written by a friend and associate of Trumbull who larded his pages with important letters. Neither Mark M. Krug, *Lyman Trumbull, Conservative Radical* (New York, 1965) nor Ralph J. Roske, *His Own Counsel: The Life and Times of Lyman Trumbull* (Reno, Nev., 1979) provide entire satisfaction: Krug is superficial, while Roske overly compressed his research. Gaillard Hunt, comp., *Israel, Elihu, and Cadwallader Washburn* (New York, 1925) prints important documents relating to Elihu Washburne (the maverick speller of the family), the influential congressman from Galena, but detailed analysis is available only in Russell K. Nelson, "The Early Life and Congressional Career of Elihu B. Washburne" (Ph.D. diss., Univ. of North Dakota, 1953). Another important Republican congressman from northern Illinois receives scholarly treatment in Edward Magdol, *Owen Lovejoy, Abolitionist in Congress* (New Brunswick, N.J., 1967).

Yet another congressman, destined for a major role in state politics, is the subject of Richard Yates and Catharine Yates Pickering, *Richard Yates, Civil War Governor* (Danville, Ill., 1966). Mark A. Plummer, "Richard J. Oglesby, Lincoln's Rail-Splitter," *Illinois Historical Journal*, 80 (Spring 1987), ably introduces Yates's successor, who was important in Lincoln's nomination in 1860. Maurice G. Baxter, *Orville H. Browning, Lincoln's Friend and Critic* (Bloomington, Ind., 1957) analyzes a major figure in the Lincoln story, who provides copious source material in *The Diary of Orville Hickman Browning*, Volume 1, *1850–1864*, Theodore Calvin Pease and James G. Randall, eds., and Volume 2, *1865–1881*, Randall, ed., in Collections of the Illinois State Historical Library, 20 and 22 (1925–33). Willard L. King, *Lincoln's Manager, David Davis* (Cambridge, Mass., 1960) taps without exhausting the massive David Davis papers in the Illinois State Historical Library. Clint Clay Tilton, "Lincoln and Lamon, Partners and Friends," *Transactions of the Illinois State Historical Society for the Year 1931*, 138, an unannotated and not fully reliable account, can be supplemented by Lavern M. Hamand, "Lincoln's Particular Friend," in Donald F. Tingley, ed., *Essays in Illinois History in Honor of Glenn Huron Seymour* (Carbondale, 1968), an outgrowth of the author's "Ward Hill Lamon . . . " (Ph.D. diss., Univ. of Illinois, 1949). Harry C. Blair and Rebecca Tarshis, *The Life of Colonel Edward D. Baker, Lincoln's Constant Ally* (Portland, Oreg., 1960) serves as a reminder that Baker deserves more attention, some of which he receives in Gayle Anderson Braden, "The Public Career of Edward Dickinson Baker" (Ph.D. diss., Vanderbilt Univ., 1960). Members of Lincoln's Illinois circle still demanding initial biographical treatment include Norman B. Judd and Leonard Swett.

Thomas J. McCormack, ed., *Memoirs of Gustave Koerner, 1809–1896* . . . (2 vols., Cedar Rapids, Iowa, 1909), which Paul M. Angle rightly labeled "a neglected American classic," reveals the importance of German immigrants in Illinois politics and society. Frederick C. Luebke, ed., *Ethnic Voters and the Election of Lincoln* (Lincoln, Nebr., 1971) includes two articles that deal exclusively with German voting in Illinois; one by Jay Monaghan is reprinted from the *Journal of the Illinois State Historical Society*, 35 (June 1942), but James

M. Bergquist's essay is unavailable elsewhere, and the surrounding essays place the problem in context. Other immigrant groups are more in need of scholarly attention, as are the interactions of immigrants with others. Robert P. Sutton, "Against the 'drunken Dutch and low Irish': Nativism and Know-Nothings in Illinois," in Sutton, ed., *The Prairie State: A Documentary History of Illinois* . . . , 1 (2 vols., Grand Rapids, 1976), explores a topic that demands further work. See also Thomas M. Keefe's articles, "Chicago's Flirtation with Political Nativism, 1854–1856," *Records of the American Catholic Historical Society of Philadelphia*, 82 (Sept. 1971), and "The Catholic Issue in the *Chicago Tribune* before the Civil War," *Mid-America*, 57 (Oct. 1975).

Victor B. Howard's two-part study of "The Illinois Republican Party," including "A Party Organizer for the Republicans in 1854" and "The Party Becomes Conservative, 1855–1856," *Journal of the Illinois State Historical Society*, 64 (Summer and Autumn 1971), discusses the topic all too briefly. Two doctoral dissertations remain valuable: Don E. Fehrenbacher, "Illinois Political Attitudes, 1854–1861" (Univ. of Chicago, 1951) and Harold Preston James, "Lincoln's Own State in the Election of 1860" (Univ. of Illinois, 1943). John Shup Wright, "The Background and Formation of the Republican Party in Illinois, 1846–1860" (Ph.D. diss., Univ. of Chicago, 1946) remains informative although Wright drew heavily upon it for *Lincoln and the Politics of Slavery* (Reno, Nev., 1970). The early history of the Republican party in Illinois is best approached through the Lincoln literature; the corresponding history of the Democratic party remains unwritten. Ameda Ruth King, "The Last Years of the Whig Party in Illinois, 1847 to 1856," *Transactions of the Illinois State Historical Society for the Year 1925*, 32, offers basic information on a topic that should receive more coverage. Illinois political history has been reassessed by a quantifier tracing the growth of party loyalty in Stephen L. Hansen, *The Making of the Third Party System: Voters and Parties in Illinois, 1850–1876* (Ann Arbor, 1980). Edgar F. Raines, Jr., "The American Missionary Association in Southern Illinois, 1856–1862: A Case History in the Abolition Movement," *Journal of the Illinois State Historical Society*, 65 (Autumn 1972), sheds light on a dark corner of the state and points the way toward further scholarship on other regions. The American Missionary Association collection at the Amistad Research Center, at Tulane University, has yielded fifteen reels of microfilm covering Illinois. These materials are accessible through the *Author and Added Entry Catalog of the American Missionary Association Archives* . . . (3 vols., Westport, Conn., 1970).

Railroad development transformed antebellum Illinois. The Illinois Central, the longest railroad in the nation at the time of its completion, has attracted most attention. Paul Wallace Gates, *The Illinois Central Railroad and Its Colonization Work* (Cambridge, Mass., 1934), a superb study, covers more than the title reveals. Carlton J. Corliss, *Main Line of Mid-America: The Story of the Illinois Central* (New York, 1950) provides a general survey, and Robert Mize Sutton, *The Illinois Central Railroad in Peace and War, 1858–1868* (New York, 1981), a facsimile printing of a Ph.D. dissertation (Univ. of Illinois, 1948), remains indispensable.

As Chicago developed to dominate the commerce of the Midwest, its newspapers grew to dominate its journalism. Philip Kinsley, *"The Chicago Tribune"*: *Its First Hundred Years* (3 vols., New York, 1943–46) discusses without analysis the most powerful Republican voice. Somewhat better, but still inadequate, is Lloyd Wendt, *"Chicago Tribune"*: *The Rise of a Great American Newspaper* (Chicago, 1979). Its editors are treated in Jay Monaghan, *The Man Who Elected Lincoln* (Indianapolis, 1956); Tracy Elmer Strevey, "Joseph Medill and the *Chicago Tribune* during the Civil War Period" (Ph.D. diss., Univ. of Chicago, 1930); and Joseph Logsdon, *Horace White, Nineteenth Century Liberal* (Westport, Conn., 1971). Monaghan's work is an inadequate and misleadingly titled biography of Charles H. Ray. The leading Democratic newspaper, the *Chicago Times*, is best approached through a study of its editor: Justin E. Walsh, *To Print the News and Raise Hell! A Biography of Wilbur F. Storey* (Chapel Hill, 1968). Andy Van Meter, *Always My Friend: A History of the State Journal-Register and Springfield* (Springfield, 1981) is an informal and unannotated account of both Springfield newspapers of the Civil War era.

The best studies of communities outside Chicago are Paul M. Angle, *"Here I Have Lived"*: *A History of Lincoln's Springfield, 1821–1865* (Springfield, 1935) and Don Harrison Doyle, *The Social Order of a Frontier Community: Jacksonville, Illinois, 1825–70* (Urbana, 1978). The latter could furnish a model for investigations of other towns and cities. Kenneth N. Owens, *Galena, Grant, and the Fortunes of War: A History of Galena, Illinois during the Civil War* (DeKalb, 1963) uses primary sources. New towns founded as the Illinois Central laid tracks include Carbondale, and its founder wrote an intriguing autobiography: Daniel Harmon Brush, *Growing Up with Southern Illinois, 1820 to 1861* (Chicago, 1944). Brush's book can be supplemented by John W. D. Wright, *A History of Early Carbondale, Illinois, 1852–1905* (Carbondale, 1977). The completion of the Illinois Central and the coming of the Civil War gave added importance to Cairo, for which the standard history is John M. Lansden, *A History of the City of Cairo, Illinois* (Chicago, 1910). Herman R. Lantz, *A Community in Search of Itself: A Case History of Cairo, Illinois* (Carbondale, 1972) approached the problem from a sociological perspective with mixed results; the statistics are useful. James M. Merrill, "Cairo, Illinois: Strategic Civil War River Port," *Journal of the Illinois State Historical Society*, 76 (Winter 1983), is well written and incorporates substantial research.

The advent of the Civil War changes the major focus in Illinois history from politics to the military. Research on individual soldiers or units usually begins with the *Report of the Adjutant General of the State of Illinois* (8 vols., Springfield, 1867; revised eds., by J[oseph] W. Vance and J[asper] N. Reece, respectively, Springfield, 1886 and 1900–l). Each person who served should be listed by regiment and company, with residence and dates of enlistment and discharge. Remarks on wounds, desertions, and promotions sometimes follow.

Original muster rolls on which these compilations are based at the Illinois State Archives contain additional information and often serve to correct errors in the printed compilation, even as revised at the turn of the century. Another starting point, alphabetically arranged, is the *Index to Compiled Service Records of Volunteer Union Soldiers Who Served in Organizations from the State of Illinois*, National Archives Microfilm Publications, M539 (101 reels).

The *Report of the Adjutant General* also contains a brief account of the service of each regiment, which can be supplemented through C[harles] E. Dornbusch, *Regimental Publications and Personal Narratives of the Civil War: A Checklist; Vol. 1, Northern States; Part 1, Illinois*, Military Bibliography of the Civil War (3 vols., New York, 1961–72; reprinted, using the series title, New York, 1971). The Illinois listing is augmented in Dornbusch, *Military Bibliography of the Civil War*, 4 (Dayton, Ohio, 1987). Garold L. Cole, *Civil War Eyewitnesses: An Annotated Bibliography of Books and Articles, 1955–1986* (Columbia, S.C., 1988) provides helpful comments on an abundance of Illinois sources. A useful guide to regiments broken down by county is Civil War Centennial Commission of Illinois, *Illinois Military Units in the Civil War* (Springfield, 1962). Information about unprinted material is in William L. Burton, *Descriptive Bibliography of Civil War Manuscripts in Illinois* (Evanston, 1966). Officers who served in the U.S. Army and regimental field officers (colonel, lieutenant colonel, and major) who served from Illinois are listed in Francis B. Heitman, *Historical Register and Dictionary of the United States Army from Its Organization, September 29, 1789, to March 2, 1903* (2 vols., Washington, D.C., 1903). Data on desertions, based on the Adjutant General's *Report*, is presented in Bob Sterling, "Discouragement, Weariness, and War Politics: Desertions from Illinois Regiments during the Civil War," *Illinois Historical Journal*, 82 (Winter 1989).

Immediately after the end of the war, T[homas] M. Eddy compiled a massive record of *The Patriotism of Illinois . . .* (2 vols., Chicago, 1865–66), which remains useful for its biographical sketches and reprinted documents. In later years, reminiscences of veterans were collected in *Military Essays and Recollections: Papers Read before the Commandery of the State of Illinois, Military Order of the Loyal Legion of the United States* (4 vols., Chicago, 1891–1907).

The overall military contribution of Illinois to the Civil War receives narrative treatment in Victor Hicken, *Illinois in the Civil War* (Urbana, 1966). As for its leading contribution, *Personal Memoirs of U. S. Grant* (2 vols., New York, 1885–86) offers little about Grant's prewar life in Galena, a topic best handled in Lloyd Lewis, *Captain Sam Grant* (Boston, 1950). Lewis planned a multivolume biography but died even before completing the first volume. Bruce Catton carried the work through the Civil War in *Grant Moves South* and *Grant Takes Command* (Boston, 1960–69). A less friendly view of Grant is William S. McFeely, *Grant: A Biography* (New York, 1981). What Grant wrote and the letters he received are in John Y. Simon, ed., *The Papers of Ulysses S. Grant* (16 vols., Carbondale, 1967–88), a mammoth project which has reached the end of 1866 in chronological presentation but will cover the remainder of Grant's life.

Of the other Illinois generals, those with the most political involvement yield the richest ore for state history. Wallace J. Schutz and Walter N. Trenerry, *Abandoned by Lincoln: A Military Biography of General John Pope* (Urbana, 1990) champions a figure occasionally overlooked as an Illinoisan. Victor Hicken, "From Vandalia to Vicksburg: The Political and Military Career of John A. McClernand" (Ph.D. diss., Univ. of Illinois, 1955) presents a flamboyant leader whose military record remains controversial. James P. Jones, *"Black Jack": John A. Logan and Southern Illinois in the Civil War Era* (Tallahassee, 1967) begins a biography completed with *John A. Logan, Stalwart Republican from Illinois* (Tallahassee, 1982). Both are mines of factual material. William H. Leckie and Shirley A. Leckie, *Unlikely Warriors: General Benjamin H. Grierson and His Family* (Norman, Okla., 1984) describes the successes of a cavalry officer. Jeffrey N. Lash, "Stephen Augustus Hurlbut, a Military and Diplomatic Politician, 1815–1882" (Ph.D. diss., Kent State Univ., 1980) surprises by its hostility to Hurlbut and its assiduous research. A sample is available in Lash, "A Politician Turned General: Stephen A. Hurlbut and Military Patronage in Illinois, 1861–1862," in Illinois State Historical Society, *Selected Papers in Illinois History, 1981*.

On the home front, the key issue was loyalty. The perennial debate over whether opponents of the war were dangerous subversives or ineffective grumblers portrayed as traitors by hysterical Republicans receives diametrically opposed answers in Wood Gray, *The Hidden Civil War: The Story of the Copperheads* (New York, 1942) and Frank L. Klement, *The Copperheads in the Middle West* (Chicago, 1960). Klement, who finds little evidence of danger, deals with Illinois directly in "Copperhead Secret Societies in Illinois during the Civil War," *Journal of the Illinois State Historical Society*, 48 (Summer 1955). See also Klement, *Dark Lanterns: Secret Political Societies, Conspiracies, and Treason Trials in the Civil War* (Baton Rouge, 1984). The area in which most disloyalty existed receives superb scholarly treatment in Jasper William Cross, Jr., "Divided Loyalties in Southern Illinois during the Civil War" (Ph.D. diss., Univ. of Illinois, 1942). Only a bit of this research surfaces in Cross, "The Civil War Comes to 'Egypt,' " *Journal of the Illinois State Historical Society*, 44 (Summer 1951). Other aspects of the same problem appear in Robert E. Sterling, "Civil War Draft Resistance in Illinois," ibid., 64 (Autumn 1971), and Charles H. Coleman and Paul H. Spence, "The Charleston Riot, March 28, 1864," ibid., 33 (Mar. 1940).

Other perspectives on the problem come from David Wallace Adams, "Illinois Soldiers and the Emancipation Proclamation," *Journal of the Illinois State Historical Society*, 67 (Sept. 1974), and Craig D. Tenney, "To Suppress or Not to Suppress: Abraham Lincoln and the *Chicago Times*," *Civil War History*, 27 (Sept. 1981). One battlefield of this struggle is analyzed in O[liver]

M. Dickerson, *The Illinois Constitutional Convention of 1862*, University Studies, Vol. 1, No. 9 (Urbana, 1905), while Stanley L. Jones, "Agrarian Radicalism in Illinois' Constitutional Convention of 1862," *Journal of the Illinois State Historical Society*, 48 (Autumn 1955), focuses on new issues. Another perspective is used in Jack Nortrup, "Yates, the Prorogued Legislature, and the Constitutional Convention," ibid., 62 (Spring 1969), an article derived from Nortrup's "Richard Yates, Civil War Governor of Illinois" (Ph.D. diss., Univ. of Illinois, 1960). Wartime politics receives sprightly and detailed analysis in Harry E. Pratt, "The Repudiation of Lincoln's War Policy in 1862: Stuart-Swett Congressional Campaign," *Journal of the Illinois State Historical Society*, 24 (Apr. 1931). Regarding 1864, see Paul Gaylord Hubbard, "The Lincoln-McClellan Presidential Election in Illinois" (Ph.D. diss., Univ. of Illinois, 1949). An unexploited source for wartime Illinois is reproduced in *Internal Revenue Assessment Lists for Illinois, 1862–1866*, National Archives Microfilm Publications, M764 (63 reels).

Treatment of prisoners of war in Chicago is analyzed in E. B. Long, "Camp Douglas: 'A Hellish Den'?" *Chicago History*, 1 (Fall 1970). See also Joseph L. Eisendrath, Jr., "Chicago's Camp Douglas, 1861–1865," *Journal of the Illinois State Historical Society*, 53 (Spring 1960). William S. Peterson, "A History of Camp Butler, 1861–1866," *Illinois Historical Journal*, 82 (Summer 1989), brings together contemporary references to the camp near Springfield.

The immediate postwar period is covered in John H. Keiser, *Building for the Centuries: Illinois, 1865 to 1898* (Urbana, 1977). Keiser's intriguing topical history will disappoint those looking for conventional political narrative, who will be better served by Harris L. Dante, "Reconstruction Politics in Illinois, 1860–1872" (Ph.D. diss., Univ. of Chicago, 1950). Dante's research led to two major articles, "Western Attitudes and Reconstruction Politics in Illinois, 1865–1872," *Journal of the Illinois State Historical Society*, 49 (Summer 1956), and "The *Chicago Tribune*'s 'Lost' Years, 1865–1874," ibid., 58 (Summer 1965). Michael C. Robinson, "Illinois Politics in the Post–Civil War Era: The Liberal Republican Movement; A Test Case" (Ph.D. diss., Univ. of Wyoming, 1973) is also useful for Reconstruction politics. Edgar F. Raines, Jr., "The Ku Klux Klan in Illinois, 1867–1875," *Illinois Historical Journal*, 78 (Spring 1985), is an excellent piece of research and analysis.

Cole's *Era of the Civil War* strikes most modern readers as especially deficient in its treatment of blacks and women, but seventy years of subsequent scholarship have done little to repair matters. Nothing printed covers the topic better than N[orman] Dwight Harris, *The History of Negro Servitude in Illinois* . . . (Chicago, 1904), but readers should consult Charles N. Zucker, "The Free Negro Question: Race Relations in Ante-Bellum Illinois, 1801–1860" (Ph.D. diss., Northwestern Univ., 1972) and Dennis Frank Ricke, "Illinois Blacks through the Civil War: A Struggle for Equality" (M.A. thesis, Southern Illinois Univ., Carbondale, 1972), the latter a massive accumulation of data, weak in interpretation. Eugene H. Berwanger, *The Frontier Against Slavery:*

*Western Anti-Negro Prejudice and the Slavery Extension Controversy* (Urbana, 1967) and V[ictor] Jacque Voegeli, *Free but Not Equal: The Midwest and the Negro during the Civil War* (Chicago, 1967) contain considerable Illinois material and handle it well. See also John M. Rozett, "Racism and Republican Emergence in Illinois, 1848–1860: A Re-evaluation of Republican Negrophobia," *Civil War History*, 22 (June 1976). The "Emancipation Centennial Issue" of the *Journal of the Illinois State Historical Society*, 56 (Autumn 1963), has a scattering of pertinent articles. Charles A. Gliozzo, "John Jones: A Study of a Black Chicagoan," *Illinois Historical Journal*, 80 (Autumn 1987), introduces the most important Illinois black leader of his generation but explores only some dimensions of his multifaceted career. Roger D. Bridges, "Equality Deferred: Civil Rights for Illinois Blacks, 1865–1885," *Journal of the Illinois State Historical Society*, 74 (Summer 1981), a masterful study, promises future work in black history that the topic deserves. Another model effort is Joanne Wheeler, "Together in Egypt: A Pattern of Race Relations in Cairo, Illinois, 1865–1915," in Orville Vernon Burton and Robert C. McMath, Jr., eds., *Toward a New South? Studies in Post–Civil War Southern Communities* (Westport, Conn., 1982).

As for women's history, there is little reason to peruse the relevant sections of Adade Mitchell Wheeler, *The Roads They Made: Women in Illinois History* (Chicago, 1977) except to see how little is there. Biographies and autobiographies of prominent women remain the chief resource. Mary A. Livermore, *My Story of the War . . .* (Hartford, 1888) portrays the relief work of women. The career of a dedicated nurse from Galesburg is delineated in Nina Brown Baker, *Cyclone in Calico: The Story of Mary Ann Bickerdyke* (Boston, 1952) and Martin Litvin, *The Young Mary, 1817–1861 . . .* (Galesburg, 1977). Ruth Painter Randall, *Mary Lincoln: Biography of a Marriage* (Boston, 1953) defends her subject vigorously, at one point denouncing Lincoln's "backwoods relatives" as "a drag . . . to him and his wife" (p. 129). Ishbel Ross, *The President's Wife, Mary Todd Lincoln: A Biography* (New York, 1973) is better balanced but dull. Jean H. Baker, *Mary Todd Lincoln: A Biography* (New York, 1987) is now standard. Justin G. Turner and Linda Levitt Turner, *Mary Todd Lincoln: Her Life and Letters* (New York, 1972) has little life but a copious harvest of letters. Mary Lincoln deserves an unsympathetic modern biography. Relatively little Illinois material appears in John Y. Simon, ed., *The Personal Memoirs of Julia Dent Grant . . .* (New York, 1975) or Ishbel Ross, *The General's Wife: The Life of Mrs. Ulysses S. Grant* (New York, 1959). Mrs. John A. [Mary] Logan, *Reminiscences of a Soldier's Wife: An Autobiography* (New York, 1913; abridged ed., *Reminiscences of the Civil War and Reconstruction*, Carbondale, 1970) remains an important source. See also Sandra J. Fenger, "Mary Logan, Nineteenth Century Feminine Politician" (M.A. thesis, Southern Illinois Univ., Carbondale, 1977).

A brief survey can only touch on a few highlights of a copious literature. Those even vaguely aware of the great mass remaining unlisted must shudder at the prospect of even trying to master so much. At the same time, dozens of major topics demand further work, and dozens of others remain untouched. Cole's long supremacy as the standard survey remains a tribute to him but a reproach to his successors.

# 5

# THE GILDED AGE, 1870–1900

## MARK A. PLUMMER

THE GILDED AGE in Illinois was symbolized by the polished dome being built over the state capitol, by the state's miles of shining rails which led the nation in track mileage, by its bountiful, golden corn harvests, and by the glittering success of its agriculture-related industries. Yet the capitol was completed by spending money in excess of that allowed under the Constitution of 1870, and many of the state's political leaders became involved in the questionable political activities typical of the age. The railroads that brought prosperity to Illinois also brought grief, and the state took the lead in their regulation, albeit somewhat ineffectively. Crop overproduction and certain corporate and governmental policies greatly reduced the promised riches for many farmers. And industries such as Harvester and Pullman became the focal point for some of America's most excruciating labor problems. Not surprisingly, much has been written about Illinois in the Gilded Age. The politician-generals, the Grangers, the Liberal Republicans, the Haymarket bombing, and the Pullman strike all captured the attention of the nation. Yet much remains to be written regarding the state in the late nineteenth century.

The indispensable book on Illinois in the Gilded Age is John H. Keiser, *Building for the Centuries: Illinois, 1865 to 1898* (Urbana, 1977). Keiser's comprehensive work includes chapters on the people, government, politics, agriculture, transportation, industry, labor, and culture of the state, and on Chicago. The book is also a useful guide to the sources, with rich endnotes and a lengthy bibliography. Keiser's volume supersedes much of Ernest Ludlow Bogart and Charles Manfred Thompson, *The Industrial State, 1870–1893* (Springfield, 1920) and of Bogart and John Mabry Mathews, *The Modern Commonwealth, 1893–1918* (Springfield, 1920), two rather dull surveys of the period which, however, provide considerable factual material and some helpful documentation.

Earlier compilations are often useful both for "facts and figures" and for "anecdotes and incidents." Alexander Davidson and Bernard Stuvé, *A Complete History of Illinois* . . . (Springfield, 1874; enlarged ed., Springfield, 1884) and John Moses, *Illinois, Historical and Statistical* . . . (2 vols., Chicago, 1889–92; revised ed., Chicago, 1895) cover successive gubernatorial administrations down to the time of publication. The "statistical tables" or lists in Moses's appendix add to the value of his work. Another contemporary account is D[avid] W. Lusk, *Politics and Politicians* . . . (Springfield, 1884; three enlarged eds., the third with the cover title *Eighty Years of Illinois*, Springfield, 1886–89). Partisan politics provided the incentive for other works. Green B. Raum, *History of Illinois Republicanism* . . . (Chicago, 1900) and Charles A. Church, *History of the Republican Party in Illinois, 1854–1912* . . . (Rockford, 1912) are essentially anecdotal, but they contain information not available elsewhere, including biographies of Republican party leaders. *Prominent Democrats of Illinois: A Basic History of the Rise and Progress of the Democratic Party of Illinois* . . . (Chicago, 1899) and Walter A. Townsend, *Illinois Democracy: A History of the Party and Its Representative Members, Past and Present* (4 vols., Springfield, 1935) are mainly biographical; as histories, they are less useful than their Republican counterparts, reflecting perhaps the lack of Democratic victories in the period.

A new constitution, ratified in 1870, provides a convenient, if arbitrary, watershed in Illinois history. William Robert Thompson, "Illinois Constitutions" (Ph.D. diss., Univ. of Illinois, 1960) contends that the Constitution of 1870 was adopted because it was relatively non-partisan. A participant's view of its formation is in Elliott Anthony, *The Constitutional History of Illinois* (Chicago, 1891). See also *Debates and Proceedings of the Constitutional Convention of the State of Illinois* . . . (2 vols., Springfield, 1870).

A more meaningful watershed for Illinois politics of the period is the Liberal Republican movement of 1872. According to Michael C. Robinson, "Illinois Politics in the Post–Civil War Era: The Liberal Republican Movement; A Test Case" (Ph.D. diss., Univ. of Wyoming, 1973), the insurgents of 1872 came from the "moribund wing" of the Republican party. Having led the party before and during the Civil War, they had been displaced by younger soldier-politicians. Robinson epitomizes this view in "After Lincoln: The Transformation of the Illinois Republican Party, 1865–1872," in Illinois State Historical Society, *Selected Papers in Illinois History, 1982*. The growing importance of party allegiance is further explored in Gary Lee Cardwell, "The Rise of the Stalwarts and the Transformation of Illinois Republican Politics, 1860–1880" (Ph.D. diss., Univ. of Virginia, 1976).

Among the prominent Republicans who defected to the Liberal Republican-Democratic coalition in 1872 were many party leaders of the previous two decades. Those who had entered politics as Democrats and then become Republicans included Lyman Trumbull (U.S. Sen., 1855–73), Gustave Koerner (Lt. Gov., 1853–57), and John M. Palmer (Gov., 1869–73). Trumbull has been studied repeatedly. In addition to the published biographies cited in the preceding chapter, see, for example, Ralph Joseph Roske, "The Post Civil War Career of Lyman Trumbull" (Ph.D. diss., Univ. of Illinois, 1949) and Mario R. DiNunzio, "Lyman Trumbull, United States Senator" (Ph.D. diss., Clark Univ., 1964). Koerner's role as the Liberal Republican–Democratic candidate for governor in 1872 is described in Thomas J. McCormack, ed., *Memoirs of Gustave Koerner, 1809–1896* . . . (2 vols., Cedar Rapids, Iowa, 1909). There is an urgent need for a full and objective biography of Palmer, who was both a Republican governor and, from 1891 to 1897, a Democratic U.S. senator. *Personal Recollections of John M. Palmer: The Story of an Earnest Life* (Cincinnati, 1901) should be used with care. In *A Conscientious Turncoat: The Story of John M. Palmer, 1817–1900* (New Haven, 1941), his grandson, George Thomas Palmer, incorporates some letters of the period into a sketchy narrative. Virginia Rose Grollemond, "The Administration of Governor John M. Palmer of Illinois, 1869–1873" (M.A. thesis, Univ. of Illinois, 1955) briefly covers the topic.

Palmer, Richard J. Oglesby, and John A. Logan, three of Gen. Ulysses S. Grant's politician-generals, emerged after the Civil War to build the new Republican party. All three used the power of the Grand Army of the Republic for their political advantage. According to Mary R. Dearing, *Veterans in Politics: The Story of the G.A.R.* (Baton Rouge, 1952), Oglesby secretly founded the organization. If so, he did not use it as well as either Palmer or Logan did. Except for Shelby Cullom, every governor from the Civil War to 1893 was a Republican veteran. There is as yet no adequate biography of Oglesby, who served at three points, 1865–69, 1873, and 1885–89, cutting short his second term to become a U.S. senator, 1873–79. By contrast, Cullom's career is well documented, partly in George Cullom Davis, Jr., "Governor Shelby M. Cullom, 1877–1883" (M.A. thesis, Univ. of Illinois, 1961) and especially in James W. Neilson, *Shelby M. Cullom, Prairie State Republican* (Urbana, 1962), which analyzes his extraordinary longevity in the U.S. Senate, 1883–1913. See also *Fifty Years of Public Service: Personal Recollections of Shelby M. Cullom* . . . (Chicago, 1911).

John A. Logan and Cullom established a party hierarchy that used federal patronage to control state politics, according to James William Fullinwider, "The Governor and the Senator: Executive Power and the Structure of the Illinois Republican Party, 1880–1917" (Ph.D. diss., Washington Univ., 1974). Logan, a late but steadfast convert to the Republican party, seemed to regard Washington as more important than Springfield. Aspiring to be senator rather than governor, he used the statewide base of a congressman-at-large to take Richard Yates's place in the Senate in 1871. Defeated in 1877 by U.S. Supreme Court Justice David

Davis, who was selected as an independent, Logan returned to the Senate in 1879 and gained the Republican vice-presidential nomination in 1884. His career is well covered in James Pickett Jones, *John A. Logan, Stalwart Republican from Illinois* (Tallahassee, 1982) and William Gene Eidson, "John Alexander Logan, Hero of the Volunteers" (Ph.D. diss., Vanderbilt Univ., 1967).

John Peter Altgeld was the only Illinois Democratic governor in the Gilded Age and the state's most famous political figure in the period after Lincoln and Grant. Harry Barnard, *"Eagle Forgotten": The Life of John Peter Altgeld* (Indianapolis, 1938) is the best-known biography, but Howard Fast's fictionalized account, *The American: A Middle Western Legend* (New York, 1946), has been widely read. Both books are rather dated, as are the articles by Harvey Wish, including "Altgeld and the Progressive Tradition," *American Historical Review*, 46 (July 1941); "John Peter Altgeld and the Background of the Campaign of 1896," *Mississippi Valley Historical Review*, 24 (Mar. 1938); and "John Peter Altgeld and the Election of 1896," *Journal of the Illinois State Historical Society*, 30 (Oct. 1937). Some sources are collected in Henry M. Christman, ed., *The Mind and Spirit of John Peter Altgeld: Selected Writings and Addresses* (Urbana, 1960). Not only Altgeld but other Illinois Democrats held major offices in the 1890s, including John M. Palmer as U.S. senator and Adlai E. Stevenson as vice-president under Grover Cleveland. Stevenson's career is outlined in Leonard Schlup, "Gilded Age Politician: Adlai E. Stevenson of Illinois and His Times," *Illinois Historical Journal*, 82 (Winter 1989), while his personality comes through in his own account, *Something of Men I Have Known . . .* (Chicago, 1909).

Altgeld's term of office was bracketed by two Republicans, Joseph W. Fifer (1889–93) and John R. Tanner (1897–1901), who warrant biographies. The existing literature is rather anecdotal. Fifer survived to entertain interviewers; see A. L. Bowen, "Personal Reminiscences of Joseph W. Fifer . . . ," *Blue Book of the State of Illinois, 1925–1926*, and James O'Donnell Bennett, *"Private Joe" Fifer . . .* (Bloomington, Ill., 1936). Tanner's celebrated marriage on the eve of his inauguration is charmingly told in John Thomas Trutter and Edith English Trutter, *The Governor Takes a Bride . . .* (Carbondale, 1977). Other Republican governors who remain obscure include John L. Beveridge (1873–77) and John M. Hamilton (1883–85), the lieutenant governors who were promoted when Oglesby and Cullom resigned to take Senate seats. Two skillful politicians who became senators, Charles B. Farwell (1887–91) and William E. Mason (1897–1903), have also gone unnoticed. Studies of Illinois' Gilded Age congressmen, such as David Earl Robbins, Jr., "The Congressional Career of William Ralls Morrison" (Ph.D. diss., Univ. of Illinois, 1963), are in short supply.

Satisfactory biographies exist, however, for several Illinoisans who were nationally prominent in the period. One such volume is Willard L. King, *Melville Weston Fuller, Chief Justice of the United States, 1888–1910* (New York, 1950). John S. Goff, *Robert Todd Lincoln: A Man in His Own Right* (Norman, Okla.,

1968) ably describes the career of Abraham Lincoln's son as secretary of war, minister to England, and president of the Pullman Company. Chester McArthur Destler, *Henry Demarest Lloyd and the Empire of Reform* (Philadelphia, 1963) traces the life of a persistent critic of industrial capitalism. C[larence] H. Cramer, *Royal Bob: The Life of Robert G. Ingersoll* (Indianapolis, 1952) is the best of many biographies of late nineteenth-century America's most famous orator. For the great agnostic's political aspirations in Illinois, see Mark A. Plummer, *Robert G. Ingersoll, Peoria's Pagan Politician* (Macomb, 1984).

Not only biographies but other studies illuminate the political history of the Gilded Age. An old standard for the first agrarian protest of the period is Solon Justus Buck, *The Granger Movement: A Study of Agricultural Organization and Its Political, Economic, and Social Manifestations, 1870–1880* (Cambridge, Mass., 1913), which covers the formation of the Patrons of Husbandry and their victories in the Constitution of 1870. It may be supplemented by George H. Miller, *Railroads and the Granger Laws* (Madison, 1971), one chapter of which traces regulatory legislation in the state which culminated in the landmark case of *Munn v. Illinois*. Roy V. Scott, *The Agrarian Movement in Illinois, 1880–1896* (Urbana, 1962) carries the story through the Greenback, Alliance, and Populist eras. Important figures in the movement are sketched in Scott, "John Patterson Stelle, Agrarian Crusader from Southern Illinois," *Journal of the Illinois State Historical Society*, 55 (Autumn 1962), and Alfred W. Newcombe, "Alson J. Streeter, an Agrarian Liberal," ibid., 38 (Dec. 1945) and 39 (Mar. 1946).

Relatively few Illinois farmers took up the Populist cause, but their identity and relationship to the labor movement have raised important historical issues. An early approach was Chester McArthur Destler, "The People's Party in Illinois, 1888–1896: A Phase of the Populist Revolt" (Ph.D. diss., Univ. of Chicago, 1932), part of which was incorporated into Destler's *American Radicalism, 1865–1901: Essays and Documents* (New London, Conn., 1946). More recently, Joanne Elizabeth Wheeler drew on her doctoral dissertation, "The Origins of Populism in the Political Structure of a Midwestern State: Partisan Preference in Illinois, 1876–1892" (State Univ. of New York, Buffalo, 1976), for a study of "Populists and Other People: An Illinois Portrait," in Milton Plesur, ed., *An American Historian: Essays to Honor Selig Adler* (Buffalo, 1980). In this analysis, the "agricultural equation" is less decisive in political behavior than is the clash between evangelical and liturgical perspectives. For a similar study of an earlier decade, see Richard Jensen, "The Religious and Occupational Roots of Party Identification: Illinois and Indiana in the 1870's," *Civil War History*, 16 (Dec. 1970).

Students in courses on Chicago and Illinois history have for years enjoyed the portrait of reformers in Ray Ginger, *Altgeld's America: The Lincoln Ideal versus Changing Realities* (New York, 1958). But newly developed statistical methods have allowed historians to undertake collective biography of another kind and to widen their grasp of political culture in the period. The outstanding example of this genre is Richard Jensen's regional study, *The Winning of the*

*Midwest: Social and Political Conflict, 1888–1896* (Chicago, 1971). Jensen concludes that the upheavals of the 1890s resulted in a realignment of the electorate under the Republican party's "new spirit of pluralism," a pluralism that "found roles for men of every occupation and status" and that appealed to both evangelical and liturgical voters (p. 308). In *Representative Democracy: Public Policy and Midwestern Legislatures in the Late Nineteenth Century* (Cambridge, Mass., 1980), Ballard C. Campbell uses multivariate analysis of roll call votes in Illinois, Iowa, and Wisconsin to study legislative issues rather than the personalities of the leaders. Thomas R. Pegram considers a range of reform issues between the constitutional conventions of 1869–70 and 1920–22 in "Progressivism and Partisanship: Reformers, Politicians, and Public Policy in Illinois, 1870–1922" (Ph.D. diss., Brandeis Univ., 1987).

Illinois farming in the late nineteenth century, as earlier, is authoritatively discussed in Allen G. Bogue, *From Prairie to Corn Belt . . .* (Chicago, 1963). Large-scale agriculture in central Illinois has been well studied, especially in Paul W. Gates, *Landlords and Tenants on the Prairie Frontier . . .* (Ithaca, 1973) and in Margaret Beattie Bogue, *Patterns from the Sod: Land Use and Tenure in the Grand Prairie, 1850–1900*, Collections of the Illinois State Historical Library, 34 (1959). The latter book takes particular note of Matthew T. Scott. For the leading agricultural entrepreneur of the period, see Homer E. Socolofsky, *Landlord William Scully* (Lawrence, Kans., 1979). Hiram Sibley is conspicuous in Roger Andrew Winsor, "Artificial Drainage of East Central Illinois, 1820–1920" (Ph.D. diss., Univ. of Illinois, Urbana-Champaign, 1975). Other aspects of agriculture in the period are studied in James W. Whitaker, *Feedlot Empire: Beef Cattle Feeding in Illinois and Iowa, 1840–1900* (Ames, Iowa, 1975); Mary Yeager, *Competition and Regulation: The Development of Oligopoly in the Meat Packing Industry* (Greenwich, Conn., 1981); and Margaret Walsh, *The Rise of the Midwestern Meat Packing Industry* (Lexington, Ky., 1982).

The rich land of Illinois created a demand for farm implements that certain entrepreneurs met. The story of one such business is told at length in Wayne G. Broehl, Jr., *John Deere's Company: A History of Deere & Company and Its Times* (New York, 1984), some three hundred pages of which relate to the period from 1837 to 1907. An early but exemplary study of a rival is William T. Hutchinson, *Cyrus Hall McCormick . . .* (2 vols., Chicago, 1930–35). The extensive records of the McCormick Company and its successor have also supported the twin economic histories of Robert Ozanne, *A Century of Labor-Management Relations at McCormick and International Harvester* (Madison, 1967) and *Wages in Practice and Theory: McCormick and International Harvester, 1860–1960* (Madison, 1968). Margaret R. Hafstad, ed., *Guide to the McCormick Collection at the State Historical Society of Wisconsin* (Madison, 1973) is an invitation to further work. J[ames] Sanford Rikoon, *Threshing in the Midwest, 1820–1940: A Study of Traditional Culture and Technological Change* (Bloomington, Ind., 1988) traces the role of farmers in agricultural mechanization.

Coal mining was a major industry in Gilded Age Illinois, but the subject so far lacks a full-scale account. Much of the literature to date has concerned specific labor disputes. Coal-mining communities in northeastern Illinois are studied in Herbert G. Gutman, "The Braidwood Lockout of 1874," *Journal of the Illinois State Historical Society*, 53 (Spring 1960); Richard Patrick Joyce, "Miners of the Prairie: Life and Labor in the Wilmington, Illinois, Coal Field, 1866–1897" (M.A. thesis, Illinois State Univ., 1980); and John H. M. Laslett, *Nature's Noblemen: The Fortunes of the Independent Collier in Scotland and the American Midwest, 1855–1889* (Los Angeles, 1983). Clashes at mines elsewhere in the state are described in Fred W. Soady, Jr., "Little Mine Riot of 1894: A Study of a Central Illinois Labor Dispute" (M.S. thesis, Illinois State Univ., 1962), regarding a strike near Pekin, and Victor Hicken, "The Virden and Pana Mine Wars of 1898," *Journal of the Illinois State Historical Society*, 52 (Summer 1959). Hicken's "Mine Union Radicalism in Macoupin and Montgomery Counties," *Western Illiniois Regional Studies*, 3 (Fall 1980), and John H. Keiser, "The Union Miners Cemetery at Mt. Olive, Illinois: A Spirit-Thread of Labor History," *Journal of the Illinois State Historical Society*, 62 (Autumn 1969), trace aspects of the story into the twentieth century. Jensen's *Winning of the Midwest* contains a stimulating chapter on "Conflict in Coal: Labor Militancy and the Politics of Hardship." Studies of labor leaders who were shaped by the disputes of the 1890s include Elsie Glück, *John Mitchell, Miner: Labor's Bargain with the Gilded Age* (New York, 1929); Joseph Michael Gowaskie, "John Mitchell: A Study in Leadership" (Ph.D. diss., Catholic Univ. of America, 1968); and Lorin Lee Cary, "Adolph Germer and the 1890's Depression," *Journal of the Illinois State Historical Society*, 68 (Sept. 1975). Another perspective on coal-mine production, ending with legislation in the wake of the Cherry Mine disaster, is Amy Zahl Gottlieb, "The Regulation of the Coal Mining Industry in Illinois, with Special Reference to the Influence of British Miners and British Precedents, 1870–1911" (Ph.D. diss., Univ. of London, 1975). There is a clear need for a comprehensive history of coal mining in the state, one that uses available studies, investigates new questions, and rationalizes the entire topic.

Labor disputes concerning railroads loom large in Illinois history. These difficulties are studied in context by Shelton Stromquist, *A Generation of Boomers: The Pattern of Railroad Labor Conflict in Nineteenth-Century America* (Urbana, 1987). Philip S. Foner, *The Great Labor Uprising of 1877* (New York, 1977) emphasizes the role of the Workingmen's party in the "great strike." Further study of the National Guard, which was formed in 1877, is warranted. A good starting point is Roy Turnbaugh, "Ethnicity, Civic Pride, and Commitment: The Evolution of the Chicago Militia," *Journal of the Illinois State Historical Society*, 72 (May 1979). Donald L. McMurry, *The Great Burlington Strike of 1888: A Case Study in Labor Relations* (Cambridge, Mass., 1956) shows how injunctions were used to break labor union boycotts. Almont Lindsey, *The Pullman Strike: The Story of a Unique Experiment and of a Great Labor Upheaval* (Chicago, 1942) is a well-documented account of the 1894 conflict. A useful localized study is Harry Jebsen, Jr., "The Role of Blue Island in the Pullman Strike of 1894," *Journal of the Illinois State Historical Society*, 67 (June 1974). All these strikes are described from a national perspective in Gerald G. Eggert, *Railroad Labor Disputes: The Beginnings of Federal Strike Policy* (Ann Arbor, 1967). Important studies that utilize new approaches to the subject include Paul V. Black, "The Development of Management Personnel Policies on the Burlington Railroad, 1860–1900" (Ph.D. diss., Univ. of Wisconsin, Madison, 1972) and David L. Lightner, *Labor on the Illinois Central Railroad, 1852–1900: The Evolution of an Industrial Environment* (New York, 1977). Another study, treating a "traditional" topic, a trade union, in new terms, is Richard Schneirov and Thomas J. Suhrbur, *Union Brotherhood, Union Town: The History of the Carpenters' Union of Chicago, 1863–1987* (Carbondale, 1988).

Much has been written about the Haymarket affair of 1886. Until recently the principal account was Henry David, *The History of the Haymarket Affair: A Study in the American Social-Revolutionary and Labor Movements* (New York, 1936). The new standard is Paul Avrich, *The Haymarket Tragedy* (Princeton, 1984). Both books exceed five hundred pages, and both are objective, although somewhat sympathetic to the anarchists. Specialized articles include Francis X. Busch, "The Haymarket Riot and the Trial of the Anarchists," *Journal of the Illinois State Historical Society*, 48 (Autumn 1955); Mark Plummer, "Governor Richard J. Oglesby and the Haymarket Anarchists," in Illinois State Historical Society, *Selected Papers in Illinois History, 1981*; and Harvey Wish, "Governor Altgeld Pardons the Anarchists," *Journal of the Illinois State Historical Society*, 31 (Dec. 1938). Dave Roediger and Franklin Rosemont, eds., *Haymarket Scrapbook* (Chicago, 1986) is an anthology of sources and commentary to mark the Haymarket centennial.

Present-day scholars, although conscious of their predecessors' neglect of black history, have written very little on Illinois in particular. Roger D. Bridges, "Equality Deferred: Civil Rights for Illinois Blacks, 1865–1885," *Journal of the Illinois State Historical Society*, 74 (Summer 1981), is a pioneering work. John H. Keiser, "Black Strikebreakers and Racism in Illinois, 1865–1900," ibid., 65 (Autumn 1972), is also important. Shirley J. Carlson, "Black Migration to Pulaski County, Illinois, 1860–1900," *Illinois Historical Journal*, 80 (Spring 1987), examines a county bordering on the Ohio River. The racial politics and policies of the Tanner administration are reflected in studies by Willard B. Gatewood, Jr., "An Experiment in Color: The Eighth Illinois Volunteers, 1898–1899," *Journal of the Illinois State Historical Society*, 65 (Autumn 1972), and *"Smoked Yankees" and the Struggle for Empire: Letters from Negro Soldiers, 1898–1902* (Urbana, 1971). The field clearly needs more attention.

Somewhat the same situation exists for women's history, although certain leaders have been well studied. Ruth Bordin, *Frances Willard: A Biography* (Chapel Hill, 1986) updates the literature regarding the president of the Woman's Christian Temperance Union. Articles on other reformers include Ralph Scharnau, "Elizabeth Morgan, Crusader for Labor Reform," *Labor History*, 14

(Summer 1973), and Sandra D. Harmon, "Florence Kelley in Illinois," *Journal of the Illinois State Historical Society*, 74 (Autumn 1981). A well-known matrix for such leadership is examined in Kathryn Kish Sklar, "Hull House in the 1890s: A Community of Women Reformers," *Signs: Journal of Women in Culture and Society*, 10 (Summer 1985). Collective biographies include Lana Ruegamer, " 'The Paradise of Exceptional Women': Chicago Women Reformers, 1863–1893" (Ph.D. diss., Indiana Univ., 1982) and Rebecca Louise Sherrick, "Private Visions, Public Lives: The Hull–House Women in the Progressive Era" (Ph.D. diss., Northwestern Univ., 1980). See also Meredith Tax, *The Rising of the Women: Feminist Solidarity and Class Conflict, 1880–1917* (New York, 1980).

In summary, readers have an up-to-date single-volume history of Illinois in the Gilded Age. They also have satisfactory biographies of many of the state's political leaders such as Lyman Trumbull, John A. Logan, Shelby M. Cullom, and John Peter Altgeld. Yet many governors, senators, and representatives have passed virtually unnoticed. There is a respectable literature regarding agrarian movements in the state, the agricultural experience, and the careers of certain landlords. But in this field there is room for new approaches. Studies of blacks and women in Illinois in the late nineteenth century are especially needed. As for the complex processes of industrialization in the state, most of what has been written has concerned labor conflicts in coal mining, railroading, and manufacturing. But these accounts are narrowly focused, gaps remain, and the field clearly needs a synthesis. Illinois industrialization was more than the Pullman strike and the Haymarket affair, and it should be studied from a broader perspective.

# 6

# THE PROGRESSIVE ERA, 1900–20

JOHN D. BUENKER

IN ILLINOIS, AS elsewhere in the United States, the first two decades of the twentieth century were characterized by so many efforts to "reform" society and to promote "progress" that contemporaries and historians alike have called the period the Progressive era. During this complex and volatile era, Illinoisans struggled to adapt to life in a rapidly emerging industrial, urban, multicultural society. Their efforts resulted in a proliferation of voluntary associations, many of which entered the political arena. Concurrently, they sponsored "reform" candidates who produced an outpouring of "progressive" legislation. Although the Prairie State did not achieve the reputation accorded Wisconsin, Oregon, or a handful of other "progressive" states, it clearly earned a place within the mainstream of reform. Indeed, as John D. Buenker contends, in "Illinois and the Four Progressive-Era Amendments to the United States Constitution," *Illinois Historical Journal*, 80 (Winter 1987), the state played a crucial role in making the income tax, direct election of U.S. senators, prohibition, and woman suffrage the law of the land.

Despite Illinois' size and importance, there is no comprehensive history of the Progressive era in the state. Ernest Ludlow Bogart and John Mabry Mathews, *The Modern Commonwealth, 1893–1918* (Springfield, 1920) is a detailed narrative, but it lacks analysis or interpretation. Donald F. Tingley, *The Structuring of a State: The History of Illinois, 1899 to 1928* (Urbana, 1980) provides a topical approach to the period, reviewing in turn industry, agriculture, labor, and transportation but devoting the longest chapter to politics, which is described as a "bewildering confusion of factions and bosses combined with occasional excursions into reform" (p. 130). These books are useful as a starting point for many subjects, but a thorough understanding of the era can be gained only by reading a myriad of monographs, articles, and dissertations. Although part of this literature is discussed here, many studies of the period are cited elsewhere, especially in the chapter on Chicago. Throughout the era, Chicago remained the center of the state's reform enterprises, producing most of its intellectual, economic, and organizational leadership, while functioning as the seat of power for nearly every important political faction. Not surprisingly, the centrality of the Windy City is reflected in the literature, which is relatively thin in its treatment of downstate developments.

The reformist currents of the Progressive era permeated both major parties, cutting across their shifting alignments. They affected especially the Republican party, which was initially divided into two sometimes overlapping factions: a "federal" group, including Shelby M. Cullom, Joseph G. Cannon, and Charles G. Dawes, and the Chicago "machine," controlled at different times by William "Blond Boss" Lorimer and William Hale "Big Bill" Thompson. James W. Neilson, *Shelby M. Cullom, Prairie State Republican* (Urbana, 1962) skillfully reviews the Springfield politician's career through five terms in the U.S. Senate, ending in 1913. Blair Bolles, *Tyrant from Illinois: Uncle Joe Cannon's Experiment with Personal Power* (New York, 1951) is the best account of the Danville conservative's rise and fall as Speaker of the U.S. House of Representatives, 1903–11. Dawes, a Chicago banker who led the party in support of William McKinley for president in 1896 and who was elected vice-president under Calvin Coolidge in 1924, is studied in John E. Pixton, Jr., "The Early Career of Charles G. Dawes" (Ph.D. diss., Univ. of Chicago, 1952). For Dawes' own highly interesting comments on Illinois politics from 1893 to 1913, see Bascom N. Timmons, ed., *A Journal of the McKinley Years* (Chicago, 1950). Joel Arthur Tarr, *A Study in Boss Politics: William Lorimer of Chicago* (Urbana, 1971) is an outstanding work, emphasizing Lorimer's role in helping immigrant minorities, tracing his career in Congress, and defending him against old-stock reformers who brought about his ouster from the Senate in 1912. Lloyd Wendt and Herman Kogan, *Big Bill of Chicago* (Indianapolis, 1953) is descriptive, anecdotal, and popularized, but it accurately conveys Mayor Thompson's success formula: an alliance with business, a wide-open attitude toward liquor and vice, and ethnocultural appeals, especially to blacks.

Within the Republican party, pushing for more reform than the machine would accommodate, were insurgents, many of whom in time formed the Progressive party. One such reformer was Harold L. Ickes, a journalist and attorney who left a lively account in *The Autobiography of a Curmudgeon* (New York, 1943) and who is thoughtfully assessed in Linda J. Lear, *Harold L. Ickes, the Aggressive Progressive, 1874–1933* (New York, 1981). Another reformer, Charles E. Merriam, a political scientist at the University of Chicago, exemplified the academic community's interest in politics and public policy. His *Chicago: A More Intimate View of Urban Politics* (New York, 1929) exhibits a rare and judicious blend of scholarly expertise and practical political experience. The Republican nominee for mayor in 1911, he was nearly elected. See Michael P. McCarthy, "Prelude to Armageddon: Charles E. Merriam and the Chicago Mayoral Election of 1911," *Journal of the Illinois State Historical Society*, 67 (Nov. 1974). The Bull Moose movement of 1912 brought about a schism between regular and insurgent Republicans. The course of the reformers in this split, and their subsequent return to the Republican party, is plotted in Ralph Arthur Straetz, "The Progressive Movement in Illinois, 1910–1916" (Ph.D. diss., Univ. of Illinois, 1951).

Except in 1912, Republicans won every gubernatorial election in the period, leading to terms for Richard Yates (1901–5), Charles S. Deneen (1905–13), and Frank O. Lowden (1917–21). Yates and Deneen have not attracted biographers, but the title of Yates's sketchy autobiography indicates how he ran on his name: John H. Krenkel, ed., *Serving the Republic: Richard Yates, Illinois Governor and Congressman, Son of Richard Yates, Civil War Governor* . . . (Danville, Ill., 1968). Deneen carefully toed the line between reform and regularity, while Lowden began as a Lorimerite congressman and became a moderate reformer. William T. Hutchinson, *Lowden of Illinois: The Life of Frank O. Lowden* . . . (2 vols., Chicago, 1957) is not only an excellent biography but a useful political history of the period.

Illinois Democrats in the Progressive era were divided into three Chicago-based factions, led by Carter Harrison II, Roger C. Sullivan, and Edward F. Dunne. *Stormy Years: The Autobiography of Carter H. Harrison* . . . (Indianapolis, 1935) presents an articulate, witty, and thoroughly self-interested picture of his five mayoral terms. Samuel Alvin Lilly, "The Political Career of Roger C. Sullivan" (M.A. thesis, Eastern Illinois Univ., 1964) sketches the shifting course of a powerful boss. Dunne, a lawyer and judge, was elected mayor of Chicago and then governor of the state, the only Illinoisan ever to hold both offices. His secretary, William L. Sullivan, edited *Dunne: Judge, Mayor, Governor* (Chicago, 1916), a collection of his judicial and political statements, and Dunne gave his own administrations considerable space in *Illinois: The Heart of the Nation* (5 vols., Chicago, 1933). The Chicago political scene through Dunne's mayoral term is outlined in Ralph R. Tingley, "From Carter Harrison II to Fred Busse: A Study of Chicago Political Parties and Personages from 1896 to 1907" (Ph.D. diss., Univ. of Chicago, 1950). John D. Buenker, "Edward F. Dunne: The Urban New Stock Democrat as Progressive," *Mid-America*, 50 (Jan. 1968), points to numerous reform measures during Dunne's term as governor, 1913–17. Richard Allen Morton, "Justice and Humanity: The Politics of Edward F. Dunne" (Ph.D. diss., Univ. of Illinois, Urbana-Champaign, 1988) provides a positive assessment of his career.

According to John D. Buenker, "The New-Stock Politicians of 1912," *Journal of the Illinois State Historical Society*, 62 (Spring 1969), the Democratic party, more than the Republican or Progressive parties, was open to candidates who represented ethnic and religious minorities. Furthermore, they often provided crucial support for labor, welfare, regulatory, and tax reform measures, a point established in Buenker, "Urban Immigrant Lawmakers and Progressive Reform in Illinois," in Donald F. Tingley, ed., *Essays in Illinois History* . . . (Carbondale, 1968). Although ethnic communities often opposed prohibition and other expressions of legislated conformity, they shared with old-stock Americans a substantial record on behalf of reform in the period.

The factional politics of the major parties were occasionally complicated by third-party candidates. Four Chicago Socialists were elected to the legislature in 1912, but their voting records are almost indistinguishable from those of other working-class representatives, according to John D. Buenker, "Illinois Socialists and Progressive Reform," *Journal of the Illinois State Historical Society*, 63 (Winter 1970). Similarly moderate were the Socialists who gained office in local contests. See, for example, Errol Wayne Stevens, "The Socialist Party of America in Municipal Politics: Canton, Illinois, 1911–1920," ibid., 72 (Nov. 1979). John Howard Keiser, "John Fitzpatrick and Progressive Unionism, 1915–1925" (Ph.D. diss., Northwestern Univ., 1965) describes the pragmatic efforts of the president of the Chicago Federation of Labor to advance working-class power. Fitzpatrick led the Labor party in the state, running as its candidate for mayor of Chicago in 1919.

William Booth Philip, "Chicago and the Down State: A Study of Their Conflicts, 1870–1934" (Ph.D. diss., Univ. of Chicago, 1940) considers the deepest, most persistent schism in Illinois politics. Questions of legislative apportionment, consolidation and home rule for Chicago, traction franchises, the drainage canal and the Illinois River, and taxation all divided legislators in the Progressive era. The careers of particular congressmen illustrate the diversity of districts within the state. Long-term representatives of the period, two Chicago Republicans and a downstate Democrat, are studied in L. Ethan Ellis, "James Robert Mann, Legislator Extraordinary," *Journal of the Illinois State Historical Society*, 46 (Spring 1953); Thomas Robert Bullard, "From Businessman to Congressman: The Careers of Martin B. Madden" (Ph.D. diss., Univ. of Illinois, Chicago, 1973); and, on Henry T. Rainey, Robert A. Waller, *Rainey of Illinois: A Political Biography, 1903–34* (Urbana, 1977).

Beginning in the late nineteenth century, Chicago's politicians were confronted by an array of reform-minded civic associations. To an extent, these organizations drew their support from middle-class neighborhoods that had been annexed to Chicago, notably in 1889, but their relative success depended upon their willingness to build bridges to the residents of ethnic working-class neighborhoods, according to Michael P. McCarthy, "The New Metropolis: Chicago, the Annexation Movement, and Progressive Reform," in Michael H. Ebner and Eugene M. Tobin, eds., *The Age of Urban Reform: New*

*Perspectives on the Progressive Era* (Port Washington, N.Y., 1977). Donald D. Marks, "Polishing the Gem of the Prairie: The Evolution of Civic Reform Consciousness in Chicago, 1874–1900" (Ph.D. diss., Univ. of Wisconsin, Madison, 1974) suggests that the Citizens' Association and the Civic Federation unintentionally broadened the base of political involvement by espousing not only voluntary reform but governmental intervention. As indicated by Sidney I. Roberts, "The Municipal Voters' League and Chicago's Boodlers," *Journal of the Illinois State Historical Society*, 53 (Summer 1960), the league was particularly effective in upgrading the quality of Chicago aldermen. Hoyt King, *Citizen Cole of Chicago* (Chicago, 1931) and Alan B. Gould, "Walter L. Fisher: Profile of an Urban Reformer, 1880–1910," *Mid-America*, 57 (July 1975), concern early leaders of the Municipal Voters' League.

Chicago was prominently featured in the muckraking exposés that helped to initiate reforms in the Progressive era. William T. Stead, *If Christ Came to Chicago . . .* (Chicago, 1894) graphically portrayed the connections among business, politics, vice, and poverty, and aroused the city's respectable elements in support of remedial efforts. Upton Sinclair, *The Jungle* (New York, 1906; best ed., Urbana, 1988), a socialist novel, depicted conditions among the immigrants in Chicago's packinghouses and provided ammunition for meat inspection laws. In *The Titan* (Cleveland, 1914), Theodore Dreiser thinly fictionalized the machinations of the city's traction magnate, Charles T. Yerkes, who built a system opposed by mayors from Harrison to Dunne. According to [Joseph] Lincoln Steffens, in *The Shame of the Cities* (New York, 1904), Chicago, through the efforts of its civic associations, was "half-free and fighting on." In *The Struggle for Self-Government . . .* (New York, 1906), Steffens argued that the reform currents that had originated in Chicago were spreading to the rest of Illinois.

Chicago's newspapers took the lead in shaping public opinion in support of reform. The fullest account of this process is John Edward Erickson, "Newspapers and Social Values: Chicago Journalism, 1890–1910" (Ph.D. diss., Univ. of Illinois, Urbana-Champaign, 1973). The *Tribune* and the *Daily News*, two of the six papers analyzed by Erickson, are compared with two St. Louis papers in David Paul Nord, *Newspapers and New Politics: Midwestern Municipal Reform, 1890–1900* (Ann Arbor, 1981), a study that relates the "new politics" of urban reform to the mass communication of the press. Royal J. Schmidt, "The *Chicago Daily News* and Traction Politics, 1876–1920," *Journal of the Illinois State Historical Society*, 64 (Autumn 1971), describes Victor Lawson's impact on a leading issue of the day. James Weber Linn, *James Keeley, Newspaperman* (Indianapolis, 1937) presents the editor of the *Tribune*. An important source of reform ideas, more radical than the mainline newspapers, is noted in Dominic Candeloro, "*The Public* of Louis F. Post and Progressivism," *Mid-America*, 56 (Apr. 1974). By all odds, however, Chicago's most famous journalist was Finley Peter Dunne, who chided and cajoled reformers and boodlers alike in the thick Irish brogue of his alter ego, Mr. Dooley. The best of Dunne's columns before he moved to New York can be found in Barbara C. Schaaf, *Mr. Dooley's Chicago* (Garden City, N.Y., 1977). See also Charles Fanning, *Finley Peter Dunne and Mr. Dooley: The Chicago Years* (Lexington, Ky., 1978).

Perhaps the most active, effective, and respected reformers in the Progressive era were those who founded Hull House, Chicago Commons, and similar institutions designed to aid immigrants, ethnic minorities, and the underprivileged. The settlement house workers lived among these people, tried to understand their traditions and values, and sought to integrate them into American life without destroying their sense of identity or self-esteem. Although primarily engaged in educational, recreational, and cultural activities, settlement house leaders occasionally became involved in political campaigns, unionization drives, and reform causes. The importance of the settlement movement in Chicago, New York, and Boston is established in Allen F. Davis, *Spearheads for Reform: The Social Settlements and the Progressive Movement, 1890–1914* (New York, 1967). In his introduction to a new edition of this book (New Brunswick, N.J., 1984), Davis sets an agenda for studies of social welfare in the period, suggesting more attention to the purposes of settlement workers and to the "point of view of the client, the inmate, the tenement dweller, and the factory worker" (p. xxiii). Robert A. Woods and Albert J. Kennedy, eds., *Handbook of Settlements* (New York, 1911) includes a chapter listing downstate as well as Chicago settlements.

The literature on Chicago's most celebrated settlement house resident, Jane Addams of Hull House, is voluminous. Her own writings, especially *Twenty Years at Hull-House, with Autobiographical Notes* (New York, 1910; best ed., Urbana, 1990) and *Democracy and Social Ethics* (New York, 1902; best ed., Cambridge, Mass., 1964), are fundamental. Important biographies include Daniel Levine, *Jane Addams and the Liberal Tradition* (Madison, 1971) and Allen F. Davis, *American Heroine: The Life and Legend of Jane Addams* (New York, 1973). Her early experience in politics, described in Davis's "Jane Addams *vs.* the Ward Boss," *Journal of the Illinois State Historical Society*, 53 (Autumn 1960), may be compared to the political career of another leading reformer, the subject of Davis's "Raymond Robins: The Settlement Worker as Municipal Refomer," *Social Service Review*, 33 (June 1959).

Some of the complexities of charitable endeavors in the period are discussed in Helen L. Horowitz, "Varieties of Cultural Experience in Jane Addams' Chicago," *History of Education Quarterly*, 14 (Spring 1974), and John A. Mayer, "Relief Systems and Social Controls: The Case of Chicago, 1890–1910," *Old Northwest*, 6 (Fall 1980). There are numerous studies focusing on particular efforts of settlement house reformers. Lynn Gordon, "Women and the Anti–Child Labor Movement in Illinois, 1890–1920," *Social Service Review*, 51 (June 1977), describes one of Florence Kelley's concerns. Robert L. Buroker, "From Voluntary Association to Welfare State: The Illinois Immigrants' Protective League, 1908–1926," *Journal of American History*, 58 (Dec. 1971), and Henry

B. Leonard, "The Immigrants' Protective League of Chicago, 1908–1921," *Journal of the Illinois State Historical Society*, 66 (Nov. 1973), assess an organization founded by Jane Addams and Grace Abbott. Anthony R. Travis, "The Origin of Mothers' Pensions in Illinois," ibid., 68 (Nov. 1975), relates to the work of Sophonisba Breckinridge and Edith Abbott. See also Joseph L. Candela, Jr., "The Struggle to Limit the Hours and Raise the Wages of Working Women in Illinois, 1893–1917," *Social Service Review*, 53 (Mar. 1979).

Social welfare reformers cooperated with civic and business leaders in creating parks and playgrounds for Chicago's diverse population, a development traced in Benjamin McArthur, "The Chicago Playground Movement: A Neglected Feature of Social Justice," *Social Service Review*, 49 (Sept. 1975), and in Michael P. McCarthy, "Politics and the Parks: Chicago Businessmen and the Recreation Movement," *Journal of the Illinois State Historical Society*, 65 (Summer 1972). Chicago also became known for large-scale city planning. John James Pauly, Jr., "The City Builders: Chicago Businessmen and Their Changing Ethos, 1871–1909" (Ph.D. diss., Univ. of Illinois, Urbana-Champaign, 1979) sketches the background of this movement, the culmination of which was the *Plan of Chicago* . . . (Chicago, 1909), prepared by Daniel H. Burnham and Edward H. Bennett for the Commercial Club of Chicago.

Chicago was also the focal point for cultural reforms which frequently split the city along ethnic and religious lines. Liquor, gambling, vice, and even the emerging medium of motion pictures became moral issues that separated people who had been allies in other matters. John D. Buenker, "The Illinois Legislature and Prohibition, 1907–1919," *Journal of the Illinois State Historical Society*, 62 (Winter 1969), finds that "wets" and "drys" were typically divided not so much between Chicago and Downstate or by party and class as between new-stock Catholics and Jews and old-stock Protestants. Anti-gambling and vice crusades were often pressed by civic associations and the Protestant clergy, and resisted by professional politicians with ethnic working-class constituencies. Walter C. Reckless, *Vice in Chicago* (Chicago, 1933) relies upon the work of the Chicago and Illinois vice commissions to document the alliance of politicians, policemen, and the underworld in defense of an open city. Mark H. Haller, "Police Reform in Chicago, 1905–1935," *American Behavioral Scientist*, 13 (May–Aug. 1970), argues that the predominantly Irish Catholic police force often refused to cooperate with vice crusaders because they pointed to police corruption and politicization as thwarting their efforts to end prostitution and gambling. Haller's "Organized Crime in Urban Society: Chicago in the Twentieth Century," *Journal of Social History*, 5 (Winter 1971–72), considers the connections between particular ethnic groups and specific criminal activities. Kathleen D. McCarthy, "Nickel Vice and Virtue: Movie Censorship in Chicago, 1907–1915," *Journal of Popular Film*, Vol. 5, No. 1 (1976), outlines the reactions of civic reformers to the spread of motion pictures. The history of the city's film industry is skillfully reconstructed in William Franklin Grisham, "Modes, Movies, and Magnates:

Early Filmmaking in Chicago" (Ph.D. diss., Northwestern Univ., 1982).

Women played a significant role in many reform efforts of the period, especially in the settlement house movement and in the quest for political equality. In "Side Lights on Illinois Suffrage History," *Journal of the Illinois State Historical Society*, 13 (July 1920), Grace Wilbur Trout, president of the Illinois Equal Suffrage Association, recounts the passage of the state's suffrage act of 1913 and its ratification of the Nineteenth Amendment in 1919. Adade Mitchell Wheeler, "Conflict in the Illinois Woman Suffrage Movement of 1913," ibid., 76 (Summer 1983), describes the split between those who sought the vote for its own sake and those who planned to use the ballot to effect other more radical changes. These competing objectives are analyzed over a longer period in Steven M. Buechler, *The Transformation of the Woman Suffrage Movement: The Case of Illinois, 1850–1920* (New Brunswick, N.J., 1986), an important study.

Tingley's *Structuring of a State* includes a chapter surveying the experience of blacks in Illinois in the early twentieth century. As with other topics, more specialized accounts emphasize developments in Chicago. See, for example, Steven J. Diner, "Chicago Social Workers and Blacks in the Progressive Era," *Social Service Review*, 44 (Dec. 1970), and Philip Jackson, "Black Charity in Progressive Era Chicago," ibid., 52 (Sept. 1978). Arvarh E. Strickland, *History of the Chicago Urban League* (Urbana, 1966) traces an important organization that began in the period. The most devastating event for the black community is assessed in William M. Tuttle, Jr., *Race Riot: Chicago in the Red Summer of 1919* (New York, 1970) and Arthur I. Waskow, *From Race Riot to Sit-In, 1919 and the 1960s . . .* (Garden City, N.Y., 1966). Racial tensions also erupted in riots downstate. The first such violence is briefly described in James Krohe, Jr., *Summer of Rage: The Springfield Race Riot of 1908* (Springfield, 1973) and more fully analyzed in Roberta Senechal, *The Sociogenesis of a Race Riot: Springfield, Illinois in 1908* (Urbana, 1990). Elliott M. Rudwick, *Race Riot at East St. Louis, July 2, 1917* (Carbondale, 1964) not only covers that outbreak in detail but also locates it within the larger context of race relations in the period.

A perennial issue of the Progressive era concerned the transportation system in the state, especially roads and electric railways to link communities mainly connected by steam railroads. The proliferation of automobiles, trucks, and buses depended upon a network of concrete highways, the first stages of which are described in David R. Wrone, "Illinois Pulls Out of the Mud," *Journal of the Illinois State Historical Society*, 58 (Spring 1965). As discussed in Norman T. Moline, *Mobility and the Small Town, 1900–1930: Transportation Change in Oregon, Illinois* (Chicago, 1971), the car not only stimulated the good roads movement but also hastened other changes begun by the electric interurban, including different travel patterns and a new sense of distances between cities in the state. Robert A. Waller, "The Illinois Waterway from Conception to Completion, 1908–1933," *Journal of the Illinois State Historical Society*, 65

(Summer 1972), reviews the controversial effort to build a deep waterway from the Great Lakes to the Mississippi River.

World War I disrupted the lives of many Illinoisans, and the state's contribution to the war effort was a milestone in its development. Marguerite Edith Jenison (Pease), *The War-Time Organization of Illinois*, Illinois in the World War, 5 (Springfield, 1923), is the essential study of the State Council of Defense, which coordinated the efforts of agriculture, industry, and labor; sponsored war bond drives; and drew women into the work force. Numerous leaders on the homefront are sketched in J[osiah] Seymour Currey, *Illinois Activities in the World War* . . . (3 vols., Chicago, 1921).

The war raised the issue of loyalty for many German-Americans, socialists, and pacifists. Edgar Bernhard et al., *Pursuit of Freedom: A History of Civil Liberty in Illinois, 1787–1942* (Chicago, 1942) examines the efforts of the fledgling Chicago Civil Liberties Committee to defend the rights of dissenters. Arthur W. Thurner, "The Mayor, the Governor, and the People's Council: A Chapter in American Wartime Dissent," *Journal of the Illinois State Historical Society*, 66 (Summer 1973), reviews the split between Thompson and Lowden over Thompson's defense of the People's Council of America for Democracy and Peace, a coordinating agency for local organizations seeking an early peace. Joan M. Jensen, *The Price of Vigilance* (Chicago, 1968) focuses on the activities of the American Protective League, a volunteer organization founded in Chicago to aid federal authorities in ferreting out radicals and other "disloyal" persons. Although there were many instances of discrimination and violence against German-Americans during the war, perhaps the most reprehensible was the lynching in Collinsville of Robert Praeger, an immigrant with socialist leanings. See Donald R. Hickey, "The Praeger Affair: A Study in Wartime Hysteria," *Journal of the Illinois State Historical Society*, 62 (Summer 1969). Frederick C. Luebke, *Bonds of Loyalty: German-Americans and World War I* (DeKalb, 1974) uses the Praeger incident to introduce larger questions regarding German-Americans during the war.

In 1917, despite the atmosphere of superpatriotism in the state, six Illinois congressmen voted against U.S. involvement in the war. See Philip R. Vander Meer, "Congressional Decision-Making and World War I: A Case Study of Illinois Congressional Opponents," *Congressional Studies*, Vol. 8, No. 2 (1981). In 1920, in another landmark vote, both Illinois senators, Medill McCormick and Lawrence Y. Sherman, opposed U.S. entry into the League of Nations. See Ralph A. Stone, "Two Illinois Senators among the Irreconcilables," *Mississippi Valley Historical Review*, 50 (Dec. 1963).

Despite the large body of literature that examines the Progressive era in the state, it is clear that there are significant gaps that should be filled. Most obvious is the relative dearth of studies on downstate Illinois, as opposed to the wealth of material on Chicago. Although the metropolis certainly played the central role, developments in smaller cities and in towns and rural areas ought to be investigated. There is also a great need for detailed studies of the gubernatorial administrations of the period. Similarly, it is clear that the origins and impact of many reforms have yet to be closely examined. There is little danger that studies of the Progressive period in Illinois will reach the saturation point at any time in the near future.

# 7

# PROSPERITY, DEPRESSION, AND WAR, 1920–45

RALPH A. STONE

EXCEPT FOR GENERAL surveys, there is no single volume that examines Illinois history between 1920 and 1945. Monographic literature for these years is rather thin, especially so in works that are broadly conceived or that attempt to apply interpretations of national events to the Illinois scene. Much of the writing, however, falls into periodizations found at the national level: the 1920s, the Depression and New Deal, and World War II.

The place to begin for Illinois history in the 1920s is Donald F. Tingley, *The Structuring of a State: The History of Illinois, 1899 to 1928* (Urbana, 1980). Tingley's approach is comprehensive, and he takes care to set Illinois history in the context of national events, though in doing so he sometimes loses the thread of state development. There is considerable material on the activities of ordinary people, with amusing anecdotes gleaned from newspapers. The book's title suggests the author's theme for these years: life in virtually every area became more structured. Industry grew more concentrated and subject to control by a few firms; political machines became more sophisticated and able to manipulate the voters; labor's future, if not its current status, rested on its ability to form unions; cities found it necessary to organize recreation and other activities; sports became more professionalized. For most Illinoisans, Tingley concludes, life was better materially in 1928 than in earlier years, but certain freedoms had been lost in the process of change.

As Tingley notes, Illinois and the nation had much in common in the 1920s. Politics provides a good illustration. Like the nation, Illinois was served by less than sterling leaders, and the odor of corruption hung over Springfield as it did over Washington, D.C.

Neither of the Republican governors of the period, Len Small (1921–29) and Louis L. Emmerson (1929–33), has been the subject of a biography, although Small's voluminous papers have been available at the Illinois State Historical Library since 1963. Probably the best introduction to state politics in the 1920s is Carroll Hill Wooddy, *The Case of Frank L. Smith: A Study in Representative Government* (Chicago, 1931). Smith was the Small-appointed chairman of the Illinois Commerce Commission who in 1926 sought the Republican nomination for the U.S. Senate. In the course of his campaign, Smith accepted huge contributions from Samuel Insull, the utilities magnate, whose companies' rates were set by the commission. Smith was elected, but the Senate, after an investigation, barred him from taking his seat. Wooddy is very critical of Smith, Insull, and Small, as well as of the assorted "payrollers and job-hungry henchmen" of Small and William Hale "Big Bill" Thompson, Chicago's mayor, but he assigns responsibility for the state's corrupt politics to many elements (p. 248). Wooddy's book is much broader than the title indicates. There are excellent descriptions of the workings of the political machines at the state and local levels, including the shifting alliances among political factions and the role of patronage, favors, loyalty, and money in Illinois politics. The book also contains shrewd observations about political corruption and sharply drawn portraits of the leading political figures of the time.

William H. Stuart, *The Twenty Incredible Years* (Chicago, 1935) provides a far different perspective on the politics of the era. While Wooddy looks unfavorably upon the political wheeling and dealing, Stuart is almost celebratory of it. Stuart is largely concerned with the career of Big Bill Thompson between 1915 and 1935, but there is necessarily much in the book about state politics. Stuart was apparently quite close to Thompson, and he does not hide his partisanship, lambasting all "reformers" and "internationalists" who challenged the mayor and his allies. Among those drawing his fire are Wooddy and his fellow University of Chicago professors. Indeed, Stuart makes some useful corrections to Wooddy's account of the 1926 primary campaign, which was first put forward in Wooddy, *The Chicago Primary of 1926: A Study of Election Methods* (Chicago, 1926). Additional information on the subject of money and politics in the 1920s can be found in M[orris] R. Werner, *Julius Rosenwald: The Life of a Practical Humanitarian* (New York, 1939). As head of Sears, Roebuck and Company, Rosenwald used his wealth freely in an effort to shape public policy.

A well-researched article on the 1924 election reveals the complexity of Illinois politics beyond the matter of corruption. In "Norman L. Jones versus Len Small in the Illinois Gubernatorial Campaign of 1924," *Journal of the Illinois State Historical Society*, 72 (Aug. 1979), Robert A. Waller notes that issues such as anti-labor court injunctions, reform of governmental procedures, traction fares, and public education were vigorously debated in 1924 but often without clear identification with the respective party standard-bearers. Small, the conservative

Republican, pictured himself as something of a populist, while his Democratic opponent's background suggested sympathy for business interests. The political waters were further muddied by highly emotional debates over prohibition and the Ku Klux Klan. Corruption, to be sure, was an issue in 1924. Small had earlier been indicted by a grand jury for having embezzled money when he was state treasurer. But on election day, voters found Small's positive attributes, especially his program of hard road building, coupled with Jones's weaknesses, more important than Small's alleged crimes of the past. Additional insights into the state's political infighting are provided in Kristie Miller, "Ruth Hanna McCormick and the Senatorial Election of 1930," *Illinois Historical Journal*, 81 (Autumn 1988). McCormick, long active in Republican politics and the first woman nominated to the U.S. Senate by a major political party, had been elected the state's first congresswoman in 1928.

Other general works contain information on politics in the twenties. William T. Hutchinson, *Lowden of Illinois: The Life of Frank O. Lowden . . .* (2 vols., Chicago, 1957) is unfriendly to the Thompson-Small combine without being overly partial to Lowden. The book is strong on agricultural politics, a prime interest of Lowden's. Alex Gottfried, *Boss Cermak of Chicago: A Study of Political Leadership* (Seattle, 1962) considers machine politics from the Democratic side, showing Cermak's skillful appeals to ethnic groups and his exploitation of the prohibition issue. While Thompson claimed to be "wetter than the Atlantic Ocean," Cermak championed the wet cause more single-mindedly. For a narrow but detailed study of Cermak, see Aaron Smith, "The Administration of Mayor Anton J. Cermak, 1931-1933" (M.A. thesis, Univ. of Illinois, 1956). The precise relationship between ethnic groups and the rise of the Democratic party in the late 1920s is thoughtfully explored in John M. Allswang, *A House for All Peoples: Ethnic Politics in Chicago, 1890–1936* (Lexington, Ky., 1971).

Little has been written about business in Illinois during the 1920s. Tingley's *Structuring of a State* skillfully utilizes materials on the national economy as well as a few local studies to show the growth of chain stores, installment buying, and the automobile industry within the state. For the electric power industry, Forrest McDonald, *Insull* (Chicago, 1962) is informative but uncritical, whether of Insull's holding company empire or of his ventures into politics. Alfred H. Kelly, *A History of the Illinois Manufacturers' Association* (Chicago, 1940), a part of his doctoral dissertation of the same title (Univ. of Chicago, 1938), examines the influence of that conservative body on social legislation in the state.

The story of labor has fared somewhat better. Two older books, Eugene Staley, *History of the Illinois State Federation of Labor* (Chicago, 1930) and Earl R. Beckner, *A History of Labor Legislation in Illinois* (Chicago, 1929), are still quite worthy but need updating. John Hunter Walker, president of the Illinois Federation of Labor in the 1920s and earlier president of the United Mine Workers of America, District 12 (Illinois), is the subject of an insightful article by John H. Keiser, "John H. Walker, Labor Leader from Illinois," in

Donald F. Tingley, ed., *Essays in Illinois History* . . . (Carbondale, 1968). Also useful is Anthony Barger Barrette, "John H. Walker, Labor Leader of Illinois, 1905–1933" (M.A. thesis, Eastern Illinois Univ., 1967). Walker was a close friend of the legendary labor agitator Mary Harris "Mother" Jones, and letters to and from him are published in Edward M. Steel, ed., *The Correspondence of Mother Jones* (Pittsburgh, 1985). Although she is buried at Mt. Olive, next to her "boys" who died in the Virden mine war, Mother Jones was less influential in Illinois than in more troubled mining regions such as West Virginia and Colorado.

The UMWA was one of the nation's most radical labor organizations, and the Illinois miners were the most militant group within the parent body. Harold William Perrigo has examined aspects of this story in "Factional Strife in District No. 12, United Mine Workers of America, 1919–1933" (Ph.D. diss., Univ. of Wisconsin, 1933). A sympathetic early account of left-wing elements in District 12 is Sylvia Kopald (Selekman), *Rebellion in Labor Unions* (New York, 1924). Kopald and others have argued that the 1920s saw a conservative retrenchment within the labor movement. This view is challenged in John H. M. Laslett's sophisticated study, "Swan Song or New Social Movement? Socialism and Illinois District 12, United Mine Workers of America, 1919–1926," in Donald T. Critchlow, ed., *Socialism in the Heartland: The Midwestern Experience, 1900–1925* (Notre Dame, Ind., 1986). Laslett contends that while voting statistics indicate a decline in leftist strength during the decade, the Illinois miners created a partially new radical movement based upon a broad concern for economic democracy.

A thorough work on the Illinois miners would be a signal contribution to national as well as state history. Until that time, students can turn to Melvyn Dubofsky and Warren Van Tine, *John L. Lewis: A Biography* (New York, 1977; abridged ed., Urbana, 1986) and to McAlister Coleman, *Men and Coal* (New York, 1943). Coleman was a reporter in the 1920s on the *Illinois Miner*, District 12's brilliantly edited newspaper.

An almost forgotten activity of the Illinois labor movement in the first third of the twentieth century was its sponsorship of consumer cooperatives. In *The Consumers' Co-operative Movement in Illinois* (Chicago, 1926), Colston Estey Warne provides a rich account of the hundreds of cooperative stores started primarily by the miners. By the end of the 1920s, most of the stores had folded, victims of internal dissension and the depressed conditions of the mines. For an analysis of the leadership of the Illinois miners in the national consumer cooperative movement, see Ralph A. Stone, "Illinois Miners and the Birth of the Cooperative League U.S.A.," in Illinois State Historical Society, *Selected Papers in Illinois History, 1981*.

Farmers as well as miners experienced declining fortunes in the 1920s. Rural Illinoisans protested against falling farm prices and rising property taxes, against urban corruption and the undermining of traditional values. Were these protests irrational, the result of a status revolution that had elevated city dwellers at the expense of rural Americans? That thesis, advanced, for instance, in Richard Hofstadter, *The Age of Reform: From Bryan to F. D. R.* (New York, 1955), is questioned by Don S. Kirschner in *City and Country: Rural Responses to Urbanization in the 1920s* (Westport, Conn., 1970). In a provocative analysis of farm issues in Iowa and Illinois, Kirschner argues that farmers had legitimate grievances. As state and local government grew, so did the costs. Those costs were borne disproportionately by rural property owners, whose crops were bringing in far less than they were only a few years before. Farmers tried but failed to enact a state income tax which would shift the burdens of government toward corporate interests. Kirschner acknowledges that farmers were also suffering from a loss of prestige and that their way of life was being eroded by an urban-dominated culture. Still, their concerns over taxes, expenditures, and other economic issues absorbed far more of their attention than did cultural conflicts with the cities. Nor does Kirschner find the Ku Klux Klan and religious fundamentalism to have been the overriding issues in rural Illinois that they were in some states such as Indiana. Kirschner's book, which combines legislative roll call analysis with a subtle reading of the rural press, is one of the most challenging interpretations of Illinois history in the 1920s.

Rural life is also illuminated by James F. Evans, *"Prairie Farmer" and WLS: The Burridge D. Butler Years* (Urbana, 1969). According to Evans, the great popularity of the *Prairie Farmer* and of WLS (Chicago) was due in large part to considering their readers and listeners as one big family. Radio in particular seemed to fill a void in farmers' lives. Whether it was the Saturday night barn dance, market reports, or the Little Brown Church of the Air, WLS was one urban institution that conveyed understanding and respect for rural values. A different kind of agricultural history is found in John J. Lacey, *Farm Bureau in Illinois: History of Illinois Farm Bureau* (Bloomington, Ill., 1965). Lacey, who was associated with the American and Illinois farm bureaus for more than two decades, offers insights into its shifting attitudes toward government subsidy programs. The importance of science and technology in the development of Illinois agriculture is illustrated in Helen M. Cavanagh, *Seed, Soil, and Science: The Story of Eugene D. Funk* (Chicago, 1959). Funk was the person most responsible for the success of the Funk Brothers Seed Company near Bloomington.

Another book on the 1920s, which has become a classic in Illinois literature, is Paul M. Angle, *Bloody Williamson: A Chapter in American Lawlessness* (New York, 1952). In beautiful prose, Angle describes the people of southern Illinois, many of them migrants from the hill regions of Kentucky and Tennessee: "generous, hospitable, hardy, independent, brave, and intelligent, but undisciplined by education" (p. 72). They were also proud, superstitious, racist, prejudiced against Catholics and Jews, and not slow to take the law into their own hands. Angle analyzes the growth of the union movement in the southern coal fields; the companies' use of black strikebreakers and the ensuing violence; prostitution, gambling, and bootlegging; and gang wars, corrupt law enforcement, and the Ku Klux Klan's orgy of terror. Daniel J. Prosser, whose "Coal Towns in Egypt: Portrait of an Illinois Mining Region, 1890–1930" (Ph.D. diss., Northwestern Univ., 1973) covers some of the same ground as Angle's book, maintains that when the coal industry collapsed in the 1920s, the tensions inherent in the conflicting values and heterogeneous character of the people of southern Illinois came to the fore. For a localized study of the Klan, see Carl V. Hallberg, " 'For God, Country, and Home': The Ku Klux Klan in Pekin, 1923–1925," *Journal of the Illinois State Historical Society*, 77 (Summer 1984).

There is as yet no book on the Great Depression and New Deal comparable to Tingley's history of the 1920s. For now, a biography of Gov. Henry Horner must suffice: Thomas B. Littlewood, *Horner of Illinois* (Evanston, 1969). Based on the Horner Papers at the Illinois State Historical Library and spiced with personal interviews, this work is strongest in its portrayal of political combat between Chicago and Downstate. Littlewood is less successful in analyzing the economic conditions that shaped the years of Horner's administration. Horner, Illinois' first Jewish governor, emerges as an idealist who, in his first term of office, succeeded in steering several New Deal measures through the General Assembly. In 1936, however, following an unsuccessful attempt by the Chicago machine of Mayor Edward J. Kelly to prevent Horner's reelection, the governor became vindictive, a "strong hater," almost irrational, and with a diminished capacity for leadership (p. 187). Horner died in office in 1940, the victim, many thought, of the attacks waged on him by the Chicago bosses. Thus, in death if not in life, in Littlewood's view, Horner helped to produce a cleaner politics in the state.

Horner's victory in the 1932 election is considered in Arvarh E. Strickland, "The New Deal Comes to Illinois," *Journal of the Illinois State Historical Society*, 63 (Spring 1970). Strickland notes that the anti-Semitism employed by Big Bill Thompson to defeat Horner backfired in certain quarters and that many Republicans switched to the Democratic nominee because he promised to repeal prohibition, aid the farmers, and support tax reform. Strickland believes that the subsequently adopted state sales tax, which Horner backed, while regressive, was "probably the best of the possible alternatives" (p. 61).

While Littlewood and Strickland view Horner as a liberal, Gene DeLon Jones strikes a different note, arguing in "The Origin of the Alliance between the New Deal and the Chicago Machine," *Journal of the Illinois State Historical Society*, 67 (June 1974), that Horner appeared more progressive than he was because of his enemies, including "a hostile Republican minority in the legislature, a rapacious Chicago machine, and a municipal press noted nationally for its attacks on unemployment relief and the New Deal." Jones claims that Horner "was not above sabotaging the relief structure of the state or using the relief issue for personal advantage" in his struggle with the Chicago Democrats (p. 257). Moreover, according to Jones, Horner failed to effect a good working relationship with Harry Hopkins, Washington's chief relief administrator. The result was to weaken Horner's ability to accomplish his goals.

Several doctoral dissertations relate to the 1930s, the most comprehensive of which is Philip Garth Bean, "Illinois Politics during the New Deal" (Univ. of Illinois, Urbana-Champaign, 1976). Bean takes issue with Horner's critics, contending instead that Horner was not so preoccupied with the Kelly machine in Chicago as to prevent him from enacting reform legislation in the form of old age pensions, wages and hours laws, improved workers compensation, and restrictions on public utilities. Bean admits, however, that most of these accomplishments came before 1936. After his split with Kelly, Horner had to turn to downstate Democrats whose interest in reform was lukewarm. It was also significant, Bean indicates, that national issues such as collective bargaining, social security, public housing, and public power never penetrated deeply into Illinois politics. Instead, scandals and economy in government remained the main topics of debate for many years.

The Chicago side of the Horner-Kelly dispute is treated in [William] Roger Biles, *Big City Boss in Depression and War: Mayor Edward J. Kelly of Chicago* (DeKalb, 1984). Biles sets out to redeem Kelly from the tag of being incompetent and ideologically uncommitted to New Deal principles. Instead, he sees Kelly as manifesting great concern for the underprivileged, notably in his strong support for housing and educational programs for black Chicagoans. Nevertheless, Biles concedes that Kelly remained linked to the Chicago underworld and that his administration was not free of corruption.

There are several studies of the economic impact of the Depression on Illinois, but none of them is fully satisfactory. David J. Maurer, "Unemployment in Illinois during the Great Depression," in Tingley, *Essays in Illinois History*, analyzes the reports of the Illinois Emergency Relief Administration to show the type and extent of relief given during the thirties. Arthur Parker Miles, *Federal Aid and Public Assistance in Illinois* (Chicago, 1941) assesses the statewide administration of federal programs such as the Reconstruction Finance Corporation and the Federal Emergency Relief Administration. The major state relief agency is surveyed in Frank Z. Glick, *The Illinois Emergency Relief Commission: A Study of Administrative and Financial Aspects of Emergency Relief* (Chicago, 1940). Malcolm Brown and John N. Webb, *Seven Stranded Coal Towns: A Study of an American Depressed Area*, Work Projects Administration Research Monograph 23 (Washington, D.C., 1941), has excellent statistical and photographic documentation of the devastating conditions in Franklin, Saline, and Williamson counties. A more detailed sociological investigation of the same region, with particular attention to Zeigler, is Herman R. Lantz, *People of Coal Town* (New York, 1958). David E. Conrad and Glen M. Jones, "Town Life in Southern Illinois during the Great Depression," *ICarbS* (Morris Library, Southern Illinois Univ., Carbondale), 1 (Spring–Summer 1974), compares depression conditions in towns with four different economic bases. In some ways, the best economic report is the lengthy unpublished manuscript by

Paul Mattick, "Unemployment and Relief in Illinois," prepared for the Federal Writers' Project in 1938 or 1939 and subsequently deposited in the Illinois State Historical Library.

The exciting labor struggles of the 1930s have not received their due. There are no first-rate accounts of the Progressive Mine Workers of America or the bloody clashes between the Progressives and the United Mine Workers. For the moment, however, see Dallas M. Young, "A History of the Progressive Miners of America, 1932–1940" (Ph.D. diss., Univ. of Illinois, 1940); Young, "Origin of the Progressive Mine Workers of America," *Journal of the Illinois State Historical Society*, 40 (Sept. 1947); and Harriet D. Hudson, *The Progressive Mine Workers of America: A Study in Rival Unionism* (Urbana, 1952). Stephane Elise Booth, "A Coal-Mining Activist in the Fields of Southern Illinois, 1932–1938," in Illinois State Historical Society, *Selected Papers in Illinois History, 1981*, examines the career of the Progressives' newspaper editor Gerry Allard. Also informative is Lorin Lee Cary, "The Reorganized United Mine Workers of America, 1930–1931," *Journal of the Illinois State Historical Society*, 66 (Autumn 1973).

Efforts to document life in Illinois in the twentieth century, with considerable attention to working-class experiences between the wars, have led to oral history transcriptions in many libraries. The Chicago Polonia and Italians in Chicago projects left major collections of this sort. Another set of interviews became the basis for Adria Bernardi, *Houses with Names: The Italian Immigrants of Highwood, Illinois* (Urbana, 1990), enriching the history of a North Shore community, while a successful downstate project culminated in Michael G. Matejka and Greg Koos, eds., *Bloomington's C&A Shops: Our Lives Remembered* (Bloomington, Ill., 1987). See also Mark Wyman, "Railroaders' Town: Bloomington's Shopmen Look Back," *Labor's Heritage*, 1 (Jan. 1989).

Hostile reaction to the reform and radical currents of the 1930s can be followed in Edgar Bernhard et al., *Pursuit of Freedom: A History of Civil Liberty in Illinois, 1787–1942* (Chicago, 1942), which describes vigilante attacks on unemployed councils in Decatur and Danville, depredations of the Klan, and anti-Communist bills passed by the General Assembly. The legislative investigation of subversive activity at the University of Chicago ("crème de la Kremlin") is skewered in Milton Mayer, "The Red Room," *Massachusetts Review*, 16 (Summer 1975).

The careers of two Illinois congressmen illustrate the sharp differences in the 1930s over the issue of communism. Noah Mason, Republican from LaSalle, served as a member of the House Committee on Un-American Activities from 1938 to 1943 and later became a strong supporter of Sen. Joseph McCarthy. By contrast, Kent Keller, a Southern Illinois Democrat, had his ten-year legislative career cut short in 1940, in part because he was branded by the *Chicago Tribune* and like-minded newspapers as a member of the "Pink Squadron" for his opposition to that committee. See Jack A. Samosky, "Congressman Noah Morgan Mason, Illinois' Conservative Spokesman," *Journal of the Illinois State*

*Historical Society*, 76 (Spring 1983), and Stuart Weiss, "Kent Keller, the Liberal Bloc, and the New Deal," ibid., 68 (Apr. 1975).

As might be expected, Illinois during World War II has generated less scholarly inquiry than earlier periods. However, the one book on the subject, Mary Watters, *Illinois in the Second World War* . . . (2 vols., Springfield, 1951–52), is an outstanding achievement. In nearly a thousand pages, Watters delineates an overall picture of life in Illinois unsurpassed by any other study for a comparable span of time in the twentieth century. No author more assiduously mines government documents and local newspapers for the telling details that add concreteness and color to the story. At the same time her sweep is broad. There is much in the book on Illinois from World War I through the 1930s, and she follows the effects of World War II to 1950. The Selective Service System in the state is chronicled in Victor Kleber, *Selective Service in Illinois, 1940–1947* . . . (Springfield, 1949).

A revealing sociological study of the Illinois river town of Seneca during World War II is Robert J. Havighurst and H. Gerthon Morgan, *The Social History of a War-Boom Community* (New York, 1951). Although the town grew from 1,200 to 6,600 in two years, becoming a shipbuilding center for Landing Ship Tanks, Senecans maintained about the same values throughout the war. They remained distrustful of experts and suspicious of public works projects. Another sociological work on an Illinois community during the war is W[illiam] Lloyd Warner, *Democracy in Jonesville: A Study in Quality and Inequality* (New York, 1949). The fictional Jonesville is actually Morris.

Political history since 1940 would benefit from a careful biography of Gov. Dwight H. Green (Rep., 1941–49). Robert J. Casey and W. A. S. Douglas, *The Midwesterner: The Story of Dwight H. Green* (Chicago, 1948) is woefully inadequate, apparently an effort to promote Green's presidential and vice-presidential ambitions in 1948. Even Green's dog comes in for high praise. Republican party success in the 1940s owed much to the disunity within the Democratic party, which resulted, in turn, from the Horner-Kelly clashes. For evidence on this point, see Iwan Morgan, "The 1942 Mid-Term Elections in Illinois," *Journal of the Illinois State Historical Society*, 76 (Summer 1983). Among those Republicans winning reelection in 1942 were two prominent isolationists, C. Wayland Brooks to the Senate and Stephen Albion Day to the post of congressman-at-large. While their victories did not necessarily foretell a resurgence of isolationism, it was nonetheless true that foreign affairs had come to assume far more importance in the lives of Illinoisans.

Future research on this period of Illinois history will have to give more attention to foreign policy. Neither Jerome E. Edwards, *The Foreign Policy of Col. McCormick's "Tribune," 1929–1941* (Reno, Nev., 1971) nor Frank C. Waldrop, *McCormick of Chicago: An Unconventional Portrait of a Controversial Figure* (Englewood Cliffs, N.J., 1966) does justice to the influence of the newspaper or its owner. A detailed analysis of Illinois attitudes on foreign affairs in the late 1930s could test long-held assumptions about the prevalence of Midwestern isolationism. James C. Schneider, *Should America Go to War? The Debate over Foreign Policy in Chicago, 1939–1941* (Chapel Hill, 1989) is suggestive of what needs to be done on a statewide basis.

There are other areas of Illinois life during these years that deserve further research. There should be much more on the history of women. Quantitative studies of social conditions are wanting. A major investigation of the Chicago/Downstate conflict would certainly help. And more studies that compare Illinois history to that of other states and the nation at large should be undertaken.

# 8

# ILLINOIS
# SINCE 1945

CULLOM DAVIS

BIBLIOGRAPHIC STUDIES OF contemporary history are a perilous enterprise. They suffer under the double risk of instant obsolescence and myopic perspective. Each new review journal, publisher's catalog, and dissertation list introduces additional items for consideration, so that any bibliographic essay is doomed to miss a growing number of pertinent works. It is also difficult to assess the quality and enduring contribution of recent studies on contemporary subjects; the direction of research and the patterns of interpretation are too unclear and unstable to permit definitive analysis.

Many noteworthy events, personalities, and issues since 1945 have contributed to Illinois history, yet few have so far received careful and serious attention. Like any contemporary subject, their initial treatment has largely been in the hands of headline historians and popular biographers. Most of the serious historical effort has focused on government and politics, with limited attention devoted to topics such as education and urban affairs. Economic and cultural history have been slighted. There are as yet no broad thematic studies or syntheses of the period.

The modern era roster of prominent Illinois political figures is lengthy, but only Adlai E. Stevenson and Richard J. Daley have been extensively studied. Governor William G. Stratton (Rep., 1953–61) is covered in David Kenney, *A Political Passage: The Career of Stratton of Illinois* (Carbondale, 1990), while Robert E. Hartley, *Big Jim Thompson of Illinois* (Chicago, 1979) is a dated popular life of Gov. James R. Thompson (Rep., 1977–91), who headed the longest administration in the state's history. Governors Otto Kerner (Dem., 1961–68), Samuel H. Shapiro (Dem., 1968–69), Richard B. Ogilvie (Rep., 1969–73), and Dan Walker (Dem., 1973–77) await full-length accounts.

Several biographies of Gov. Adlai E. Stevenson (Dem., 1949–53), twice his party's nominee for president, deserve attention. Kenneth S. Davis, *The Politics of Honor: A Biography of Adlai E. Stevenson* (New York, 1967) is an affectionate but useful portrait that benefited from Stevenson's active cooperation as well as access to family sources and acquaintances. Davis revised and expanded an earlier study for this comprehensive view of mid-century America's "dominant political figure" (p. 11). John Bartlow Martin, *The Life of Adlai E. Stevenson*, in two volumes subtitled *Adlai Stevenson of Illinois* and *Adlai Stevenson and the World* (New York, 1976–77), is widely respected as a definitive biography, a meticulous and balanced treatment of a complex leader. Based on exhaustive study of voluminous records and numerous interviews, Martin chronicles Stevenson's life in almost smothering detail. A recent account, emphasizing the post-gubernatorial years, is Porter McKeever, *Adlai Stevenson: His Life and Legacy* (New York, 1989).

Walter Johnson, ed., *The Papers of Adlai E. Stevenson* (8 vols., Boston, 1972–79) is an indispensable collection. With the assistance of Stevenson's long-time secretary Carol Evans, Johnson assembled and annotated selected letters and statements of a gifted writer and public speaker. Volume 2 carries Stevenson through the war years and his upset gubernatorial victory in 1948. Volume 3 covers his term as governor, and volume 4 documents the presidential race of 1952. See also Michael Maher, ed., *An Illinois Legacy: Gubernatorial Addresses of Adlai E. Stevenson, 1949–1952* (Bloomington, Ill., 1985). Walter Johnson, *How We Drafted Adlai Stevenson* (New York, 1952) is a detailed account of the governor's first presidential nomination. For a flattering assessment of a Chicago Democrat's role in this event, see Roger Biles, "Jacob M. Arvey, Kingmaker: The Nomination of Adlai E. Stevenson in 1952," *Chicago History*, 8 (Fall 1979).

Richard J. Daley, mayor of Chicago from 1955 to 1976, was the dominant force, if not the dominant personality, in Illinois politics for a quarter century. He combined intense privacy in his personal life with a blustering public manner, making him a favorite for popular biographers. Perhaps fittingly, many works about him combine a lengthy text with a short, punchy title: e.g., *Boss*, *Clout*, *Requiem*, and *Legend*. Most of his biographers have been working journalists, and most of their evidence has been from personal observation or the direct testimony of others. This latter characteristic is likely to persist, as most of what anyone can and will ever know about the Daley mayoralty and Cook County organization will come from eyewitness recollections and newspaper coverage rather than from public documents and official papers.

There is merit in nearly all of the studies of Daley, although most of them betray the shortcomings of limited detachment and perspective. Among the best is Mike Royko's early effort, *Boss: Richard J. Daley of Chicago* (New York, 1971). Royko captures the distinctive personality and political genius of the man. Len O'Connor contributed two books to Daleyana. In *Clout: Mayor Daley and His City* (Chicago, 1975), he combines grudging admiration with sharp criticism. His conclusions add little to what Royko wrote, but they are based on fresh and revealing anecdotes. His *Requiem: The Decline and Demise of Mayor Daley and His Era* (Chicago, 1977) attempts to assess the man and his lingering influence. Additional anecdotes fill the pages of Frank Sullivan, *Legend: The Only Inside Story about Mayor Richard J. Daley* (Chicago, 1989). More serious and less gossipy is Eugene Kennedy, *Himself! The Life and Times of Mayor Richard J. Daley* (New York, 1978). Kennedy applies psychological insight and an Irish Catholic perspective in explaining Daley's behavior and success. Also useful on the ethnic theme is Patrick Victor Power, "Mayor Daley's Other Home: The Irish Connection," *Studies: An Irish Quarterly Review* (Dublin), 69 (Spring 1980).

Two valuable contributions to understanding Daley came from a political scientist, Milton L. Rakove: *Don't Make No Waves, Don't Back No Losers: An Insider's Analysis of the Daley Machine* (Bloomington, Ind., 1975) and *We Don't Want Nobody Nobody Sent: An Oral History of the Daley Years* (Bloomington, Ind., 1979). Eschewing the complex methodology of behavioralist political science, Rakove simply gathered all the evidence that he could find and employed common sense and city machine instincts to understand the man. His first book describes and dissects the Daley organization's *modus operandi*, wittily examining each component as well as such alien nuisances as independents and the Republican opposition. *We Don't Want Nobody* uses this framework for a series of intimate glimpses by those who knew, loved, feared, and despised him. Included in this oral history patchwork are the recollections of such groups as Daley loyalists, young turks in the organization, suburban orphan Democrats, and various dissidents. Particularly good on the challenge that Daley faced from emergent political independents is Joe Mathewson, *Up Against Daley* (LaSalle, Ill., 1974).

Samuel K. Gove and Louis H. Masotti, eds., *After Daley: Chicago Politics in Transition* (Urbana, 1982) is an early effort to assess the post-Daley era. Melvin A. Kahn and Frances J. Majors, *The Winning Ticket: Daley, the Chicago Machine, and Illinois Politics* (New York, 1984), an account of Kahn's quest for statewide office in 1969, also describes the Daley machine's fragile ethnic coalition and its slide since 1976 from accommodation to polarization.

The state's U.S. Senate delegation in recent years has included prominent and important figures. Senator Scott Lucas (Dem., 1939–51) is introduced in Edward L. Schapsmeier and Frederick H. Schapsmeier, "Scott W. Lucas of Havana: His Rise and Fall as Majority Leader in the United States Senate," *Journal of the Illinois State Historical Society*, 70 (Nov. 1977). The authors trace Lucas's early political career and rapid rise in his second Senate term as party whip and then majority leader. His loyal and largely effective support for

Harry Truman's liberal domestic program and expansive internationalism led to defeat in 1950 because it kept him too busy to mend fences at home and identified him with an increasingly unpopular president.

Senator Paul Douglas (Dem., 1949–67) deserves a good biography. The best available reading is still his own six-hundred-page account, *In the Fullness of Time: The Memoirs of Paul H. Douglas* (New York, 1972). Douglas applied the same diligence and honesty to this informative book as he did to national issues during his academic and political careers. A brief sketch focusing on Douglas's changing posture on foreign affairs is Edward L. Schapsmeier and Frederick H. Schapsmeier, "Paul H. Douglas: From Pacifist to Soldier-Statesman," *Journal of the Illinois State Historical Society*, 67 (June 1974).

In *Dirksen: Portrait of a Public Man* (New York, 1970), Neil MacNeil, a veteran Washington reporter, favorably assesses Sen. Everett McKinley Dirksen (Rep., 1951–69). His colorful career and unique style also receive appreciative treatment in Edward L. Schapsmeier and Frederick H. Schapsmeier, *Dirksen of Illinois, Senatorial Statesman* (Urbana, 1985). Robert E. Hartley, *Charles H. Percy: A Political Perspective* (Chicago, 1975) is a useful but dated popular biography of Sen. Percy (Rep., 1967–85).

Turning from political personalities to political events, the student of contemporary Illinois finds much less literature of enduring value. The one conspicuous exception is the Constitutional Convention of 1969–70, known as Con Con, which is the most carefully chronicled and analyzed event in modern Illinois history. Useful surveys of the topic include Samuel K. Gove and Thomas R. Kitsos, *Revision Success: The Sixth Illinois Constitutional Convention*, State Constitutional Convention Studies, 8 (New York, 1974), and Elmer Gertz and Joseph P. Pisciotte, *Charter for a New Age: An Inside View of the Sixth Illinois Constitutional Convention* (Urbana, 1980). Pisciotte also edited Studies in Illinois Constitution Making, a series on selected themes and issues. These books, which vary in depth and originality, include Jane G. Buresh, *A Fundamental Goal: Education for the People of Illnois* (Urbana, 1975); Ian D. Burman, *Lobbying at the Illinois Constitutional Convention* (Urbana, 1973); Rubin G. Cohn, *To Judge with Justice: History and Politics of Illinois Judicial Reform* (Urbana, 1973); Joyce D. Fishbane and Glenn W. Fisher, *Politics of the Purse: Revenue and Finance in the Sixth Illinois Constitutional Convention* (Urbana, 1974); Elmer Gertz, *For the First Hours of Tomorrow: The New Illinois Bill of Rights* (Urbana, 1972); Alan S. Gratch and Virginia H. Ubik, *Ballots for Change: New Suffrage and Amending Articles for Illinois* (Urbana, 1973); David Kenney et al., *Roll Call! Patterns of Voting in the Sixth Illinois Constitutional Convention* (Urbana, 1975); and JoAnna M. Watson, *Electing a Constitution: The Illinois Citizen and the 1970 Constitution* (Urbana, 1980).

Also useful are the special reports and studies that preceded the convention, such as Victoria Ranney, ed., *Con-Con: Issues for the Illinois Constitutional Convention* (Urbana, 1970). Sensitive to the historic purpose and nature of their work, the delegates cooperated in recording and publishing their deliberations and committee actions. These can be found in Illinois Secretary of State, *Record of Proceedings: Sixth Illinois Constitutional Convention* (7 vols., Springfield, 1972). An uncritical sketch of the president of the convention is Elmer Gertz and Edward S. Gilbreth, *Quest for a Constitution: A Man Who Wouldn't Quit; A Political Biography of Samuel Witwer of Illinois* (Lanham, Md., 1984).

Several doctoral dissertations in political science make important contributions to Con Con literature: Charles R. Pastors, "Constitution-Making in Illinois: A Case of Traditional Illinois Politics" (Univ. of Chicago, 1972); Paula Wolff, "Principles of Government in the Political Arena: An Analysis of the Sixth Illinois Constitutional Convention" (Univ. of Chicago, 1972); and Janet Morrissey Clark, "Constitution Making in Illinois: A Comparison of Two Conventions, 1920 and 1970" (Univ. of Illinois, Urbana-Champaign, 1973). Thematic studies of the same kind include Thomas Robert Kitsos, "State Constitutional Revision and the Urban Crisis: The Sixth Illinois Constitutional Convention" (Univ. of Illinois, Urbana-Champaign, 1972) and Robert Walter Kustra, "The Formulation of Constitutional Home Rule in Illinois" (Univ. of Illinois, Urbana-Champaign, 1975).

Later work examines legal and political consequences of the Constitution of 1970. For example, David R. Miller, *1970 Illinois Constitution Annotated for Legislators* (Springfield, 1983) covers each constitutional provision in light of subsequent court and attorney general opinions, while papers from a symposium on the constitution, and a bibliography about it, appear in a special issue of *Northern Illinois University Law Review*, Vol. 8, No. 3 (1988).

Illinois political institutions, particularly the state legislature and selected agencies, are reasonably well covered in the literature. A continuing source of statistical, descriptive, and historical information is *Illinois Issues*, published monthly since 1975 by Sangamon State University. This magazine reports on newsworthy personalities, events, and issues, with regular and careful coverage of each branch of state government as well as numerous agencies, boards, and commissions. It also publishes collections of articles on specific themes, e.g., Paul M. Green et al., *Illinois Elections* (3rd ed., Springfield, 1986), updating editions in 1979 and 1982. For an informative overview of modern state government, see Edgar G. Crane, Jr., ed., *Illinois: Political Processes and Governmental Performance* (Dubuque, 1980). This collection of over thirty essays is uneven in quality but nevertheless valuable on a variety of subjects including the formal organs of authority, electoral behavior, local government, interest groups, the media, and selected policy areas.

The Illinois General Assembly has undergone dramatic development and change in the generation since 1945. This has had the double effect of dating many sound earlier studies and creating a need for contemporary research and analysis. Still a valuable standard is Samuel K. Gove et al., *The Illinois Legislature: Structure and Process* (Urbana, 1976). For a fresher perspective that addresses recent structural and procedural changes, see Jack R. Van Der

Slik and Kent D. Redfield, *Lawmaking in Illinois: Legislative Politics, People, and Processes* (Springfield, 1986).

Two useful studies of reapportionment are James Lynn McDowell, "Changes in the Apportionment System: The Illinois General Assembly, 1963–1967" (Ph.D. diss., Univ. of Illinois, Urbana-Champaign, 1972) and Thomas Vocino, "Assessing the Impact of the 1965 Reapportionment on the Politics and Policies of the Illinois General Assembly" (Ph.D. diss., Southern Illinois Univ., Carbondale, 1973). Both works deemphasize the political consequences of reapportionment. Although the Constitution of 1970 left intact the state's unique, century-old cumulative voting system, it fell a decade later as part of an amendment to reduce the size of the House. The system that was superseded is evaluated with different results in George S. Blair, *Cumulative Voting: An Effective Electoral Device in Illinois Politics* (Urbana, 1960) and Charles W. Dunn, "Cumulative Voting Problems in Illinois Legislative Elections," *Harvard Journal on Legislation*, 9 (May 1972). The electoral change itself is described in J. Michael Lennon and Caroline M. Gherardini, eds., *The Cutback Amendment* (Springfield, 1982), a special report of *Illinois Issues*, and Anna J. Merritt, ed., *Redistricting: An Exercise in Prophecy* (Urbana, 1982), while Paul Kleppner et al., *Political Atlas of Illinois* (DeKalb, 1988) contains a map and statistical data for each new legislative district.

The appropriations and revenue processes prior to reforms wrought by Con Con and the Ogilvie administration are cogently analyzed in Thomas J. Anton, *The Politics of State Expenditure in Illinois* (Urbana, 1966) and Glenn W. Fisher, *Taxes and Politics: A Study of Illinois Public Finance* (Urbana, 1969). A landmark political battle after the Cutback Amendment is described in Joan A. Parker, *The Illinois Tax Increase of 1983: Summit and Resolution* (Springfield, 1984). For a study of long-term trends, see Bennett S. Stark, "The Political Economy of State Public Finance: A Model of the Determinants of Revenue Policy; The Illinois Case, 1850–1970" (Ph.D. diss., Univ. of Wisconsin, Madison, 1982).

The full extent of reform and modernization in the Illinois legislature since 1945 needs careful analysis. Much of that reform agenda was outlined in an important study by the Illinois Commission on the Organization of the General Assembly, *Improving the State Legislature* . . . (Urbana, 1967). Personal eyewitness recollections of that subject and the panorama of modern legislative life are available in the Illinois Statecraft series of oral history memoirs. Sponsored by the Illinois Legislative Research Unit and Sangamon State University's Oral History Office, this program since 1979 has recorded extensive life history interviews with a representative group of thirty-five former legislators, yielding over twenty thousand pages of autobiographical transcript. Nearly all of these memoirs are published in book form, and there is a separate master index for the series. A companion project has gathered the recollections of several dozen executive branch officials and other veterans of state politics. To date, some twenty-one memoirs in this series are published.

Regrettably, state offices and agencies no longer take the trouble to compile and publish detailed annual reports of their operations. Students of nineteenth-century Illinois history have discovered a treasure of useful statistical and narrative information in the reports of that period. Today such products are a rarity. Among the small number of relatively worthwhile efforts are the annual reports of the Administrative Office of the Illinois Courts and most of the state's code departments; periodic management, compliance, and financial audits of the Illinois Office of the Auditor General; and the biennial *Illinois Blue Book* released by the Illinois Secretary of State. Two specialized institutional studies worthy of note are James B. Jacobs, *Stateville: The Penitentiary in Mass Society* (Chicago, 1977) and Peter Li-Chung Hsin, "Historical Development of Chester Mental Health Center from Custodial to Therapeutic Care of the Mentally Disordered Offenders of Illinois from 1879 to 1980" (Ph.D. diss., Southern Illinois Univ., Carbondale, 1980). A more dramatic event, for which the Illinois Bureau of Mines and Minerals was partly blamed, is described in Catherine Anne Phee, "The Centralia Mine Disaster of 1947" (Ph.D. diss., St. Louis Univ., 1971).

Relatively few political events in recent Illinois history have been studied as thoroughly as have many facets of the state's constitutional and governmental framework. Kenneth O'Reilly, "Adlai E. Stevenson, McCarthyism, and the FBI," *Illinois Historical Journal*, 81 (Spring 1988), supplements the Illinois pages in James Truett Selcraig, *The Red Scare in the Midwest, 1945–1955: A State and Local Study* (Ann Arbor, 1982). In *The Hodge Scandal* (New York, 1963), George Thiem, an investigative reporter, recounts his role in uncovering Orville E. Hodge's embezzlement of state funds, for which the popular state auditor was imprisoned. In *Courthouse over White House: Chicago and the Presidential Election of 1960* (Orlando, Fla., 1988), Edmund F. Kallina, Jr., concludes that Mayor Daley's machine was primarily concerned with the race for state's attorney, not president, in 1960 and that voting irregularities in Chicago at that time more clearly affected the outcome of the former than the latter contest. Hank Messick, *The Politics of Prosecution: Jim Thompson, Marje Everett, Richard Nixon, and the Trial of Otto Kerner* (Ottawa, Ill., 1978) dramatizes Gov. Kerner's conviction in a racetrack stock scandal, while David E. Woodard, "Reflections on Otto Kerner as a Civil Rights Leader," in the 1986–87 *Transactions of the Illinois State Historical Society*, briefly describes his attention to civil rights, culminating in 1967–68 in his work as chairman of a presidential panel to study civil disorders, known as the Kerner Commission. David Farber, *Chicago '68* (Chicago, 1988) is a detailed account of the 1968 Democratic national convention in Chicago, which was marred by confrontations between protesters and police. A potentially explosive issue during 1977–78 was the dispute over American Nazi demands to stage a march in suburban Skokie, whose inhabitants include many Holocaust refugees. One of many studies of this event is Donald Alexander Downs, *Nazis in Skokie: Freedom, Community, and the First Amendment* (Notre Dame, Ind., 1985).

Several essays in Peter F. Nardulli, ed., *Diversity, Conflict, and State Politics: Regionalism in Illinois* (Urbana, 1989) consider certain wider issues of political significance, some predating the modern period. Another collaborative work, important for political as well as economic history, is Milton Derber, *Labor in Illinois: The Affluent Years, 1945–80* (Urbana, 1989).

The full body of historical literature on Chicago is treated in another chapter, but a few studies warrant mention here. Unscholarly but irresistibly stimulating is the general exposé by Michael Kilian et al., *Who Runs Chicago?* (New York, 1979). The authors display originality and insight in devising social categories for Chicago's power brokers and elites. A vastly different group of individuals is profiled in Jeffrey Sweet, *Something Wonderful Right Away* (New York, 1978), an oral history of the Second City and the Compass Players, and in Donna McCrohan, *The Second City . . .* (New York, 1987). These accounts of the improvisational groups that launched talented performers from Mike Nichols to John Belushi capture the flavor of a distinctive Chicago cultural phenomenon.

Works on black Chicago also command attention. The new edition of St. Clair Drake and Horace R. Cayton, *Black Metropolis: A Study of Negro Life in a Northern City* (2 vols., New York, 1962) includes an appendix bringing the analysis forward to 1961. This enduring monograph covers all aspects of South Side life. More narrowly focused is R. Lincoln Keiser, *The Vice Lords, Warriors of the Streets* (New York, 1969; fieldwork ed., New York, 1979), which delineates the social organization of a well-known youth gang. The related subject of neighborhood organizing is impressively treated in John Hall Fish, *Black Power/White Control: The Struggle of the Woodlawn Organization in Chicago* (Princeton, 1973); Robert Bailey, Jr., *Radicals in Urban Politics: The Alinsky Approach* (Chicago, 1974); and Carole Goodwin, *The Oak Park Strategy: Community Control of Racial Change* (Chicago, 1979). Numerous interviews inform Sanford D. Horwitt, *Let Them Call Me Rebel: Saul Alinsky; His Life and Legacy* (New York, 1989), while Jerome Don Harris, "Grass-Roots Organizing in the City of Chicago" (Ph.D. diss., Univ. of Illinois, Chicago, 1980) is a comparative study of twenty-five Alinsky-style community organizations.

There are only a few noteworthy contemporary studies of smaller cities and towns in Illinois. Rich in original thought and detail are two works by Daniel J. Elazar: *Cities of the Prairie: The Metropolitan Frontier and American Politics* (New York, 1970) and *Cities of the Prairie Revisited: The Closing of the Metropolitan Frontier* (Lincoln, Nebr., 1986). These seminal studies of American federalism use historical and quantitative information drawn from a dozen medium-size Illinois cities, thereby characterizing their distinctive political cultures. A worthwhile but less ambitious companion is Daniel Milo Johnson and Rebecca Monroe Veach, eds., *The Middle-Size Cities of Illinois: Their People, Politics, and Quality of Life* (Springfield, 1980), which outlines the history, demographics, economy, and government of eight urban areas in the state. A gossipy probe in the Middletown tradition is Joseph P. Lyford, *The*

*Talk in Vandalia* (Santa Barbara, Calif., 1962). As with all such community studies, this purports to represent a category of social experience, in this case small midwestern towns. For East St. Louis and its ills, see Dennis R. Judd and Robert E. Mendelson, *The Politics of Urban Planning: The East St. Louis Experience* (Urbana, 1973) as well as other revealing studies by Mendelson. A contemporary glimpse of the equally troubled and racially tense city of Cairo appeared in a special issue of *Focus/Midwest*, Vol. 8, No. 54 (1971). One steadily growing source of contemporary community history is tape-recorded recollections or oral history. Over 150 projects and an estimated 10,000 separate interviews are identified in Kathryn Wrigley, comp., *Directory of Illinois Oral History Resources* (Springfield, 1981).

The growth of publicly supported education, especially higher education, since World War II has attracted the attention of researchers. Paul E. Peterson, *School Politics, Chicago Style* (Chicago, 1976) employs organization theory to analyze three issues that troubled Chicago public education in the 1960s: desegregation, collective bargaining, and decentralization. For an interesting comparative study of educational politics in Illinois, Michigan, and Missouri, see Nicholas A. Masters et al., *State Politics and the Public Schools: An Exploratory Analysis* (New York, 1964). There is a contemporary examination of the impact of unionization, from a conservative viewpoint, in John B. Parrish, "Unionization and Education: Lessons from the Illinois Schoolrooms," *Journal of Social, Political, and Economic Studies*, 6 (Fall 1981).

Mixing religion with public education was not much of a controversy in the 1940s until an issue originating in Champaign made headlines. A local practice for encouraging religious observance sparked an effort by the McCollum family that finally reached the U.S. Supreme Court. A personal and revealing account of the case is Vashti Cromwell McCollum, *One Woman's Fight* (Garden City, N.Y., 1951; revised ed., Boston, 1961). Another useful contribution is Dannel Angus McCollum, "Origins of the 'Champaign System': Prelude to the McCollum Case, 1945–1948," *Journal of the Illinois State Historical Society*, 75 (Summer 1982).

The recent development of public higher education is chronicled in various general university histories. One special report for a young campus is David L. Butler, *Retrospect at a Tenth Anniversary: Southern Illinois University at Edwardsville* (Carbondale, 1976). A useful study of some fateful decisions for both education and Chicago is George Rosen, *Decision-Making Chicago-Style: The Genesis of a University of Illinois Campus* (Urbana, 1980). For an insider's meticulous account of the dramatic growth of community colleges, see Gerald W. Smith, *Illinois Junior-Community College Development, 1946–1980* (Springfield, 1980).

Except for Thomas B. Littlewood, *Coals of Fire: The Alton Telegraph Libel Case* (Carbondale, 1988), most of the thoughtful analysis of communications and media since 1945 remains in the form of unpublished doctoral dissertations. Among the better studies are Richard Allen Hatch, "Reporters and Legislators in

Illinois: Their Roles and How They Interact" (Univ. of Illinois, Urbana–Champaign, 1969); Theodore Lynn Nielsen, "A History of Chicago Television News Presentation, 1948–1968" (Univ. of Wisconsin, Madison, 1971); and Ronald Dean Mulder, "The Effects of Televised Political Advertising: The 1975 Chicago Mayoral Election" (Univ. of Chicago, 1975).

The unfinished business of post-1945 Illinois history is substantial, and it keeps growing as the beginning point recedes in time. There are encouraging signs that the field is ripe for careful investigation and that interest among historians is quickening. One indicator of this is the attention paid to contemporary history in the pages of the *Illinois Historical Journal*. Eventually, the pioneering but impermanent work of the headline historians and popular biographers will give way to a body of thoughtful scholarship.

# 9

# PEOPLES OF ILLINOIS

MARK WYMAN

STUDIES OF ILLINOIS' diverse peoples generally suffer from the draw-backs that afflict such works across the nation. Immigrant histories too often have been plagued with filiopietism, an excessive emphasis on the greatness of the forefathers. They also have tended to cast a net that is either too broad or too narrow. Furthermore, recent breakthroughs in the field have generally not been followed by similar studies for Illinois. The state still lacks a book such as June Drenning Holmquist, ed., *They Chose Minnesota: A Survey of the State's Ethnic Groups* (1981), published by the Minnesota Historical Society, or even a series of booklets such as the State Historical Society of Wisconsin has issued, including Richard H. Zeitlan, *Germans in Wisconsin* (1977); Frederick Hale, *Danes in Wisconsin* (1981); and Phillips G. Davies, *The Welsh in Wisconsin* (1982). Such a project would make possible the presentation of a broader view, for in historical writing on Illinois' peoples the sum of the parts—at least the *published* parts—still falls short of the whole.

Several general works on Illinois history, it must be noted, include brief but worthwhile surveys of ethnic, economic, religious, and other groups. John H. Keiser offers this in *Building for the Centuries: Illinois, 1865 to 1898* (Urbana, 1977). Ernest Ludlow Bogart and John Mabry Mathews provide it as well in *The Modern Commonwealth, 1893–1918* (Springfield, 1920), as does Richard J. Jensen, *Illinois: A Bicentennial History* (New York, 1978). The topic is approached from other angles in Alden Cutshall, "Historical Geography," and Albert Larson and Siim Sööt, "Population and Social Geography," in Ronald

E. Nelson, ed., *Illinois: Land and Life in the Prairie State* (Dubuque, 1978).

The early French declined in importance as the colonial era drew to a close, but their role as survivors in early Illinois under American sovereignty is deftly sketched in Solon Justus Buck, *Illinois in 1818* (Springfield, 1917). The long-term *survivance* of the French-Canadian settlement at Bourbonnais in the Kankakee River country is taken up by Edward R. Kantowicz, "A Fragment of French Canada on the Illinois Prairies," *Journal of the Illinois State Historical Society*, 75 (Winter 1982). But the French soon had to yield to other incoming groups, especially to Southerners coming from the Upper South and to New Englanders and others coming from the East.

Several authors have analyzed each of these newer groups of the early nineteenth century. For the Southerners, see the articles by Douglas K. Meyer, "Southern Illinois Migration Fields: The Shawnee Hills in 1850," *Professional Geographer*, 28 (May 1976), and "Native-Born Immigrant Clusters on the Illinois Frontier," *Proceedings of the Association of American Geographers*, 8 (1976). See also Theodore Calvin Pease, *The Frontier State, 1818–1848* (Springfield, 1918) and Arthur Charles Cole, *The Era of the Civil War, 1848–1870* (Springfield, 1919). An informative collection of Southerners' letters from Illinois is provided in James W. Patton, ed., "Letters from North Carolina Emigrants in the Old Northwest, 1830–1834," *Mississippi Valley Historical Review*, 47 (Sept. 1960).

Two older works on New Englanders in Illinois are still worthwhile for basic information: Lois Kimball Mathews (Rosenberry), *The Expansion of New England: The Spread of New England Settlement and Institutions to the Mississippi River, 1620–1865* (Boston, 1909) and Carrie Prudence Kofoid, "Puritan Influences in the Formative Years of Illinois History," *Transactions of the Illinois State Historical Society for the Year 1905*, 10. Pease's *Frontier State* and Cole's *Era of the Civil War* are also useful on this subject, as is Albert J. Larson, "Northern Illinois as New England Extended: A Preliminary Report," *Pioneer America*, 7 (Jan. 1975).

Groups from Europe were present as well in the antebellum era. Revolutions and famine combined with improved means of transportation to direct a massive stream of foreigners to Illinois. Irish and Germans were most numerous, although Scandinavian and British groups also came. The Old World backgrounds of these groups, and major immigration trends and routes, are described in Stephan Thernstrom, ed., *Harvard Encyclopedia of American Ethnic Groups* (Cambridge, Mass., 1980). Mark Wyman, *Immigration History and Ethnicity in Illinois: A Guide* (Springfield, 1990), the bibliography of which largely duplicates this chapter, sketches the ethnic history of the state.

The general buildup of population from Europe, the South, and the East is discussed in William V. Pooley, *The Settlement of Illinois from 1830 to 1850*, Bulletin of the University of Wisconsin, History Series, 1 (Madison, 1908), and Mark Wyman, *Immigrants in the Valley: Irish, Germans, and Americans in the Upper Mississippi Country, 1830–1860* (Chicago, 1984). Different groups and their conflicts in Chicago are described in Bessie Louise Pierce, *A History of Chicago* (3 vols., Chicago, 1937–57). Church groups and their activities in Illinois—usually tied to ethnic or regional backgrounds—are documented in William Warren Sweet's landmark collection, *Religion on the American Frontier* . . . (4 vols., New York and Chicago, 1931–46).

One of the smaller ethnic group settlements in the early pioneer era, the English Settlement in Edwards County, has received a disproportionate amount of attention from historians due to the prolific literary output of its leaders. An interesting view of this and other early English groups is Grant Foreman, "English Settlers in Illinois," *Journal of the Illinois State Historical Society*, 34 (Sept. 1941), which includes letters sent home in the 1840s.

Scandinavians in Illinois are covered in Kendric Charles Babcock's basic account, *The Scandinavian Element in the United States*, University of Illinois Studies in the Social Sciences, 3 (Urbana, 1914). The early nucleus of Norwegians is discussed in Carlton C. Qualey, "The Fox River Norwegian Settlement," *Journal of the Illinois State Historical Society*, 27 (July 1934), while Odd S. Lovoll, *A Century of Urban Life: The Norwegians in Chicago before 1930* (Urbana, 1988) is a full-length study. Finns, especially in Chicago, DeKalb, and Waukegan, are chronicled in Esa Arra, *The Finns in Illinois* (New York Mills, Minn., 1971). See also Philip S. Friedman, "The Americanization of Chicago's Danish Community, 1850–1920," *Chicago History*, 9 (Spring 1980).

For the Swedes, a good starting point is Conrad Bergendoff, "The Beginnings of Swedish Immigration into Illinois a Century Ago," *Journal of the Illinois State Historical Society*, 41 (March 1948). Ulf Beijbom, *Swedes in Chicago: A Demographic and Social Study of the 1846–1880 Immigration* (Stockholm, 1971) is an outstanding work, combining letters, census materials, church and medical records, and other sources. For an introduction to Bishop Hill, a Swedish colony in Henry County, see the lectures and bibliography collected in a special issue of *Western Illinois Regional Studies*, 12 (Fall 1989). Studies of other Swedish communities downstate include Hugh E. McIntosh, "How the Swedes Came to Paxton," *Swedish Pioneer Historical Quarterly*, 30 (Jan. 1979), and Carl V. Hallberg, "Soperville: An Immigrant Community in Knox County," *Journal of the Illinois State Historical Society*, 74 (Spring 1981). A pivotal period for Swedish–American identity is analyzed in Sture Lindmark, *Swedish America, 1914–1932: Studies in Ethnicity with Emphasis on Illinois and Minnesota* (Stockholm, 1971).

Germans and Irish were far more numerous than Swedes but have been less studied, although surveys of Illinois history as well as broader examinations of both groups have touched on their experiences in the state. Thomas J. McCormack, ed., *The Memoirs of Gustave Koerner, 1809–1896* . . . (2 vols., Cedar Rapids, Iowa, 1909) illuminates German immigrant life in the period. For German-language readers, the *Belleviller Zeitung* (Belleville) and the *Illinois Staats-Zeitung* (Chicago) are gold mines of raw material. Ada M. Klett, "Belleville Germans Look at America, 1833–1845," *Journal of the Illinois State*

*Historical Society*, 40 (Mar. 1947), examines some immigrant letters home. Arrivals of other Europeans in colonies sponsored by the Roman Catholic Church are described in Mary Gilbert Kelly, *Catholic Immigrant Colonization Projects in the United States, 1815–1860* (New York, 1939). The intricate processes of "chain migration" as they brought Germans to central Illinois are detailed in Robert W. Frizzell, "Migration Chains to Illinois: The Evidence from German-American Church Records," *Journal of American Ethnic History*, 7 (Fall 1987). The world of German laborers in Chicago, especially its radical side, is examined in Hartmut Keil, "The German Immigrant Working Class of Chicago, 1875–90: Workers, Labor Leaders, and the Labor Movement," in Dirk Hoerder, ed., *American Labor and Immigration History, 1877–1920s: Recent European Research* (Urbana, 1983). Lawrence J. McCaffrey et al., *The Irish in Chicago* (Urbana, 1987) is a collection of essays touching on politics, religion, and literature.

By the end of the nineteenth century, the population of Illinois, as of the nation, was changing markedly. But while the "New Immigration" from South and East Europe has been studied for years, recent works have shown that miners from the British Isles had a great impact at the same time. See Amy Zahl Gottlieb's excellent analyses of this phenomenon: "The Influence of British Trade Unionists on the Regulation of the Mining Industry in Illinois, 1872," *Labor History*, 19 (Summer 1978), and "British Coal Miners: A Demographic Study of Braidwood and Streator, Illinois," *Journal of the Illinois State Historical Society*, 72 (Aug. 1979). Phillips G. Davies, ed., "Early Welsh Settlements in Illinois," ibid., 70 (Nov. 1977), is a translation of an 1872 account that points to the importance of this British group in the post-Civil War years. For a survey of the nationalities of Illinois coal miners, see the U.S. Immigration Commission (Dillingham Commission) report of 1910, *Immigrants in Industries* (Immigration Commission reports, Vols. 6–25; Senate Doc. 633, 61st Cong., 2nd Sess., 1909–10; Washington, D.C., 1910–11), 6 (Part 1, Vol. I, part III). This study picks out ten Illinois coal-mining communities for closer analysis.

The New Immigration's role in Illinois is sketched in such general works as Kaiser's *Building for the Centuries*; Donald F. Tingley, *The Structuring of a State: The History of Illinois, 1899 to 1928* (Urbana, 1980); and Ernest L. Bogart, "The Movement of the Population of Illinois, 1870–1910," *Transactions of the Illinois State Historical Society for the Year 1917*, 23. See also Stanley B. Kimball, *East Europeans in Southwestern Illinois: The Ethnic Experience in Historical Perspective* (Edwardsville, 1981) and Stephane Elise Booth, "The Relationship between Radicalism and Ethnicity in Southern Illinois Coal Fields, 1870–1940" (D.A. diss., Illinois State Univ., 1983).

Not surprisingly, most writing on the New Immigration in Illinois has concentrated on Chicago. Chicago had both teeming diversity and enormous numbers—from Back of the Yards to Swedetown, from Maxwell Street to Polonia. Jane Addams, *Twenty Years at Hull-House* . . . (New York, 1910) provides fascinating glimpses of some of these new and often bewildered "peoples of Illinois." And hidden in the statistical tables and summaries of the Dillingham Commission reports are important stories of the occupational life of many New Immigrant groups in Chicago—for example, in clothing manufacturing (*Immigrants in Industries*, 11, Part 6, part IV) and meat packing (ibid., 13, Part 11, part II). For an intriguing look at nationalities in twelve different Chicago neighborhoods, see *Immigrants in Cities* . . . (Immigration Commission reports, Vols. 26–27; Senate Doc. 338, 61st Cong., 2nd Sess.), 26 (part III).

Similar gems regarding Italians in particular are found between the lines in Carroll D. Wright (U.S. Commissioner of Labor), Ninth Special Report, *The Italians in Chicago: A Social and Economic Study* (Washington, D.C., 1897). Included in this account of occupations, school attendance, and literacy are data on the diets of individual workingmen, down to their nickel's worth of beer. Two general studies are Giovanni E. Schiavo, *The Italians in Chicago: A Study in Americanization* (Chicago, 1928) and Humbert S. Nelli, *Italians in Chicago, 1880–1930: A Study in Ethnic Mobility* (New York, 1970). See also Rudolph J. Vecoli, "The Formation of Chicago's 'Little Italies,' " *Journal of American Ethnic History*, 2 (Spring 1983).

The role of Greeks is examined in Grace Abbott, "A Study of the Greeks in Chicago," *American Journal of Sociology*, 15 (Nov. 1909), although it is apparent that this view is limited to what was visible from the steps of Hull House. The much-touted importance of the work of Hull House with Greeks, Italians, and Russian Jews is challenged in Rivka Lissak, "Myth and Reality: The Pattern of Relationship between the Hull House Circle and the 'New Immigrants' on Chicago's West Side, 1890–1919," *Journal of American Ethnic History*, 2 (Spring 1983). An interesting personal view of Jews in the city is Philip P. Bregstone, *Chicago and Its Jews: A Cultural History* (Chicago, 1933). See also Thomas Randolph Hall, "The Russian Community of Chicago," in Illinois State Historical Society, *Papers in Illinois History and Transactions for the Year 1937*.

Luckily for today's students of Chicago's ethnic diversity, there is an excellent collection of essays regarding many groups: Peter d'A. Jones and Melvin G. Holli, eds., *Ethnic Chicago* (Grand Rapids, 1981; revised ed., Holli and Jones, eds., Grand Rapids, 1984). For Mexicans, who joined the Chicago labor pool in large numbers from World War I onwards, see Mark Reisler, "The Mexican Immigrant in the Chicago Area during the 1920's," *Journal of the Illinois State Historical Society*, 66 (Summer 1973), and two articles in *Aztlán*, 7 (Summer 1976): Francisco Arturo Rosales, "The Regional Origins of Mexicano Immigrants to Chicago during the 1920s" and Juan R. Garcia, "History of Chicanos in Chicago Heights."

America's growing interest in its ethnic past, in its "roots," has produced an outpouring of recent studies that open new doors to understanding. This is also true with studies of the peoples of Illinois. Historical writing on the state's ethnic groups has had its shortcomings, but it generally provides a solid basis for more detailed and substantial works in the future.

# 10

# CHICAGO

PERRY R. DUIS

    JOSEPH BALESTIER STARTED it all. In 1840, when Chicago's city
charter was only three years old, the twenty-five-year-old lawyer delivered an
oration that became the first history of the city. The purpose of *The Annals
of Chicago* . . . , reprinted as the first number in Fergus' Historical Series
(Chicago, 1876), was clear: the past would help to establish the legitimacy of
the present, which was then racked by severe economic depression. This small
book also established the idea that history should serve some other master, a
course that many others would follow during the remainder of the nineteenth
century. For William Bross, *History of Chicago* . . . (Chicago, 1876), the past
was but a prelude to the economic boom of mid-century. The creation of the
Chicago Historical Society in 1856 and the publications that would flow from it
were meant to preserve the story of the founding members' contributions for later
generations, as well as to teach Americanism to the city's polyglot population.
Similarly, the spate of instant accounts following the Great Fire of 1871 used
history to reassure their readers of the inevitability of the city's rebuilding and
its return to its former greatness. Every word had its purpose.
    By the late nineteenth century, history began to play a role in the efforts to
create a sense of celebration and civic unity amidst economic discord and labor
violence. The publication of A[lfred] T[heodore] Andreas's monumental *History
of Chicago from the Earliest Period to the Present Time* (3 vols., Chicago,
1884–86) was the first milestone. While his books were a commercial venture,

the sales of which depended in part on the number of people whose biographies he could squeeze between the covers, Andreas also saw as his mission the collection of reminiscences of the fast-disappearing generation of pioneers. With the loss of the Historical Society's collections in 1871 and again in a major conflagration in 1874, much of the city's early history had to be reassembled from oral sources, but the young men of the 1830s and 1840s were now aged, so he approached his task with a sense of urgency.

Andreas soon had his imitators, who hoped to cash in on the excitement surrounding the World's Columbian Exposition of 1893. These works vary in quality, with Joseph Kirkland, *The Story of Chicago* (2 vols., Chicago, 1892–94) and John Moses and Joseph Kirkland, eds., *History of Chicago, Illinois* (2 vols., Chicago, 1895) being the best. Later, J[osiah] Seymour Currey compiled *Chicago: Its Makers and Its Builders; A Century of Marvelous Growth* (5 vols., Chicago, 1912). Currey's work, like its predecessors, is uncritical, and heavily biographical—historians call such volumes "mugbooks." This tradition survived into the 1920s with Paul Gilbert and Charles Lee Bryson, *Chicago and Its Makers . . .* (Chicago, 1929), a great celebration of that decade's optimism.

By the late 1920s, however, such massive histories were beginning to give way to markedly different genres. One was the popular survey for mass audiences, the best example of which is Lloyd Lewis and Henry Justin Smith, *Chicago: The History of Its Reputation* (Chicago, 1929), which provides a delightfully written portrait of the city. Another was the academic study of the city's past, pioneered by Bessie Louise Pierce, who arrived at the University of Chicago in 1929. Her anthology, *As Others See Chicago: Impressions of Visitors, 1673–1933* (Chicago, 1933), was followed by *A History of Chicago* (3 vols., Chicago, 1937–57), the first scholarly history of an American city. Although her emphasis on economic matters reflected the Great Depression during which it was researched and planned, her work was balanced and comprehensive. Sadly, however, she did not live to complete her study beyond 1893, but she did raise local history to new levels of respectability and accuracy. Perry R. Duis provides an estimate of her career in "Bessie Louise Pierce: Symbol and Scholar," *Chicago History*, 5 (Fall 1976), and an account of Chicago's urban biographies in "Chicago Chronicles," ibid., 14 (Winter 1985–86).

Specialized studies of the city have followed a logic of their own, while multiplying in huge numbers. Frank Jewell, *Annotated Bibliography of Chicago History* (Chicago, 1979) includes over twenty-eight thousand entries and could be supplemented by hundreds of references in recent years.

Chicago, however, still lacks the one-volume synthesis that covers all topics. Emmett Dedmon, *Fabulous Chicago* (New York, 1953) is highly readable but thin beyond colorful personalities and, though enlarged (New York, 1981), still skimpy on the twentieth century. Harold M. Mayer and Richard C. Wade, *Chicago: Growth of a Metropolis* (Chicago, 1969) is the standard brief account of the physical city but says too little about the people of Chicago. Historical geographers have considered the evolution of the city in

Irving Cutler, *Chicago: Metropolis of the Mid-Continent* (Chicago, 1973; revised ed., Dubuque, 1982) and Brian J. L. Berry, ed., *Chicago: Transformations of an Urban System* (Cambridge, Mass., 1976). Paul M. Green and Melvin G. Holli, eds., *The Mayors: The Chicago Political Tradition* (Carbondale, 1987), which recounts the lives of Joseph Medill, mayor after the Fire of 1871, and all of the elected twentieth-century mayors from Carter Harrison II to Harold Washington, provides an excellent biographical approach to large parts of the city's history.

Chapters in Pierce and Andreas remain the best surveys of life in the nineteenth century. No one has reinterpreted the formation of government since Samuel Edwin Sparling, *Municipal History and Present Organization of the City of Chicago*, Bulletin of the University of Wisconsin, No. 23: Economics, Political Science, and History Series, Vol. 2 (Madison, 1898), and the lesser known but superior work by Hugo S. Grosser, *Chicago: A Review of Its Governmental History from 1837 to 1906*, 10th Annual Convention of the League of American Municipalities . . . (Chicago, 1906). There are a few specialized studies of specific municipal functions, including James S. McQuade, ed., *A Synoptical History of the Chicago Fire Department* . . . (Chicago, 1908), a brief chronology issued by the Benevolent Association of the Paid Fire Department of Chicago.

Questions of health, which posed a constant threat to early Chicagoans, have enjoyed more adequate treatment. Thomas Neville Bonner, *Medicine in Chicago, 1850–1950* . . . (Madison, 1957) is a model history, which may be supplemented by Ruth E. Parsons, "The Department of Health of the City of Chicago, 1894–1914" (M.A. thesis, Univ. of Chicago, 1939) and David Fricke Simonson, "The History of the Department of Health of Chicago, 1947–1956" (Ph.D. diss., Univ. of Chicago, 1962). Two scholars have provided valuable insights into the question of water supplies, a critical part of public health. Louis P. Cain, *Sanitation Strategy for a Lakefront Metropolis: The Case of Chicago* (DeKalb, 1978) is a fine summary of his detailed "The Sanitary District of Chicago: A Case Study of Water Use and Conservation" (Ph.D. diss., Northwestern Univ., 1969), while a pamphlet by James C. O'Connell, *Chicago's Quest for Pure Water* (Washington, D.C., 1976), was a preview of his "Technology and Pollution: Chicago's Water Policy, 1833–1930" (Ph.D. diss., Univ. of Chicago, 1980).

Until recently, the literature dealing with the earliest period existed in the shadows of that written by the city's founders. For example, Mrs. John H. [Juliette] Kinzie, *Wau-Bun, the "Early Day" in the North-West* (New York, 1856; best ed., Chicago, 1932), which was written to establish her family as Chicago's founders, is more fiction than fact. The biographical approach, which emphasized the deeds of the few rather than the contributions of the many, remained largely unchallenged until Milo Milton Quaife, *Chicago and the Old Northwest, 1673–1835* . . . (Chicago, 1913) showed the importance of subjects rather than personalities. His work, and Pierce's first volume, which covers 1673–1848, remain the best accounts of the period.

In recent decades, the pioneer era has received less attention than other periods, not only because of the high quality of Pierce but also because of the declining interest in the once-popular field of frontier history, of which early Chicago was a part. Yet exceptions have begun to appear. The rise of black consciousness during the 1960s contributed to the ascension of DuSable to his rightful place as founder, but the literature about him remains as thin as the sources. Thomas A. Meehan, "Jean Baptiste Point du Sable, the First Chicagoan," *Journal of the Illinois State Historical Society*, 56 (Autumn 1963), is still the best study. The most useful work on the period before 1850 is Alfred H. Meyer, "Circulation and Settlement Patterns of the Calumet Region of Northwest Indiana and Northeast Illinois . . . ," *Annals of the Association of American Geographers*, 44 (Sept. 1954) and 46 (Sept. 1956). Glen E. Holt, "The Birth of Chicago: An Examination of Economic Parentage," *Journal of the Illinois State Historical Society*, 76 (Summer 1983), shows the region's dependence on the federal government. An important reinterpretation of the early city is Jacqueline Peterson, " 'Wild' Chicago: The Formation and Destruction of a Multi-racial Community on the Midwestern Frontier, 1816–1837," in Melvin G. Holli and Peter d'A. Jones, eds., *The Ethnic Frontier: Essays in the History of Group Survival in Chicago and the Midwest* (Grand Rapids, 1977). Recently discovered records of the city council are used in Robin Leigh Einhorn, "Before the Machine: Municipal Government in Chicago, 1833–1872" (Ph.D. diss., Univ. of Chicago, 1988).

The development of mid-nineteenth-century social life is dominated by a concentration on great leaders. Don E. Fehrenbacher, *Chicago Giant: A Biography of "Long John" Wentworth* (Madison, 1957) focuses more on the early mayor's congressional career than on his life in Chicago. Joseph Medill looms large in Lloyd Wendt, *"Chicago Tribune": The Rise of a Great American Newspaper* (Chicago, 1979), while a bitter rival is the subject of Justin E. Walsh, *To Print the News and Raise Hell! A Biography of Wilbur F. Storey* (Chapel Hill, 1968). Other studies have concentrated on collective biography and intellectual attitudes. Craig Buettinger, "Economic Inequality in Early Chicago, 1849–1850," *Journal of Social History*, 11 (Spring 1978), attempts to demonstrate statistically that there was a fairly rigid inequality at an early date, while Frederic Cople Jaher, *The Urban Establishment: Upper Strata in Boston, New York, Charleston, Chicago, and Los Angeles* (Urbana, 1982) argues that entry into the local elite was easier for *nouveau riche* in Chicago than for those in Gotham and the Hub.

Popular ideas about the mid-nineteenth-century city were dominated by the boosters' quest for regional economic hegemony, as Chicagoans struggled to present a positive image to the rest of the world. For years, the standard works were Lloyd Lewis, *John S. Wright, Prophet of the Prairies* (Chicago, 1941) and Wyatt Winton Belcher, *The Economic Rivalry between St. Louis and Chicago, 1850–1880* (New York, 1947). More recently, others have reexamined the subject. John Denis Haeger, "Eastern Money and the Urban Frontier:

Chicago, 1833–1842," *Journal of the Illinois State Historical Society*, 64 (Autumn 1971), and J. Christopher Schnell, "Chicago versus St. Louis: A Reassessment of the Great Rivalry," *Missouri Historical Review*, 71 (Apr. 1977), each attack Belcher on different grounds, the former stressing ties to Atlantic fortunes and the latter defending St. Louis against charges that it was conservative, rejecting railroads in favor of river commerce. Carl Abbott, *Boosters and Businessmen . . .* (Westport, Conn., 1981) treats the pre–Civil War competition among Chicago, Cincinnati, Indianapolis, and Galena. Two Ph.D. dissertations also consider the city's economic development: Patrick Edward McLear, "Chicago and the Growth of a Region, 1832 through 1848" (Univ. of Missouri, Columbia, 1974) and Rima Lunin Schultz, "The Businessman's Role in Western Settlement: The Entrepreneurial Frontier, Chicago, 1833–1872" (Boston Univ., 1984). William J. Cronon, "To Be the Central City: Chicago, 1848–1857," *Chicago History*, 10 (Fall 1981), is a seminal interpretation of the city's quest for regional leadership.

Despite the puffery about Chicago, it is interesting to note the early and strong desire of many Chicagoans to live on the suburban fringe which, they claimed, was everything that Chicago was not. Carl Abbott, " 'Necessary Adjuncts to Its Growth': The Railroad Suburbs of Chicago, 1854–1875," *Journal of the Illinois State Historical Society*, 73 (Summer 1980), explores the ideology of suburbanization. Barbara M. Posadas, "Suburb into Neighborhood: The Transformation of Urban Identity on Chicago's Periphery; Irving Park as a Case Study, 1870–1910," *Journal of the Illinois State Historical Society*, 76 (Autumn 1983), deals with the economic relationship of city and hinterland. Other approaches to suburban history are evident in Michael H. Ebner, *Creating Chicago's North Shore: A Suburban History* (Chicago, 1988), which gracefully interprets the similarities and differences among towns along one critical corridor of fringe development, and Anne Durkin Keating, *Building Chicago: Suburban Developers and the Creation of a Divided Metropolis* (Columbus, Ohio, 1988), which examines the governmental aspects of town building in outlying areas.

While the literature of boosterism and suburban anti-urbanism is good and getting better, other literature on the economic development of the city is far thinner, and the reader must still depend on such venerable works as *Industrial Chicago . . .* (6 vols., Chicago, 1891–96) and J[osiah] Seymour Currey, *Manufacturing and Wholesale Industries of Chicago* (3 vols., Chicago, 1918), both of which are largely compilations of uninterpretive corporate histories. Elmer A. Riley, *The Development of Chicago and Vicinity as a Manufacturing Center Prior to 1880* (Chicago, 1911) is still of some use, while much of Mary Oona Marquardt, "Sources of Capital of Early Illinois Manufacturers, 1840–1880" (Ph.D. diss., Univ. of Illinois, 1960) deals with Chicago. Jonathan Lurie, *The Chicago Board of Trade, 1859–1905: The Dynamics of Self–Regulation* (Urbana, 1979) and William G. Ferris, *The Grain Traders: The Story of the Chicago Board of Trade* (East Lansing, 1988) replace part, but not all, of Charles H. Taylor, ed., *History of the Board of Trade of the City of Chicago* (3 vols., Chicago, 1917). F[rank] Cyril James, *The Growth of Chicago Banks* . . . (2 vols., Chicago, 1938) has withstood the test of later scholarship because of its quality, as has William T. Hutchinson, *Cyrus Hall McCormick* . . . (2 vols., Chicago, 1930–35), a model of economic history as well as biography.

The railroad was *the* essential element in mid-century growth, but there has been precious little of scholarly value done about it. George H. Douglas, *Rail City: Chicago, U.S.A.* (San Diego, 1981), which suffers from a weak text balanced by excellent illustrations, is the sole attempt at a synthesis. The rest of Chicago's railway history must be culled from studies of individual companies. One wave of this literature appeared after World War II, as the various lines began celebrating centennials, and included Robert J. Casey and W. A. S. Douglas, *Pioneer Railroad: The Story of the Chicago and North Western System* (New York, 1948); Carlton J. Corliss, *Main Line of Mid-America: The Story of the Illinois Central* (New York, 1950); August Derleth, *The Milwaukee Road: Its First Hundred Years* (New York, 1948); William Edward Hayes, *Iron Road to Empire: The History of 100 Years of the Progress and Achievements of the Rock Island Lines* (New York, 1953); and James Marshall, *Santa Fe: The Railroad That Built an Empire* (New York, 1945). During the 1960s another wave of railroad books appealed to rail buffs, advertisements for which may be found in such magazines as *Trains*. Most of these books contain a text rehashed from old sources and many, many illustrations. Meanwhile, academic rail history has developed more slowly, but luckily the leading scholars have studied lines with close Chicago ties. Robert C. Overton, *Burlington Route: A History of the Burlington Lines* (New York, 1965) and John F. Stover, *History of the Illinois Central Railroad* (New York, 1975) are outstanding works. See also Stover, *History of the Baltimore and Ohio Railroad* (West Lafayette, Ind., 1987) and H[arry] Roger Grant, *The Corn Belt Route: A History of the Chicago Great Western Railroad Company* (DeKalb, 1984).

The mid-century decades reveal an odd fact about local historical writing: the more important events are often the least studied by scholars. The Civil War and the Great Fire illustrate this. The former was essential to Chicago's quick rise to economic power, but the vast Civil War literature virtually ignores the city. Lester Harold Cook, "Anti-Slavery Sentiment in the Culture of Chicago, 1844–1858" (Ph.D. diss., Univ. of Chicago, 1952) is very useful, as are Stanley L. Jones, "John Wentworth and Anti-Slavery in Chicago to 1856," *Mid-America*, 36 (July 1954), and Meredith M. Dytch, " 'Remember Ellsworth!' Chicago's First Hero of the Civil War," *Chicago History*, 11 (Spring 1982). Beyond that, the appropriate chapters of Pierce's second volume, 1848–71, are the best.

The Great Fire of 1871 is a problem in itself. Its literature is voluminous and consists of several types. There were many instant reports that rolled off the presses before the ashes cooled. Elias Colbert and Everett Chamberlin, *Chicago and the Great Conflagration* (Cincinnati, 1871) is probably the best. Later, Mabel McIlvaine compiled different accounts of the disaster in *Reminiscences of Chicago during the Great Fire* (Chicago, 1915). Another category consists of popular narratives, such as Robert Cromie, *The Great Chicago Fire* (New York, 1958). H. A. Musham, "The Great Chicago Fire, October 8–10, 1871," in Illinois State Historical Society, *Papers in Illinois History and Transactions for the Year 1940*, is a lengthy but little-used account that bridges the gap between popular and scholarly works. Karen Sawislak, "Smoldering City," *Chicago History*, 17 (Fall–Winter 1988–89), reviews the efforts to rebuild Chicago. Christine Meisner Rosen, *The Limits of Power: Great Fires and the Process of City Growth in America* (New York, 1986) compares conflagrations in Boston and Baltimore with the Great Fire in Chicago as they affected land use and reconstruction. Yet the opening chapter of Pierce's third volume remains the best general study.

The Chicago literature covering the years between the Fire of 1871 and the World's Columbian Exposition of 1893 has been dominated by the story of economic expansion and the response of workers. These studies, however, are unevenly balanced. Phyllis Bate, "The Development of the Iron and Steel Industry of the Chicago Area, 1900–1920" (Ph.D. diss., Univ. of Chicago, 1948) covers the pre–1900 period only in passing, but it remains the most useful work. By contrast, there is a substantial body of information about the packing industry. For years, Chicagoans read Louis F. Swift's useful but uncritical *The Yankee of the Yards: The Biography of Gustavus Franklin Swift* (Chicago, 1927), until Louis Unfer's pioneering "Swift and Company: The Development of the Packing Industry, 1875 to 1912" (Ph.D. diss., Univ. of Illinois, 1951) put the family in proper perspective. More recently, Louise Carroll Wade, *Chicago's Pride: The Stockyards, Packingtown, and Environs in the Nineteenth Century* (Urbana, 1987) contributed to an understanding of how Chicago bested its packing rivals. Other studies have emphasized the life of the workers. Dominic A. Pacyga, "Villages of Packinghouses and Steel Mills: The Polish Worker on Chicago's South Side, 1880 to 1921" (Ph.D. diss., Univ. of Illinois, Chicago, 1981) skillfully compares two communities which also represented Chicago's two largest industries. Robert A. Slayton, *Back of the Yards: The Making of a Local Democracy* (Chicago, 1986) deals with twentieth-century social history in part through the use of oral traditions. James R. Barrett, *Work and Community in the Jungle: Chicago's Packinghouse Workers, 1894–1922* (Urbana, 1987) is a factual substitute for Upton Sinclair's famous novel.

The stockyards labor literature is finally taking its place alongside the more sensational, and thus more thoroughly studied, labor violence that contributed to Chicago's negative reputation. There is no adequate study of the 1877 railway riots, but the reader should see the chapter in Howard Barton Myers, "The Policing of Labor Disputes in Chicago: A Case Study" (Ph.D. diss., Univ. of Chicago, 1929), a lengthy review of local industrial violence through 1925. It is helpful to seek a balance of accounts of the Haymarket and Pullman bloodshed. For the former, Hutchinson's *McCormick* is somewhat less pro-labor than either Henry David, *The History of the Haymarket Affair* . . . (New York, 1936) or Harry Barnard, *"Eagle Forgotten": The Life of John Peter Altgeld* (Indianapolis,

1938). A similar match of views can be found between Stanley Buder, *Pullman: An Experiment in Industrial Order and Community Planning, 1880–1930* (New York, 1967), a book attacked for being not anti-Pullman enough, and Almont Lindsey, *The Pullman Strike . . .* (Chicago, 1942), a more traditional view. Other perspectives on the period come from Richard Schneirov, "The Knights of Labor in the Chicago Labor Movement and in Municipal Politics, 1877–1887" (Ph.D. diss., Northern Illinois Univ., 1984); Bruce C. Nelson, *Beyond the Martyrs: A Social History of Chicago's Anarchists, 1870–1900* (New Brunswick, N.J., 1988); and Ralph W. Scharnau, "Thomas J. Morgan and the Chicago Socialist Movement, 1876–1901" (Ph.D. diss., Northern Illinois Univ., 1969).

The remaining economic literature is scattered and specialized. Retailing is dominated by mail-order merchandising and department stores. The former field is exemplified by Boris Emmet and John E. Jeuck, *Catalogues and Counters: A History of Sears, Roebuck and Company* (Chicago, 1950) and James C. Worthy, *Shaping an American Institution: Robert E. Wood and Sears, Roebuck* (Urbana, 1984). The latter topic is treated in Robert W. Twyman, *History of Marshall Field & Co., 1852–1906* (Philadelphia, 1954), which is more scholarly but less readable on Field's than Lloyd Wendt and Herman Kogan, *Give the Lady What She Wants . . .* (Chicago, 1952). Sharon S. Darling approaches Chicago industry through artifacts that were left behind, and what emerges is a unique kind of economic history: *Chicago Metalsmiths: An Illustrated History* (Chicago, 1977); *Chicago Ceramics and Glass: An Illustrated History from 1871 to 1933* (Chicago, 1979); and *Chicago Furniture: Art, Craft, and Industry, 1833–1983* (New York, 1984).

Like the Great Fire, the World's Columbian Exposition has yet to enjoy a truly adequate interpretation. Historians have thought the fire too simplistic to study, while the exposition seems to have been too complex. David F. Burg, *Chicago's White City of 1893* (Lexington, Ky., 1976) starts off well but lapses into a too-detailed guidebook description, while [Rodney] Reid Badger, *The Great American Fair: The World's Columbian Exposition and American Culture* (Chicago, 1979) is a bit broader but fails to examine the impact on the city. Specialized aspects of the exposition have fared better. Jeanne Madeline Weimann, *The Fair Women* (Chicago, 1981) is an undocumented but scholarly look at the exposition's impact on American women. See also Elliott M. Rudwick and August Meier, "Black Man in the 'White City': Negroes and the Columbian Exposition, 1893," *Phylon*, 26 (Winter 1965). The origins of the "Windy City" nickname lay in Chicago's boastfulness, not its weather. For a discussion of how Chicago won the fair, see Robert D. Parmet, "Competition for the World's Columbian Exposition: The New York Campaign," and Francis L. Lederer II, " . . . The Chicago Campaign," *Journal of the Illinois State Historical Society*, 65 (Winter 1972). Rossiter Johnson, ed., *A History of the World's Columbian Exposition Held in Chicago in 1893* (4 vols., New York, 1897–98) remains the place to begin any search for information on the fair.

While the Fire and the world's fair were the most traumatic events during Chicago's first hundred years, the real transformation of the city came in its outward dispersal, the annexation of 125 square miles in 1889, and the creation of an industrial society. Despite the exciting changes going on in the neighborhoods, such historians as Pierce and the army of monograph writers virtually ignored them in favor of what might be called the "Loop Synthesis"—that is, an emphasis on City Hall politics, downtown shopping magnates, and major industrialists. This is not unlike the "Presidential Synthesis" in national history, where *all* events tended to be shaped to fit between the watersheds of quadrennial elections. For years, the story of outlying events was left to sociologists, economists, and social workers, many of them affiliated with the University of Chicago. That institution sponsored the *Local Community Fact Book . . .* (5 vols., Chicago, 1935–84), based on each census since 1930 and containing excellent community area histories. This series began with the *District Fact Book . . .* , which was revised and retitled in 1938. The most recent compilation, using the 1970 and 1980 censuses, was undertaken by the Chicago Fact Book Consortium, based in the Department of Sociology of the University of Illinois at Chicago.

Some classic sociological studies also answer historical questions, while providing lively contemporary views, including Harvey Warren Zorbaugh, *Gold Coast and Slum: A Sociological Study of Chicago's Near North Side* (Chicago, 1929); Frederic M. Thrasher, *The Gang: A Study of 1,313 Gangs in Chicago* (Chicago, 1927; abridged ed., Chicago, 1963); and Louis Wirth, *The Ghetto* (Chicago, 1928). For the academic milieu of these studies, see Martin Bulmer, *The Chicago School of Sociology: Institutionalization, Diversity, and the Rise of Sociological Research* (Chicago, 1984).

Homer Hoyt, *One Hundred Years of Land Values in Chicago: The Relationship of the Growth of Chicago to the Rise in Its Land Values, 1830–1933* (Chicago, 1933) remains the most useful single book on the physical development of the city. Its companion, Earl Shepard Johnson, "The Natural History of the Central Business District with Particular Reference to Chicago" (Ph.D. diss., Univ. of Chicago, 1941), was unfortunately left unpublished, as were many wartime theses. Hoyt and Johnson were economists, while Edith Abbott was one of America's leading social welfare experts. Her book, *The Tenements of Chicago, 1908–1935* (Chicago, 1936), remains the best study of slum conditions in any city.

More recently, a new generation of historians has attempted to investigate Chicago social history without the Loop Synthesis. The results have been mixed. Richard Sennett, *Families against the City: Middle Class Homes of Industrial Chicago, 1872–1890* (Cambridge, Mass., 1970) is a failure because of faulty research crammed into an unworkable idea. Carrol Hunter Quenzel, " 'Society' in New York and Chicago, 1888–1900" (Ph.D. diss., Univ. of Wisconsin, 1938), a study of the elite, is uninterpretive but still very useful. Gwendolyn Wright, *Moralism and the Modern Home: Domestic Architecture and Cultural Conflict in Chicago, 1873–1913* (Chicago, 1980) interprets social history through the artifact of housing. Perry R. Duis, *The Saloon: Public Drinking in Chicago and Boston, 1880–1920* (Urbana, 1983) demonstrates the importance of that institution but also establishes a hierarchy of social class based on the ability of people to privatize their lives as the city dispersed outward. Glen E. Holt and Dominic A. Pacyga, *Chicago: A Historical Guide to the Neighborhoods; The Loop and the South Side* (Chicago, 1979) provides area-by-area portraits. Pacyga teamed with Ellen Skerrett to write *Chicago: City of Neighborhoods; Histories and Tours* (Chicago, 1986), an excellent guide to selected areas.

The historiographical tension between the Loop and the neighborhoods, as well as the transition from history written by other social scientists to that produced by historians, can be found in the burgeoning literature on reform in Chicago. This field also demonstrates that scholars, like electricity or water, seek the paths of least resistance. Two factors have been responsible: not only were reformers literate people who retained good records of their careers, but such institutions as the Chicago Historical Society and the University of Illinois at Chicago began to amass large archival collections in the mid–1960s. Their first acquisitions focused on social reformers, just as a generation of graduate students was discovering the new field of urban history. The tendency toward academic specialization has also meant that the resulting literature has cut the reform pie into narrow slices. There is still no synthesis of the Progressive era in Chicago and no reliable general work to chart the course for others.

The treatment of the poor is a case in point. For years, the standard works were James Brown, *The History of Public Assistance in Chicago, 1833 to 1893* (Chicago, 1941) and Sophonisba P. Breckinridge, *The Illinois Poor Law and Its Administration* (Chicago, 1939), both written by social work experts. The shadow of Jane Addams and her contemporaries attracted the earliest attention of historians. Allen Freeman Davis, "Spearheads for Reform: The Social Settlements and the Progressive Movement, 1890–1914" (Ph.D. diss., Univ. of Wisconsin, 1959), later reorganized topically instead of by city and published under the same title (New York, 1967), led the way. In 1969, Davis and Mary Lynn McCree (Bryan) edited a marvelous collection of documents, now available as *100 Years at Hull-House* (Bloomington, Ind., 1990), while Davis's interpretation culminated in *American Heroine: The Life and Legend of Jane Addams* (New York, 1973). John C. Farrell, *Beloved Lady: A History of Jane Addams' Ideas on Reform and Peace*, Johns Hopkins University Studies in Historical and Political Science, Ser. 85, No. 2 (Baltimore, 1967), is an intellectual biography based on the subject's voluminous writings, including her famous autobiography. Jane Addams is reexamined in Rivka Shpak Lissak, *Pluralism and Progressives: Hull House and the New Immigrants, 1890–1919* (Chicago, 1989).

The second most important figure in local social reform was Graham Taylor, and Louise C. Wade, *Graham Taylor, Pioneer for Social Justice, 1851–1938* (New York, 1964) is an excellent account of his life. The lesser stars in the Chicago reform constellation are subjects, for the most part, of older books and articles written primarily by social workers: Josephine Goldmark, *Impatient Crusader: Florence Kelley's Life Story* (Urbana, 1953); Howard E. Wilson, *Mary McDowell, Neighbor* (Chicago, 1928); Jane Addams, *My Friend, Julia Lathrop* (New York, 1935); and Eleanor K. Taylor, "The Edith Abbott I Knew," *Journal of the Illinois State Historical Society*, 70 (Aug. 1977). Lela B. Costin, *Two Sisters for Social Justice: A Biography of Grace and Edith Abbott* (Urbana, 1983) updates the trend of social workers writing about fellow social workers.

Gradually, historians have come to grips with social work and philanthropy as a whole. Louise C. Wade, "The Heritage from Chicago's Early Settlement Houses," *Journal of the Illinois State Historical Society*, 60 (Winter 1967), is a particularly good summary, as is Kenneth L. Kusmer, "The Functions of Organized Charity in the Progressive Era: Chicago as a Case Study," *Journal of American History*, 60 (Dec. 1973). Kathleen D. McCarthy, *Noblesse Oblige: Charity and Cultural Philanthropy in Chicago, 1849–1929* (Chicago, 1982) is the most comprehensive interpretation to date. More particular studies include Steven J. Diner, *A City and Its Universities: Public Policy in Chicago, 1892–1919* (Chapel Hill, 1980), which emphasizes the reform activities of the University of Chicago faculty, and Arthur Edward Anderson, "The Institutional Path of Old Age in Chicago, 1870–1912" (Ph.D. diss., Univ. of Virginia, 1983), which describes the homes in which ethnic and occupational groups sheltered their dependent aged population apart from the poorhouse. Many nineteenth-century problems persist, as shown by Charles Hoch and Robert A. Slayton, *New Homeless and Old: Community and the Skid Row Hotel* (Philadelphia, 1989).

Since the mid–1960s, researchers in many different fields have tended to study reformers rather than what they were trying to reform. In the case of women, for example, we still know too little about housewives. Joanne J. Meyerowitz, *Women Adrift: Independent Wage Earners in Chicago, 1880–1930* (Chicago, 1988) and Lisa Michelle Fine, " 'The Record Keepers of Property': The Making of the Female Clerical Labor Force in Chicago, 1870–1930" (Ph.D. diss., Univ. of Wisconsin, Madison, 1985) fill an enormous void through their studies of anonymous working women. Biographies of women in the labor movement include Carolyn Ashbaugh, *Lucy Parsons, American Revolutionary* (Chicago, 1976) and Elizabeth Anne Payne, *Reform, Labor, and Feminism: Margaret Dreier Robins and the Women's Trade Union League* (Urbana, 1988). The best work on the garment trades is N. Sue Weiler, "Walkout: The Chicago Men's Garment Workers' Strike, 1910–1911," *Chicago History*, 8 (Winter 1979–80). Opposing sides of the suffrage struggle emerge in Catherine Cole Mambretti, "The Battle against the Ballot: Illinois Woman Antisuffragists," ibid., 9 (Fall 1980), and Steven M. Buechler, *The Transformation of the Woman Suffrage Movement: The Case of Illinois, 1850–1920* (New Brunswick, N.J., 1986). Finally, women's clubs were important centers of reform, as seen in two uninterpretive works, Henriette Greenebaum Frank and Amalie Hofer Jerome, comps., *Annals of the Chicago Woman's Club for the First Forty Years of Its Organization, 1876–1916* (Chicago, 1916) and Dorothy Edwards Powers,

"The Chicago Woman's Club" (M.A. diss., Univ. of Chicago, 1939). Another uncritical account of another club is Muriel Beadle et al., *The Fortnightly of Chicago: The City and Its Women, 1873–1973* (Chicago, 1973).

Scholars who have researched the 1890–1915 era have tended to tie almost everything to the reform ethos. The Burnham Plan, for instance, was once regarded as a detached topic. Robert Averill Walker, *The Planning Function in Urban Government* (Chicago, 1941; enlarged ed., Chicago, 1950) remains a little-used but perceptive study, while Lois Wille, *Forever Open, Clear, and Free: The Historic Struggle for Chicago's Lakefront* (Chicago, 1972) shows more advocacy than research. The standard biographies, Charles Moore, *Daniel H. Burnham: Architect, Planner of Cities* (2 vols., Chicago, 1921) and Thomas S. Hines, *Burnham of Chicago, Architect and Planner* (New York, 1974), may be supplemented by Roger P. Akeley, Jr., "Implementing the 1909 Plan of Chicago: An Historical Account of Planning Salesmanship" (M.S. thesis, Univ. of Tennessee, Knoxville, 1973), a fine study, and the thinner Michael P. McCarthy, "Chicago Businessmen and the Burnham Plan," *Journal of the Illinois State Historical Society*, 63 (Autumn 1970).

Reformers regarded the parks as a critical link between the ideals of social uplift and the reality of the slums, but the idea was late in arriving. Galen Cranz, "Models for Park Usage: Ideology and the Development of Chicago's Public Parks" (Ph.D. diss., Univ. of Chicago, 1971) shows how the expectations of park functions changed. Her dissertation is more useful for Chicago topics than is her book, *The Politics of Park Design: A History of Urban Parks in America* (Cambridge, Mass., 1982). Daniel M. Bluestone, "Landscape and Culture in Nineteenth-Century Chicago" (Ph.D. diss., Univ. of Chicago, 1984) is a major study of attitudes toward parks, skyscrapers, and other aspects of the urban environment. Recent attention to the archives of the Chicago Park District augurs well for further work in the field.

There has always been a thin line between the literature of crime and that of moral reform in Chicago, in large part because the city's criminal image is so deeply rooted in the problems of prostitution and gambling. This was not always so, however, as the city's earliest police history, John J. Flinn, *History of the Chicago Police* . . . (Chicago, 1887; best ed., Montclair, N.J., 1973), was really a semiofficial propaganda piece in the aftermath of the Haymarket Riot. This book, along with the brief sections of Andreas and Pierce, stood as the only police history until scholars recently began to place the subject in a wider context. One such study is Frank Morn, *"The Eye That Never Sleeps": A History of the Pinkerton National Detective Agency* (Bloomington, Ind., 1982). David R. Johnson, *Policing the Urban Underworld: The Impact of Crime on the Development of the American Police, 1800–1887* (Philadelphia, 1979) argues that police reform came as a response to the changing nature of crime. Mark H. Haller's articles, "Urban Crime and Criminal Justice: The Chicago Case," *Journal of American History*, 57 (Dec. 1970), and "Historical Roots of Police Behavior: Chicago, 1890–1925," *Law and Society Review*, 10 (Winter 1976), are perceptive on local policing, but we still lack a good general history of the Chicago Police Department.

The largest share of Chicago crime and anti-crime literature focuses on the so-called "victimless crimes" of prostitution, gambling, liquor law violations, and pornography. Here, academic historians have had to chart a course between two extremes in the rest of the published work. Herbert Asbury, *Gem of the Prairie: An Informal History of the Chicago Underworld* (New York, 1940; best ed., DeKalb, 1986) started what might be called the "Lovable Scoundrel School" of crime historiography by scouring newspaper files for an affectionate portrait of colorful thieves, whoremasters, and gamesters. Lloyd Wendt and Herman Kogan, *Lords of the Levee: The Story of Bathhouse John and Hinky Dink* (Indianapolis, 1943; reprinted as *Bosses in Lusty Chicago* . . . , Bloomington, Ind., 1967) followed Asbury in emphasizing anecdote rather than analysis, but both books are carefully researched in the newspapers, which often constitute the only source available. To counter this trend, the former head of the Chicago Crime Commission, Virgil W. Peterson, wrote *Barbarians in Our Midst: A History of Chicago Crime and Politics* (Boston, 1952), which emphasized the viciousness of criminals and challenged the notion of victimless criminality. Although academic historians have leaned toward Peterson's viewpoint, they have tended to see such crimes as prostitution only in a reform context. Joseph O. Baylen, "A Victorian's 'Crusade' in Chicago, 1893–1894," *Journal of American History*, 51 (Dec. 1964), tells the story of William T. Stead, whose *If Christ Came to Chicago* . . . (Chicago, 1894) is the supreme indictment of urban immorality. Eric Anderson, "Prostitution and Social Justice: Chicago, 1910–15," *Social Service Review*, 48 (June 1974), and Mark Thomas Connelly, *The Response to Prostitution in the Progressive Era* (Chapel Hill, 1980) both focus on the anti-vice reformers, while Ruth Rosen, *The Lost Sisterhood: Prostitution in America, 1900–1918* (Baltimore, 1982) is a feminist view of the white slave as victim.

The bulk of the literature on Chicago politics from the Great Fire through 1920 has examined the reformer rather than the unreformed, the major exceptions being Wendt and Kogan's *Lords of the Levee* and Claudius O. Johnson, *Carter Harrison I, Political Leader* (Chicago, 1928). Much of the later work has been influenced by contemporary studies by some of the partisans, in particular Charles Edward Merriam, *Chicago: A More Intimate View of Urban Politics* (New York, 1929) and Harold F. Gosnell, *Machine Politics, Chicago Model* (Chicago, 1937; best ed., Chicago, 1968). Bruce Grant, *Fight for a City: The Story of the Union League Club of Chicago and Its Times, 1880–1955* (Chicago, 1955) is an uncritical commemorative history, but it, along with the accumulation of reformers' papers, books, and articles, helped to launch a string of theses and dissertations on municipal reform. Sidney I. Roberts, "Businessmen in Revolt: Chicago, 1874–1900" (Ph.D. diss., Northwestern Univ., 1960) was the first, followed by Joan S. Miller, "The Politics of Municipal Reform in Chicago during the Progressive Era: The Municipal Voters' League as a Test Case, 1896–1920" (M.A. thesis, Roosevelt Univ., 1966), a short but influential work.

Robert L. Woodbury, "William Kent, Progressive Gadfly, 1864–1928" (Ph.D. diss., Yale Univ., 1967) enjoyed the benefit of Kent's papers at Yale. Nick Alexander Komons, "Chicago, 1893–1907: The Politics of Reform" (Ph.D. diss., George Washington Univ., 1961) is thin, while Richard Edward Becker, "Edward Dunne, Reform Mayor of Chicago, 1905–1907" (Ph.D. diss., Univ. of Chicago, 1971) focuses on the city's only reform mayor in the Progressive era. The literature generally followed two scholarly models, holding either that monied interests wanted government to operate with businesslike efficiency or that some reformers were primarily committed to "structural reform" of governmental apparatus, while others focused on the "social reform" needs of the poor and exploited.

During the 1970s, another framework began to appear, one that emphasized the ethnic dimension to Chicago politicians and reformers. John M. Allswang, *A House for All Peoples: Ethnic Politics in Chicago, 1890–1936* (Lexington, Ky., 1971) provided a statistical overview, while Joel Arthur Tarr, *A Study in Boss Politics: William Lorimer of Chicago* (Urbana, 1971) focused on ethnocultural factors in what is, so far, the best account of a ward boss. Paul Michael Green, "The Chicago Democratic Party, 1840–1920: From Factionalism to Political Organization" (Ph.D. diss., Univ. of Chicago, 1975) deals heavily with Irish ethnicity, while Edward Herbert Mazur, "Minyans for a Prairie City: The Politics of Chicago Jewry, 1850–1940" (Ph.D. diss., Univ. of Chicago, 1974) and Edward R. Kantowicz, *Polish-American Politics in Chicago, 1888–1940* (Chicago, 1975) are exemplary studies. Maureen A. Flanagan, *Charter Reform in Chicago* (Carbondale, 1987) also treats ethnic politics, but the most influential study has been John D. Buenker, *Urban Liberalism and Progressive Reform* (New York, 1973), which demonstrates that most ethnic politicians were by no means machine hacks but rather contributed to urban reform movements.

The rise of ethnic political studies is only one dimension to the growing interest among academic historians in Chicago's foreign-born communities, and here, too, the groundwork was established by people outside of the field. Filiopietistic works—seldom analytical, documented, or critical—dominated this area for years. Hyman L. Meites, ed., *History of the Jews of Chicago* (Chicago, 1924) was typical of a tradition that continues with such works as David Fainhauz, *Lithuanians in Multi-Ethnic Chicago until World War II* (Chicago, 1977). During the 1920s and 1930s, however, graduate students at the University of Chicago began to investigate ethnic groups. The influence of Bessie Louise Pierce in legitimizing academic attention to Chicago's history and the interest in the university's sociology department in ethnicity and neighborhood life inspired these studies of Chicago's foreign-born. The massive compilation of foreign language press translations under the Works Progress Administration gave scholars lacking language skills the ability to research ethnic topics. The result was a seemingly endless number of studies from the Midway, beginning with Jakub Horak, "Assimilation of Czechs in Chicago" (Ph.D. diss., 1920). There soon followed Tin-Chiu Fan, *Chinese Residents in Chicago* (San Francisco, 1974, from M.A. thesis, 1926); Anita Edgar Jones, *Conditions Surrounding Mexicans in Chicago* (San Francisco, 1971, from M.A. thesis, 1928); Ruth Margaret Piper, "The Irish in Chicago, 1848 to 1871" (M.A. thesis, 1936); Gustav Elwood Johnson, "The Swedes in Chicago" (Ph.D. diss., 1940); and Eugene McCarthy, "The Bohemians in Chicago and Their Benevolent Societies, 1875–1946" (M.A. thesis, 1950). Andrew Jacke Townsend, *The Germans of Chicago* (Chicago, 1932) also began as a Chicago dissertation. By today's standards, these works are not very interpretive or comparative. They compartmentalized each group into social, economic, political, religious, and cultural chapters and treated the subjects in isolation. Surprisingly little from this Chicago School, in fact, dealt with comparative ethnicity other than Paul Frederick Creesey, "Population Succession in Chicago, 1898–1930," *American Journal of Sociology*, 44 (July 1938), which merely traced the outward movement of different groups.

Scholarly writing about Chicago ethnics produced since 1950 has tended to be more interpretive and to treat narrower subjects in greater detail. The story of Italo-Americans has been the center of a debate: Rudolph J. Vecoli, "Chicago's Italians Prior to World War I: A Study of Their Social and Economic Adjustment" (Ph.D. diss., Univ. of Wisconsin, 1962) emphasizes the retention of village ways and lack of geographical mobility, while Humbert S. Nelli, *Italians in Chicago, 1880–1930: A Study in Ethnic Mobility* (New York, 1970) stresses the speed of acculturation and dispersal. Andrew Thomas Kopan, "Education and Greek Immigrants in Chicago, 1892–1973: A Study in Ethnic Survival" (Ph.D. diss., Univ. of Chicago, 1974) is broader than its title implies. Louise Año Nuevo Kerr, "The Chicano Experience in Chicago, 1920–1970" (Ph.D. diss., Univ. of Illinois, Chicago, 1976) studies the deep local roots of Mexican-Americans. Michael F. Funchion, *Chicago's Irish Nationalists, 1881–1890* (New York, 1976) demonstrates the impact of international events on local affairs, as does Leslie Vincent Tischauser, "The Burden of Ethnicity: The German Question in Chicago, 1914–1941" (Ph.D. diss., Univ. of Illinois, Chicago, 1981). Much of Hartmut Keil and John B. Jentz, eds., *German Workers in Industrial Chicago, 1850–1910: A Comparative Perspective* (DeKalb, 1983) and Keil, ed., *German Workers' Culture in the United States, 1850 to 1920* (Washington, D.C., 1988) grew out of an innovative German-sponsored research project. Keil and Jentz also edited *German Workers in Chicago: A Documentary History of Working-Class Culture from 1850 to World War I* (Urbana, 1988).

Recent studies of ethnic Chicago have tended to emphasize cultural pluralism rather than the melting pot, quite unlike the University of Chicago studies, 1920–50, which stressed assimilation, perhaps as a reaction to the immigration exclusion controversies and wartime patriotism. Contemporary scholars feel less need to justify their work in that manner. It is also clear that the two largest groups still lack comprehensive surveys of their history. Rudolf A. Hofmeister, *The Germans of Chicago* (Champaign, 1976) adds little to the old Townsend work, while Lawrence J. McCaffrey et al., *The Irish in Chicago* (Urbana, 1987) omits many topics. Finally, Chicago still lacks an interpretation of where all of the ethnic groups fit into the city's history. Robert E. T. Roberts, "Ethnic Groups," in Walter Kloetzli, ed., *Chicago Lutheran Planning Study*, 1 (3 vols., Chicago, 1965), is brief but useful. Melvin G. Holli and Peter d'A. Jones, eds., *Ethnic Chicago* (revised ed., Grand Rapids, 1984) is a combination of Jones and Holli, eds., *Ethnic Chicago* (Grand Rapids, 1981) and the six chapters on Chicago in their earlier collection, *The Ethnic Frontier*. The most recent book includes essays on Irish, Jewish, Greek, Ukrainian, Polish, Italian, Mexican, Black, German, and Japanese groups in Chicago, as well as a useful section of ethnic statistics. This work breaks new ground in local ethnic history, but the synthesis is still missing. Studies of the religious history of Chicago, which have paralleled the literature on ethnic groups, are reviewed in the next chapter, which also treats the educational history of the city.

The writings on black Chicago have followed a different pattern from that of the foreign-born communities. The filiopietistic literature was small, including Frederic H. Robb, ed., *The Negro in Chicago* . . . (2 vols., Chicago, 1927–29), and many of the later works have focused on the 1919 riot. That cataclysmic event was the reason for the lengthy report of the Chicago Commission on Race Relations, *The Negro in Chicago: A Study of Race Relations and a Race Riot* (Chicago, 1922), and it inspired one of the best books on black Chicago, William M. Tuttle, Jr., *Race Riot: Chicago in the Red Summer of 1919* (New York, 1970). It is the ending point for another excellent study, Allan H. Spear, *Black Chicago: The Making of a Negro Ghetto, 1890–1920* (Chicago, 1967), and a central event in the classic by St. Clair Drake and Horace R. Cayton, *Black Metropolis: A Study of Negro Life in a Northern City* (New York, 1945; enlarged ed., 2 vols., New York, 1962). Besides several sociological studies during the 1930s, the most notable being E[dward] Franklin Frazier, *The Negro Family in Chicago* (Chicago, 1932), the other large body of work has focused on black politics. Harold F. Gosnell, *Negro Politicians: The Rise of Negro Politics in Chicago* (Chicago, 1935) was motivated in part by the switch of black party allegiance from the Republicans to the Democrats. Perry R. Duis, "Arthur W. Mitchell, New Deal Negro in Congress" (M.A. thesis, Univ. of Chicago, 1966) studies a key figure in that transformation, while Charles Russel Branham, "The Transformation of Black Political Leadership in Chicago, 1864–1942" (Ph.D. diss., Univ. of Chicago, 1981) is a detailed survey of the subject. The literature is enriched by James R. Grossman, *Land of Hope: Chicago, Black Southerners, and the Great Migration* (Chicago, 1989).

While few Chicagoans can be proud of the city's treatment of racial and ethnic minorities, they can be pleased with its creative achievements. Literature, art, architecture, and music are covered later in this volume, but certain studies, so often neglected, deserve mention here. There is no generalized synthesis on Chicago culture, although Helen Lefkowitz Horowitz, *Culture and the City: Cultural Philanthropy in Chicago from the 1880s to 1917* (Lexington, Ky., 1976) builds a persuasive interpretation around the idea that the arts were central to the uplift of the poor. Perry Duis, *Chicago: Creating New Traditions* (Chicago,

1976) shows how innovation in several areas of economic, social, and cultural life were interconnected and often spurred by the profit motive. The same author's study, " 'Where Is Athens Now?' . . . " and " 'All Else Passes—Art Alone Endures' . . . ," *Chicago History*, 6 (Summer 1977) and 7 (Spring 1978), discusses the Fine Arts Building as an artistic center between 1898 and 1930.

Much of the literature on creative Chicago is compartmentalized and narrow. For example, there is no synthesis of theater history, but two doctoral dissertations at the University of Illinois, Jay Ferris Ludwig, "McVicker's Theatre, 1857–1896" (1958) and Bernard Frank Dukore, "Maurice Brown and the Chicago Little Theatre" (1957), are excellent. Other works are confined to major organizations. Paul M. Angle, *The Chicago Historical Society, 1856–1956: An Unconventional Chronicle* (Chicago, 1956) should have been more conventional and informative. Also of note are Gwladys Spencer, *The Chicago Public Library: Origins and Backgrounds* (Chicago, 1943) and Herman Kogan, *A Continuing Marvel: The Story of the Museum of Science and Industry* (Garden City, N.Y., 1973).

Chicago's cultural activities and institutions have provided important ties and bindings in a city composed of a patchwork of ethnic groups, neighborhoods, and economic interests. This subject is only one of several in which the reader senses in twentieth-century Chicago a tense balance between unifying and disintegrating forces of urban life. Other examples come from the history of transportation and utilities. Besides the voluminous popular literature for buffs, Chicagoans are blessed with several excellent scholarly studies on the impact of transportation. Robert David Weber, "Rationalizers and Reformers: Chicago Local Transportation in the Nineteenth Century" (Ph.D. diss., Univ. of Wisconsin, Madison, 1971) details riders' complaints and corporate machinations. Sidney I. Roberts, "Portrait of a Robber Baron: Charles T. Yerkes," *Business History Review*, 35 (Autumn 1961), portrays the transit mogul as someone so widely hated that he unified the city. By contrast, Homer Charles Harlan, "Charles Tyson Yerkes and the Chicago Transportation System" (Ph.D. diss., Univ. of Chicago, 1975) is more charitable. All three works note the way in which transit dispersed the city, as does James Leslie Davis, *The Elevated System and the Growth of Northern Chicago*, Northwestern University Studies in Geography, 10 (Evanston, 1965). Paul Barrett, *The Automobile and Urban Transit: The Formation of Public Policy in Chicago, 1900–1930* (Philadelphia, 1983) not only explains why the car displaced public transportation but also outlines the neighborhood-Loop economic tensions that underlay the transition. Finally, Forrest McDonald, *Insull* (Chicago, 1962) glorifies the career of the object of another Chicago love/hate relationship. Insull's electric lines knitted together the city, as did his support of opera, but his true importance may be in his role as one of a threesome of characters symbolic of Chicago in the 1920s.

The other central figures were Al Capone and Mayor William Hale "Big Bill" Thompson. The public's fascination with gangsters is an underlying theme in John Kobler, *Capone: The Life and World of Al Capone* (New York, 1971), an excellent biography, and in Fred D. Pasley, *Al Capone: The Biography of a Self-Made Man* (Garden City, N.Y., 1930), the title of which reflects its view of "Big Al" as part of the business ethos of the decade. John Landesco, *Organized Crime in Chicago* (Chicago, 1968) reprints Part 3 of *The Illinois Crime Survey* (Chicago, 1929) and worries about the public's insatiable interest in the mob life-style.

Chicago's colorful leader from 1915 to 1923 and from 1927 to 1931 is important not only for the attention his antics drew to himself but also because the city's mayors in this century have tended to be stronger personalities with much more power than their nineteenth-century counterparts. The pre-Daley mayoral literature is spotty but improving. Lloyd Wendt and Herman Kogan, *Big Bill of Chicago* (Indianapolis, 1953) is still the best general account, while Douglas Bukowski, "According to Image: William Hale Thompson and the Politics of Chicago, 1915–1931" (Ph.D. diss., Univ. of Illinois, Chicago, 1989) is a refreshing reinterpretation. John R. Schmidt, *"The Man Who Cleaned Up Chicago": A Political Biography of William E. Dever* (DeKalb, 1989) discusses the unfortunate man who served as mayor between Thompson's second and third terms.

Thompson's demagoguery drew support to his political campaigns, but it also helped to divide the city, which was already fracturing in several ways. The work of the University of Chicago sociologists, some of which has been mentioned, emphasized social dysfunction, deviance, and, most importantly, the mapping of social divisions. Robert E. L. Faris, *Chicago Sociology, 1920–1932* (San Francisco, 1967) makes this point. Daniel J. Prosser, "Chicago and the Bungalow Boom of the 1920s," *Chicago History*, 10 (Summer 1981), explains the lure of small homes on the fringe, while Celia Hilliard, " 'Rent Reasonable to Right Parties': Gold Coast Apartment Buildings, 1906–1929," ibid., 8 (Summer 1979), notes class distinctions in apartment living. Lizabeth Cohen, "Encountering Mass Culture at the Grassroots: The Experience of Chicago Workers in the 1920s," *American Quarterly*, 41 (Mar. 1989), provides an index to the ethnic and racial diversity of the period.

The press and radio provide another example of the tension of unity and division. The question is as old as the city but has been intensified in this century. Newspapers have frequently been outward projections of their owners' personalities. Charles H. Dennis, *Victor Lawson: His Time and His Work* (Chicago, 1935) examines the dominant personality of the early *Chicago Daily News*, a bastion of quality journalism. John Tebbel, *An American Dynasty: The Story of the McCormicks, Medills, and Pattersons* (Garden City, N.Y., 1947) chronicles the *Chicago Tribune*'s leading family, but there is still no worthy biography of Col. Robert R. McCormick, largely because his papers are not yet available.

The principal citywide newspapers have been dying, and their replacements reflect specialization of interests and division. Morris Janowitz, *The Community Press in an Urban Setting* (Glencoe, Ill., 1952) provides a sociologist's view of the neighborhood and ethnic press. Roi Ottley, *The Lonely Warrior: The Life and Times of Robert S. Abbott* (Chicago, 1955) tells the story of the founder of the *Chicago Defender*. The development of broadcasting's increasingly focused programming toward specific demographic and geographical groups can be traced to the early days of that medium. Bruce A. Linton, "A History of Chicago Radio Station Programming, 1921–1931, with Emphasis on Stations WMAQ and WGN" (Ph.D. diss., Northwestern Univ., 1953) demonstrates this, as does Joel Barry Sternberg, "A Descriptive History and Critical Analysis of the Chicago School of Television: Chicago Network Programming in the Chicago Style from 1948 to 1954" (Ph.D. diss., Northwestern Univ., 1973), a huge, encyclopedic work.

Even though Chicago has suffered through decades of mediocre teams, sports still constitute a major social adhesive in a city of disunity. Most of the team histories are little better than their subjects. Autobiographies are much more successful, beginning with Adrian C. ["Cap"] Anson, *A Ball Player's Career* . . . (Chicago, 1900) and including *Veeck—as in Wreck: The Autobiography of Bill Veeck* (Chicago, 1962) and *Halas by Halas: The Autobiography of George Halas* (New York, 1979). Amos Alonzo Stagg, *Touchdown!* (New York, 1927) is an excellent introduction to the history of college football, but happily there is as well Robin Lester, "The Rise, Decline, and Fall of Intercollegiate Football at the University of Chicago, 1890–1940" (Ph.D. diss., Univ. of Chicago, 1974). Steven A. Riess, *Touching Base: Professional Baseball and American Culture in the Progressive Era* (Westport, Conn., 1980) and his *City Games: The Evolution of American Urban Society and the Rise of Sports* (Urbana, 1989) are major studies, with many pages on Chicago.

The years between the Great Crash and 1945 also illustrate the tension between harmony and disunity in Chicago. Social work during the Depression is well documented by *Social Service Review*, edited at the University of Chicago, and by other studies originating there, but historians have not yet given the period much attention or formulated a synthesis of the literature. Ann Banks, ed., *First-Person America* (New York, 1980) and [Louis] Studs Terkel, *Hard Times: An Oral History of the Great Depression* (New York, 1970) include Chicago interviews. Penny Joan Lipkin, "Payless Paydays: Financial Crisis of the Chicago Board of Education, 1930–1934" (M.A. thesis, Columbia Univ., 1967) is an excellent piece on one aspect of the suffering, while Saul D. Alinsky, *Reveille for Radicals* (Chicago, 1946) demonstrates how his ideas of community organization grew out of the 1930s. August Meier and Elliott M. Rudwick, "Negro Protest at the Chicago World's Fair, 1933–1934," *Journal of the Illinois State Historical Society*, 59 (Summer 1966), reveals how even a unifying event such as an exposition can create disunity. Lenox R. Lohr, *Fair Management: The Story of A Century of Progress Exposition* . . . (Chicago, 1952) is the best account of the fair in general, while Folke Tyko Kihlstedt, "Formal and Structural Innovations in American Exposition Architecture, 1901–1939" (Ph.D. diss., Northwestern Univ., 1973) puts its innovative design into a larger context.

The Depression era also provided labor historians with spectacular events about which to write. Donald G. Sofchalk, "The Chicago Memorial Day Incident: An Episode in Mass Action," *Labor History*, 6 (Winter 1965), is a solid and detailed account. Barbara Warne Newell, *Chicago and the Labor Movement: Metropolitan Unionism in the 1930's* (Urbana, 1961) is a portrait of union bureaucracy rather than the work place. William H. Harris, *Keeping the Faith: A. Philip Randolph, Milton P. Webster, and the Brotherhood of Sleeping Car Porters, 1925–37* (Urbana, 1977) strikes an ideal balance between detail and readability.

The political ramifications of the Depression extend to the present in the form of the Cook County Democratic Organization, and the scholarly literature on a half century of machine rule is amazingly good. Besides the studies of black politics already mentioned, Alex Gottfried, *Boss Cermak of Chicago: A Study of Political Leadership* (Seattle, 1962) provides a political scientist's view of the organization's founder. Gene DeLon Jones, "The Local Political Significance of New Deal Relief Legislation in Chicago, 1933–1940" (Ph.D. diss., Northwestern Univ., 1970) indicates how federal relief projects strengthened the machine in Chicago while killing political organizations elsewhere. [William] Roger Biles, *Big City Boss in Depression and War . . .* (DeKalb, 1984) is the first full biography of Mayor Edward J. Kelly, 1933–47, while Peter Joseph O'Malley, "Mayor Martin H. Kennelly of Chicago: A Political Biography" (Ph.D. diss., Univ. of Illinois, Chicago, 1980) chronicles Kelly's successor until 1955. Thus, with no small irony, the social disorganization of the Depression spawned one of history's most sophisticated political organizations. There are a number of political references in Mary Watters, *Illinois in the Second World War . . .* (2 vols., Springfield, 1951–52), which is a superb narrative of Chicago as well as Downstate during the war.

The unity/division theme also underlies the literature on two final stops in this bibliographical odyssey. One concerns Mayor Richard J. Daley and the survival of the machine. Edward C. Banfield, *Political Influence* (New York, 1961); Peter H. Rossi and Robert A. Dentler, *The Politics of Urban Renewal: The Chicago Findings* (New York, 1961); and Martin Meyerson and Edward C. Banfield, *Politics, Planning, and the Public Interest: The Case of Public Housing in Chicago* (Glencoe, Ill., 1955) are all studies in political science that have since become valuable historical portraits of power during the 1950s.

The Daley literature of the following years was dominated by Mike Royko's critical biography, *Boss: Richard J. Daley of Chicago* (New York, 1971), and Bill Gleason's defensive *Daley of Chicago: The Man, the Mayor, and the Limits of Conventional Politics* (New York, 1970). Len O'Connor's two books, *Clout: Mayor Daley and His City* (Chicago, 1970) and *Requiem: The Decline and Demise of Mayor Daley and His Era* (Chicago, 1977), are clumsily written but filled with insight. Milton L. Rakove's two books, *Don't Make No Waves, Don't Back No Losers: An Insider's Analysis of the Daley Machine* (Bloomington, Ind., 1975) and *We Don't Want Nobody Nobody Sent: An Oral History of the Daley*

*Years* (Bloomington, Ind., 1979), credit the machine with being more pragmatic and multi-ethnic than it was.

Some of the more recent studies of blacks in Chicago have related to city politics. Alan B. Anderson and George W. Pickering, *Confronting the Color Line: The Broken Promise of the Civil Rights Movement in Chicago* (Athens, Ga., 1986) provides copious detail but few generalizations about the confrontations between Mayor Daley and Martin Luther King, Jr. Dianne M. Pinderhughes, *Race and Ethnicity in Chicago Politics: A Reexamination of Pluralist Theory* (Urbana, 1987) is a political scientist's dissection of the subject. The literature on Mayor Daley's successors is dominated by Harold Washington and includes not only the early analysis by Paul Kleppner, *Chicago Divided: The Making of a Black Mayor* (DeKalb, 1985) but also such contrasting assessments as Melvin G. Holli and Paul M. Green, *Bashing Chicago Traditions: Harold Washington's Last Campaign, Chicago, 1987* (Grand Rapids, 1989) and Dempsey J. Travis, *"Harold," the People's Mayor: An Authorized Biography of Mayor Harold Washington* (Chicago, 1989).

The last major question is that of race, which has become the most important division in Chicago society during the last several decades. Housing has been the root determinant of many other aspects of segregation. Thomas Lee Philpott, *The Slum and the Ghetto: Neighborhood Deterioration and Middle-Class Reform; Chicago, 1880–1930* (New York, 1978) is a passionate denunciation of reformers, while Arnold R. Hirsch, *Making the Second Ghetto: Race and Housing in Chicago, 1940–1960* (New York, 1983) is an excellent portrait of the relationship between urban renewal and segregation. A seldom-cited book, Brian J. L. Berry, *The Open Housing Question: Race and Housing in Chicago, 1966–1976* (Cambridge, Mass., 1979), chronicles the issue through the end of Mayor Daley's years. Another excellent study, Devereaux Bowly, Jr., *The Poorhouse: Subsidized Housing in Chicago, 1895–1976* (Carbondale, 1978), shows the ideological links between modern public housing and its private philanthropic predecessors. Gregory D. Squires et al., *Chicago: Race, Class, and the Response to Urban Decline* (Philadelphia, 1987) summarizes the problems of a segregated society.

Chicago history has served many masters since Joseph Balestier rose to deliver his oration. It has functioned as a rallying point for early settlers, as a way to assure old-timers that they would not be forgotten, as a source of security in the "burnt city" of 1871, and as a bulwark of identity in a multi-ethnic and multi-racial metropolis. It made money for the authors of "mugbooks." It provided background for academic sociologists and pleasureful popular reading for the multitudes. And, more recently, it has become the focus of scholars, who have examined and interpreted it in small segments.

# 11

# RELIGION AND EDUCATION

RICHARD S. TAYLOR

COMPREHENSIVE HISTORIES OF religion and education in Illinois have yet to appear. Neither university-trained scholars nor non-academic historians have attempted a synthesis of the widely divergent beliefs, practices, and traditions embraced by Illinoisans in either field. Most authors have cultivated instead their particular interests, producing an enormous number of "house histories," admiring biographies, and other celebratory accounts. Scholars more concerned with larger patterns of historical change have likewise eschewed state history, choosing rather to analyze specific institutions, individuals, or locales, most often Chicago. Their case study approach, while less ostensibly colored by piety or pedagogical special pleading, has tended to distort in its zeal for typicality and generalization. The overall result is a vast, badly fragmented, and highly partisan literature well beyond the scope of this essay. Yet by focusing on the larger picture, it still is possible to discern some of the ever-shifting patterns of religious and educational diversity that have shaped Illinois history.

An understanding of those patterns has been, above all, distorted by enduring institutions. Successful churches and schools sponsor histories and preserve the manuscript collections that influence the research interests of otherwise independent scholars, while less enduring institutions and ideals often vanish, leaving barely a trace. The Indians who once occupied Illinois, for example, left little evidence with which to reconstruct their spiritual lives or educational practices. No attempt has been made to replace Clarence Walworth Alvord's badly dated and ethnocentric synthesis, *The Illinois Country, 1673–1818* (Springfield, 1920), which characteristically dismisses the spiritual life of the Illinois Indians as "in a state lower than that of the Homeric Greeks" (p. 47). An introduction to what little may be surmised about Indian religion and education from archaeological evidence is available in the Smithsonian Institution's *Handbook of North American Indians*, specifically Volume 15, Bruce G. Trigger, ed., *Northeast* (Washington, D.C., 1978), and useful though obviously biased accounts may be found in Reuben Gold Thwaites, ed., *The Jesuit Relations and Allied Documents* . . . (73 vols., Cleveland, 1896–1901), which should be used in tandem with Joseph P. Donnelly, *Thwaites' Jesuit Relations: Errata and Addenda* (Chicago, 1967).

Roman Catholicism was the first European religious tradition transplanted to Illinois. Arriving with missionary priests in the late seventeenth century, Catholicism became a ubiquitous presence in the lives of the early French settlers. Charles Edwards O'Neill, *Church and State in French Colonial Louisiana: Policy and Politics to 1732* (New Haven, 1966) provides context by describing the French monarchy's religious policies in its Mississippi Valley colony. Thwaites' *Jesuit Relations* is a rich source for the missionary order that predominated in Illinois, but see also Sister Mary Borgias Palm's mission-by-mission chronicle, *The Jesuit Missions of the Illinois Country, 1673–1763* (Cleveland, 1933). Gilbert J. Garraghan surveys early Chicago-area missions in the first chapters of *The Catholic Church in Chicago, 1763–1871: An Historical Sketch* (Chicago, 1921). These last two volumes exemplify a genre of Illinois Catholic church history that emerged in the 1920s and 1930s as university-trained priests and nuns reacted to the romantic piety of earlier studies by producing carefully researched works of self-conscious scholarship. Their histories, while only lightly tinged with spiritual chauvinism, are generally narrow in scope and devoid of interpretive design. Other works written in the same spirit include Thomas Francis Cleary, "The History of the Catholic Church in Illinois from 1763 to 1844" (Ph.D. diss., Univ. of Illinois, 1932) and Fintan Glenn Walker, *The Catholic Church in the Meeting of Two Frontiers: The Southern Illinois Country, 1763–1793* (Washington, D.C., 1935).

Studies of individual missionary priests abound, particularly in the pages of the *Illinois Catholic Historical Review*, a rich but filiopietistic publication, begun in 1918 and renamed *Mid-America* in 1929. Before 1936, when this quarterly came under the auspices of Loyola University's Institute of Jesuit History, its articles drew heavily on Thwaites' *Jesuit Relations* and two nineteenth-century classics, John Gilmary Shea, *Discovery and Exploration of the Mississippi River* . . . (Redfield, N.Y., 1852) and Francis Parkman, *The Discovery of the Great West* (Boston, 1869; later eds., *La Salle and the Discovery of the Great West*). See also J. B. Culemans, "Catholic Explorers and Pioneers of Illinois," *Catholic Historical Review*, 4 (July 1918).

No missionary priest has received more attention than has Jacques Marquette, a Jesuit, whose exploits have generated a controversial literature animated by a lively competition between religious orders. Reuben Gold Thwaites, *Father Marquette* (New York, 1902) is still regarded by some Catholic scholars as the best biography, but in the late 1920s Francis Borgia Steck, a Franciscan, touched off a multifaceted debate when he argued in *The Jolliet-Marquette Expedition, 1673* (Washington, D.C., 1927) that Marquette neither discovered the Mississippi nor wrote the narrative traditionally attributed to him. The ensuing controversy is nicely summarized in Joseph P. Donnelly's sentimental *Jacques Marquette, S. J., 1637–1675* (Chicago, 1968) and Raphael N. Hamilton's scholarly *Marquette's Explorations: The Narratives Reexamined* (Madison, 1970), two defenses of the missionary by modern Jesuits.

Marion A. Habig, a Franciscan scholar, argues that historians preoccupied with the Jesuits have either neglected or misrepresented members of his order. See *The Franciscan Père Marquette: A Critical Biography of Father Zénobe Membré, O.F.M., La Salle's Chaplain and Missionary Companion . . .* (New York, 1934). Accounts of La Salle's explorations published by another Franciscan, Louis Hennepin, have long been regarded as plagiarized. Jean Delanglez, a Jesuit, reviews the historiography and evaluates the evidence in *Hennepin's Description of Louisiana: A Critical Essay* (Chicago, 1941). A final biography worth noting is Joseph P. Donnelly, *Pierre Gibault, Missionary, 1737–1802* (Chicago, 1971).

Catholicism's preeminent role in the lives of French villagers in early Illinois is abundantly clear in most of the publications cited in the first chapter of this book. For the history of one particularly important parish, established by priests from Quebec's Seminary of Foreign Missions, see Joseph P. Donnelly, ed., "The Founding of the Holy Family Mission and Its History in the Eighteenth Century: Documents," in John Francis McDermott, ed., *Old Cahokia: A Narrative and Documents Illustrating the First Century of Its History* (St. Louis, 1949), and Donnelly, *The Parish of the Holy Family, Cahokia, Illinois, 1699–1949* (Belleville, Ill., 1949). Evidence of a mid-eighteenth-century chapel built on an artificial earthen Indian mound near Cahokia is presented in John A. Walthall and Elizabeth D. Benchley, *The River L'Abbe Mission: A French Colonial Church for the Cahokia Illini on Monks Mound* (Springfield, 1987). The Trappist community that lived at this location from 1809 to 1813 is discussed in Raymond H. Hammes, ed., "The Cantine Mounds of Southern Illinois . . . ," *Journal of the Illinois State Historical Society*, 74 (Summer 1981), and in Gilbert J. Garraghan, "The Trappists of Monks Mound," *Records of the American Catholic Historical Society*, 36 (Mar. 1925), reprinted in Garraghan, *Chapters in Frontier History: Research Studies in the Making of the West* (Milwaukee, 1934).

Educational developments in French Illinois remain largely terra incognita despite scattered references to Catholic mission schools in writings on the colonial period. As a rule, accounts of education in Illinois begin with the appearance of the first American schools in the 1780s, an approach that originated with professional schoolmen who wrote the state's first educational histories. See, for example, Samuel Willard, "Brief History of Early Education in Illinois,"

*Fifteenth Biennial Report of the Superintendent of Public Instruction of the State of Illinois, July 1, 1882–June 30, 1884* (Springfield, 1884). William L. Pillsbury contributed similar articles, "Sketch of the Permanent Public School Funds of Illinois" and "Early Education in Illinois," to the fourteenth and sixteenth biennial reports. Willard and Pillsbury compiled facts and chronicled events with little conscious attention to synthesis and interpretation. Yet their emerging sense of professional identity led them to present the educational history of Illinois as the story of the rise and triumph of the state's public school system. This perspective also informs John Williston Cook, *Educational History of Illinois: Growth and Progress in Educational Affairs of the State . . .* (Chicago, 1912), an encyclopedic collection of institutional sketches and individual biographies. For Cook's career at Illinois State Normal University and Northern Illinois State Normal School, see Charles L. Sears, "The Educational Influence of John Williston Cook" (Ed.D. diss., Northern Illinois Univ., 1978).

Paul E. Belting, *The Development of the Free Public High School in Illinois to 1860* (Springfield, 1919) marked an important transition in the historiography of Illinois education. Completed as a doctoral dissertation in the famous Columbia University Teachers College history of education program, Belting's work, which covers the whole history of antebellum education in Illinois despite its title, was the first of many studies produced by professional educators with graduate training in history. Although Belting departed from his predecessors by synthesizing his story within the larger framework of Illinois history and by probing beneath the surface for causes, his interpretation simply made explicit assumptions left unstated in older studies. Thus, he argued that the state's public school system was the work of forward-looking reformers—pious New Englanders and Jeffersonian southerners—who overcame opposition from unenlightened southern obstructionists.

Most subsequent studies of antebellum education in Illinois have followed Belting's celebratory lead. Examples include John Donald Pulliam, "A History of the Struggle for a Free Common School System in Illinois from 1818 to the Civil War" (Ed.D. diss., Univ. of Illinois, 1965); W. G. Walker, "The Development of the Free Public High School in Illinois during the Nineteenth Century," *History of Education Quarterly*, 4 (Dec. 1964); Robert Gehlmann Bone, "Education in Illinois before 1857," *Journal of the Illinois State Historical Society*, 50 (Summer 1957); Charles E. Peterson, Jr., "The *Common School Advocate*: Molder of the Public Mind," ibid., 57 (Autumn 1964); and James E. Herget, "Democracy Revisited: The Law and School Districts in Illinois," ibid., 72 (May 1979).

Historians preoccupied with public schooling as a democratic success story have left uncharted vast areas of the antebellum educational landscape. The suggestive essays in Paul H. Mattingly and Edward W. Stevens, Jr., eds., " *. . . Schools and the Means of Education Shall Forever Be Encouraged"*: *A History of Education in the Old Northwest, 1787–1880* (Athens, Ohio, 1987) point to the educational diversity and conflicts over schooling described on a local level by Thomas O. Jewett, "The Early History of Belleville Public Schools, 1679–1917" (Ph.D. diss., St. Louis Univ., 1985). Little is known of the era's intriguing mélange of tiny local private, quasi-public, and public schools staffed by a floating population of teachers, especially women. For one example, see Jack Nortrup, "The Troubles of an Itinerant Teacher in the Early Nineteenth Century," *Journal of the Illinois State Historical Society*, 71 (Nov. 1978).

The powerful opposition to state-regulated education in Illinois has received little serious attention, but it now seems inappropriate simply to dismiss common school critics as narrow-minded southerners. Resistance to publicly controlled schooling sprang from a wide range of often legitimate concerns. Such "public" education was anything but progressive or democratic to the religious groups described in Daniel W. Kucera's suggestive but sketchy *Church-State Relationships in Education in Illinois*, Catholic University of America, Educational Research Monographs, Vol. 19, No. 1 (Washington, D.C., 1955). Moreover, proponents of public education in Illinois appear somewhat less than enlightened in Donald F. Tingley, "Anti-intellectualism on the Illinois Frontier," in Tingley, ed., *Essays in Illinois History* . . . (Carbondale, 1968).

Although special education in Illinois has its roots in the pre–Civil War period, little is available beyond a few studies of state-supported institutions. Minnie Wait Cleary, "History of the Illinois School for the Deaf," *Journal of the Illinois State Historical Society*, 35 (Dec. 1942), describes the first such school, opened in 1846, while Walter B. Hendrickson, *From Shelter to Self-reliance: A History of the Illinois Braille and Sight Saving School* (Jacksonville, Ill., 1972) documents an institution established in 1849. Lyceums, institutes, and other voluntary associations that educated outside the classroom have been equally neglected, as have museums. Worthwhile exceptions include Hendrickson, "Nineteenth-Century Natural History Organizations in Illinois," *Journal of the Illinois State Historical Society*, 54 (Autumn 1961); Hendrickson and William J. Beecher, "In the Service of Science: The History of the Chicago Academy of Sciences," *Bulletin of the Chicago Academy of Sciences*, Vol. 11, No. 7 (Sept. 1972); and Milton D. Thompson, *The Illinois State Museum: Historical Sketch and Memoirs* (Springfield, 1988).

Higher education was dominated in antebellum Illinois by small church-related colleges. A reluctant legislature incorporated the first private colleges in 1835, and three of the four schools chartered that year survived to sponsor house histories. Charles Henry Rammelkamp's classic, *Illinois College: A Centennial History, 1829–1929* (New Haven, 1928), is by far the best, overshadowing the undocumented sequels by Charles E. Frank, *Pioneer's Progress: Illinois College, 1829–1979* (Carbondale, 1979) and Iver F. Yeager, ed., *Sesquicentennial Papers: Illinois College* (Carbondale, 1982). Also worthwhile is Harold E. Gibson, *Sigma Pi Society of Illinois College, 1843–1971: A History of a Literary Society* (Jacksonville, Ill., 1972). Illinois College was established by missionary-minded Presbyterians and Congregationalists allied with local boosters. Baptist efforts to found and sustain Shurtleff College, which closed in 1956, are described in Austen Kennedy de Blois, *The Pioneer School: A History of Shurtleff College, the Oldest Educational Institution in the West* (Chicago, 1900), while Methodist labors at McKendree are recounted in W. C. Walton, "Centennial History of McKendree College," in Joseph Guandolo, ed., *Centennial: McKendree College, with St. Clair County History* (Lebanon, Ill., 1928). For McKendree's origins as an academy, see Oscar A. Weil, "The Movement to Establish Lebanon Seminary, 1833–1835," *Journal of the Illinois State Historical Society*, 59 (Winter 1966), and for a later period, see William Eaton, " 'Scholarship, Virtue, and Religion': Robert Allyn and McKendree College, 1863–1874," *Illinois Historical Journal*, 78 (Summer 1985).

Knox College, founded by Presbyterians and Congregationalists in 1837, is particularly well served by Earnest Elmo Calkins, *They Broke the Prairie: Being Some Account of the Settlement of the Upper Mississippi Valley by Religious and Educational Pioneers, Told in Terms of One City, Galesburg, and of One College, Knox* (New York, 1937; best ed., Urbana, 1989) and Hermann R. Muelder, *Missionaries and Muckrakers: The First Hundred Years of Knox College* (Urbana, 1984). Two other Presbyterian schools, Blackburn and Lake Forest, were established in 1857. See Thomas Rinaker, "Gideon Blackburn, the Founder of Blackburn University," *Journal of the Illinois State Historical Society*, 17 (Oct. 1924), and the unpublished essays by Eric R. Riedel, based on research at the University of Chicago, on file at the Lake Forest College archives. The story of Monmouth College, sponsored for a time by the Associate Reformed Presbyterian Church, is told in F[rancis] Garvin Davenport, *Monmouth College: The First Hundred Years, 1853–1953* (Cedar Rapids, Iowa, 1953) and William Urban, *A History of Monmouth College through Its Fifth Quarter Century* (Monmouth, Ill., 1979). The Disciples of Christ founded Eureka College in 1855, and Lombard College opened in 1851 as a Universalist school. See Harold Adams, *History of Eureka College* (Eureka, Ill., 1982) and James A. Swanson, *A History of Lombard College, 1851–1930* (Macomb, 1955).

Episcopalian-sponsored Jubilee College opened in 1840. Roma Louise Shively, *Jubilee: A Pioneer College* (Elmwood, Ill., 1935); Percy V. Norwood, "Jubilee College, Illinois," *Historical Magazine of the Protestant Episcopal Church*, 12 (Mar. 1943); and David R. Pichaske, "Jubilee College: Bishop Chase's School of Prophets," *Old Northwest*, 2 (Sept. 1976), are the best of several brief studies. Methodists obtained a charter for Northwestern in 1851 and for Illinois Wesleyan in 1853. See Harold F. Williamson and Payson S. Wild, *Northwestern University: A History, 1850–1975* (Evanston, 1976) and Elmo Scott Watson, *The Illinois Wesleyan Story, 1850–1950* (Bloomington, Ill., 1950). Harry E. Pratt, "Peter Cartwright and the Cause of Education," *Journal of the Illinois State Historical Society*, 28 (Jan. 1936), defends Methodist educational accomplishments in the period against the tendency of historians to exaggerate Presbyterian and Congregationalist contributions.

The only general survey of higher education for women in antebellum Illinois is Clarence P. McClelland, "The Education of Females in Early Illinois," *Journal of the Illinois State Historical Society*, 36 (Dec. 1943), a rambling account. Methodist efforts to establish a woman's college in Jacksonville are detailed in Mary Watters, *The First One Hundred Years of MacMurray College* (Springfield, 1947), a superb study, and in Walter B. Hendrickson, *Forward in the Second Century of MacMurray College: A History of 125 Years* (Jacksonville, Ill., 1972). The story of Monticello College, a Presbyterian-Congregationalist school opened in 1838, is recounted in Griffith A. Hamlin, *Monticello: The Biography of a College* (Fulton, Mo., 1976), a work commissioned by the school's foundation after the college closed in 1971. Rockford Female Seminary, now Rockford College, began under Presbyterian auspices in 1847, and Baptist-oriented Almira College, now Greenville College, dates from 1855. See C. Hal Nelson, ed., *Rockford College: A Retrospective Look* (Rockford, 1980) and Donald C. Jordahl, "John Brown White and Early Women's Education: A History of Almira College," *Journal of the Illinois State Historical Society*, 72 (May 1979). Rockford and Almira both survived in altered form, but most early women's schools simply vanished, as Grace Partridge Smith, "Wayland Female Institute, Alton, 1853–1856," ibid., 38 (Mar. 1945), and Dwight F. Clark, "A Forgotten Evanston Institution: The Northwestern Female College," ibid., 35 (June 1942), show.

Many historians trace the blend of piety and learning found in pre–Civil War colleges to New England precedents. See, for example, Travis Keene Hedrick, Jr., "Julian Monson Sturtevant and the Moral Machinery of Society: The New England Struggle against Pluralism in the Old Northwest, 1829–1877" (Ph.D. diss., Brown Univ., 1974); Daniel T. Johnson, "Financing the Western Colleges, 1844–1862," *Journal of the Illinois State Historical Society*, 65 (Spring 1972); and Richard S. Taylor, "Western Colleges as 'Securities of Intelligence & Virtue': The Towne-Eddy Report of 1846," *Old Northwest*, 7 (Spring 1981). Indeed, religion and education were so closely linked in these colleges that some scholars have depicted them as strictly denominational schools pursuing narrowly sectarian goals in isolation from the mainstream of American life. For influential formulations of this thesis, see Donald G. Tewksbury, *The Founding of American Colleges and Universities before the Civil War* . . . (New York, 1932), which includes data on twelve Illinois schools, and Richard Hofstadter and Walter P. Metzger, *The Development of Academic Freedom in the United States* (New York, 1955), the classic description of religion as a retrogressive influence in higher education before the Civil War.

Denominational considerations seem much less decisive in light of more recent studies. According to David B. Potts, in "American Colleges in the Nineteenth Century: From Localism to Denominationalism," *History of Education Quarterly*, 11 (Winter 1971), the institutions of the period were not isolated and narrowly sectarian but served important local and secular needs. While concurring that antebellum colleges were not primarily denominational, Timothy L. Smith, in "Uncommon Schools: Christian Colleges and Social Idealism in Midwestern America, 1820–1950," *Indiana Historical Society Lectures, 1976–1977: The*

*History of Education in the Middle West* (Indianapolis, 1978), contends that such schools were indigenous expressions of Christian idealism, not simply New England transplants. James Findlay presents a similar picture in "Agency, Denominations, and the Western Colleges, 1830–1860: Some Connections between Evangelicalism and American Higher Education," *Church History*, 50 (Mar. 1981), and " 'Western' Colleges, 1830–1870: Educational Institutions in Transition," *History of Higher Education Annual*, 2 (1982).

The antebellum period in Illinois was, according to some scholars, an era of evangelical Protestant hegemony. A good introduction to this perspective and to the early history of the largest evangelical denominations in the state is provided by William Warren Sweet's series, *Religion on the American Frontier . . . A Collection of Source Material[s]*, the volume titles and dates of which are *The Baptists, 1783–1830*; *The Presbyterians, 1783–1840*; *The Congregationalists, 1783–1850*; and *The Methodists, 1783–1840* (New York and Chicago, 1931–46). Sweet, who spent his most productive years at the Divinity School of the University of Chicago, pioneered in the development of American church history as an academic discipline by striving to emancipate religious history from the narrowly denominational perspectives that had dominated the field. Writing with particular attention to larger spiritual trends and related cultural patterns, he described evangelical Protestantism as a typically American religious style that arose on the midwestern frontier to play a decisive role in the nation's development. James L. Ash, Jr., "American Religion and the Academy in the Early Twentieth Century: The Chicago Years of William Warren Sweet," *Church History*, 50 (Dec. 1981), and Sidney E. Mead, "Prof. Sweet's Religion and Culture in America: A Review Article," ibid., 22 (Mar. 1953), evaluate Sweet's work in its personal and professional contexts.

Sweet's evangelical synthesis is now out of fashion due, in part, to his neglect of such significant frontier religious groups as Lutherans, Catholics, and Universalists. Wesley Norton, *Religious Newspapers in the Old Northwest to 1861: A History, Bibliography, and Record of Opinions* (Athens, Ohio, 1977) suggests something of the stubborn diversity that characterized religious life in frontier Illinois. But scholars appreciative of that diversity have found it far easier to criticize Sweet than to suggest viable alternatives. Peter W. Williams, for example, turns to ethnicity and regionalism in "Religion and the Old Northwest: A Bibliographical Essay," *Old Northwest*, 5 (Spring 1979), while Myron J. Fogde sorts religious groups into two ideal types in "Primitivism and Paternalism: Early Denominational Approaches in Western Illinois," *Western Illinois Regional Studies*, 3 (Fall 1980).

Methodist growth in Illinois before the Civil War exceeded that of all other denominations, and Illinois Methodists possess one of the state's finest denominational histories in J[ohn] Gordon Melton, *Log Cabins to Steeples: The Complete Story of the United Methodist Way in Illinois, including All Constituent Elements of the United Methodist Church* (Nashville, Tenn., 1974), a well-documented and thoughtfully organized work. Melton's study nicely encapsulates Illinois Methodism's particularly rich historiography, which begins with a short shelf of colorful memoirs penned by or about pioneer circuit riders. By far the best known is the *Autobiography of Peter Cartwright, the Backwoods Preacher* (Cincinnati, 1856; modern ed., Nashville, Tenn., 1956). See Robert Bray, "Beating the Devil: Life and Art in Peter Cartwright's *Autobiography*," *Illinois Historical Journal*, 78 (Autumn 1985), for a perceptive analysis. Helen Hardie Grant, *Peter Cartwright, Pioneer* (New York, 1931), the most adequate published biography, relies too heavily on the preacher's own recollections. Theodore Lee Agnew, Jr., "Peter Cartwright and His Times: The First Fifty Years, 1785–1835" (Ph.D. diss., Harvard Univ., 1953) is a scholarly account of the flamboyant circuit rider's early years. Although Peter Akers rivaled Cartwright in his influence on early Illinois Methodism, he left no memoir, and very little is known of him beyond what T. Walter Johnson includes in "Peter Akers, Methodist Circuit Rider and Educator, 1790–1886," *Journal of the Illinois State Historical Society*, 32 (Dec. 1939). Clarence P. McClelland, "William Henry Milburn, Blind Man Eloquent," ibid., 48 (Summer 1955), recounts the career of an Illinois circuit rider and author who became chaplain of Congress.

The first histories of Illinois Methodism were mostly compilations of memoirs, but one early effort to study the subject in its cultural context is John D. Barnhart, Jr., "The Rise of the Methodist Episcopal Church in Illinois from the Beginning to the Year 1832," *Journal of the Illinois State Historical Society*, 12 (July 1919). Far less perceptive are several conference histories, including Joseph Calvin Evers, *The History of the Southern Illinois Conference, the Methodist Church* (Nashville, Tenn., 1964); John Bunyan Robinson, *History of Rock River Conference* (DeLand, Fla., 1908); and Almer M. Pennewell, *The Methodist Movement in Northern Illinois* (Sycamore, Ill., 1942). Methodists founded Garrett Biblical Institute, now Garrett-Evangelical Theological Seminary, in 1853. See Frederick A. Norwood, *Dawn to Midday at Garrett* (Evanston, 1978).

Several small independent churches in the Wesleyan tradition were well represented in antebellum Illinois, and Melton's *Log Cabins to Steeples* includes good brief histories both of the groups that eventually merged with the United Methodist Church and of those that remained independent. For longer accounts of two merging groups, see Lynn W. Turner, "The United Brethren Church in Illinois," in Illinois State Historical Society, *Papers in Illinois History and Transactions for the Year 1939*, and John G. Schwab, *History of the Illinois Conference of the Evangelical Church, 1837–1937* (Harrisburg, Pa., 1937). One still-independent Methodist offshoot with a particularly significant early Illinois history is the Free Methodist Church, a product of the holiness revival of the late 1850s. See Joseph Goodwin Terrill's books, *The St. Charles Camp-Meeting . . .* (Chicago, 1883) and *The Life of Rev. John Wesley Redfield, M.D.* (Chicago, 1890).

Baptists also prospered in pre–Civil War Illinois, ranking second only to Methodists in the state's 1850 religious census. Myron D. Dillow, "A History of Baptists in Illinois, 1786–1845" (Th.D. diss., Southwestern Baptist Theological

Seminary, 1965) provides the best introduction to the topic, despite a sometimes disjointed presentation. Superior, though narrower in scope, is Roger D. Bridges, "Founding the Illinois Baptist Convention, 1830–1834," *American Baptist Quarterly*, 3 (Sept. 1984). Edward P. Brand, *Illinois Baptists: A History* (Bloomington, Ill., 1930) is marred in its discussion of antebellum developments by a preoccupation with twentieth-century issues.

The centerpiece of early Baptist historiography is Rufus Babcock, ed., *Forty Years of Pioneer Life: Memoir of John Mason Peck, D.D.* (Philadelphia, 1864; modern ed., Carbondale, 1965), a selection from the letters and journals of a missionary Baptist preacher who aspired to become the first historian of religion in Illinois. Helen Louise Jennings, "John Mason Peck and the Impact of New England on the Old Northwest" (Ph.D. diss., Univ. of Southern California, 1961) includes a good though incomplete bibliography of numerous articles, sermons, letters, and books written by Peck, while Matthew Lawrence's sometimes inaccurate *John Mason Peck, the Pioneer Missionary* (New York, 1940) is the best of several published biographies. See also John T. Flanagan, ed., "Letters by John Mason Peck," *Journal of the Illinois State Historical Society*, 47 (Autumn 1954), and Roger D. Bridges, ed., "John Mason Peck on Illinois Slavery," ibid., 75 (Autumn 1982).

Many early Baptist histories reflect that group's long-standing commitment to local autonomy. In the late nineteenth century, local pride prompted several regional associations to publish their histories, including W[illiam] P. Throgmorton, *History of Franklin Association of United Baptists* (Benton, Ill., 1880) and Edwin S. Walker, *History of the Springfield Baptist Association . . .* (Springfield, 1881). A more recent example, C[arl] George Ericson, *Harvest on the Prairies: Centennial History of the Baptist Conference of Illinois, 1856–1956* (Chicago, 1956), blends ethnicity with localism in telling the story of Swedish Baptists in northeastern Illinois.

Doctrinal differences spawned several small Baptist denominations in antebellum Illinois. Achilles Coffey, *A Brief History of the Regular Baptists, Principally of Southern Illinois* (Paducah, Ky., 1877) and Robert Louis Webb, *Walk about Zion: A History of the Primitive Baptists of Illinois, 1796–1976* (Burlington, Iowa, 1976) describe two groups with roots in the antimission controversy, while George A. Gordon, *The Life and Labors of Rev. Henry S. Gordon, Founder of the Free Baptist Church in Southern Illinois . . .* (Campbell Hill, Ill., 1901) and J. W. McKinney, *A Brief History of Free Baptists in Southern Illinois* (Johnston City, Ill., 1939) mix local pride with doctrinal considerations in discussing a small Free Will Baptist movement that appeared in Illinois in the 1850s.

An 1801 agreement between eastern Congregationalists and Presbyterians to pool their resources in western missions gave to those denominations a common early history in Illinois. See Edward Marvin Blumenfeld, "The Plan of Union in Illinois" (M.A. thesis, Northwestern Univ., 1961). The Presbyterian-Congregational alliance contributed to the formation in 1826 of the American

Home Missionary Society, which launched an aggressive western campaign. Illinois developments are conspicuous in Frederick Irving Kuhns, "The Operations of the American Home Missionary Society in the Old Northwest, 1826–1861" (Ph.D. thesis, Univ. of Chicago, 1947), several chapters of which constitute "A Glimpse of Home Missionary Activities in the Old Northwest, 1826–1861," in *Journal of the Presbyterian Historical Society*, 27 (June 1949). For one particularly well-known Missionary Society effort, see John Randolph Willis, *God's Frontiersmen: The Yale Band in Illinois* (Washington, D.C., 1979).

Still the best statewide history of mainstream Presbyterianism is A[ugustus] T. Norton, *History of the Presbyterian Church in the State of Illinois* (St. Louis, 1879). Norton incorporates selections from fugitive books, autobiographical articles, memorial booklets, and anniversary sermons that are basic sources for Presbyterianism in Illinois. The denomination's organizational history is traced in William Irvine Blair, *The Presbyterian Synods of Illinois* (Mattoon, 1952). Victor B. Howard, "The Slavery Controversy and a Seminary for the Northwest," *Journal of Presbyterian History*, 43 (Dec. 1965), describes circumstances surrounding the establishment of a Presbyterian seminary in Chicago, while James G. K. McClure, *The Story of the Life and Work of the Presbyterian Theological Seminary, Chicago, Founded by Cyrus H. McCormick* (Chicago, 1929) provides a more general account. Other studies include John Frederick Lyons, *Centennial Sketch of the History of the Presbytery of Chicago* (Chicago, 1947) and two papers by the Illinois Historical Records Survey, Work Projects Administration, *Inventory of the Church Archives of Illinois: Presbyterian Church in the United States of America, Presbytery of Cairo* and . . . *Presbytery of Springfield* (Chicago, 1941–42). Illinois' role in the formation of a small dissenting Presbyterian group is pictured in William L. Fisk, "The Associate Reformed Church in the Old Northwest: A Chapter in the Acculturation of the Immigrant," *Journal of Presbyterian History*, 46 (Sept. 1968).

Congregationalism's Illinois history is well covered in Matthew Spinka, ed., *A History of Illinois Congregational and Christian Churches* (Chicago, 1944), an outstanding collection of essays useful as a guide to older works. Spinka's volume includes a brief sketch of the Illinois State Christian Conference, which merged in 1931 with the Congregationalists. As Samuel Campbell Pearson, Jr., indicates, both in "The Growth of Denominational Self-consciousness among American Congregationalists, 1801–1852" (Ph.D. diss., Univ. of Chicago, 1964) and in "From Church to Denomination: American Congregationalism in the Nineteenth Century," *Church History*, 38 (Mar. 1969), Congregationalists in Illinois as elsewhere came late to an awareness of their unique identity as a denomination. This awareness led in 1855 to the creation of a Congregational (now United Church of Christ) seminary. See Arthur Cushman McGiffert, Jr., *No Ivory Tower: The Story of the Chicago Theological Seminary* (Chicago, 1965). Iver F. Yeager, *Church and College on the Illinois Frontier: The Beginnings of Illinois College and the United Church of Christ in Central Illinois, 1829 to 1867* (Jacksonville, Ill., 1980) is valuable for its chapters on each of the groups that eventually merged with the Congregationalists to form the United Church of Christ. One of those groups, the Evangelical Church Society of the West, is the subject of Carl E. Schneider, *The German Church on the American Frontier: A Study in the Rise of Religion among the Germans of the West* . . . (St. Louis, 1939). Heavily influenced by Sweet's evangelical synthesis, Schneider wrote from an assimilationist perspective now unfashionable among students of immigrant religion, but his richly detailed and scholarly account of the Church Society, a loosely organized association of pastors and laymen centered in the St. Louis–southwestern Illinois area in the mid–nineteenth century, is of enduring value.

Accounts of two small evangelical denominations, both transplanted from Kentucky and Tennessee, that played significant roles on the Illinois frontier may be found in J. B. Logan, *History of the Cumberland Presbyterian Church in Illinois* . . . (Alton, Ill., 1878); Illinois Historical Records Survey, *Inventory of the Church Archives of Illinois: Cumberland Presbyterian Church* (Chicago, 1942); and Nathaniel S. Haynes, *History of the Disciples of Christ in Illinois, 1819–1914* (Cincinnati, 1915).

Although evangelicals appear to have been in the majority, several small but vocal groups of non-evangelicals exerted an influence entirely out of proportion to their numbers. *The New Church and Chicago: A History* (Chicago, 1906), compiled by Rudolph Williams, gives a chronological account of Chicago's first Swedenborgian congregation, while early Unitarianism in Illinois is described in Charles H. Lyttle's scholarly *Freedom Moves West: A History of the Western Unitarian Conference, 1852–1952* (Boston, 1952), which also touches on Universalist developments.

Less vocal were the Brethren, Mennonites, Amish, and Quakers. Links between the German Baptist Brethren and Universalism in Illinois are explored in David B. Eller, "The Pietist Origins of Sectarian Universalism in the Midwest," *Old Northwest*, 12 (Spring 1986). Other works on the Church of the Brethren include John Heckman and J. E. Miller, *Brethren in Northern Illinois and Wisconsin* (Elgin, 1941); Minnie S. Buckingham, ed., *Church of the Brethren in Southern Illinois* . . . (Elgin, 1950); and David B. Eller, "George Wolfe and the 'Far Western' Brethren," *Illinois Historical Journal*, 80 (Summer 1987). Mennonite and Amish developments are fully covered in Harry F. Weber, *Centennial History of the Mennonites of Illinois, 1829–1929* (Goshen, Ind., 1931); Willard H. Smith, *Mennonites in Illinois* (Scottsdale, Pa., 1983); and Clyde Browning, *Amish in Illinois: Over One Hundred Years of the "Old Order" Sect of Central Illinois* (Decatur, 1971). Illinois Friends have received less attention, but see Errol T. Elliott, *Quakers on the American Frontier* . . . (Richmond, Ind., 1969) and Marion Lundy Dobbert and Helen Jean Nelson, *The Friends at Clear Creek, 1830–1930* (DeKalb, 1975).

Episcopalianism's missionary period in Illinois is usually associated with Philander Chase, whose work as first bishop of the Illinois Diocese is briefly described in Francis J. Hall, *A History of the Diocese of Chicago, including a History of the Undivided Diocese of Illinois* . . . (Dixon, Ill., 1902). The second edition of *Bishop Chase's Reminiscences: An Autobiography* . . . (2 vols., Boston, 1848) includes excerpts from Chase's letters and journals that depict Illinois Episcopalianism after he came to the state in 1835, but documents in Percy V. Norwood, "The Primary Convention of the Diocese of Illinois," *Historical Magazine of the Protestant Episcopal Church*, 24 (Sept. 1955), establish that Episcopalian missionary work in Illinois predated Chase's arrival. See also Walter B. Hendrickson, "A Church on the Prairie: The Founding and Early Years of Trinity in Jacksonville, Illinois, 1832–1838," ibid., 44 (Mar. 1975); Nils William Olsson, "Peter Arvedson, Early Swedish Immigrant Episcopalian Missionary in Illinois," *Swedish Pioneer Historical Quarterly*, 27 (Apr. 1976); Paul Elmen, "Unonius and the Swope Affair," ibid.; and Olsson, ed., *A Pioneer in Northwest America, 1841–1858: The Memoirs of Gustaf Unonius* (2 vols., Minneapolis, 1950–60), a source valuable not only for Episcopalianism but also for general religious developments among the state's Swedish immigrants.

Catholicism's fortunes in Illinois faded with France's colonial empire only to reemerge in the antebellum period as a succession of western bishops sent missionary priests to the state's widely scattered congregations. Garraghan's Chicago history and Cleary's Illinois study, already cited, cover those developments, as does Robert Frederick Trisco, *The Holy See and the Nascent Church in the Middle Western United States, 1826–1850* (Rome, 1962). An early but unusually rich account is John Rothensteiner, *History of the Archdiocese of St. Louis in Its Various Stages of Development from A.D. 1673 to A.D. 1928* (2 vols., St. Louis, 1928).

Catholic missions in nineteenth-century Illinois were supplied by religious orders whose histories are chronicled in memoirs, articles, and commemorative books too numerous to mention. But Gilbert J. Garraghan, *The Jesuits of the Middle United States* (3 vols., New York, 1938); Marion A. Habig, *Heralds of the King: The Franciscans of the St. Louis-Chicago Province, 1858–1958* (Chicago, 1958); Louise Callan, *The Society of the Sacred Heart in North America* (New York, 1937); and Sister Thomas Aquinas Winterbauer, *Lest We Forget: The First Hundred Years of the Dominican Sisters, Springfield, Illinois* (Chicago, 1973) stand somewhat above the rest. Such works also contain useful histories of schools and colleges founded and supported by these orders. Garraghan, for example, covers the earliest years of Loyola University of Chicago, while Habig includes brief sketches of Quincy College and of St. Joseph College at Teutopolis, Illinois.

The best available study of anti-Catholicism in antebellum Illinois is still Sister M. Evangeline Thomas, *Nativism in the Old Northwest, 1850–1860* (Washington, D.C., 1936), which argues that the state's Catholics suffered less from prejudice than did their eastern brethren. Her perspective is modified, however, by studies such as Mark Wyman, *Immigrants in the Valley: Irish, Germans, and Americans in the Upper Mississippi Country, 1830–1860* (Chicago,

1984) that suggest the ways in which ethnicity contributed to religious conflicts in the state. One particularly influential Illinois anti-Catholic was Charles P. T. Chiniquy, an ex-priest whose work is described in Caroline B. Brettell, "From Catholics to Presbyterians: French-Canadian Immigrants in Central Illinois," *American Presbyterians: Journal of Presbyterian History*, 63 (Fall 1985).

Another instance of immigrant religiosity, the Swedish utopian community at Bishop Hill, has received far more attention than its tiny size and evanescent history warrant. Paul Elmen, *Wheat Flour Messiah: Eric Jansson of Bishop Hill* (Carbondale, 1976) provides an excellent account of the religious vision that gave birth to that colony. For older studies, see Elmen's citations and two annotated lists by E. Gustav Johnson, "A Selected Bibliography of Bishop Hill Literature" and "Bishop Hill Bibliography: Additional Entries," in *Swedish Pioneer Historical Quarterly*, 15 (July 1964) and 16 (Jan. 1965).

The history of Lutheranism in Illinois is entangled in a maze of shifting and overlapping synodical jurisdictions based largely on competing Old World spiritual and geographical loyalties. These nineteenth-century loyalties gradually yielded in the twentieth century to an intra-Lutheran ecumenism that inspired a series of synodical mergers.

The best account of the state's pioneer Lutheran congregations, established not by German or Swedish immigrants but by North Carolina missionaries, is E. Duane Elbert, "The American Roots of German Lutheranism in Illinois," *Illinois Historical Journal*, 78 (Summer 1985). Among numerous studies that focus on particular strands of Illinois Lutheranism's complex history are Lee M. Heilman, *Historic Sketch of the Evangelical Lutheran Synod of Northern Illinois* (Philadelphia, 1892); Martin L. Wagner, *The Chicago Synod and Its Antecedents* (Waverly, Iowa, 1909); Mrs. Armin G. [Helga] Weng, ed., *Progress of a Century: A History of the Illinois Synod of the United Lutheran Church in America, 1851–1951* (Chicago, 1951); and Robert C. Wiederaenders, "A History of Lutheranism in Chicago . . . ," in Walter Kloetzli, ed., *Chicago Lutheran Planning Study*, 2 (3 vols., Chicago, 1965). Kalmer K. Klammer, "Illinois State University and the Early Lutheran Church of Springfield, Illinois," *Concordia Historical Institute Quarterly*, 54 (Winter 1980), recounts the efforts of the Synod of Northern Illinois to sustain a small school that offered preparatory, collegiate, and seminary training, first at Hillsboro and then at Springfield. The synod also sponsored Carthage College, which moved from Carthage, Illinois to Kenosha, Wisconsin in 1962. See Harold H. Lentz, *The Miracle of Carthage: History of Carthage College, 1847–1974* (Lima, Ohio, 1975).

In 1860, Scandinavians withdrew from the Synod of Northern Illinois to form the Augustana Synod. That synod's authorized history is G[othard] Everett Arden, *Augustana Heritage: A History of the Augustana Lutheran Church* (Rock Island, 1963), which synthesizes numerous early studies. For accounts of the college and seminary sponsored by the synod, see Arden, *The School of the Prophets: The Background and History of Augustana Theological Seminary,*

*1860–1960* (Rock Island, 1960) and Conrad Bergendoff, *Augustana: A Profession of Faith; A History of Augustana College, 1860–1935*, Augustana Library Publications, 33 (Rock Island, 1969). Bergendoff translated selected chapters of an important early study by Eric Norelius, in *The Pioneer Swedish Settlements and Swedish Lutheran Churches in America, 1845–1860*, Augustana Historical Society Publications, 31 (Rock Island, 1984). Swedish Lutheranism in Illinois is especially well documented due in part to the active synodical publications program described in Daniel Nystrom, *A Ministry of Printing: History of the Publication House of Augustana Lutheran Church, 1889–1962* . . . (Rock Island, 1962).

George M. Stephenson's classic work, *The Religious Aspects of Swedish Immigration: A Study of Immigrant Churches* (Minneapolis, 1932), still ranks, in many ways, as the best account of several Illinois Swedish communions—Lutheran, Methodist, Baptist, Episcopalian, and Mission Covenant. Yet Stephenson's assimilationist perspective has been replaced in more recent studies by the view that Swedish churches served to maintain rather than eradicate ethnic differences. For critiques of Stephenson's interpretation, see Ulf Beijbom, "The Historiography of Swedish America," *Swedish Pioneer Historical Quarterly*, 31 (Oct. 1980), and Robert S. Salisbury, "Swedish-American Historiography and the Question of Americanization," ibid., 29 (Apr. 1978).

German Lutherans came to Illinois in far greater numbers than did their Swedish brethren, but much of their history in the state remains to be written. The only account of many congregations is in Johannes Deindörfer, *Geschichte der Evangel.-Luth. Synode von Iowa und anderen Staaten* (Chicago, 1897). Illinois congregations belonging to the Lutheran Church–Missouri Synod are, however, described in Louis J. Schwartzkopf, *The Lutheran Trail: A History of the Synodical Conference, Lutheran Churches in Northern Illinois* (St. Louis, 1950) and August R. Suelflow, *The Heart of Missouri: A History of the Western District of the Lutheran Church–Missouri Synod, 1854–1954* (St. Louis, 1954). The synod's special sensitivity to educational concerns is documented in a five-part series by Albert G. Merkens, "Early Lutheran Settlers and Schools in Northern Illinois," in *Concordia Historical Institute Quarterly*, 21 (July 1948)–22 (July 1949); Alfred J. Freitag, *College with a Cause: A History of Concordia Teachers College* (River Forest, Ill., 1964); and Carl S. Meyer, *Log Cabin to Luther Tower: Concordia Seminary* . . . *1839–1964* (St. Louis, 1965).

Not all of the spiritual tensions that played themselves out on the Illinois frontier can be traced to ethnic differences, for no group aroused more violent animosities than did the Mormons, disciples of an indigenous American religious movement. Richard D. Poll, "Nauvoo and the New Mormon History: A Bibliographical Survey," *Journal of Mormon History*, 5 (1978), and Glen M. Leonard, "Recent Writing on Mormon Nauvoo," *Western Illinois Regional Studies*, 11 (Fall 1988), review a voluminous literature surrounding the Mormon effort to build a utopian community in western Illinois. Robert Bruce Flanders, *Nauvoo: Kingdom on the Mississippi* (Urbana, 1965) is the best single study of the subject, but its secular focus should be supplemented by recent interpretations that attribute to religion much of the conflict that had been seen as political. Two such works are Klaus J. Hansen, *Quest for Empire: The Political Kingdom of God and the Council of Fifty in Mormon History* (East Lansing, 1967) and Marvin S. Hill, "Mormon Religion in Nauvoo: Some Reflections," *Utah Historical Quarterly*, 44 (Spring 1976), which differ in portraying Mormonism as either an aggressive, imperialistic religion or a defensive, refuge-seeking faith. T. Edgar Lyon presents a straightforward account of "Doctrinal Development of the Church during the Nauvoo Sojourn, 1839–1846" in *Brigham Young University Studies*, 15 (Summer 1975). The largest of several small Mormon groups that did not accept Brigham Young's leadership was headquartered for many years in Illinois. See Richard P. Howard, "The Reorganized Church in Illinois, 1852–82: Search for Identity," *Dialogue: A Journal of Mormon Thought*, 5 (Spring 1970), and Roger D. Launius, *Joseph Smith III, Pragmatic Prophet* (Urbana, 1988).

Religious ideas and ideals contributed in important ways to the several reform movements that agitated antebellum Illinoisans. Arthur Charles Cole, *The Era of the Civil War, 1848–1870* (Springfield, 1919) is still the best survey of those developments, but see also Joseph Lee Lukonic, " 'Evangelicals in the City': Evangelical Protestant Social Concerns in Early Chicago, 1837–1860" (Ph.D. diss., Univ. of Wisconsin, Madison, 1979). F. Roger Dunn, "Formative Years of the Chicago Y.M.C.A.: A Study in Urban History," *Journal of the Illinois State Historical Society*, 37 (Dec. 1944), and Emmett Dedmon, *Great Enterprises: 100 Years of the YMCA of Metropolitan Chicago* (Chicago, 1957) focus on an important manifestation of antebellum Protestantism's social vision.

Many accounts of the connection between religion and reform stress the church's contribution to the antislavery movement. For example, Hermann R. Muelder, *Fighters for Freedom: The History of Anti-Slavery Activities of Men and Women Associated with Knox College* (New York, 1959) describes abolitionism in Illinois as revivalism's offspring. Merton L. Dillon, however, regards religion as only one of several factors contributing to the state's antislavery impulse, in "Sources of Early Antislavery Thought in Illinois," *Journal of the Illinois State Historical Society*, 50 (Spring 1957); "Abolitionism Comes to Illinois," ibid., 53 (Winter 1960); and *Elijah P. Lovejoy, Abolitionist Editor* (Urbana, 1961). Religious institutions became the primary organizational focus for Illinois abolitionists, according to Linda Jeanne Evans, "Abolitionism in the Illinois Churches, 1830–1865" (Ph.D. diss., Northwestern Univ., 1981), which stresses the radical character of Christian abolitionism. Other accounts depict antislavery churchmen in Illinois as social conservatives. See, for example, Robert Merideth, *The Politics of the Universe: Edward Beecher, Abolition, and Orthodoxy* (Nashville, Tenn., 1968); Richard S. Taylor, "Seeking the Kingdom: A Study in the Career of Jonathan Blanchard, 1811–1892" (Ph.D. diss., Northern Illinois Univ., 1977); and Taylor, "Beyond Immediate Emancipation: Jonathan Blanchard, Abolitionism, and the Emergence of American Fundamentalism,"

*Civil War History*, 27 (Sept. 1981). See also Clyde S. Kilby, *Minority of One: The Biography of Jonathan Blanchard* (Grand Rapids, 1959).

In the late nineteenth century, the Roman Catholic Church became the largest religious body in Illinois, but its modern history, like that of other denominations, is far better developed for Chicago than for Downstate. Although parish annals, biographies, and chronicles of religious orders are plentiful, the only comprehensive works not focused on Chicago are a handful of diocesan histories that vary greatly in quality. See, for example, Frederick Beuckman, *History, Diocese of Belleville, 1700–1914*, Volume 1, *St. Clair County* (Belleville, Ill., 1914); Joseph J. Thompson, comp., *Diamond Jubilee History: The Diocese of Springfield in Illinois* (Springfield, 1928); Robert R. Miller, *That All May Be One: A History of the Rockford Diocese* (Rockford, 1976); and Alice O'Rourke, *The Good Work Begun: Centennial History of Peoria Diocese* (Chicago, 1977). More particular investigations include David Francis Sweeney, *The Life of John Lancaster Spalding, First Bishop of Peoria, 1840–1916* (New York, 1965), the best of several Spalding studies, and Francis G. McManamin, "Peter J. Muldoon, First Bishop of Rockford, 1862–1927," *Catholic Historical Review*, 48 (Oct. 1962), a sketchy but suggestive portrait.

For Chicago, Charles Shanabruch, *Chicago's Catholics: The Evolution of an American Identity* (Notre Dame, Ind., 1981) is the most comprehensive of several newer works that eschew the traditional institutional approach represented most recently by Harry C. Koenig, ed., *A History of the Parishes of the Archdiocese of Chicago . . .* (2 vols., Chicago, 1980), a good church-sponsored compilation of individual parish histories. Shanabruch's study is useful for citations both to a large older literature and to newer accounts that explore patterns of religious conflict within Chicago's immigrant enclaves. The latter approach is best exemplified by Joseph John Parot, *Polish Catholics in Chicago, 1850–1920: A Religious History* (DeKalb, 1981). See also Victor Greene, *For God and Country: The Rise of Polish and Lithuanian Ethnic Consciousness in America, 1860–1910* (Madison, 1975) and Ellen Skerrett, "The Development of Catholic Identity among Irish Americans in Chicago, 1880 to 1920," in Timothy J. Meagher, ed., *From Paddy to Studs: Irish-American Communities in the Turn of the Century Era, 1880 to 1920* (Westport, Conn., 1986). Edward Kantowicz, "Church and Neighborhood," *Ethnicity*, 7 (Dec. 1980), describes the Catholic church's role in Bridgeport, an important multi-ethnic community.

Studies of Chicago's Catholic bishops provide another approach to the denomination's post–Civil War history. James P. Gaffey, "Patterns of Ecclesiastical Authority: The Problem of Chicago Succession, 1865–1881," *Church History*, 42 (June 1973), describes conflicts attending Bishop James Duggan's tenure. Edward R. Kantowicz, *Corporation Sole: Cardinal Mundelein and Chicago Catholicism* (Notre Dame, Ind., 1983) traces the efforts of George Cardinal Mundelein to bring order and efficiency to the diocese during his administration, 1916–39. Charles W. Dahm, *Power and Authority in the Catholic Church: Cardinal Cody in Chicago* (Notre Dame, Ind., 1981) is a flawed account of the conflict after Vatican Council II between John Cardinal Cody and reformers within the church.

Catholic institutional responses to urbanization are discussed in John Patrick Walsh, "The Catholic Church in Chicago and Problems of an Urban Society, 1893–1915" (Ph.D. diss., Univ. of Chicago, 1948). Timothy Walch places Chicago Catholicism in a regional context in "Catholic Social Institutions and Urban Development: The View from Nineteenth-Century Chicago and Milwaukee," *Catholic Historical Review*, 64 (Jan. 1978), and in "The Catholic Press and the Campaign for Parish Schools: Chicago and Milwaukee, 1850–1885," *U.S. Catholic Historian*, 3 (Spring 1984). Mary Agnes Amberg, *Madonna Center: Pioneer Catholic Social Settlement* (Chicago, 1976) illustrates that Chicago's secular settlement house movement had its Catholic counterpart, while another significant strand of Catholic social activism is illuminated by Francis Joseph Sicius, "The Chicago Catholic Worker Movement, 1936 to the Present" (Ph.D. diss., Loyola Univ., Chicago, 1979).

Chicago's Catholic school system is well documented in James W. Sanders, *The Education of an Urban Minority: Catholics in Chicago, 1833–1965* (New York, 1977). This study may be supplemented by Sister Mary Innocenta Montay, *The History of Catholic Secondary Education in the Archdiocese of Chicago* (Washington, D.C., 1953), which includes information on Catholic education outside of Chicago, as does Norma A. Paul, *Study and Memos: Religious Orders and Their Schools in Illinois, 1834–1939* . . . (Chicago, 1970). Brief histories of Catholic colleges and universities in the Archdiocese of Chicago may be found in Harry C. Koenig, ed., *Caritas Christi Urget Nos: A History of the Offices, Agencies, and Institutions of the Archdiocese of Chicago* (2 vols., Chicago, 1981), but see also Carole Zucco Chambers, "The Presidential Years of Sister Ann Ida Gannon, BVM, Mundelein College, 1957–1975" (Ph.D. diss., Loyola Univ., Chicago, 1977); Sister Aurelia Altenhofen, *Rosary College: Transition and Progress, 1949–1974* (River Forest, Ill., 1977); and Lester Francis Goodchild, "The Mission of the Catholic University in the Midwest, 1842–1980: A Comparative Case Study of the Effects of Strategic Policy Decisions upon the Mission of the University of Notre Dame, Loyola University of Chicago, and DePaul University" (Ph.D. diss., Univ. of Chicago, 1986).

Histories of Illinois Protestantism since the late nineteenth century also focus on Chicago. Many scholars have been intrigued by the relationship between religion and the rise of the city. For example, Thomas Emerson Lenhart, "Methodist Piety in an Industrializing Society: Chicago, 1865–1914" (Ph.D. diss., Northwestern Univ., 1981) argues that Methodists responded to urbanization by sacrificing their older moralistic piety to a new piety of adaptation and service. Paul H. Heidebrecht, "Chicago Presbyterians and the Businessman's Religion, 1900–1920," *American Presbyterians: Journal of Presbyterian History*, 64 (Spring 1986), discusses Presbyterian responses as lay-oriented, pragmatic, masculine, and inclusive. Tensions between lay leaders and religious professionals shaped the burgeoning city's spiritual life in a fundamental way, according to L. David Lewis, "The Efficient Crusade: Lay Protestantism in Chicago, 1874–1925" (Ph.D. diss., Univ. of Chicago, 1979), a wide-ranging and informative study.

Baptist developments are popularly recounted in Perry J. Stackhouse, *Chicago and the Baptists: A Century of Progress* (Chicago, 1933), while John Henry Hopkins, *The Great Forty Years in the Diocese of Chicago, A.D. 1893 to 1934* (Chicago, 1936) records diverse institutional aspects of Episcopalianism's urban ministry. One especially significant Episcopalian parish is examined in Rima Lunin Schultz, *The Church and the City: A Social History of 150 Years at Saint James, Chicago* (Chicago, 1986), which stands out among countless individual church histories for its analytical approach. Chicago Episcopalians opened Western Theological Seminary in 1885 and then transplanted the school to Evanston in the 1920s. Seabury Divinity School was moved from Minnesota to merge with Western in 1933. See Frank Arthur McElwain et al., "Seabury-Western Theological Seminary: A History," *Historical Magazine of the Protestant Episcopal Church*, 5 (Dec. 1936).

Despite the wide range of Protestant strategies for coping with Chicago's challenge, scholars have until recently lavished their attention on theological liberalism. William R. Hutchison, "Disapproval of Chicago: The Symbolic Trial of David Swing," *Journal of American History*, 59 (June 1972), uses a controversy within the Presbyterian church to argue that Protestant liberalism was indigenous to late nineteenth-century Chicago and not an eastern import. Such liberalism in this century owed much to theologians at the Divinity School of the University of Chicago. See Charles Harvey Arnold, *Near the Edge of Battle: A Short History of the Divinity School and the "Chicago School of Theology," 1866–1966* (Chicago, 1966) and Leonard I. Sweet, "The University of Chicago Revisited: The Modernization of Theology, 1890–1940," *Foundations: A Baptist Journal of History, Theology, and Ministry*, 22 (Oct.–Dec. 1979). Also associated with the Chicago theology were scholars at the Disciples Divinity House. Founded in 1894, the Divinity House was the first of several major seminaries to locate near the University of Chicago, and the school's first seventy-five years are reviewed in William Barnett Blakemore, *Quest for Intelligence in Ministry* . . . (Chicago, 1970). Protestant liberalism's inability to cope with challenges posed by the Great Depression is the focus of Jacob H. Dorn, "Religion and Reform in the City: The Re-Thinking Chicago Movement of the 1930s," *Church History*, 55 (Sept. 1986). See also Stephen C. Rowe, "Denominational Practices and the Religion of Democracy: The Church Federation of Greater Chicago and Metropolitan Issues, 1945–1968" (Ph.D. diss., Univ. of Chicago, 1974).

Chicago's liberal social gospel movement has been of particular interest to scholars. There is a good overview in Louise C. Wade, *Graham Taylor, Pioneer for Social Justice, 1851–1938* (Chicago, 1964), a fine scholarly biography of the social gospel minister who chaired the nation's first Department of Christian Sociology at Chicago Theological Seminary and founded Chicago Commons, a Christian social settlement. Worthwhile studies of two Methodist social gospelers are Stephen George Cobb, "William H. Carwardine and the Pullman Strike" (Ph.D. diss., Northwestern Univ., 1970) and Robert Moats Miller, *How Shall They Hear Without a Preacher? The Life of Ernest Fremont Tittle* (Chapel Hill, 1971), while the story of Chicago's most prominent Unitarian activist is told in Richard Harlan Thomas, "Jenkin Lloyd Jones, Lincoln's Soldier of Civic Righteousness" (Ph.D. diss., Rutgers Univ., 1967). Richard W. Schwarz, "Dr. John Harvey Kellogg as a Social Gospel Practitioner," *Journal of the Illinois State Historical Society*, 57 (Spring 1964), describes Kellogg's medical missions in Chicago, and Paula Benkart, "Paul Fox, Presbyterian Mission, and Polish Americans," *Journal of Presbyterian History*, 60 (Winter 1982), explores the implications of a liberal Protestant Polish immigrant's educational and religious missions. David Lee Smith, *Community Renewal Society . . .* (Chicago, 1982) is a centennial history of an organization founded by Congregationalists, which at first directed its programs toward German and Bohemian immigrants.

Conservative Protestants experimented with an equally diverse range of urban strategies. Harrold C. Shiffler, "The Chicago Church-Theater Controversy of 1881–1882," *Journal of the Illinois State Historical Society*, 53 (Winter 1960), and Clarence N. Roberts, "The Crusade against Secret Societies and the National Christian Association," ibid., 64 (Winter 1971), recount two attempts to rejuvenate antebellum reform crusades. A unique blend of tract society tradition and settlement house programs is described in Thomas J. Dorst, "Sowing the Seeds of Reform: The Chicago Tract Society, 1889–1910," *Chicago History*, 12 (Spring 1983), while Darrel M. Robertson, *The Chicago Revival, 1876: Society and Revivalism in a Nineteenth-Century City* (Metuchen, N.J., 1989) focuses on revivalism's divisive social impact. An inaccurate stereotype of conservatives or evangelicals as so preoccupied with soul saving as to be insensitive to temporal suffering has caused scholars to overlook numerous evangelical urban social welfare agencies. For one well-known example, see Allan Whitworth Bosch, "The Salvation Army in Chicago, 1885–1914" (Ph.D. diss., Univ. of Chicago, 1965).

Evangelicalism's continuing vitality in Illinois is particularly evident in James F. Findlay, Jr.'s superb biography of the Gilded Age's premier evangelist, *Dwight L. Moody, American Evangelist, 1837–1899* (Chicago, 1969). Moody spent several critical apprenticeship years in Illinois and later returned to found Chicago's Moody Bible Institute. Dorothy Martin, *Moody Bible Institute: God's Power in Action* (Chicago, 1977) presents the school's history from its own fundamentalist perspective. Histories of the lesser known but numerous Bible colleges scattered throughout Illinois have yet to be published.

Evangelicalism's appeal to Gilded Age Illinoisans owed much to a renewed interest in the doctrine of holiness. See Carl Oblinger, *Religious Mimesis: Social Bases for the Holiness Schism in Late Nineteenth-Century Methodism; The Illinois Case, 1869–1885* (Evanston, 1973), a sketchy but suggestive study of the Western Holiness Association. The largest holiness denomination among several to emerge from the movement was the Church of the Nazarene. It is well represented in Illinois, as Mark R. Moore, ed., *Fifty Years . . . and Beyond: A History of the Chicago Central District, Church of the Nazarene* (Kankakee, Ill., 1954) shows.

Conservative resistance to the rise of theological liberalism and a liberal social gospel movement divided several Illinois denominations, nowhere with more enduring consequences than among Illinois Baptists. The schism that led in 1907 to the creation of the Illinois Baptist State Association, now affiliated with the Southern Baptist Convention, is discussed in Lamire Holden Moore, *Southern Baptists in Illinois* (Nashville, Tenn., 1957), while Charles Chaney explores long-standing cultural, doctrinal, and ecclesiological differences that occasioned the split in "Diversity: A Study in Illinois Baptist History to 1907," *Foundations: A Baptist Journal of History and Theology*, 7 (Jan. 1964).

Many Illinois Baptist conservatives elected not to join the Southern Baptist movement. Northern Baptist Theological Seminary in Lombard and Judson College in Elgin grew out of the efforts of Chicago-area conservatives to counter liberalism's influence within what is now the American Baptist Churches in the U.S.A. The seminary's undergraduate division became Judson College when the schools moved from Chicago to separate suburban campuses in 1963. See Warren Cameron Young, *Commit What You Have Heard: A History of Northern Baptist Theological Seminary, 1913–1988* (Wheaton, Ill., 1988), which opens with a brief but informative overview of developments leading to the seminary's creation. There are many other studies, published and unpublished, of Illinois Baptists in this century, including T[homas] J. Wheeler and Harmon Etter, comps., *History of Illinois Baptist State Association* (Carbondale, 1940); Robert J. Hastings, *We Were There: An Oral History of the Illinois Baptist State Association, 1907–1976* (Springfield, 1976); and Leland D. Hine, "Aspects of Change in the Churches of the Chicago Baptist Association, 1931–1955" (Ph.D. diss., Univ. of Pennsylvania, 1958).

Free thought's largely unwritten Illinois history makes it difficult to cast liberal/conservative religious differences in an urban/rural or Chicago/Downstate mold. Robert Ingersoll, the state's most popular Gilded Age freethinker, resided in Peoria and found receptive audiences in both city and countryside. See Orvin Larson, *American Infidel: Robert G. Ingersoll* (New York, 1962). Free thought periodicals were not uncommon in rural Illinois as well as in Chicago, as references scattered through Marshall G. Brown and Gordon Stein, *Freethought in the United States: A Descriptive Bibliography* (Westport, Conn., 1978) suggest. See also Robert Rewalt Roberts, "Freethought Movement of Chicago, 1875–1914" (M.A. thesis, Univ. of Chicago, 1947) and Robert W. Frizzell, "German Freethinkers in Bloomington: Sampling a Forgotten Culture," in the 1984–85 *Transactions of the Illinois State Historical Society*.

Because more than 90 percent of Illinois Jews live in the Chicago area, the state's Jewish history is largely a Chicago story. Hyman L. Meites, ed., *History of the Jews of Chicago* (Chicago, 1924) is an elegantly appointed but undocumented panegyric to Jewish Chicago published by the Jewish Historical Society of

Illinois, an organization established in 1918 amidst a flush of filiopietistic enthusiasm surrounding the state's centennial. Among the society's founders was Bernhard Felsenthal, a German immigrant who became the first rabbi of Chicago's Reform congregation and a spokesman for Reform Judaism in America. See Victor Leifson Ludlow, "Bernhard Felsenthal: Quest for Zion" (Ph.D. diss., Brandeis Univ., 1979). Arriving later than their German brethren, eastern European Jews generally held more orthodox views, and Mitchell Alan Horwich, *Conflict and Child Care Policy in the Chicago Jewish Community, 1893–1942: The Early Years of the Jewish Children's Bureau of Chicago* (Chicago, 1977) documents one aspect of the clash between the two groups.

Useful histories of the Chicago Jewish community include Morris A. Gutstein, *A Priceless Heritage: The Epic Growth of Nineteenth Century Chicago Jewry* (New York, 1953); Simon Rawidowicz, ed., *The Chicago Pinkas* (Chicago, 1952); and J. I. Fishbein, ed., *The Sentinel's History of Chicago Jewry, 1911–1986* (Chicago, 1986). Louis Wirth, *The Ghetto* (Chicago, 1928) is the best known of several sociological studies of Jewish Chicago, but see Erich Rosenthal's criticisms in "Acculturation without Assimilation? The Jewish Community in Chicago, Illiniois," *American Journal of Sociology*, 66 (Nov. 1960), and "This Was North Lawndale: The Transplantation of a Jewish Community," *Jewish Social Studies*, 22 (Apr. 1960). For Downstate, see Oscar Fleishaker, *The Illinois-Iowa Jewish Community on the Banks of the Mississippi River* (printed version of D.H.L. diss., Yeshiva Univ., 1957), which deals with Rock Island and Moline, and Asa Rubenstein, "Midwestern Jewish Commitment and Practical American Idealism: The Early History of Sinai Temple, Champaign, Illinois," *Journal of the Illinois State Historical Society*, 75 (Summer 1982).

Chicago has dominated accounts of black religious life in Illinois, insofar as the topic has been studied at all. Miles Mark Fisher, "Negro Churches in Illinois: A Fragmentary History with Emphasis on Chicago," *Journal of the Illinois State Historical Society*, 56 (Autumn 1963), provides a starting point and is indebted to St. Clair Drake, *Churches and Voluntary Associations in the Chicago Negro Community* (Chicago, 1940). The history of Chicago's Black Muslim movement, interpreted as a utopian phenomenon, is described in William A. Marshall, "Education in the Nation of Islam during the Leadership of Elijah Muhammad, 1935–1975" (Ed.D. diss., Loyola Univ., Chicago, 1976).

Equally neglected in the historiography of Illinois religion are the various "alternative altars" that have dotted the state's spiritual landscape since the late nineteenth century. Paul R. Anderson, *Platonism in the Midwest* (New York, 1963) documents an interest in philosophical idealism sparked by Hiram K. Jones in Jacksonville and Quincy. The branch of theosophy that established its national headquarters at Wheaton is described in Joy Mills, *100 Years of Theosophy: A History of the Theosophical Society in America* (Wheaton, Ill., 1987). Another emanation of Gilded Age idealism, Christian Science, proved more lasting. References to Chicago in Robert Peel's work, *Mary Baker Eddy:*

*The Years of Trial* (New York, 1971) and *Mary Baker Eddy: The Years of Authority* (New York, 1977), show that both Christian Science and its first cousin, New Thought, were well established in Illinois by 1900. See also Richard S. Taylor, "New Thought in the Twenties: The Case of Springfield, Illinois," *The Historian*, 49 (May 1987).

Religious utopianism did not vanish from Illinois with Nauvoo and Bishop Hill. Grant Wacker, "Marching to Zion: Religion in a Modern Utopian Community," *Church History*, 54 (Dec. 1985), describes John Alexander Dowie's much studied experiment at Zion. Lesser known communities are covered in Harold D. Fine, "The Koreshan Unity: The Chicago Years of a Utopian Community," *Journal of the Illinois State Historical Society*, 68 (June 1975), and H[arry] Roger Grant, *Spirit Fruit: A Gentle Utopia* (DeKalb, 1988). For recent ventures, see William Lawrence Smith, "Urban Communitarianism in the 1980's: Seven Religious Communes in Chicago" (Ph.D. diss., Univ. of Notre Dame, 1984).

Spiritualism's popularity in late nineteenth-century Illinois led in 1896 to the formation of the Illinois State Spiritualists' Association. See Victoria Barnes, comp., *Centennial Book of Modern Spiritualism in America* (Chicago, 1948). The story of one downstate spiritualist congregation is covered in *Life and Times of S. H. West, with an Appendix on Evolution, Religion, and Spiritual Phenomena* (Bloomington, Ill., 1908), an autobiography, while David St. Clair, *Watseka: America's Most Extraordinary Case of Possession and Exorcism* (Chicago, 1977) is a fictionalized account of one Gilded Age episode. Brad Steiger, *Psychic City: Chicago, Doorway to Another Dimension* (Garden City, N.Y., 1976) documents the mid-twentieth-century explosion of interest in the occult, suggesting something of the rich complexity of religious life in contemporary Illinois.

Several faiths trace their Illinois origins to the World's Parliament of Religions, which is described in Richard H. Seager, "The World's Parliament of Religions, Chicago, Illinois, 1893: America's Religious Coming of Age" (Ph.D. diss., Harvard Univ., 1986) and interpreted as a symptom of the ambiguous, experimental nature of the era's religious life in Paul A. Carter, *The Spiritual Crisis of the Gilded Age* (DeKalb, 1971). The World's Parliament introduced Bahá'í to Illinois. Robert H. Stockman, *The Bahá'í Faith in America: Origins, 1892–1900* (Wilmette, Ill., 1985) gives considerable attention to Chicago as the first major center of Bahá'í activity in North America, while Bruce W. Whitmore, *The Dawning Place: The Building of a Temple, the Forging of a North American Bahá'í Community* (Wilmette, Ill., 1984) is a history of the Bahá'í house of worship in Wilmette. Hinduism owes its Illinois origins to Swami Vivekananda of India, whose travels in the Chicago area following the 1893 meeting are recounted in Marie Louise Burke, *Swami Vivekananda in the West: New Discoveries; His Prophetic Mission*, 1 (2 vols., Calcutta, 1983).

Numerous institutional studies and a preoccupation with Chicago mark the historiography of education in modern Illinois. Public elementary and secondary education expanded rapidly in the post–Civil War era, an important but generally neglected period. The period is briefly covered in the opening chapter of Henry C. Johnson, Jr., and Erwin V. Johanningmeier, *Teachers for the Prairie: The University of Illinois and the Schools, 1868–1945* (Urbana, 1972), a work that narrows in later chapters to focus on the university's College of Education. Illinois developments are scattered through Wayne E. Fuller, *The Old Country School: The Story of Rural Education in the Middle West* (Chicago, 1982), an excellent study focusing on the late nineteenth century. The evolution of rural schooling in one locale is covered in Mona Garland Kaegi, "An Historical Study of an Educational Microcosm: Hardin County, Illinois, 1839–1977" (Ph.D. diss., Southern Illinois Univ., Carbondale, 1978). Chautauquas, annual summer gatherings that featured lecturers and classes as well as entertainment and recreation, provided outdoor educational opportunities for many rural Illinoisans. See, for example, Katharine Aird Miller and Raymond H. Montgomery, *A Chautauqua to Remember: The Story of Old Salem* (Petersburg, Ill., 1987). Other general works on education in the period include Albert Victor Lockhart, "The Popularization of Public Secondary Education in Illinois, 1885–1944" (Ph.D. diss., Univ. of Chicago, 1948) and Carl Green, "School Legislation in Illinois" (Ph.D. diss., Univ. of Illinois, 1930).

Symbolic of public education's progress was the growth of the state office of public instruction. Victor H. Sheppard provides the authorized account in *A Brief History of the Office of Public Instruction* (Springfield, 1957) and a *Supplement . . . 1955–63* (Springfield, 1962), and two academic works focus narrowly on administrative strategies: John William McLure, "The Illinois Superintendent of Public Instruction, 1854–1894: A Study in Educational Leadership" (Ph.D. diss., Univ. of Illinois, Urbana-Champaign, 1968) and William Browne Gillies III, "The Illinois Office of the Superintendent of Public Instruction: An Analysis of Effectiveness and Influence, 1854–1920" (Ph.D. diss., Univ. of Chicago, 1977). For admiring portraits of Gilded Age administrators, see William Edward Simonds, "Newton Bateman, State Superintendent of Public Instruction and President of Knox College," *Illinois State Historical Society Transactions for the Year 1935*, 42, and Burt Weed Loomis, *The Educational Influence of Richard Edwards*, George Peabody College for Teachers, Contributions to Education, 106 (Nashville, Tenn., 1932). An 1889 compulsory education law bearing Edwards's name provoked a sharp reaction from many Illinoisans not particularly enamored of public education. See Charles Shanabruch, "The Repeal of the Edwards Law: A Study of Religion and Ethnicity in Illinois Politics," *Ethnicity*, 7 (Sept. 1980), and Peter Pousma De Boer, "A History of the Early Compulsory School Attendance Legislation in the State of Illinois" (Ph.D. diss., Univ. of Chicago, 1968).

The standard history of public schooling in Chicago is Mary J. Herrick, *The Chicago Schools: A Social and Political History* (Beverly Hills, Calif., 1971), a fine comprehensive account that provides a good guide to an extensive older literature, but the author, a former teacher, tends to stereotype school controversies as battles fought by right-thinking educators and their reform-minded allies against obstructionist administrators and power-seeking politicians. For an alternative to that manichaean vision, see David John Hogan, *Class and Reform: School and Society in Chicago, 1880–1930* (Philadelphia, 1985). Chicago's modern school system had its roots in the Progressive era, a period that has received a disproportionate share of attention from educational historians, and Hogan's Marxist work is a good but thesis-ridden introduction to that literature and to the issues at stake. Relating educational reform to economic change, he analyzes administrative centralization, vocational education, and the Progressive education movement as part of the "structuration and class formation" that accompanied the "market revolution" of the period (p. xx). His complex definition of "class" differs from that employed by Julia Wrigley in *Class Politics and Public Schools: Chicago, 1900–1950* (New Brunswick, N.J., 1982), but both pointedly reject the thesis that public schooling was imposed on the working classes by social elites for essentially repressive purposes, an idea popular among revisionist historians of the 1960s and 1970s. Revisionism performed a useful function by raising questions of class and power in educational decision making. Its emphasis on social control, however, failed to account for the complex motives and often contradictory results of battles over public education waged by labor leaders, businessmen, and civic reformers. Some attention is now being given to ways in which students themselves have influenced educational policymaking. See, for example, Thomas W. Gutowski, "Student Initiative and the Origins of the High School Extracurriculum: Chicago, 1880–1915," *History of Education Quarterly*, 28 (Spring 1988).

Studies of Chicago's Progressive educators abound. The best of several assessments of John Dewey's educational philosophy as it developed during his Chicago years is Melvin C. Baker, *Foundations of John Dewey's Educational Theory* (New York, 1955), while the story of Dewey's laboratory school is covered in Katherine Camp Mayhew and Anna Camp Edwards, *The Dewey School: The Laboratory School of the University of Chicago, 1896–1903* (New York, 1936), a lively account by former staff members. The best study of Francis W. Parker, whom Dewey called the "father of Progressive education," is Jack W. Campbell, *Colonel Francis W. Parker, the Children's Crusader* (Chicago, 1967). Gilbert A. Harrison, *A Timeless Affair: The Life of Anita McCormick Blaine* (Chicago, 1979) provides a sensitive portrait of the philanthropist who supported Parker. See also Marie Kirchner Stone, ed., *Between Home and Community: Chronicle of the Francis W. Parker School, 1901–1976* (Chicago, 1976). Chicago's first woman superintendent of schools is the subject of Joan K. Smith's admiring *Ella Flagg Young: Portrait of a Leader* (Ames, Iowa, 1979). Ellen Condliffe Lagemann, ed., *Jane Addams on Education* (New York, 1985) includes a sketch of her life as well as selections from her writings.

Modern teachers organizations are rooted in the Progressive era. Teachers were professionalizing when they organized the Chicago Teachers' Federation, according to Robert Louis Reid in "The Professionalization of Public School

Teachers: The Chicago Experience, 1895–1920" (Ph.D. diss., Northwestern Univ., 1968) and in his introduction to *Battleground: The Autobiography of Margaret A. Haley* (Urbana, 1982), a lively and revealing account by the federation's long-time leader. By contrast, Wayne J. Urban, *Why Teachers Organized* (Detroit, 1982) contends that the federation was a working-class organization, not an association of middle-class professionals. See also Marjorie Murphy, "Taxation and Social Conflict: Teacher Unionism and Public School Finance in Chicago, 1898–1934," *Journal of the Illinois State Historical Society*, 74 (Winter 1981). The federation's successor is examined in Francis M. Landwermeyer, "Teacher Unionism—Chicago Style: A History of the Chicago Teachers Union, 1937–1972" (Ph.D. diss., Univ. of Chicago, 1978). Outside of Chicago, the teachers union movement is poorly documented, but see Robert Arthur Nottenberg, "The Relationship of Organized Labor to Public School Legislation in Illinois, 1880–1948" (Ph.D. diss., Univ. of Chicago, 1950) and James Logsdon Fletcher, "The Judicial and Legislative History of Public School Employee Collective Bargaining in Illinois, 1921–1971" (Ph.D. diss., Northwestern Univ., 1971).

There are numerous published and unpublished histories of state-level professional associations for teachers and administrators, all of which lack depth and interpretive perspective when compared with the Chicago literature. See, for example, George Propeck and Irving F. Pearson, *The History of the Illinois Education Association* . . . (Springfield, 1961).

Racial segregation, a phenomenon only recently studied by historians of education in the state, is explored in Robert L. McCaul, *The Black Struggle for Public Schooling in Nineteenth-Century Illinois* (Carbondale, 1987). See also August Meier and Elliott M. Rudwick, "Early Boycotts of Segregated Schools: The Alton, Illinois Case, 1897–1908," *Journal of Negro Education*, 36 (Fall 1967). School segregation in twentieth-century Chicago is examined in Judy Jolley Mohraz, *The Separate Problem: Case Studies of Black Education in the North, 1900–1930* (Westport, Conn., 1979) and Michael W. Homel, *Down from Equality: Black Chicagoans and the Public Schools, 1920–41* (Urbana, 1984). Recent issues are analyzed in Catherine Sardo Weidner, "Debating the Future of Chicago's Black Youth: Black Professionals, Black Labor, and Educational Politics during the Civil Rights Era, 1950–1965" (Ph.D. diss., Northwestern Univ., 1989).

Publicly funded universities emerged in Illinois during the Civil War era. The best account of this development is Winton U. Solberg, *The University of Illinois, 1867–1894: An Intellectual and Cultural History* (Urbana, 1968). The antebellum roots of tax-supported higher education are analyzed in Jon Francis McKenna, "Disputed Destiny: The Political and Intellectual Origins of Public-supported Higher Education in Illinois" (Ph.D. diss., Univ. of Illinois, Urbana-Champaign, 1973). Much of the historiography focuses on the role of Jonathan Baldwin Turner, at one time regarded as the originator of the land-grant college ideal. Donald R. Brown, "Jonathan Baldwin Turner and the Land-Grant Idea," *Journal of the Illinois State Historical Society*, 55 (Winter 1962), surveys the issues, but the best review of the literature is Earle D. Ross, "The 'Father' of the Land-Grant College," *Agricultural History*, 12 (Apr. 1938), which refutes such older works as Mary Turner Carriel, *The Life of Jonathan Baldwin Turner* (Jacksonville, Ill., 1911). Judith Ann Hancock, "Jonathan Baldwin Turner, 1805–1899: A Study of an Educational Reformer" (Ph.D. diss., Univ. of Washington, 1971) is the most adequate modern biography.

There is as yet no sequel to Solberg's history other than several presidential studies and numerous accounts of particular academic programs. Harry A. Kersey, Jr., *John Milton Gregory and the University of Illinois* (Urbana, 1968) and Ronald M. Johnson, "Schoolman among Scholars: Andrew S. Draper at the University of Illinois, 1894–1904," *Illinois Historical Journal*, 78 (Winter 1985), focus on two early heads of the institution, while Richard Allen Swanson, "Edmund J. James, 1855–1925: A 'Conservative Progressive' in American Higher Education" (Ph.D. diss., Univ. of Illinois, Urbana-Champaign, 1966) and Karl Max Grisso, "David Kinley, 1861–1944: The Career of the Fifth President of the University of Illinois" (Ph.D. diss., Univ. of Illinois, Urbana-Champaign, 1980) describe their immediate successors. Jerome Leon Rodnitzky's work on university public relations includes "President James and His Campaigns for University of Illinois Funds," *Journal of the Illinois State Historical Society*, 63 (Spring 1970). Exemplifying a plethora of program studies are Beverly Bartow, "Isabel Bevier at the University of Illinois and the Home Economics Movement," ibid., 72 (Feb. 1979); Benjamin F. Shearer, "An Experiment in Military and Civilian Education: The Students' Army Training Corps at the University of Illinois," ibid., 72 (Aug. 1979); and Richard Gordon Moores, *Fields of Rich Toil: The Development of the University of Illinois College of Agriculture* (Urbana, 1970).

State normal schools came into their own in the late nineteenth century. Illinois State Normal University, founded in 1857, had been the state's first tax-supported institution of higher education. Charles A. Harper, *Development of the Teachers College in the United States with Special Reference to the Illinois State Normal University* (Bloomington, Ill., 1935) describes the school's growth and significance in its larger context, while Helen E. Marshall, *Grandest of Enterprises: The Illinois State Normal University, 1857–1957* (Normal, Ill., 1956) supersedes older histories of the institution. See also her continuation, *The Eleventh Decade: Illinois State University, 1957–1967* (Normal, Ill., 1967), and Roger J. Champagne, *A Place of Education: Illinois State University, 1967–1977* (Normal, Ill., 1978).

For the early history of Southern Illinois State Normal University, chartered in 1869, see Eli G. Lentz, *Seventy Five Years in Retrospect: From Normal School to Teachers College to University; Southern Illinois University, 1874–1949* (Carbondale, 1955). George Kimball Plochmann, *The Ordeal of Southern Illinois University* (Carbondale, 1959) and Betty Mitchell, *Delyte Morris of SIU* (Carbondale, 1988) describe the school's modern transformation. James

W. Neckers, *The Building of a Department: Chemistry at Southern Illinois University, 1927–1967* (Carbondale, 1979) is representative of a proliferating literature on particular academic programs at Carbondale, while Keith A. Wadell, "The Establishment of Southern Illinois University at Edwardsville" (Ph.D. diss., Southern Illinois Univ., Carbondale, 1983) describes the creation of SIU's Edwardsville campus.

Charles H. Coleman, *Eastern Illinois State College: Fifty Years of Public Service* (Charleston, Ill., 1950) and Donald F. Tingley, ed., *The Emerging University: A History of Eastern Illinois University, 1949–74* (Charleston, Ill., 1974) cover the evolution of the institution chartered in 1895 as Eastern Illinois State Normal School. Northern Illinois State Normal School was also established in 1895. See Earl W. Hayter, *Education in Transition: The History of Northern Illinois University* (DeKalb, 1974). For the development of Western Illinois State Normal School, founded in 1899, see Victor Hicken, *The Purple and the Gold: The Story of Western Illinois University* (Macomb, 1970). Also part of the educational scene were county normal schools, some of which are described in Cook's *Educational History of Illinois*, already cited. Although most disappeared, Cook County Normal, founded in 1869, survived to become Chicago State University. See Edmund W. Kearney and E. Maynard Moore, *A History: Chicago State University, 1867–1979* (Chicago, 1979). Melvin R. George, "Northeastern Illinois University: The History of a Comprehensive State University" (Ph.D. diss., Univ. of Chicago, 1979) traces the evolution of another Chicago school, begun in 1961 as a municipal teachers college. Edna Dean Baker, *An Adventure in Higher Education: The Story of National College of Education* (Evanston, 1956) documents an Evanston-based private college, now National-Louis University, founded in 1886 to train kindergarten teachers.

The junior college movement in Illinois traces its roots to the Progressive era and evolved through several stages before entering a period of rapid expansion in the 1960s. The best published account is Thomas L. Hardin, "The University of Illinois and the Community-Junior College Movement, 1901–1965," *Illinois Historical Journal*, 79 (Summer 1986). See also Matthew Meisterheim, "A History of the Public Junior College in Illinois, 1900–1965" (Ed.D. diss., Northern Illinois Univ., 1975).

The rise of publicly funded institutions of higher education should not obscure the regularity with which church-related colleges continued to appear. For Wheaton College, chartered in 1861 as a nondenominational school with fraternal ties to the Congregational church, see Paul M. Bechtel, *Wheaton College: A Heritage Remembered, 1860–1984* (Wheaton, Ill., 1984). The Evangelical Association of North America founded what is now North Central College in 1861, while the Cumberland Presbyterian Church obtained a charter for Lincoln College in 1865. See Clarence N. Roberts, *North Central College: A Century of Liberal Education, 1861–1961* (Naperville, Ill., 1960) and Andrew Lindstrom, *Lincoln, the Namesake College: A Centennial History of Lincoln College, 1865–1965* (Lincoln, Ill., 1965). A[aron] E. Prince, *History of Ewing College*

(Collinsville, Ill., 1961) tells the story of an institution, now defunct, which began in 1867 as a Baptist high school. Peter F. Mizera, *Czech Benedictines in America, 1877–1901* (Lisle, Ill., 1969) covers the early years of St. Procopius College, now Illinois Benedictine College. North Park College opened in 1891 under the auspices of the Evangelical Covenant Church of America, and Almira became Greenville College after being purchased in 1892 by the Free Methodists. See Leland H. Carlson, *A History of North Park College, Commemorating the Fiftieth Anniversary, 1891–1941* (Chicago, 1941) and Mary A. Tenney, *"Still Abides the Memory"* (Greenville, Ill., 1942). Calvin B. Hanson, *"The Trinity Story"* (Minneapolis, 1983) traces the histories of Trinity College and Trinity Evangelical Divinity School, established in 1897 by the Evangelical Free Church of America. In 1898, Christian Scientists founded the school that became Principia College. See Edwin S. Leonard, Jr., *As the Sowing: The First Fifty Years of The Principia* (St. Louis, 1948; abridged ed., St. Louis, 1951). Presbyterians opened Millikin University in 1901, and Olivet Nazarene University, now sustained by the Nazarene Church, was established in 1909 as Illinois Holiness University. See the *Autobiography of Albert Reynolds Taylor . . .* (Decatur, 1929) for Millikin, and Carl S. McClain, *I Remember: My Fifty-seven Years at Olivet Nazarene College* (Kansas City, Mo., 1983).

Although religion clearly continued to influence higher education in Gilded Age Illinois, historians have differed over the extent to which the traditional link between piety and learning persisted. Why it did so at Wheaton College but not at Knox is the subject of Thomas A. Askew, Jr., "The Liberal Arts College Encounters Intellectual Change: A Comparative Study of Education at Knox and Wheaton Colleges, 1837–1925" (Ph.D. diss., Northwestern Univ., 1969), while the origins of Wheaton's conservative religious character are further explored in Richard S. Taylor, "Religion and Higher Education in Gilded Age America: The Case of Wheaton College," *American Studies*, 22 (Spring 1981). See also William Bryan Adrian, Jr., "Changes in Christian Emphasis among Selected Church-related Colleges in Illinois" (Ph.D. diss., Univ. of Denver, 1967), an analysis of twentieth-century continuities and changes in the religious character of eight schools, specifically Augustana, Aurora, Concordia, Elmhurst, Illinois Wesleyan, Millikin, North Central, and Olivet Nazarene.

Piety and higher education remained closely connected in some private colleges, but more secular ideals prevailed elsewhere. The background of Roosevelt University, which opened in 1945, is studied in Thomas Charles Lelon, "The Emergence of Roosevelt College of Chicago: A Search for an Ideal" (Ph.D. diss., Univ. of Chicago, 1973). Bradley University and Illinois Institute of Technology both trace their origins to the technical education and manual training movement of the 1890s. See Louis A. R. Yates, *A Proud Heritage: Bradley's History, 1897–1972* (Peoria, 1974) and Irene Macauley, *The Heritage of Illinois Institute of Technology* (Chicago, 1978). Northwestern and the University of Chicago also embraced secular ideals as they evolved into modern universities with complex departmental structures. There are many studies of individual programs at Northwestern. Among the best are Michael W. Sedlak and Harold F. Williamson, *The Evolution of Management Education: A History of the Northwestern University J. L. Kellogg Graduate School of Management, 1908–1983* (Urbana, 1983) and Lynn Miller Rein, *Northwestern University School of Speech: A History* (Evanston, 1981).

Richard J. Storr, *Harper's University: The Beginnings; A History of the University of Chicago* (Chicago, 1966) focuses on the relationship between Chicago's first president, William Rainey Harper, and its principal benefactor, John D. Rockefeller. William Michael Murphey and D. J. R. Bruckner, eds., *The Idea of the University of Chicago: Selections from the Papers of the First Eight Chief Executives of the University of Chicago from 1891 to 1975* (Chicago, 1976) carries the university's story beyond its early years. There are the many studies of individual presidents and faculty members. An outstanding recent example is Harry S. Ashmore, *Unseasonable Truths: The Life of Robert Maynard Hutchins* (Boston, 1989), an account of the controversial educator who presided over the university from 1929 to 1951. Another approach to the institution's history is through research on particular programs. One example is Woodie T. White, Jr., "The Decline of the Classroom and the Chicago Study of Education, 1909–1929," *American Journal of Education*, 90 (Feb. 1982), which argues that the study of education at the University of Chicago became increasingly removed from classroom concerns as academics and white male school administrators used the program for careerist ends. Other program histories include John Richardson, Jr., *The Spirit of Inquiry: The Graduate Library School at Chicago, 1921–51* (Chicago, 1982) and Barry D. Karl, *Charles E. Merriam and the Study of Politics* (Chicago, 1974). For the most studied department, see Lester R. Kurtz, *Evaluating Chicago Sociology: A Guide to the Literature, with an Annotated Bibliography* (Chicago, 1984).

Scholars employed in academia and preoccupied with their own institutional roots have thus contributed substantially to the unwieldy historiography of education in Illinois, and the literature is no less cumbersome for religion. A definitive review in either field would require an entire volume similar to L[avere] C. Rudolph and Judith E. Endelman, *Religion in Indiana: A Guide to Historical Sources* (Bloomington, Ind., 1986). Institutional histories, biographies, and other works devoted to particular religious or educational movements in Illinois will no doubt continue to proliferate, but their authors would do well to strive for a more appropriate balance between narrative detail and interpretive generalization than is currently the norm. David Tyack and Thomas James, in "State Government and American Public Education: Exploring the 'Primeval Forest,' " *History of Education Quarterly*, 26 (Spring 1986), point to the need for state-level histories of education, and a similar case might be made for religion. Yet scholars aspiring to produce synoptic histories of either religion or education in Illinois will still face the difficult challenge of doing justice to the stubborn diversity of institutions, practices, and traditions found in the state while simultaneously weaving those diverse strands into coherent patterns.

# 12

# LITERATURE

## JAMES HURT

STUDENTS OF ILLINOIS literature find themselves in something like the position of early travelers to the state. The maps available are sketchy, with large areas marked "terra incognita." The study of Illinois literature has lagged far behind the study of other state literatures, including several in the Midwest, notably those of Indiana, Iowa, and Michigan. It is not clear why this should be so. Certainly it is not for any thinness in the state's literary heritage. The early nineteenth-century travelers' accounts and "guides for emigrants," many of high literary quality; the speeches not only of Abraham Lincoln but of such other notable orators as Stephen A. Douglas, Owen Lovejoy, and Robert G. Ingersoll; such memorable autobiographies as those of Peter Cartwright, Ulysses S. Grant, and Jane Addams; such permanently valuable products of the Chicago Renaissance as Edgar Lee Masters' *Spoon River Anthology* (1915), Carl Sandburg's *Chicago Poems* (1916), and the poems of Vachel Lindsay; the tough "Chicago novels" of James T. Farrell, Richard Wright, and Nelson Algren; and a contemporary tradition that includes the works of Saul Bellow, Gwendolyn Brooks, William Maxwell, and Harry Mark Petrakis—these amount to a remarkably rich and provocative body of Illinois writing.

Of course, few of these writers could be fairly labeled "neglected" or "forgotten"; many of them have received and continue to receive voluminous critical attention. It is only as Illinois writers, as writers exploring a sense of place and reflecting or rejecting a certain distinctive intellectual and artistic tradition, that they could be said to be neglected. And even here, a partial exception should be made in the case of the literature of Chicago, which has attracted the recurring attention of literary historians and critics since the Chicago Renaissance of the years around World War I. Paradoxically, though, the study of Chicago literature has, if anything, diverted attention from the broader study of Illinois literature, preserving the split, so pervasive in Illinois life, between Chicago and Downstate, despite the intimate relationship that can be shown to exist between Chicago's distinctive literary voices and the rural, prairie experiences that anticipated and echoed them.

What can be gained by dividing literature along state lines, for thinking sometimes of "Illinois literature," rather than "midwestern literature," "American literature," or even "world literature"? Certainly political boundaries do not necessarily imply distinctive or unified cultural or artistic values, and a state-line approach to literature runs the risk of critical incoherence and a narrow boosterism. Nevertheless, carried on intelligently, the study of the literature of Illinois can offer a great deal to both the historian and the critic. A novel like Theodore Dreiser's *Sister Carrie* (1900) or Frank Norris's *The Pit* (1903) can provide many details of everyday life in a past age hard to recover from other sources. And more important, it can give insight into inner reality as well, what it felt like to live at that time and in that place. The literary critic, too, can gain from the study of a range of literature rooted in the same place a heightened sense of the complex interplay between history and art.

Attempts to define and survey the literature of Illinois have been few and far between. The most comprehensive account is Robert Bray, ed., *A Reader's Guide to Illinois Literature* (Springfield, 1985). This publication of the state-sponsored Read Illinois program contains essays on nonfiction, fiction to 1915, fiction since 1915, poetry, and women, along with annotated bibliographies of both primary and secondary material. Blair Whitney, "The Garden of Illinois," in John E. Hallwas and Dennis J. Reader, eds., *The Vision of This Land . . .* (Macomb, 1976), though it deals directly only with Lindsay, Masters, and Sandburg, provides some generalizations that can be extended to Illinois writing as a whole. James Hurt, "Life in Prairie Land: The Literature of Illinois," *Illinois English Bulletin*, 70 (Spring 1983), offers a brief overview and an attempt at definition.

A full-length critical history of Illinois writing is clearly needed. The closest approach to such a history thus far is Robert C. Bray, *Rediscoveries: Literature and Place in Illinois* (Urbana, 1982), though Bray makes no attempt at inclusiveness, dealing primarily with fiction and stopping at about the time of World War I. Nevertheless, *Rediscoveries* is a tough-minded, critically sophisticated book that provides thoughtful, complex readings of some major Illinois books and sets a high standard for future studies.

Anthologies of Illinois writing have been as rare as critical overviews. The most inclusive one is John E. Hallwas, ed., *Illinois Literature: The Nineteenth Century* (Macomb, 1986). This volume contains selections from nearly fifty writers, with brief historical-critical introductions and bibliographies. In commemoration of the Illinois sesquicentennial, Southern Illinois University Press published E[dward] Earle Stibitz, ed., *Illinois Poets: A Selection* (Carbondale, 1968) and Howard W. Webb, Jr., ed., *Illinois Prose Writers: A Selection* (Carbondale, 1968). Both are well edited and have thoughtful introductions but are too brief and selective to be fully satisfactory. Paul M. Angle, ed., *Prairie State: Impressions of Illinois, 1673–1967, by Travelers and Other Observers* (Chicago, 1968) is a readable book well described by its title. A fine collection restricted to Chicago is Albert Halper, ed., *This Is Chicago: An Anthology* (New York, 1952).

Bibliographers have served Illinois literature rather better than literary historians and anthologists have. The Illinois Association of Teachers of English produced a fifty-six page inventory, "Illinois Authors," compiled by J[ulius] N. Hook et al., *Illinois English Bulletin*, 54 (Nov.–Dec. 1966). Birth and death dates and a list of major works appear with each entry. This bibliography is still useful though not altogether satisfactory, marred as it is by one kind of excessive inclusiveness, incorporating authors whose only connection with Illinois is that they were born in the state, and another kind of unwarranted exclusiveness, restricting coverage to authors of belles-lettres, rather narrowly defined. Thus, Edna Ferber and Ernest Hemingway are given prominent treatment, while George Flower and Eliza Farnham are omitted.

The Illinois entries in Gerald Nemanic, ed., *A Bibliographical Guide to Midwestern Literature* (Iowa City, 1981) are more analytical, and therefore more useful, than the list of "Illinois Authors." Nemanic has a healthy disinclination to define literature too narrowly and includes sections not only on literature and language but on history and society, folklore, personal narratives, and architecture and graphics as well. Chicago receives separate treatment, as do black literature, Indian literature, and literary periodicals, and there are generous treatments of major individual authors.

Thomas L. Kilpatrick and Patsy-Rose Hoshiko, *Illinois! Illinois! An Annotated Bibliography of Fiction* (Metuchen, N.J., 1979) is an extraordinary listing of 1,554 novels and short-story collections dealing with Illinois, classified into five chronological periods (by subject, not by date of composition). Each item is briefly summarized. The editors lament in their introduction their suspected failure to achieve total comprehensiveness; surely their failure is not great. *Illinois! Illinois!* includes a useful subject and place name index in which, of course, by far the longest entry is for Chicago. This inventory may be supplemented by Clarence A. Andrews, "Literature of Place: Chicago," *Great Lakes Review*, 5 (Summer 1978 and Winter 1979), a listing of 875 Chicago items, including, as Kilpatrick and Hoshiko do not, plays, collections of poetry, and films. An older compilation still of some use is Chicago Public Library Omnibus Project, Work Projects Administration, *Bibliography of Illinois Poets since 1900* (Chicago, 1942).

The literature of Illinois begins with travelers' accounts of the region, emigrants' guides, and similar narratives. There are a great many such works, many of very high quality, including books by Morris Birkbeck, George Flower, William Oliver, Catherine Stewart, Eliza Farnham, and Rebecca Burlend. Much of this material remains unexplored from a literary point of view, though there has been a recent surge of interest in travelers' narratives by critics wishing to expand the academic canon of American literature, which has tended to be heavily male and narrowly belletristic.

Are such travelers' narratives "literature," and can the literary critic add anything of significance to the historian's study of them? Few of these writers conceived of themselves as producing works of art, and there is a danger of overreading what in many cases were hasty, utilitarian works tossed off in the midst of more pressing matters. But in practice the dividing line between literary and nonliterary writing is far from precise. Many of the travelers' narratives are the work of highly sophisticated and very skillful writers, and it seems unreasonable to ignore them in favor of less interesting frontier poems and tales merely on the basis of genre and intention. For an exemplary application of the methods of literary criticism to frontier personal narrative, see Bray's treatment in *Rediscoveries* of Eliza W. Farnham, *Life in Prairie Land* (New York, 1846; best ed., Urbana, 1988), a book Bray sees as "a sustained and lovely hymn to the land" (p. 16). A longer and equally excellent treatment of this book is John E. Hallwas, "Eliza Farnham's *Life in Prairie Land*," *Old Northwest*, 7 (Winter 1981–82). For a similar attempt to treat nonliterary prose from a literary point of view, see James Hurt, "Reality and the Picture of Imagination: The Literature of the English Prairie," *Great Lakes Review*, 7 (Summer 1981).

The literary study of nineteenth-century Illinois autobiography presents similar complexities. On the one hand, it is an essentially nonliterary form; on the other, it seems to have called forth some of the finest writing of the period. The *Personal Memoirs of U. S. Grant* (2 vols., New York, 1885–86) is one of the great American autobiographies. The *Autobiography of Peter Cartwright, the Backwoods Preacher* (Cincinnati, 1856) deserves more critical attention than it has received; Jane Addams, *Twenty Years at Hull-House . . .* (New York, 1910) is another American masterpiece; and even such an eccentric work as Frances E. Willard, *Glimpses of Fifty Years . . .* (Chicago, 1889) is a fascinating account of social history combined with unconscious self-revelation. One of the few assessments of the Addams book as literature is James Hurt, "Walden on Halsted Street . . . ," *Centennial Review*, 23 (Spring 1979). In a category by itself is the remarkable *Life of . . . Black Hawk* (Cincinnati, 1833).

Oratory should be added to travelers' narratives and autobiography as a major frontier genre, and it is as an orator that Lincoln, the most characteristic Illinois figure, enters the history of Illinois literature. Recognition of Lincoln's powers as a writer came early, and his law partner William Herndon's comments on his style are still valid and useful. See William H. Herndon and Jesse William Weik, *Herndon's Lincoln: The True Story of a Great Life . . .* (3 vols., Chicago, 1889). Perhaps the best general overview of Lincoln as a writer is Roy P. Basler, "Lincoln's Development as a Writer," in Basler, ed., *Abraham Lincoln: His*

*Speeches and Writings* (Cleveland, 1946), reprinted in Basler, *A Touchstone for Greatness: Essays, Addresses, and Occasional Pieces about Abraham Lincoln* (Westport, Conn., 1973). David D. Anderson, *Abraham Lincoln* (New York, 1970) considers Lincoln in the tradition of American literature. James Hurt, "All the Living and the Dead: Lincoln's Imagery," *American Literature*, 52 (Nov. 1980), attempts to trace a relationship between Lincoln's style and certain features of his personality. Study of Lincoln as a writer has focused heavily upon his poetic speeches of the war years. A larger view would take into account also the speeches of his Illinois years. It would, in other words, place him more clearly in the tradition of Western oratory. The Lincoln-Douglas debates furnish good material for such a reconsideration. A handy edition of the debates is Robert W. Johannsen's, *The Lincoln-Douglas Debates of 1858* (New York, 1965).

Stephen A. Douglas's speeches are well worth studying, too, independently of Lincoln's. Unfortunately, they have not been collected, but a good guide to those still extant is the authoritative biography by Robert W. Johannsen, *Stephen A. Douglas* (New York, 1973). The speeches of Peoria's great agnostic Robert G. Ingersoll have also been neglected, despite the light that they throw not only on the history of American public speaking but also on a curious and important strain in American intellectual history. His speeches, immensely popular in his own day, are preserved in C[linton] P. Farrell, ed., *The Works of Robert G. Ingersoll* (12 vols., New York, 1900).

The history of belles-lettres on the Illinois frontier is overshadowed by the accomplishments of such figures as Eliza Farnham, Peter Cartwright, and Abraham Lincoln, but it is important nevertheless. For an amusing and thoughtful overview, not restricted to Illinois, of early attempts to create a distinctive "Western" literature, see David Donald and Frederick A. Palmer, "Toward a Western Literature, 1820–60," in Donald, *Lincoln Reconsidered: Essays on the Civil War Era* (New York, 1956). Dorothy Anne Dondore, *The Prairie and the Making of Middle America: Four Centuries of Description* (Cedar Rapids, Iowa, 1926) remains, despite its age, a standard source of information about frontier literature. The same might be said for Ralph Leslie Rusk, *The Literature of the Middle Western Frontier* (2 vols., New York, 1925). The only critical study of early Illinois poetry is John E. Hallwas, "Illinois Poetry: The Lincoln Era," in Illinois State Historical Society, *Selected Papers in Illinois History, 1981*.

The rise of the Illinois novel is the principal subject of Bray's *Rediscoveries*. Bray includes incisive analyses of a number of novels written between 1880 and 1910, emphasizing the continuities between such downstate novels as Joseph Kirkland's *Zury: The Meanest Man in Spring County* (1887) and Francis Grierson's *The Valley of Shadows* (1909) and such Chicago novels as Frank Norris's *The Pit* (1903) and Upton Sinclair's *The Jungle* (1906).

*The Jungle* and *The Pit* bring us to the threshold of the most vital period of Illinois literature, the Chicago Renaissance. The most thorough and authoritative treatment of the Renaissance is Bernard Duffey, *The Chicago Renaissance in*

*American Letters: A Critical History* (East Lansing, 1954). A more popular but still valuable history is Dale Kramer, *Chicago Renaissance: The Literary Life in the Midwest, 1900–1930* (New York, 1966). Duffey and Kramer may be supplemented by Hugh Danziel Duncan, *The Rise of Chicago as a Literary Center from 1885 to 1920: A Sociological Essay in American Culture* (Totowa, N.J., 1964). Individual authors of the Renaissance have been voluminously treated, though perhaps the present emphasis on their relation to a continuing tradition of Illinois writing has not received sufficient attention; for bibliographies of individual authors, the reader is referred to Nemanic's *Guide*.

Treatments of Chicago literature have by no means been limited to the comparatively brief and in some ways unrepresentative period of the Chicago Renaissance. For brief, integrative overviews of Chicago literature, see Michael Anania, "A Commitment to Grit," *Chicago*, 32 (Nov. 1983); Bernard Rogers, "The Chicago Novel," *Illinois Issues*, 9 (Nov. 1983); and James Hurt, "Images of Chicago," in Roger D. Bridges and Rodney O. Davis, *Illinois: Its History and Legacy* (St. Louis, 1984). Kenny J. Williams has produced two thick volumes of Chicago literary history, *In the City of Men: Another Story of Chicago* (Nashville, Tenn., 1974) and *Prairie Voices: A Literary History of Chicago from the Frontier to 1893* (Nashville, Tenn., 1980), books followed closely by Clarence A. Andrews, *Chicago in Story: A Literary History* (Iowa City, 1982)—truly an embarrassment of riches. These studies, however, have not completely superseded Lennox Bouton Grey's encyclopedic "Chicago and 'The Great American Novel': A Critical Approach to the American Epic" (Ph.D. thesis, Univ. of Chicago, 1935).

In *Chicago and the American Literary Imagination, 1880–1920* (Chicago, 1984), Carl S. Smith traces the theme of art in a number of turn-of-the-century Chicago novels, showing the role that the image of the city played in creating a modern literature, and looks closely at the repeated treatments of the quintessential Chicago subjects of the railroad, the skyscraper, and the stockyards. The virtue of Smith's book is that he moves beyond the purely descriptive and taxonomic method of most previous treatments of the subject to thoughtful interpretation.

On the special topic of Chicago's tradition of newspaper humor, Kenny J. Williams and Bernard Duffey have edited *Chicago's Public Wits: A Chapter in the American Comic Spirit* (Baton Rouge, 1983). A critical treatment of three of the most important figures in this tradition is James DeMuth, *Small Town Chicago: The Comic Perspective of Finley Peter Dunne, George Ade, Ring Lardner* (Port Washington, N.Y., 1980).

Many of these recent critics, historians, and anthologists of Chicago literature seem to imply agreement, in varying ways, that the study of the city's literature can be enriched by leaping two gulfs, that between literary and nonliterary writing and that between Chicago and Downstate. The sometimes tiresome litany of the "Chicago canon"—Dreiser, Farrell, Algren, et al.—needs to be revised to include not only the work of such non-Naturalistic novelists as Saul Bellow but also such vital nonfiction works as Milton "Mezz" Mezzrow and Bernard Wolfe's lovely chronicle of Chicago jazz life, *Really the Blues* (New York, 1946), and Norman Mailer, *Miami and the Siege of Chicago: An Informal History of the Republican and Democratic Conventions of 1968* (New York, 1968). It also needs to be revised to consider the contributions of women. Sidney H. Bremer has "rediscovered" a number of turn-of-the-century novels by women which give a rather different interpretation of the city from canonical male novels. See her essays, "Lost Continuities: Alternative Urban Visions in Chicago Novels, 1890–1915," *Soundings*, 64 (Spring 1981), and "Willa Cather's Lost Chicago Sisters," in Susan Merrill Squier, ed., *Women Writers and the City: Essays in Feminist Literary Criticism* (Knoxville, Tenn., 1984). The oral histories of Studs Terkel and the newspaper columns of Mike Royko also deserve consideration as contemporary expressions of Chicago life. We have perhaps followed the Hogbutcher line long enough. In addition, more attention needs to be paid to Chicago's setting in the rural Midwest and to the tension, so prominent in much of the literature but often neglected in criticism, between the farm and the city. Kenny Williams suggests this interplay when she calls her "literary history of Chicago" *Prairie Voices*.

Fortunately, the prairie voices are not yet stilled, and the literature of Illinois is still very much an ongoing enterprise. An excellent starting point for the study of contemporary downstate writing is Bray's lyrical personal essay, "The Road Down from Spoon River," which forms the final chapter of *Rediscoveries*. Bray defines the spirit of much contemporary Illinois writing by exploring both its indebtedness to and its rebellion against the glum necrology of *Spoon River Anthology*, "for better or worse our classic of classics" (p. 154). Bray finds the spirit of "village virus" writing dead and in its place a regional literature that is marked by a reconciliatory humor and that employs the materials of the Illinois landscape, history, and folklore not as grounds for bitterness or grievance but as sources of strength in a more and more homogeneous world.

The "All Illinois" issue of *StoryQuarterly*, 10 (1980), and the "Chicago" issue of *TriQuarterly*, 60 (Spring–Summer 1984), also provide an introduction to current Illinois writing. Each magazine includes criticism and interviews as well as selections from leading contemporary writers. Two valuable collections of contemporary poetry are *Heartland: Poets of the Midwest* (DeKalb, 1967) and *Heartland II* . . . (DeKalb, 1975), both edited by Lucien Stryk. Though not restricted to Illinois, these volumes contain selections from a number of Illinois poets. Stryk's critical introductions are also valuable. Another fine collection is James McGowan and Lynn DeVore, eds., *Benchmark: Anthology of Contemporary Illinois Poetry* (Urbana, 1988). *Studies in Illinois Poetry*, edited by John E. Hallwas (Urban, 1989), offers five provocative essays on the subject.

Finally, however, as with any contemporary literature, the history of contemporary Illinois writing is being written every day, and anyone interested in the subject can watch it unfold in the book review pages of the state's and the nation's newspapers and magazines. Few of the state's outstanding writers would, probably, like to be known primarily as "Illinois writers," but placing their work occasionally against a long tradition of Illinois literature sometimes helps one both to define their achievements and to understand better the personal, human history of the state.

# 13

# ART, ARCHITECTURE, AND MUSIC

## TITUS M. KARLOWICZ AND SARAH HANKS KARLOWICZ

IN STUDIES OF the arts in Illinois history, both architecture and music have received more attention than painting, sculpture, and the decorative arts. Moreover, the record for Chicago is far better than that for the state as a whole. Yet the literature in every field is so extensive that this review is necessarily selective, with an emphasis on essential or representative secondary works, some of which are as valuable for their bibliographies as for their own coverage.

*Illinois: A Descriptive and Historical Guide*, compiled by the Federal Writers' Project of the Work Projects Administration (Chicago, 1939), provides in three brief chapters a good but somewhat dated synopsis of art, architecture, and music in Illinois history. Frances Cheney Bennett, ed., *History of Music and Art in Illinois . . .* (Philadelphia, 1904) includes a historical essay followed by biographical sketches of artists, musicians, and patrons throughout the state. For summaries of cultural development in specific periods, see Henry B. Fuller's chapters in Ernest Ludlow Bogart and Charles Manfred Thompson, *The Industrial State, 1870–1893* (Springfield, 1920) and Bogart and John Mabry Mathews, *The Modern Commonwealth, 1893–1918* (Springfield, 1920), and also the coverage in Donald F. Tingley, *The Structuring of a State: The History of Illinois, 1899 to 1928* (Springfield, 1980).

Betty I. Madden, *Arts, Crafts, and Architecture in Early Illinois* (Urbana, 1974) demonstrates the significance of the arts in the state's development before about 1860. A pioneering synthesis, concerned in part to trace successive incursions of refined forms onto the vernacular, the book is a well-illustrated, well-documented primer for the field. A special issue of *Chicago History*, 10 (Winter 1981–82), is devoted to the "Folk Art of Illinois." Esther Sparks, "A Biographical Dictionary of Painters and Sculptors in Illinois, 1808–1945" (Ph.D. diss., Northwestern Univ., 1971) is a gold mine of information on the spread of artistic professionalism. This work not only identifies a host of artists who practiced or taught in Illinois but also surveys at length the history of art in the state.

Several more particular studies focus on Chicago. Leslie S. Goldstein, "Art in Chicago and the World's Columbian Exposition of 1893" (M.A. thesis, Univ. of Iowa, 1970) reviews the years from 1885 to 1895. In "American Paintings and Sculpture in the Fine Arts Building of the World's Columbian Exposition, Chicago, 1893" (Ph.D. diss., Univ. of Kansas, 1976), Elizabeth Broun considers the contributions of different schools of art. Intellectual histories of an important artistic movement include Eileen Boris, *Art and Labor: Ruskin, Morris, and the Craftsman Ideal in America* (Philadelphia, 1986) and Bruce Robert Kahler, "Art and Life: The Arts and Crafts Movement in Chicago, 1897–1910" (Ph.D. diss., Purdue Univ., 1986). Sharon S. Darling ably documents the craftsmanship of Chicago in several studies, including, for example, *Chicago Ceramics and Glass: An Illustrated History from 1871 to 1933* (Chicago, 1979) and *Decorative and Architectural Arts in Chicago, 1871–1933: An Illustrated Guide to the Ceramics and Glass Exhibition* (Chicago, 1982).

In "Five Artists and the Chicago Modernist Movement, 1909–1928" (Ph.D. diss., Emory Univ., 1973), Kenneth R. Hey probes the limits of artistic taste in the city. He also discusses the first, most traditional artist of the group in "Ralph Clarkson: An Academic Painter in an Era of Change," *Journal of the Illinois State Historical Society*, 76 (Autumn 1983). J[acob] Z. Jacobson, ed., *Art of Today: Chicago, 1933* (Chicago, 1932), documenting the modernism of the period, includes "artists' statements" and biographical notes for fifty-two painters and sculptors. A similar record, especially for the 1930s and 1940s, is Louise Dunn Yochim, *Role and Impact: The Chicago Society of Artists* (Chicago, 1979). For the major venture in government support of art in the period, see George J. Mavigliano and Richard A. Lawson, *The Federal Art Project in Illinois, 1935–1943* (Carbondale, 1990). Robert J. Evans and Maureen A. McKenna, *After the Great Crash: New Deal Art in Illinois; An Exhibition of Art from the Period 1934–1943, Produced by Artists on the Various Federal Art Projects in Illinois* (Springfield, 1983) is an informative catalog which also illustrates the Illinois State Museum's attention to the history of Illinois art.

For contemporary developments, see Franz Schulze, *Fantastic Images: Chicago Art since 1945* (Chicago, 1972) and Dennis Adrian, *Sight Out of Mind: Essays and Criticism on Art* (Ann Arbor, 1985). Catalogs for exhibitions, both in Chicago and elsewhere, extend the record. Susan Regan McKillop, ed., *West Coast '76: The Chicago Connection* (Sacramento, 1976); Diane Kirkpatrick, *Chicago: The City and Its Artists, 1945–1978* (Ann Arbor, 1978);

and Tony Knipe et al., *Who Chicago? An Exhibition of Contemporary Imagists* (Sunderland, Eng., 1980) were mounted in other cities. More recently, Dennis Adrian and Richard A. Born, *The Chicago Imagist Print: Ten Artists' Works, 1958–1987* . . . (Chicago, 1987) and Judith Russi Kirshner, *Surfaces: Two Decades of Painting in Chicago; Seventies and Eighties* (Chicago, 1987) were dedicated to exhibitions in Chicago at the Smart Gallery and the Terra Museum, respectively. The catalogs include more particular lists and bibliographies.

Monographic works on Illinois painters and sculptors are rare. Lewis W. Williams II, "Lorado Taft: American Sculptor and Art Missionary" (Ph.D. diss., Univ. of Chicago, 1958) and Michael Croydon, *Ivan Albright* (New York, 1978) deal with two of the more outstanding native sons. See also Timothy J. Garvey, *Public Sculptor: Lorado Taft and the Beautification of Chicago* (Urbana, 1988). Tributes to lesser-known artists can be found, such as Adelaide N. Cooley, *The Monument Maker: A Biography of Frederick Ernst Triebel* (Hicksville, N.Y., 1978) and Shirley J. Burton, *Adelaide Johnson: To Make Immortal Their Adventurous Will* (Macomb, 1986). One might expect more.

Art in Illinois must also be considered in terms of the collections found throughout the state. One of the foremost in the United States is introduced in John Maxon, *The Art Institute of Chicago* (New York, 1970) and *Master Paintings in the Art Institute of Chicago*, selected by James N. Wood and Katharine C. Lee (Chicago, 1988). For a more particular account of the period before 1924, see Anne Felicia Cierpik, "History of the Art Institute of Chicago from Its Incorporation on May 24, 1879, to the Death of Charles L. Hutchinson" (M.A. thesis, DePaul Univ., 1957). An informal record of certain patrons may be found in Patricia Erens, *Masterpieces: Famous Chicagoans and Their Paintings* (Chicago, 1979). Terry Ann R. Neff, ed., *The Museum of Contemporary Art, Chicago: Selections from the Permanent Collection* (Chicago, 1984) illustrates the first decade of the museum's development, while Neff, ed., *A Proud Heritage: Two Centuries of American Art* . . . (Chicago, 1987) marked the opening in Chicago of the Terra Museum of American Art. Chicago is otherwise possessor of a formidable amount of sculpture in public places. For inventories of this "collection," see James L. Riedy, *Chicago Sculpture* (Urbana, 1981) and Ira J. Bach and Mary Lackritz Gray, *A Guide to Chicago's Public Sculpture* (Chicago, 1983).

Chicago is conspicuous in the literature on architecture as well as art in Illinois. There is as yet, however, no full-scale synthesis of the subject. Thomas E. Tallmadge, *Architecture in Old Chicago* (Chicago, 1941) is limited to the nineteenth century. John Zukowsky, ed., *Chicago Architecture, 1872–1922: Birth of a Metropolis* (Munich, 1987) brings together twenty essays and a host of illustrations pertaining to selected topics in the dynamic years between the Great Chicago Fire and the Tribune Tower competition. Ross Miller, *American Apocalypse: The Great Fire and the Myth of Chicago* (Chicago, 1990) provides another perspective on the period. Contemporary concerns are important in several exhibition catalogs that survey the field, including Oswald W. Grube et al., *100 Years of Architecture in Chicago: Continuity of Structure and Form* (Chicago, 1976); Stuart E. Cohen, *Chicago Architects . . .* (Chicago, 1976); and Ante Glibota, *A Guide to 150 Years of Chicago Architecture* (Chicago, 1985).

Popular guides to particular landmarks include John Drury, *Old Chicago Houses* (Chicago, 1941) and Arthur Siegel, ed., *Chicago's Famous Buildings . . .* (Chicago, 1965; 3rd ed. by Ira J. Bach, Chicago, 1980). Many buildings in Chicago and surrounding communities are charted in Bach's itineraries, *Chicago on Foot . . .* (Chicago, 1969; 4th ed. with Susan Wolfson, Chicago, 1987) and *A Guide to Chicago's Historic Suburbs on Wheels and on Foot* (Athens, Ohio, 1981). The diversity of Chicago architecture, despite the regnant styles of successive generations, is well illustrated in a thematic guide by George A. Lane, *Chicago Churches and Synagogues: An Architectural Pilgrimage* (Chicago, 1981).

One of Chicago's leading achievements after the Fire of 1871 was the construction of the tall commercial building. This subject is ably treated in Carl W. Condit, *The Rise of the Skyscraper* (New York, 1952; revised ed., *The Chicago School of Architecture: A History of Commercial and Public Building in the Chicago Area, 1875–1925*, Chicago, 1964). Condit traces many architectural advances to Chicago, not New York or other cities, a controversy discussed in "The Chicago School of Architecture: A Symposium," *Prairie School Review*, 9 (1st and 2nd Quarters, 1972). Condit continued his studies in *Chicago, 1910–29* and *Chicago, 1930–70*, each subtitled *Building, Planning, and Urban Technology* (Chicago, 1973–74). For two architects who were important in the development of the skyscraper, see Theodore Turak, *William Le Baron Jenney: A Pioneer of Modern Architecture* (Ann Arbor, 1986) and Donald Hoffmann, *The Architecture of John Wellborn Root* (Baltimore, 1973). See also John Zukowsky et al., *Chicago and New York: Architectural Interactions* (Chicago, 1984).

The literature on the World's Columbian Exposition is voluminous. A useful introduction is David F. Burg, *Chicago's White City of 1893* (Lexington, Ky., 1976), while a more concentrated view is Titus Marion Karlowicz, "The Architecture of the World's Columbian Exposition" (Ph.D. diss., Northwestern Univ., 1965). Frederick Law Olmsted and Daniel H. Burnham, two leaders in the development of Chicago's park and boulevard system, are studied in Victoria Post Ranney, *Olmsted in Chicago* (Chicago, 1972) and Thomas S. Hines, *Burnham of Chicago, Architect and Planner* (New York, 1974).

The classical architecture of the 1893 fair, perpetuated in such buildings as the Museum of Science and Industry and the Field Museum of Natural History, established the Beaux Arts tradition which lasted into the 1920s. At the same time, Chicago and the Midwest witnessed a different, more indigenous style known as the Prairie School of architecture. In Louis H. Sullivan, *The Autobiography of an Idea* (New York, 1924) and Frank Lloyd Wright, *An Autobiography* (New York, 1932; revised eds., New York, 1943 and 1977), the leading exemplars of the new school took issue with the classical tradition. Writings about their own work are extensive, but Hugh Morrison, *Louis Sullivan: Prophet of Modern*

*Architecture* (New York, 1935); Grant Carpenter Manson, *Frank Lloyd Wright to 1910: The First Golden Age* (New York, 1958); and Henry-Russell Hitchcock, *In the Nature of Materials: 1887–1941; The Buildings of Frank Lloyd Wright* (New York, 1942) remain the respected standards of reference. See also the biographies by Robert C. Twombly, *Louis Sullivan: His Life and Work* (New York, 1986) and *Frank Lloyd Wright: An Interpretive Biography* (New York, 1973; revised ed., *Frank Lloyd Wright: His Life and His Architecture*, New York, 1979).

H[arold] Allen Brooks, *The Prairie School: Frank Lloyd Wright and His Midwest Contemporaries* (Toronto, 1972) is a careful study of the architects for whom Sullivan and Wright were mentors. Several related investigations appeared in the *Prairie School Review* (13 vols., 1964–76). See also Wim de Wit, ed., *Louis Sullivan: The Function of Ornament* (New York, 1986). A single community is inventoried in Paul E. Sprague, *Guide to Frank Lloyd Wright and Prairie School Architecture in Oak Park* (Oak Park, 1976; revised ed., Oak Park, 1986).

By the time of A Century of Progress, the world's fair of 1933–34, both classical and Prairie School styles had given way to the machine age of modern architecture. More importantly, in 1938 Ludwig Mies van der Rohe was appointed director of architecture of the Armour (now Illinois) Institute of Technology, advancing the International Style of architecture. Mies's many commissions in Chicago before his death in 1969 are an important part of several biographies and exhibition catalogs, including, for example, Franz Schulze, *Mies van der Rohe: A Critical Biography* (Chicago, 1985) and John Zukowsky, ed., *Mies Reconsidered: His Career, Legacy, and Disciples* (New York, 1986). For an assessment of post-Miesian trends, see Maurizio Casari and Vincenzo Pavan, eds., *Beyond the International Style: New Chicago Architecture* (Chicago, 1981). Current work of members of the Chicago Architectural Club is included in the *Chicago Architectural Journal* (8 issues, 1981–89).

While the architectural history of Chicago is well defined, the record for Downstate is uneven and incomplete. Many buildings are pictured and briefly described in Frederick Koeper, ed., *Illinois Architecture from Territorial Times to the Present: A Selective Guide* (Chicago, 1968) and John Drury, *Old Illinois Houses* (Springfield, 1948). Drury attempted a different kind of survey in the American Aerial County History series, an effort in 1954–56 to document rural settings from the air. The series includes separate volumes for at least thirty counties in Illinois, each with a title approximating that of the first book: *This Is Macon County, Illinois: An Up-to-date Historical Narrative with County Map and Many Unique Aerial Photographs of Cities, Towns, Villages, and Farmsteads* (Chicago, 1954).

The Historic Sites Division of the Illinois Department of Conservation, which in 1985 was transferred to the Illinois Historic Preservation Agency, has undertaken more complete inventories of the state, county by county, including the Illinois Historic Landmarks Survey, the Illinois Historic Structures Survey, and the Illinois Archaeological Survey. The division prepared mimeographed summaries of this work in the mid-1970s. It also issued a useful though dated guide to its activities in Ruth Eckdish Knack, ed., *Preservation Illinois: A Guide to State and Local Resources* (Springfield, 1977). Sara Jane Herrin, "Historic Preservation in Illinois," *Southern Illinois University Law Journal* (No. 3, 1979) reviews the legal basis of the preservation movement.

Official interest in documenting historic buildings is matched by preservation efforts in many places around the state and by increased scholarly attention to the architectural history of individual communities. Examples of the ensuing literature from opposite ends of the state are Carl H. Johnson, Jr., *The Building of Galena: An Architectural Legacy* (Galena, 1977) and Susan E. Maycock, *An Architectural History of Carbondale, Illinois* (Carbondale, 1983). The Mormon legacy at Nauvoo is studied in Dolores Hayden, *Seven American Utopias: The Architecture of Communitarian Socialism, 1790–1975* (Cambridge, Mass., 1976). For an introduction to two small and rather singular communities, see Charles B. Hosmer, Jr., and Paul O. Williams, *Elsah: A Historic Guidebook* (Elsah, 1967; revised ed., Elsah, 1986) and John S. Garner, "Leclaire, Illinois: A Model Company Town, 1890–1934," *Journal of the Society of Architectural Historians*, 30 (Oct. 1971). Riverside is included in Walter L. Creese, *The Crowning of the American Landscape: Eight Great Spaces and Their Buildings* (Princeton, 1985). The rich architectural heritage of Quincy deserves more attention. James R. Allen, "Ernest M. Wood: A Provincial Testament," *Prairie School Review*, 11 (2nd Quarter, 1974), and Mara Gelbloom, "Ossian Simonds: Prairie Spirit in Landscape Gardening," ibid., 12 (2nd Quarter, 1975), provide a beginning. Other communities, including Springfield, benefited from parks designed by Jens Jensen, work that is described in Leonard K. Eaton, *Landscape Artist in America . . .* (Chicago, 1964). Charles B. Hosmer, Jr., *Preservation Comes of Age: From Williamsburg to the National Trust, 1926–1949* (2 vols., Charlottesville, Va., 1981) includes pages on New Salem and other state projects, while Ellen Huening Makowski, "Scenic Parks and Landscape Values" (Ph.D. diss., Univ. of Illinois, Urbana-Champaign, 1987) interprets the history of Starved Rock, White Pines, Pere Marquette, and Giant City state parks.

The influence of professional training in architecture and related fields is an important but neglected topic. One leading, if not legendary, figure in this area at the University of Illinois is studied in Lynn Monical Allen, "Nathan Clifford Ricker and His Students: A Legacy in Architectural Education" (M.A. thesis, Western Illinois Univ., 1971) and Wayne Michael Charney and John W. Stamper, "Nathan Clifford Ricker and the Beginning of Architectural Education in Illinois," *Illinois Historical Journal*, 79 (Winter 1986).

Another approach that could enrich the architectural history of the state is the consideration of different types of buildings. The two state capitols in Springfield, and several courthouses around the state, are noticed in Henry-Russell Hitchcock and William Seale, *Temples of Democracy: The State Capitols of the USA* (New York, 1976) and Paul Kenneth Goeldner, "Temples of Justice: Nineteenth Century County Courthouses in the Midwest and Texas" (Ph.D. diss., Columbia

Univ., 1970). Another study that could be applied to Illinois is Edward T. Price, "The Central Courthouse Square in the American County Seat," *Geographical Review*, 58 (Jan. 1968). Further research could focus on churches, opera houses, and other structures for specific purposes in communities throughout the state. There are indeed many aspects of the built environment that students of Illinois history have yet to explore.

Resources for the history of music in Illinois are less plentiful than those for architecture but are similarly concentrated on Chicago. For most purposes, the best starting point is H. Wiley Hitchcock and Stanley Sadie, eds., *The New Grove Dictionary of American Music* (4 vols., London, 1986), a cornucopia of pertinent information, combining biographical entries with articles on topics ranging from Chicago to musical styles such as jazz and blues. Robert L. Brubaker, *Making Music Chicago Style* (Chicago, 1985) is an excellent catalog for a wide-ranging exhibition at the Chicago Historical Society.

In "Music in Chicago, 1830 to 1850" (M.M. thesis, Univ. of Illinois, Urbana-Champaign, 1977), Marianne Clare Kozlowski extracts from extant newspapers a remarkable number of relevant items, prefacing this documentary record with chapters on concerts and recitals, music instruction, dancing, music merchandise, and sacred music in early Chicago. Another carefully researched study is Dena J. Epstein, *Music Publishing in Chicago before 1871: The Firm of Root & Cady, 1858–1871*, Detroit Studies in Music Bibliography, 14 (Detroit, 1969), the first chapter of which discusses "Chicago Music Publishers other than Root & Cady." George F. Root, *The Story of a Musical Life: An Autobiography* (Cincinnati, 1891) illuminates his work not only as a music publisher but as a music educator and song composer. Theodore Winton Thorson, "A History of Music Publishing in Chicago, 1850–1960" (Ph.D. diss., Northwestern Univ., 1961) surveys the subject.

W[illiam] S. B. Mathews, ed., *A Hundred Years of Music in America . . .* (Chicago, 1889) is a rich and fascinating history, national in scope but with Chicago as a point of reference. Its comprehensive approach extends to such less frequently treated topics as instrument manufacture, music festivals and auditoriums, and music teachers and critics, and many Illinoisans can be identified in its "Supplementary Dictionary of American Musicians." Chicago is also conspicuous in Mathews' journal, *Music* (1891–1902), and in his articles for *Dwight's Journal of Music*, *Étude*, and some fifteen other music periodicals of the period. His writings are studied in James Wesley Clark, "Prof. W. S. B. Mathews, 1837–1912, Self-made Musician of the Gilded Age" (Ph.D. diss., Univ. of Minnesota, 1983). Other articles on music in Chicago are listed in Joseph A. Mussulman, *Music in the Cultured Generation: A Social History of Music in America, 1870–1900* (Evanston, 1971).

The most detailed single account of early musical life in Chicago is George P. Upton, *Musical Memories: My Recollections of Celebrities of the Half Century, 1850–1900* (Chicago, 1908). Upton, music critic for the *Chicago Tribune*, discusses musical societies, symphony orchestras, opera companies, and topics ranging from music during the Civil War to music at the World's Columbian Exposition. His own career is covered in Mary Ann J. Feldman, "George P. Upton: Journalist, Music Critic, and Mentor to Early Chicago" (Ph.D. diss., Univ. of Minnesota, 1983). Upton's book may be supplemented by Florence Ffrench, comp., *Music and Musicians in Chicago* . . . (Chicago, 1899).

Undoubtedly the most important conductor in the Chicago of Mathews and Upton was Theodore Thomas. Upton edited *Theodore Thomas: A Musical Autobiography* (Chicago, 1905), adding his "Reminiscence and Appreciation" of Thomas and listing in a second volume most of Thomas's concert programs, 1855–1905. The one-volume edition of this work (New York, 1964) omits this enumeration but includes an introduction by Leon Stein and several updated lists regarding the Chicago Symphony Orchestra. After many itinerant performances in Chicago and Illinois, Thomas moved to Chicago to organize this orchestra in 1891 and to supervise the music at the world's fair of 1893. For accounts of these events, see Robert McColley, "Classical Music in Chicago and the Founding of the Symphony, 1850–1905," *Illinois Historical Journal*, 78 (Winter 1985), and Sandy R. Mazzola, "Bands and Orchestras at the World's Columbian Exposition," *American Music*, 4 (Winter 1986). Thomas's career as a "captain of musical enterprise" is studied in Ezra Schabas, *Theodore Thomas, America's Conductor and Builder of Orchestras, 1835–1905* (Urbana, 1989).

The Chicago Symphony Orchestra is further chronicled in Philo Adams Otis, *The Chicago Symphony Orchestra: Its Organization, Growth, and Development, 1891–1924* (Chicago, 1924) and Ellis A. Johnson, "The Chicago Symphony Orchestra, 1891–1942: A Study in American Cultural History" (Ph.D. diss., Univ. of Chicago, 1955). The latter work extends through the tenure of Thomas's successor, whose career is also covered in Donald Herbert Berglund, "A Study of the Life and Work of Frederick Stock . . . " (Ph.D. diss., Northwestern Univ., 1955). A brief summary of the orchestra's development to 1950 is in John H. Mueller, *The American Symphony Orchestra: A Social History of Musical Taste* (Bloomington, Ind., 1951).

Although itinerant opera performers first reached Chicago in 1850, resident companies date only from 1910. The entire subject would benefit from more scholarly attention. Edward C. Moore of the *Chicago Tribune* contributed an anecdotal account, *Forty Years of Opera in Chicago* (New York, 1930). A leading soprano and operatic director in Moore's generation is sketched in Richard D. Fletcher, " 'Our Own' Mary Garden," *Chicago History*, 2 (Spring 1972). For the period from 1922 to 1932, see John E. Hodge, "The Chicago Civic Opera Company: Its Rise and Fall," *Journal of the Illinois State Historical Society*, 55 (Spring 1962). Some achievements of the present-day company are pictured and described in Claudia Cassidy, *Lyric Opera of Chicago* (Chicago, 1979). The field as a whole is reviewed in Ronald L. Davis, *Opera in Chicago* (New York, 1966). There are as yet no unified accounts of the events that took place in numerous small town "opera houses" of the late nineteenth and early twentieth centuries, although a few research projects are indexed under "Illinois" in James R. Heintze, *American Music Studies: A Classified Bibliography of Master's Theses* (Detroit, 1984).

Church music is another subject that merits investigation. Leonard Ellinwood, *The History of American Church Music* (New York, 1953) cites a number of Chicago churches and supplies biographies of about a dozen church musicians employed at some time in the city. For an account of a durable Chicago institution, see Lawrence L. Edlund, *The Apollo Musical Club of Chicago: A Historical Sketch* (Chicago, 1946). Fannia Weingartner, ed., *Ravinia: The Festival at Its Half Century* (Chicago, 1985) is a pictorial history of a summer music center in the northern suburb of Highland Park.

Musical activities sustained by the heavily German population of a downstate community are outlined in Virginia K. Blair, "The Singing Societies and Philharmonic Orchestra of Belleville," *Journal of the Illinois State Historical Society*, 68 (Nov. 1975). Lee Margaret Trobaugh, *All They Had Was a Song: The Story of the Egyptian Choral Club, 1934–1946* (West Frankfort, Ill., 1986) preserves another chapter in the history of Illinois music. Mariesta Dodge Howland Bloom, *The Song That Didn't Die: A History of the Peoria Symphony Orchestra, 1898–1958* (Peoria, 1959) is a brief account. Aspects of music education in the state are covered in two studies at the University of Illinois, Urbana-Champaign: Calvin Earl Weber, "The Contribution of Albert Austin Harding and His Influence on the Development of School and College Bands" (Ed.D. diss., 1963) and Albert Dale Harrison, "A History of the University of Illinois School of Music, 1940–1970" (Ed.D. diss., 1986).

There is a scattering of work related to performing musicians, beginning with the period studied by Sandy R. Mazzola, "When Music Is Labor: Chicago Bands and Orchestras and the Origins of the Chicago Federation of Musicians, 1880–1902" (Ph.D. diss., Northern Illinois Univ., 1984). The state's experience with the Works Progress Administration's Federal Music Project is discussed in Vicki L. Eaklor, "The Illinois Symphony Orchestra, 1936–1942: Microcosm of a Cultural New Deal," in Illinois State Historical Society, *Selected Papers in Illinois History, 1980*. Robert D. Leiter, *The Musicians and Petrillo* (New York, 1953) recounts the unionization of musicians but tends to underplay James C. Petrillo's role in Chicago's musical life. A leader of the city's black musicians' union is interviewed in Donald Spivey, *Union and the Black Musician: The Narrative of William Everett Samuels and Chicago Local 208* (Lanham, Md., 1984).

Individual musicians from Illinois have received more attention in the twentieth century than earlier. The list of those active in Chicago alone prior to 1950 would include Felix Borowski, John Alden Carpenter, Eric DeLamarter, Rudolf Ganz, Frederick Grant Gleason, Peter C. Lutkin, Silas G. Pratt, and Leo Sowerby. Useful sources for these and other Chicagoans are Claire R. Reis, *Composers in America . . .* (New York, 1938; revised ed., New York, 1947) and Hazel Gertrude Kinscella, "Americana Index to *The Musical Quarterly*, 1915–1957," *Journal of Research in Music Education*, 6 (Fall 1958).

As a great urban center, Chicago has made important contributions to more commercially oriented musical genres such as musicals and jazz. In the early twentieth century, Chicago rivaled New York in the production of musicals, many written by Richard Carle, Joseph Howard, Gustav Luders, and Harold Orlob. A picture of their work can be extracted from Gerald Bordman, *American Musical Theatre: A Chronicle* (New York, 1978; expanded ed., New York, 1986). Another composer in this vein is remembered in Mrs. Reginald [Anna Farwell] DeKoven, *A Musician and His Wife* (New York, 1926).

In the broad field of jazz, encompassing many styles and locales, one aspect deserves mention. The period from about 1911 to 1920 witnessed an influx of New Orleans jazz musicians into Chicago, resulting in the "Chicago style." Two valuable aids in understanding this development are John Steiner, "Chicago," in Nat Hentoff and Albert J. McCarthy, eds., *Jazz: New Perspectives on the History of Jazz* . . . (New York, 1959) and Leroy Ostransky, *Jazz City: The Impact of Our Cities on the Development of Jazz* (Englewood Cliffs, N.J., 1978). See also Thomas J. Hennessey, "The Black Chicago Establishment, 1919–1930," *Journal of Jazz Studies*, 2 (Dec. 1974), and Burton W. Peretti, "White Hot Jazz," *Chicago History*, 17 (Fall–Winter 1988–89). The variegated field of blues scholarship may be approached through Charles Keil, *Urban Blues* (Chicago, 1966) and Mike Rowe, *Chicago Breakdown* (London, 1973; reprinted, *Chicago Blues: The City and the Music*, New York, 1981).

Literature on the music trade and instrument manufacture in Chicago is almost nonexistent, although a firm such as Lyon & Healy deserves study. Lester A. Weinrott, "Play That Player Piano," *Chicago History*, 4 (Summer 1975), points to the production of player pianos during their vogue in the early twentieth century.

This review of writings on music in Illinois, while not extending to native Indian or to folk and ethnic music, is fairly indicative of the subject at this time. Although the literature is interesting and significant as it stands, much basic work needs to be done. New avenues for publication are open, including the pages of *American Music*, the Sonneck Society's quarterly journal since 1983, and its *Bulletin*. This bibliography may help to suggest some opportunities for research in the field.

# 14

# ABRAHAM LINCOLN: THE ILLINOIS YEARS

## ROBERT W. JOHANNSEN

WHEN THOMAS LINCOLN led his family into Illinois from their hard-scrabble farm in southern Indiana in the spring of 1830, the state was not yet twelve years old. The three lumbering wagons on which the family's worldly goods were loaded halted on the banks of the Sangamon River, west of the town of Decatur near the northern limit of settlement in one of the state's fastest-growing areas. A cabin was quickly erected, land cleared, and corn planted. Thomas's son Abraham, just turned twenty-one, assisted in the work. After enduring one of the worst winters in memory (the "Winter of the Deep Snow"), Thomas decided to move his family to a better location, eastward to Coles County, but this time Abraham did not accompany him. Restless, stirred by ambition, and eager to leave behind the hard life of the farm, Abraham Lincoln struck out on his own. While the physical distance between Lincoln and his father from that time on was never great, the spiritual distance grew ever wider. Lincoln never saw his father again.

For the next three decades, Lincoln's life was bound to the developing fortunes of his adopted state. He found his own fortune in a career that combined law and politics, achieving a success that placed him above and apart from his countrymen. When he left Illinois early in 1861, the aspiring young country boy had become President-elect of the United States. His words, as he bade farewell to his Springfield friends and neighbors from the rear platform of the train that would take him to his new duties, carried an ominous tone. The nation was in crisis, and the task that awaited him was awesome, greater he said than that which had faced George Washington. "I now leave," he declared, "not knowing when, or whether ever, I may return." He never saw Illinois again.

During most of his life, Lincoln's world was bounded by the limits of his state. Only rarely did he travel beyond Illinois' boundaries—a trip to New Orleans as a young man, a journey to Washington as a freshman congressman, and brief excursions into neighboring states on electioneering missions. Lincoln's ambitions, however, knew no bounds; his vision transcended the immediate circumstances that surrounded him. It was a time of "boundlessness," and Abraham Lincoln was firmly in its grasp.

What were the springs of that ambition? What was the source of the vision that drove him onward? There are no simple answers. Although many of his early friends and associates remembered otherwise in later years, no one could foresee that this uninspiring product of America's backwoods would some day be chosen to lead the nation through its darkest moment. To historian George Bancroft, the nineteenth century's foremost interpreter of America's mission, Lincoln was called to leadership by God, precisely because he embodied all that America stood for. He was, as Bancroft put it in 1866, "a child of nature, a child of the West, a child of America." To America's seer, Ralph Waldo Emerson, Lincoln was "a heroic figure in the centre of a heroic epoch." It was an assessment that would have pleased Lincoln himself. To many in his generation, no less than to Lincoln, his life and career seemed to epitomize the meaning and promise of America. He was perceived as a hero in the true Carlylean sense.

The effort to define Lincoln's greatness began during his lifetime; it has continued unabated to the present day. The result has been an incredible outpouring from the pens of historians, politicians, novelists, poets, dramatists, propagandists, devoted admirers and malicious detractors, and a host of others. Every imaginable aspect of Lincoln's life (and some that are not imaginable) has been the subject of scrutiny. The facts of his life down to the most minute and intimate details, his motivations, his innermost thoughts and emotions, even his soul, have been bared to an extent unknown to any other American. Where evidence has been lacking, the gaps have been filled with fantasy, imagination, and speculation. Lincoln became larger than life, dehumanized, legendary, and even saintly, wrenched from time and space and raised to the level of abstraction.

For all the attention that he has received, however, Lincoln yet remains elusive, enigmatic, and puzzling. Much of his life is still shrouded in mystery and will likely always be so, a point convincingly demonstrated in Richard N. Current, *The Lincoln Nobody Knows* (New York, 1958). The "search for the real Lincoln," undaunted, continues. New research efforts to uncover and reveal the complexity of early nineteenth-century America, if they have not resulted in knowing the unknowable, have brought new meaning and understanding to Lincoln's life, for Lincoln if he was anything was eminently a man of his time. See Robert

W. Johannsen, "In Search of the Real Lincoln, or Lincoln at the Crossroads," *Journal of the Illinois State Historical Society*, 61 (Autumn 1968).

More than fifty years ago, James G. Randall wondered if Lincoln research had not by then reached its limits, asking "Has the Lincoln Theme Been Exhausted?" *American Historical Review*, 41 (Jan. 1936). He answered his query in the negative and, in doing so, demonstrated why he felt that Lincoln scholarship still had vitality. The same question has been repeated at intervals ever since Randall asked it and the answer has always been the same. The study of Lincoln has not only not been exhausted, it is now recognized as inexhaustible. As Mark E. Neely, Jr., has shown, in "The Lincoln Theme since Randall's Call: The Promises and Perils of Professionalism," *Papers of the Abraham Lincoln Association*, 1 (1979), Lincoln scholarship has paralleled the changing nature of historical study generally. This relationship has been assessed from time to time by others, most notably David M. Potter, *The Lincoln Theme and American National Historiography* (Oxford, 1948) and Don E. Fehrenbacher, *The Changing Image of Lincoln in American Historiography* (Oxford, 1968).

Few individuals in recent years have attempted full-length biographical studies of Lincoln, perhaps because so many aspects of Lincoln's life have been encrusted with legend or because the requirements of Lincoln biography have become greater and more complex. At the same time, the sources on which any study of Lincoln must ultimately be based have been made more easily available to the researcher. Basic to any investigation is the collection of Lincoln's own writings in Roy P. Basler et al., eds., *The Collected Works of Abraham Lincoln* (9 vols., New Brunswick, N.J., 1953–55; *Supplement, 1832–1865*, Westport, Conn., 1974; *Second Supplement, 1848–1865*, New Brunswick, N.J., 1990). See also Thomas F. Schwartz, "Lincoln's Published Writings: A History and Supplement," *Journal of the Abraham Lincoln Association*, 9 (1987).

This record is complemented by the collection in the Library of Congress of letters and other documents received by Lincoln, microfilmed (97 reels) and accessible through the *Index to the Abraham Lincoln Papers* (Washington, D.C., 1960). These papers include the Robert Todd Lincoln collection, first opened to researchers in July 1947 after having been sealed for twenty-one years following the death of Lincoln's son. The collection is described in David C. Mearns, *The Lincoln Papers: The Story of the Collection with Selections to July 4, 1861* (2 vols., Garden City, N.Y., 1948). Papers of considerable importance to Lincoln's pre-presidential years form the Herndon-Weik collection of the Library of Congress (15 reels). Gathered initially by Lincoln's law partner William H. Herndon for use in his biography of Lincoln, these papers include the recollections of Lincoln's friends and early associates. Parts of the collection were published, with varying accuracy, in Emanuel Hertz, *The Hidden Lincoln: From the Letters and Papers of William H. Herndon* (New York, 1938). For two chapters in the history of Lincoln forgeries, see John Kobler, "Yrs. Truly, A. Lincoln," *New Yorker*, 32 (Feb. 25, 1956), on Joseph Cosey, and Don E.

Fehrenbacher, *The Minor Affair* (Fort Wayne, Ind., 1979; revised in his *Lincoln in Text and Context: Collected Essays*, Stanford, 1987).

No comprehensive bibliography of published Lincoln materials has been attempted since Jay Monaghan, comp., *Lincoln Bibliography, 1839–1939*, Collections of the Illinois State Historical Library, 31–32 (1943–45). Monaghan's work, a gigantic undertaking even in 1939, is incomplete and inconsistent, but despite its weaknesses, it still serves the scholar and the collector well. It is particularly valuable for its listing of Lincoln imprints, in all their various editions. Paul M. Angle, *A Shelf of Lincoln Books: A Critical, Selective Bibliography of Lincolniana* (New Brunswick, N.J., 1946) is of limited use to the researcher but valuable to the beginning student. Current bibliographies of Lincoln studies are regularly included in the *Lincoln Herald*, published quarterly by Lincoln Memorial University, Harrogate, Tennessee, and in *Lincoln Lore*, issued monthly by the Louis A. Warren Lincoln Library and Museum, Fort Wayne, Indiana. The latter publication, currently edited by Mark E. Neely, Jr., is a treasure-house of information and commentary on Lincoln. Moreover, in *The Abraham Lincoln Encyclopedia* (New York, 1982), Neely drew on Lincoln sources and secondary literature to produce the most complete and up-to-date compendium of information about Lincoln, an indispensable reference tool for all who may be interested in him.

Lincoln scholarship has been both recognized and enriched by the programs and publications of the Abraham Lincoln Association, an organization based in Springfield that had its beginnings in 1908 when the Lincoln Centennial Association was formed to plan the observance of the one-hundredth anniversary of Lincoln's birth. The association issued first a *Bulletin* (58 numbered and 2 special issues, 1923–39) and an annual volume of *Papers* (1924–39) and then the *Abraham Lincoln Quarterly* (1940–52), publications that did much to strengthen the scholarly study of Lincoln and his times. The association ceased to exist in 1952 when all of its resources were applied to the support of the *Collected Works*, a lasting monument to the organization's determination to advance Lincoln scholarship. Revived in recent years, the association initiated an annual symposium in 1974 and resumed publication of the *Papers* in 1979. In 1987, the series was retitled the *Journal of the Abraham Lincoln Association*. Since 1982, each issue has contained a valuable review of writings and activities in the Lincoln field compiled by Frank J. Williams. Among the contributions of the association was its sponsorship of *Lincoln Day by Day: A Chronology, 1809–1865*, an ambitious work that sought to document each day of Lincoln's life, begun by Paul M. Angle, Benjamin P. Thomas, and Harry E. Pratt, and revised and expanded under the editorship of Earl Schenck Miers (3 vols., Washington, D.C., 1960).

The first biographies of Lincoln appeared during his campaign for the Presidency in 1860: William Dean Howells, *Life of Abraham Lincoln* (modern ed., Springfield, 1938) and John Locke Scripps, *Life of Abraham Lincoln* (best ed., Bloomington, Ind., 1961). Like most campaign biographies, they were sketchy, superficial, and uncritical. Their value for the researcher lies in the fact that Lincoln not only supplied information to the writers but also had the opportunity to comment on their accuracy. The first post-assassination biography of Lincoln was published in 1866 by Josiah G. Holland; from that time to the present, Lincoln has been the subject of a continuing stream of biographical writing. Some of the leading biographers have themselves been studied in Benjamin P. Thomas, *Portrait for Posterity: Lincoln and His Biographers* (New Brunswick, N.J., 1947).

One of the most important of the biographies is that by William H. Herndon, Lincoln's outspoken and often erratic law partner. Written in collaboration with Jesse William Weik, *Herndon's Lincoln: The True Story of a Great Life* . . . (3 vols., Chicago, 1889) was based on personal reminiscences and testimony diligently gathered from those who had known Lincoln. The work contains a wealth of information not readily available elsewhere, but it must be used with considerable caution. Herndon was a tangle of strong prejudices and self-delusion that often colored his judgment and obscured the truth, in spite of the claim made in his title. Every serious student of Abraham Lincoln must at some time come to terms with Herndon, winnowing fact from pseudo-fact and innuendo. See Paul M. Angle's preface to *Herndon's Life of Lincoln* . . . (Cleveland, 1930). Important to an understanding of this one man who was probably closer to Lincoln than any other is David Donald, *Lincoln's Herndon* (New York, 1948).

Biographies of Lincoln have run the gamut from the adulatory panegyrics of Lincoln's admirers to the harsh strictures of his critics, from superficial sketches dripping with legend to densely detailed tomes. When James G. Randall questioned the exhaustion of the Lincoln theme, he observed that Lincoln studies had largely been left to the amateurs. Carl Sandburg had turned from poetry to produce the most extensive biography of Lincoln ever published, the highly impressionistic, even poetic *Abraham Lincoln: The Prairie Years* and *Abraham Lincoln: The War Years* (6 vols., New York, 1926–39). See Robert W. Johannsen, "Sandburg and Lincoln: The Prairie Years," *The Frontier, the Union, and Stephen A. Douglas* (Urbana, 1989). The death in 1927 of Sen. Albert J. Beveridge, an Indiana Republican, cut short an ambitious effort to portray Lincoln truthfully and realistically in relation to his times. Beveridge's *Abraham Lincoln, 1809–1858* (2 vols., Boston, 1928) is still one of the best accounts of Lincoln's life before the Presidency, in spite of an over-reliance on Herndon.

Lincoln's first academic biographer was Nathaniel Wright Stephenson, whose *Lincoln: An Account of His Personal Life* . . . (Indianapolis, 1922) mirrored the Progressivism of the early twentieth century. By the end of the 1930s, the professionals were gradually preempting the Lincoln field. Randall himself, "the greatest Lincoln scholar of all time" according to Mark Neely, began publication of his own Lincoln biography with *Lincoln the President: Springfield to Gettysburg* (2 vols., New York, 1945). Subsequent volumes, *Lincoln the President: Midstream* (New York, 1952) and *Lincoln the President: Last Full*

*Measure* (completed by Richard N. Current; New York, 1955), carried Lincoln through the Civil War to his assassination. As the title suggests, Randall's masterful achievement focused on the presidential years, although it included considerable detail relating to Lincoln's earlier career.

Three one-volume biographies have appeared since Randall's series began that stand out for their scholarship: Benjamin P. Thomas, *Abraham Lincoln: A Biography* (New York, 1952), still a favorite of many Lincoln scholars for its literary quality and balanced, sensitive portrayal; Reinhard H. Luthin, *The Real Abraham Lincoln* . . . (Englewood Cliffs, N.J., 1960); and Stephen B. Oates, *With Malice Toward None: The Life of Abraham Lincoln* (New York, 1977). Oates followed his biography with *Abraham Lincoln: The Man behind the Myths* (New York, 1984), "an exploration into special moments and meanings of Lincoln's life."

As Potter and Fehrenbacher have pointed out, writing on Lincoln has followed the twists and turns of American historiography. Indeed, the image cast by Lincoln reveals much about the perceptions of Americans toward their past and toward themselves. Although the study of Lincoln has perhaps been less susceptible to changing fashions in historical methodology, some inroads have been made. The "unknown Lincoln" has particularly challenged those historians committed to psychological techniques of analysis to embark along new and untried pathways in an effort to discover the unknowable. Lincoln's enigmatic personality, his moodiness and periodic fits of depression, and his introspective and self-effacing attitude (what some have called his "humility complex") all seem to invite the speculations of the psychobiographers. In seeking to probe the inner recesses of Lincoln's mind, with only fragmentary and incomplete evidence to guide them, the psychobiographers have run the risk of creating a new Lincoln legend. The basis for a psychological interpretation of Lincoln was laid by George B. Forgie, *Patricide in the House Divided: A Psychological Interpretation of Lincoln and His Age* (New York, 1979). Building on Forgie's effort, although differing from him in some respects, were Charles B. Strozier, *Lincoln's Quest for Union: Public and Private Meanings* (New York, 1982) and Dwight G. Anderson, *Abraham Lincoln: The Quest for Immortality* (New York, 1982).

In 1860, in reply to a request for biographical information, Lincoln insisted that "it is a great piece of folly to attempt to make anything out of my early life." To him, those early years were utterly devoid "of all romantic and heroic elements." Obviously future generations disagreed, for it was out of Lincoln's life on the frontier, in the woods, that the Lincoln legend was born. It is ironic that those same conditions that now loom so large in the popular perception of Lincoln's character were precisely those conditions that he tried so desperately to forget. Following that first winter in Illinois, Lincoln's ambition (described by Herndon as "a little engine that knew no rest") led him away from farm and family; he seemed anxious to sever his ties with his past and to rise above his origins. Lincoln attached himself to the growing urban environment of central

Illinois when he settled in New Salem, a thriving village on the Sangamon River with good prospects for development, where the chances for social and economic advancement appeared more abundant, life less isolated. New Salem was Lincoln's home for almost six years, a formative period in which he put down the foundations for his careers in law and politics. The town's prospects, however, failed to materialize; more importantly, Lincoln simply outgrew it. His success as a lawyer-politician demanded a wider arena for his activities. The town was abandoned not long after his departure in 1837, and many of its buildings were moved to nearby Petersburg. A century later, the townsite was acquired by the state of Illinois, a state park was established, and the restoration of New Salem as it was in Lincoln's day was undertaken. The story of New Salem's rise and fall and of Lincoln's role in the town's life is ably sketched in Benjamin P. Thomas, *Lincoln's New Salem* (Springfield, 1934; revised ed., New York, 1954).

Lincoln moved to Springfield, where he resided from 1837 until his departure for Washington in 1861. It was there that he married, his children were born, and he bought the only home he ever owned. Paul M. Angle, *"Here I Have Lived": A History of Lincoln's Springfield, 1821–1865* (Springfield, 1935) is still the only full account of the city's development during the Lincoln years. Today, the Old State Capitol where Lincoln sat as a legislator and frequently spoke, the home in which he and his family lived after 1844, the law office which he occupied from 1843 to 1849, the Great Western Railroad Station from which he bade his friends farewell in 1861, and his imposing tomb in Oak Ridge Cemetery have been designated Lincoln "shrines" and regularly attract large numbers of visitors.

Lincoln's pursuit of the law brought him the social position that he sought, earning for him the reputation of one of the state's most successful lawyers by the 1850s and enabling him to live comfortably, if not lavishly. John J. Duff, *A. Lincoln, Prairie Lawyer* (New York, 1960) and John P. Frank, *Lincoln as a Lawyer* (Urbana, 1961) are the best studies of Lincoln's law career, complementary rather than repetitive.

Lincoln's success in the legal profession not only provided entry into Springfield society but also supplied him with valuable contacts throughout the state that proved indispensable to his political ambitions. His social position was further strengthened by his marriage in November 1842 to Mary Todd, the daughter of a wealthy Lexington, Kentucky banker, merchant, and Whig politician. Ruth Painter Randall's admiring *Mary Lincoln: Biography of a Marriage* (Boston, 1953), although still useful, is generally superseded by Jean H. Baker's scholarly *Mary Todd Lincoln: A Biography* (New York, 1987). For Mary Lincoln's correspondence, see Justin G. Turner and Linda Levitt Turner, eds., *Mary Todd Lincoln: Her Life and Letters* (New York, 1972).

It was not Lincoln's legal career but rather his career in politics that finally secured for him the fame and position that he so assiduously sought. He was being disingenuous in 1856 when, after comparing his career with that of Stephen A.

Douglas, he declared ruefully that "with *me*, the race of ambition has been a failure—a flat failure." If anything, the statement revealed the intensity of his political drive and the zeal with which he pursued political office. The facts of Lincoln's career in politics, the offices that he held, and the programs that he espoused have been well covered in Lincoln historiography. What has not been adequately considered is Lincoln's political thought, especially as it was influenced by the rapidly changing political scene in early nineteenth-century America. Richard N. Current, ed., *The Political Thought of Abraham Lincoln* (Indianapolis, 1967) is a very useful and balanced selection of Lincoln's own statements, illustrating his political orientation. Stanley Pargellis's survey, "Lincoln's Political Philosophy," *Abraham Lincoln Quarterly*, 3 (June 1945), is helpful. T. Harry Williams, "Abraham Lincoln: Principle and Pragmatism in Politics; A Review Article," *Mississippi Valley Historical Review*, 40 (June 1953), an analysis based on a close reading of the *Collected Works*, captures the spirit of Lincoln's political outlook. Norman A. Graebner, ed., *The Enduring Lincoln* (Urbana, 1959) offers clues to Lincoln's political philosophy.

Following his move to New Salem in 1831, the young Lincoln lost no time in offering himself as a candidate for political office. He rejected the Jacksonian faith of the frontier and its identification with the small yeoman farmer (perhaps another indication of his desire to overcome his background) and cast his lot with the party of wealth and status. He was captivated by fellow-Kentuckian Henry Clay ("my beau ideal of a statesman") and was impressed with Clay's American System, a program that provided for America's material development through the strong, dynamic intervention of the federal government. Lincoln's ambition also played a part in determining the direction of his political allegiance, for the Whig party was perceived as the party of gentility, education, and manners. Lincoln's loyalty to the Whig party and its program ran deep; indeed, he remained a Whig throughout his life, even after the party ceased to be a viable political force.

The best treatments of this affiliation are in Daniel Walker Howe, *The Political Culture of the American Whigs* (Chicago, 1979) and Joel H. Silbey, " 'Always a Whig in Politics': The Partisan Life of Abraham Lincoln," *Papers of the Abraham Lincoln Association*, 8 (1986). An important element in Lincoln's political philosophy was his concern for economic issues, in keeping with the thrust of Whig ideology but also reflecting his frontier beginnings. His economic views are analyzed in G[abor] S. Boritt, *Lincoln and the Economics of the American Dream* (Memphis, 1978). For Lincoln's particular debt to Henry Clay, see Mark E. Neely, Jr., "American Nationalism in the Image of Henry Clay: Abraham Lincoln's Eulogy on Henry Clay in Context," *Register of the Kentucky Historical Society*, 73 (Jan. 1975).

At a time when the nation was dominated by Andrew Jackson's romantic democracy, a new mass politics based on the expansion of the suffrage, and an emphasis on individualism, the Whigs valued order and stability, reason and restraint, preferring a more limited popular participation in the nation's governance. Lincoln was no exception. His voice was always the voice of caution against lending too much credence to the will of the mass. In his early political statements, he expressed his alarm at the "mobocratic spirit" that seemed to threaten the stability of the republic. His address before the Springfield Lyceum in January 1838 on "The Perpetuation of Our Political Institutions" has been widely quoted and almost as often misunderstood. His outspoken call for "law and order" epitomized Whig attitudes. One of the best treatments of this statement is Major L. Wilson, "Lincoln and Van Buren in the Steps of the Fathers: Another Look at the Lyceum Address," *Civil War History*, 29 (Sept. 1983). A valuable analysis of the ideas found in the address in a broader national perspective is George M. Fredrickson, "The Search for Order and Community," in Cullom Davis et al., eds., *The Public and Private Lincoln: Contemporary Perspectives* (Carbondale, 1979). Phillip S. Paludan's articles, "Lincoln, the Rule of Law, and the American Revolution," *Journal of the Illinois State Historical Society*, 70 (Feb. 1977), and "The American Civil War Considered as a Crisis in Law and Order," *American Historical Review*, 77 (Oct. 1972), are also useful in evaluating Lincoln's political philosophy. A preliminary effort to trace elements of Lincoln's Whiggery through his career is Robert W. Johannsen, "Lincoln, Liberty, and Equality," in John Agresto, ed., *Liberty and Equality under the Constitution* (Washington, D.C., 1983). That Lincoln's commitment to law, order, and reason was tempered by his devotion to the Declaration of Independence has been demonstrated by Thomas J. Pressly, "Bullets and Ballots: Lincoln and the 'Right of Revolution,' " *American Historical Review*, 67 (Apr. 1962). Also relevant is Otto H. Olsen, "Abraham Lincoln as Revolutionary," *Civil War History*, 24 (Sept. 1978).

Lincoln was not successful in his first political campaign, a race for a seat in the Illinois legislature in 1832, but two years later he won, and thus began a legislative career that would see him serve four terms in the state assembly. Illinois' capital, when Lincoln first entered the legislature, was Vandalia; in part through his efforts, the capital was moved to Springfield in 1837, the same year that he moved there. Lincoln's role as a legislator is revealed in William E. Baringer, *Lincoln's Vandalia: A Pioneer Portrait* (New Brunswick, N.J., 1949) and Paul Simon, *Lincoln's Preparation for Greatness: The Illinois Legislative Years* (Norman, Okla., 1965).

Lincoln's political ambition could not be confined to Illinois; as early as 1843 he was writing to friends of his strong desire to be elected to Congress. By that time he had achieved considerable power as a Whig party leader in the state, a role that has not been adequately studied. The challenge of national politics with its promise of greater renown and opportunity for reputation beckoned, and Lincoln was eager to accept it. For a Whig to be elected to Congress from an overwhelmingly Democratic state, however, was not easy. The only sure Whig district was that in which Springfield was located; Lincoln's residence there was no coincidence. As Lincoln quickly learned, he was not alone among Whigs in his desire to be chosen. An informal rotation plan was agreed upon by which he was nominated and elected to the House of Representatives in

1846, to take his seat in the Thirtieth Congress in December 1847. Donald W. Riddle's books, *Lincoln Runs for Congress* (New Brunswick, N.J., 1948) and *Congressman Abraham Lincoln* (Urbana, 1957), although now dated, provide the most complete coverage of Lincoln's single term in the House. See also *A. Lincoln: The Crucible of Congress* (New York, 1979) by Paul Findley, who was himself a representative from central Illinois.

Lincoln served in Congress just as the Mexican War was winding down; when he took his seat, the fighting had long since ended, and the peace treaty was about to be signed. Like many Whigs, Lincoln was ambivalent toward the war, regarding it as unjust and unnecessary but also encouraging the volunteers and taking pride in their victories. He would later support Zachary Taylor, the hero of the Mexican War, for the Presidency more easily and confidently than would many Whigs. Lincoln's principal speech in Congress, the statement that he hoped would make his reputation as one of the party faithful on the national level, was a denunciation of President James K. Polk for having deceived the American people when he took the nation into the conflict two years before. Although much has been made of Lincoln's position, even to the extent of regarding it as an expression of high moral principle, the ideas were neither new nor unique. Whigs had been making essentially the same point long before Lincoln got around to it. Furthermore, because Lincoln's views were patently unpopular with his constituents and because he was not returned to Congress, it has been assumed that he deliberately committed political suicide rather than give up his convictions. That legend has been refuted in recent scholarship, especially in G. S. Borit[t], "Lincoln's Opposition to the Mexican War," *Journal of the Illinois State Historical Society*, 67 (Feb. 1974), and Mark E. Neely, Jr., "Lincoln and the Mexican War: An Argument by Analogy," *Civil War History*, 24 (Mar. 1978).

When Lincoln returned to Illinois from Washington, he suddenly found himself not only without a political office but also without prospects for one. He had hoped to play a part in Zachary Taylor's patronage decisions and to secure what he called a "first class" appointment in Washington for himself, but he was disappointed on both counts. He returned to his law practice and for the next few years remained relatively inactive, while still maintaining his position as a strong Whig leader in the state. When he eventually returned to political action, it was on an entirely different platform and in a completely new direction.

Lincoln came late to the slavery question. Indeed, he once confessed that before 1854 slavery had been only a "minor question" with him. Confident that the institution was destined to "ultimate extinction," he saw little point in belaboring an issue that could only have disruptive consequences. To him, the question had been essentially a political one. On those few occasions when he had addressed the issue, his strictures against the abolitionists were as severe as those against the slave power. Yet it is Lincoln's position on slavery, and on the concomitant question of race, that has engaged most Lincoln students, to the extent that Lincoln's involvement with slavery has overshadowed, even distorted, his pre-1854 career. Furthermore, Lincoln's attitudes toward slavery and race have become entangled with the Lincoln of myth and legend, fed by uncritical adulation, prejudice, and wishful thinking. Only recently have scholars been able to probe Lincoln's beliefs in a judicious and objective manner.

Two studies stand out for their insight: Don E. Fehrenbacher, "Only His Stepchildren: Lincoln and the Negro," *Civil War History*, 20 (Dec. 1974), and George M. Fredrickson, "A Man but Not a Brother: Abraham Lincoln and Racial Equality," *Journal of Southern History*, 41 (Feb. 1975). A pioneering survey was Benjamin Quarles, *Lincoln and the Negro* (New York, 1962); more recently LaWanda Cox has analyzed Lincoln's stance, with an emphasis on the presidential years, in her superb *Lincoln and Black Freedom: A Study in Presidential Leadership* (Columbia, S.C., 1981). The Illinois perspective has been treated in Arvarh E. Strickland, "The Illinois Background of Lincoln's Attitude toward Slavery and the Negro," *Journal of the Illinois State Historical Society*, 56 (Autumn 1963), and David Lightner, "Abraham Lincoln and the Ideal of Equality," ibid., 75 (Winter 1982). Charges that Lincoln was a racist in spite of his antislavery ideals were made during the civil rights movement of the 1960s. The ensuing debate may be followed in Lerone Bennett, Jr., "Was Abe Lincoln a White Supremacist?" *Ebony*, 23 (Feb. 1968); Herbert Mitgang, "Was Lincoln Just a Honkie?" *New York Times Magazine* (Feb. 11, 1968); and Robert F. Durden, "A. Lincoln: Honkie or Equalitarian?" *South Atlantic Quarterly*, 71 (Summer 1972).

The passage of Stephen A. Douglas's Kansas-Nebraska Act in the spring of 1854 jolted Lincoln's complacency and destroyed his illusion that slavery was in the process of eradication. On the contrary, Lincoln believed that the act had given the southern institution new life and vigor. Douglas's legislation played the same role for Lincoln's political career, rekindling his ambition and opening a new arena for his talents. With speeches in Springfield and Peoria, he gave notice that he had reentered the lists, this time as the sworn enemy of slavery's extension. The issue for Lincoln, moreover, had assumed a new moral urgency. He hated slavery, he insisted, because of its "monstrous injustice"; it was a "gross outrage on the law of nature" because it denied the humanity of the black race. The extension of slavery challenged the integrity of the republic and the purity of its mission. Lincoln looked increasingly to the Declaration of Independence, which he called "the sheet anchor of American republicanism," as the source of his convictions.

Lincoln was elected once again to the state legislature but quickly resigned his seat. His eyes were on a higher goal, the U.S. Senate, and he hoped to ride the wave of anti-Nebraska sentiment into that chamber. Although disappointed that he was not selected in 1855 (the prize went to Lyman Trumbull, like Lincoln a critic of Douglas's legislation but one of Democratic antecedents), he stiffened his determination and began laying plans to challenge Douglas himself three years hence.

Lincoln's involvement in the politics of slavery has to be seen against the troubled and tortuous course of American politics after the Kansas-Nebraska Act. The nature and direction of Lincoln's ideas and activities were shaped by events in the larger arena. An indispensable guide through the political maze of the decade is David M. Potter's insightful *The Impending Crisis, 1848–1861* (completed by Don E. Fehrenbacher; New York, 1976). The breakup of the party system and the emergence of new alignments are treated in Michael F. Holt's provocative *The Political Crisis of the 1850s* (New York, 1978). The party that emerged from the protests against the Kansas-Nebraska Act, with which Lincoln hesitatingly affiliated, is studied in Eric Foner, *Free Soil, Free Labor, Free Men: The Ideology of the Republican Party before the Civil War* (New York, 1970). For Lincoln's own part in the politics of the decade, see Don E. Fehrenbacher, *Prelude to Greatness: Lincoln in the 1850's* (Stanford, 1962). Less useful is William Baringer's older *Lincoln's Rise to Power* (Boston, 1937).

The climactic episode in Lincoln's new crusade was his campaign for the Senate against Douglas in 1858. A long, hard-fought campaign, the election was highlighted by the seven joint debates between the two candidates. The campaign is described in Robert W. Johannsen, "The Lincoln-Douglas Campaign of 1858: Background and Perspective," *Journal of the Illinois State Historical Society*, 73 (Winter 1980), and in Bruce Collins, "The Lincoln-Douglas Contest of 1858 and Illinois' Electorate," *Journal of American Studies*, 20 (Dec. 1986). The debates themselves have been published in many editions since their first appearance as a Republican campaign document in 1860. The best is that of Paul M. Angle, *Created Equal? The Complete Lincoln-Douglas Debates of 1858* (Chicago, 1958; also issued in Collections of the Illinois State Historical Library, 33). An early edition, containing related material drawn from newspapers and other sources, was prepared by Edwin Erle Sparks, *The Lincoln-Douglas Debates of 1858*, Collections of the Illinois State Historical Library, 3 (1908).

The story of the debates is told in Richard Allen Heckman, *Lincoln vs. Douglas: The Great Debates Campaign* (Washington, D.C., 1967) and in the less satisfactory account of Saul Sigelschiffer, *The American Conscience: The Drama of the Lincoln-Douglas Debates* (New York, 1973). The ideas and positions advanced by each of the debaters are closely scrutinized in Harry V. Jaffa's highly analytical *Crisis of the House Divided: An Interpretation of the Issues of the Lincoln-Douglas Debates* (New York, 1959).

Lincoln did not win election to the Senate, but he achieved what was probably more important in the long run—national recognition as an able spokesman for the antislavery cause and as a leading figure in the Republican party. In the last years of the decade, he continued to carry his arguments to audiences in his own as well as other states. One of his most important excursions was his participation in Ohio's 1859 state election; Douglas also participated on behalf of Democratic candidates. See Harry V. Jaffa and Robert W. Johannsen, eds., *In the Name of the People: Speeches and Writings of Lincoln and Douglas in the Ohio Campaign of 1859* (Columbus, Ohio, 1959).

The ultimate consequence of Lincoln's new notoriety and prestige was his candidacy for the Republican nomination for President in 1860. It was an ambition that gradually grew in Lincoln's mind following the 1858 race, aided and abetted by his political associates in the state. The story of the struggle for the nomination in the Republican convention may be found in Willard L. King, *Lincoln's Manager, David Davis* (Cambridge, Mass., 1960). Lincoln owed his success to his remarkable campaign against Douglas two years before and, it might be argued, it was the Little Giant who indirectly assured his nomination for the Presidency, for if Douglas's nomination by northern Democrats had not been certain it is likely that Lincoln would not have been selected.

Lincoln's successful campaign and his election to the Presidency is analyzed in Reinhard H. Luthin, *The First Lincoln Campaign* (Cambridge, Mass., 1944). Certain salient aspects of the election are discussed in Norman A. Graebner, ed., *Politics and the Crisis of 1860* (Urbana, 1961). Unfortunately, no complete scholarly study of the contest has been written. Following his election, Lincoln remained at home in Springfield, receiving well-wishers and wrestling with the problems of the patronage, a period that is covered in William E. Baringer, *A House Dividing: Lincoln as President Elect* (Springfield, 1945) and Robert W. Johannsen, *Lincoln and the South in 1860* (Fort Wayne, Ind., 1989).

When Abraham Lincoln left Springfield in February 1861, he closed a distinct period in his life, what Sandburg called his "prairie years." In the three decades since he had entered Illinois, he had become the state's most prominent citizen. He never forgot the debt that he owed to those who had helped nurture his ambitions. Nor did Illinoisans ever forget what Abraham Lincoln did for them. He quickly became the revered object of an outpouring of affectionate reminiscence and eulogy that soon assumed the proportions of an industry. The tide, both mythical and historical, shows no sign of abating.

## PART TWO

# ARCHIVAL AND MANUSCRIPT COLLECTIONS

# INTRODUCTION

THE *GUIDE TO Depositories of Manuscript Collections in Illinois* (Chicago, 1940), based on work by the Historical Records Survey in the late 1930s, briefly described the holdings of only forty institutions in the state. In 1978, the National Historical Publications and Records Commission issued the *Directory of Archives and Manuscript Repositories in the United States*, which, as partly updated (2nd ed., Phoenix, Ariz., 1988), identified in Illinois 180 historical societies, governmental agencies, college and university libraries, and other institutions engaged in preserving the primary sources of history, and this work is only a recent addition to a shelf of directories to which students of Illinois history may turn in their research. Local historical societies are listed by the American Association of State and Local History in Mary Bray Wheeler, ed., *Directory of Historical Organizations in the United States and Canada* (14th ed., Nashville, Tenn., 1990) and by the Congress of Illinois Historical Societies and Museums in *Historical and Cultural Agencies and Museums in Illinois* (latest ed., Springfield, 1989). The *American Library Directory* . . . , now in its 43rd edition (2 vols., New York, 1990), is useful for public and special libraries and for some data as to the holdings of each institution. Many libraries provided a list of their collections for the Illinois Regional Library Council's *Illinois Libraries and Information Centers*, edited by Ellen Palmer (Chicago, 1981).

Regional directories have supplemented national and state listings in recent years. The most successful publication of this kind was issued by the Chicago Area Archivists, *Archival and Manuscript Repositories in Metropolitan Chicago and the Calumet Region of Northwest Indiana* (Chicago, 1986). Similarly, the Association of St. Louis Area Archivists issued in 1985 the *Directory of Archives and Manuscript Collections in the St. Louis Area* (2nd ed., St. Louis, 1988), which includes entries for Illinois repositories from Quincy to Marissa. Western Illinois and eastern Iowa are covered in John Caldwell, comp., "Guide to Resources for Regional Studies," *Western Illinois Regional Studies*, 6 (Spring 1983), while the Illinois Regional Library Council's *Directory of Local History Collections in Northern Illinois* (Chicago, 1981) extends across a twenty-three-county area.

More informative than all such directories is the literature relating to particular repositories in Illinois. These publications are listed in three bibliographies: Roger D. Bridges, comp., "Illinois Manuscript and Archival Collections: A Checklist of Published Guides," *Journal of the Illinois State Historical Society*, 66 (Winter 1973); Mary E. Janzen, "Archival Literature Relating to Illinois Repositories and Their Holdings, 1971–1980: A Selective Bibliography," *Illinois Libraries*, 63 (Mar. 1981); and Kevin B. Leonard, "Writings on Illinois Archives, 1980–1987: A Bibliography," ibid., 69 (Oct. 1987). The latter periodical, a publication of the Illinois State Library, has welcomed articles on manuscript collections since the 1950s, usually for an issue devoted to manuscript, archival, or special collections. Another forum for institutional reports is *M.A.C.: Newsletter of the Midwest Archives Conference*.

For information regarding individual manuscript collections, the most important source is undoubtedly the *National Union Catalog of Manuscript Collections*, sometimes known by its acronym, *NUCMC*. Initiated with a volume for manuscript collections cataloged in 1959–61 and published since the 1963–64 volume by the Library of Congress, *NUCMC* through 1984 includes descriptions of nearly fifty-five thousand manuscript collections in about thirteen hundred repositories in the United States, fifty-three of them in Illinois. The series is mainly based on reports from these repositories of their holdings and is thus uneven and less than comprehensive. Nonetheless, the value of *NUCMC* in locating primary sources is unmatched. Of the twenty-four volumes in the series through 1984, three are indexes—for 1959–62, 1975–79, and 1980–84. The indexes for 1963–74 are bound with the 1966, 1969, and 1973–74 catalogs. This six-part index contains nearly 600,000 subject and name entries, only a third of which appear in Chadwyck-Healey's *Index to Personal Names in the National Union Catalog of Manuscript Collections, 1959–1984* (2 vols., Alexandria, Va., 1988). After publishing as usual a bound catalog and a paperback index for 1985, *NUCMC* adopted a computerized format for subsequent biennial issues.

The collection entries in *NUCMC* are somewhat complemented by the depository descriptions in *A Guide to Archives and Manuscripts in the United States*, edited for the National Historical Publications Commission by Philip M. Hamer (New Haven, 1961). This work, although increasingly dated, gave an order to the holdings of each repository that a catalog of separate collections cannot provide and included many collections not yet in *NUCMC*.

The *National Inventory of Documentary Sources in the United States*, shortened to *NIDS*, is an expanding series of inventories of individual collections, begun in 1983 and published on microfiche by Chadwyck-Healey, now in Alexandria, Virginia. Although these inventories vary in length and detail, reflecting the standards of the repositories that prepared them, they generally provide more information about a collection than does an entry in *NUCMC* or in most institutional guides. The publication was at first organized in four parts: Federal Records (including the National Archives); the Manuscript Division of the Library of Congress; State Archives, State Libraries, and State Historical Societies; and Academic and Research Libraries and Other Repositories. Parts 1 and 2 each include a bound *Index*, while the index to Parts 3 and 4—merged in 1988 and now designated Part 3—is cumulated on microfiche as new units are added to the series. Whereas *NUCMC* excludes archival holdings that are located where one would expect to find them, *NIDS* includes them, thereby expanding the range of its indexes. Much of the usefulness of *NIDS* lies in the indexing because the publication includes printed as well as typed inventories and thus duplicates on microfiche what is already available in hard copy. In Part 3, for example, Illinois is represented by typed in-house summaries of 113 collections in the State Historical Library and two widely distributed publications of the State Archives. Some nine other repositories in the state have submitted inventories to *NIDS*. The access to manuscript sources promised by the series is attractive, but most libraries have found the publication prohibitively expensive.

Of the subject guides to sources, the most comprehensive is Andrea Hinding, ed., *Women's History Sources: A Guide to Archival and Manuscript Collections in the United States* (2 vols., New York, 1979). Describing materials by and about women, this work is frequently cited as equivalent to *NUCMC* in its field. Entries for Illinois repositories fill fifty three-column pages, and a host of Illinois women and topics are indexed in the second volume of the set. The holdings of the Library of Congress and of the University of Illinois at Chicago are particularly well represented. As with any broadly defined compendium, *Women's History Sources* may be extended by more focused surveys, such as Evangeline Thomas, ed., *Women Religious History Sources: A Guide to Repositories in the United States* (New York, 1983), which includes thirty-four Illinois references, double the number in the larger work. Another specialized inventory, more impressive as an archival initiative than as a list of collections, and relating to Illinois and Indiana in particular, is Darlene Clark Hine, *The Black Women in the Middle West Project: A Comprehensive Research Guide . . .* (Indianapolis, 1986).

A number of guides may facilitate the research of cultural historians. The basic index to literary sources, begun in 1960 and updated to include "both large and minuscule holdings" for nearly twenty-eight hundred authors, is J[ohn] Albert Robbins, ed., *American Literary Manuscripts: A Checklist of Holdings in Academic, Historical, and Public Libraries, Museums, and Authors' Homes in the United States* (2nd ed., Athens, Ga., 1977). Another comprehensive guide to an entire field is D[onald] W. Krummel et al., *Resources of American*

*Music History: A Directory of Source Materials from Colonial Times to World War II* (Urbana, 1981). This work is organized by repository, as is Kathleen Roy Cummings, *Architectural Records in Chicago: A Guide to Architectural Research Resources in Cook County and Vicinity* (Chicago, 1981), an excellent survey.

Congressional papers are listed in Kathryn Allamong Jacob, ed., *Guide to Research Collections of Former United States Senators, 1789–1982* (Washington, D.C., 1983), with a cumulative supplement (1987), and Cynthia Pease Miller, ed., *A Guide to Research Collections of Former Members of the United States House of Representatives, 1789–1987* (Washington, D.C., 1988). Although the Illinois State Historical Library and the Chicago Historical Society hold most "Illinois" collections, some documentation is elsewhere. The papers of Sen. William B. McKinley, for instance, are at Syracuse University. The National Historical Publications and Records Commission has sponsored an array of modern-day editorial projects, bringing together a mass of documentation, much of it political. *Historical Documentary Editions* (Washington, D.C., 1988) is a checklist of these publications. Because many Illinoisans turn up in this group of source materials, as in the microfilmed series of presidential papers in the Library of Congress, their indexes point to numerous bits of state history.

Many subject guides are based on surveys and therefore present unevenly the resources of different repositories. For example, only the Chicago Historical Society is well covered in Walter Schatz, ed., *Directory of Afro-American Resources* (New York, 1970). Similarly, the Swedish-American Historical Society's *Guide to Swedish-American Archival and Manuscript Sources in the United States* (Chicago, 1983) is best for its own archives at North Park College in Chicago and for related holdings of the Swenson Swedish Immigration Research Center at Augustana College in Rock Island. The National Endowment for the Humanities funded this work as well as the guides edited by Hinding, Thomas, Hine, Krummel, and, for instance, Melinda F. Kwedar et al., "Illinois General Store Manuscripts, 1825–1845: A Bibliography," *Illinois Libraries*, 62 (Apr. 1986), which lists only bound volumes. Another kind of inventory, including both printed and manuscript items, is exemplified by David Beck, *The Chicago American Indian Community, 1893–1988: Annotated Bibliography and Guide to Sources in Chicago* (Chicago, 1988).

Although national and subject guides provide clues to manuscript sources for Illinois history located in out-of-state repositories, the search for such materials typically requires a combination of institutional and thematic inventories, even though they cover the ground incompletely. There are usually guides for larger repositories which provide some access by state. For instance, a record book of the Willow Springs Phrenological Society, 1847–51, entered under the town's name in the *Dictionary Catalog of the Manuscript Division* of the New York Public Library (2 vols., Boston, 1967), is cross-referenced in the section for "Illinois" sources. Major repositories of materials in a particular field may also describe their holdings in an appropriate journal. Thus, an issue of *Labor History*,

23 (Fall 1982), carried such articles from thirteen institutions beyond Illinois, including the State Historical Society of Wisconsin. That repository is rich in Illinois-related sources. The best-known collection of this kind is introduced by Josephine L. Harper, *Guide to the Draper Manuscripts* (Madison, 1983), but entries for Illinoisans and Illinois topics recur frequently in the index to Part 3 of the *National Inventory of Documentary Sources*, which includes notices of no less than one thousand collections at Wisconsin, all available on microfilm.

Historical research is too complex for a single guide. Each effort to describe the sources extends, but never wholly replaces, the work of its predecessors. The following chapters constitute only an introduction to the relevant materials in the principal repositories of interest to Illinois historians. Practically every foray into the sources should be preceded by an inquiry for additional information, so that the curator or archivist at each location may not only describe the appropriate collections in more detail but also apprise the researcher of any restrictions on their use.

During the preparation of the following pages, three contributors left the state for other positions in archives and manuscripts and are thus indebted to their former colleagues and others for assistance in completing their reports. Those who should be acknowledged include Cheryl Schnirring of the Illinois State Historical Library, Robert E. Bailey of the Illinois State Archives, and several curators and archivists in other downstate repositories. More particularly, the paragraphs on sources at Knox College, initially drafted by Lynn Metz Harlan, were checked by Carley R. Robison, each in turn the college archivist; the coverage of Western Illinois University's collections was provided by Gordana Rezab, university archivist since 1975; and the summary of Sangamon State University's holdings, based on a report by Nancy Hunt, university archivist from 1981 to 1986, was updated by her successor, Thomas J. Wood. In addition, the editor is indebted to many others who in different ways contributed to this guide.

# 15

# ILLINOIS STATE
# HISTORICAL LIBRARY

LAUREL G. BOWEN

Old State Capitol
Springfield, IL 62701
(217) 782–4836

THE ILLINOIS STATE Historical Library, established by the General Assembly in 1889, is the preeminent repository for research materials that document the history of the entire state. Located since 1970 beneath the restored Old State Capitol in downtown Springfield, the library became a division of the Illinois Historic Preservation Agency in 1985. One of the library's early and continuing strengths is its Abraham Lincoln collection, including a wealth of printed Lincolniana, a copy of the Gettysburg Address in Lincoln's hand, and the largest cache of Lincoln manuscripts predating his presidency. In the late 1950s, the library began a program to microfilm Illinois newspapers, resulting in a collection that now numbers nearly sixty-five thousand reels. More generally, the library has acquired in its first century some 165,000 volumes relating to every aspect of the state's history.

In developing the manuscripts collection, the staff of the library traditionally emphasized political and military affairs during the Civil War and earlier periods of Illinois history, but around 1960 it began to give increased attention to the more recent past and to materials relating to social and economic history. Total holdings since 1962 have grown from 1,420 to nearly 12,000 linear feet, and descriptive information is now available for all of the collections. Access to the earlier acquisitions is provided by a card catalog and by detailed narrative descriptions of the larger collections, both primarily the work of curator Paul D. Spence. An expanded manuscripts staff processed the mass of material acquired in the 1970s and 1980s, preparing historical sketches, scope and content notes, and container lists for major collections and briefer descriptive abstracts for other holdings. Reports of acquisitions have appeared in issues of the *Journal of the Illinois State Historical Society* in 1958–67, 1969–76, and 1981, and in the library's annual report since the 1969–70 fiscal year, issued either in the *Journal* or separately. During the 1980s, the library microfilmed numerous collections and prepared a comprehensive inventory of "Manuscripts on Microfilm." Most of this film is available on interlibrary loan.

Several of the Manuscripts Section's outstanding nineteenth-century collections, including the Black Hawk War, Stephen A. Douglas, and Ulysses S. Grant collections, have been published as part of letterpress editions that are cited in preceding chapters. The largest body of records relating to the territorial and early statehood period has been microfilmed (28 reels, 1741–1910) and described in Kathrine Wagner Seineke, ed., *Microfilm Edition of the Pierre Menard Collection in the Illinois State Historical Library* (Springfield, 1972). Menard's activities as a fur trader, merchant, and public official are fully represented, but the collection also includes commercial papers and ledgers of his early business partner Barthelemi Tardiveau and of other mercantile firms in Kaskaskia such as Bryan and Morrison.

Several collections document the surveying, conveyance, and settlement of land in Illinois. Included are the papers of surveyors Don Alonzo Spaulding (2 ln.ft., 1818–71) and Daniel F. Hitt (1 ln.ft., 1830–1913). Other records relate to bounty land claims from the War of 1812, handled by lawyers William and Arthur McArthur (250 items, 1851–70); the land agent business of Moore, Morton and Company, in Quincy (1 ln.ft., 1818–1919); and, in Springfield, the land transactions of Ninian Wirt Edwards (280 items, 1791–1908) and the land office receivership of Pascal Enos (1 ln.ft., 1796–1868). The English Settlement in Edwards County is depicted in the George Flower and Flower family collections (1 ln.ft., 1787–1964), while the experiences of German immigrants in St. Clair County are recorded in the Engelmann-Kircher family papers (2 ln.ft., 1798–1933).

A single collection, that of Mexican War surgeon James Mahon (450 items, 1830–63), provides insights into the medical profession in mid-nineteenth-century Illinois. The development of the legal profession, however, can be studied in several collections of legal and court documents prepared by a number of prominent attorneys (2 ln.ft., 1808–97). These papers illustrate the legal practice and, in some instances, the judicial service of four lawyers who practiced with Lincoln (John T. Stuart, Stephen T. Logan, William H. Herndon, and Ward Hill Lamon), three governors of the state (Ninian Edwards,

John Reynolds, and Thomas Ford), and Stephen A. Douglas. The papers of Lucian B. Adams, a Springfield attorney and justice of the peace, are part of the Adams-Snyder family collection (11 ln.ft., 1813–1943) and include the records of businesses whose accounts were settled by Adams.

Men trained as lawyers often became leaders in politics and public life, and their papers reflect not only party politics but also the predominant state and national issues of the time. The correspondence of Henry Eddy (2 ln.ft., 1817–75), a director of the Shawneetown bank, relates in part to banking policies and land speculation in Illinois. The papers of Sidney Breese (1 ln.ft., 1731–1896), a U.S. senator and state Supreme Court judge, refer to national issues such as railroads and slavery. The state's internal improvements program is documented in Gov. Augustus C. French's papers (1 ln.ft., 1841–52). Public issues dominate letters received by Charles H. Lanphier, editor of the Democratic *Illinois State Register*, in Springfield. Most of his papers (1 ln.ft., 1838–86) are reproduced in Charles C. Patton, comp., *Glory to God and the Sucker Democracy* . . . (5 vols., Springfield, 1973).

Other sources pertain to the religious and educational history of the period. The notebooks and papers of William Royal (110 items, 1823–70), a Methodist circuit rider, document the growth of church membership in the Fox River Mission, between the Fox and Des Plaines rivers. The diaries of Levi Spencer (1 ln.ft., 1837–53), a Congregational minister and abolitionist, describe his experiences in Canton, Bloomington, and Peoria. A group of Hancock County circuit court records (1 ln.ft., 1804–58) supplements about two dozen manuscripts (1839–43) relating to Joseph Smith and the Mormon experience at Nauvoo. Bishop Philander Chase's papers (1.5 ln.ft., 1813–69) concern his efforts on behalf of Jubilee College, an Episcopal school which is further documented by the Chase collection at Bradley University. Education, abolition, and religion are only a few of the themes in the John Russell family papers (1 ln.ft., 1792–1927), a rich and varied collection, and in the Julius Willard family papers (200 items, 1783–1883). The Jonathan Baldwin Turner papers (1 ln.ft., 1836–95), which complement collections at Illinois College and the University of Illinois, document his campaign for publicly supported higher education as well as his innovations in agriculture. The papers of John A. and Robert Kennicott (18 reels, 1830–1913), transcriptions of which are available at the Grove National Historic Landmark in Glenview, Illinois, reflect their horticultural and scientific endeavors.

The Manuscripts Section's holdings for the Civil War era and Gilded Age are unusually rich, diverse, and numerous. They include the papers of leading public officials in the period such as U.S. Sen. Lyman Trumbull, in the Trumbull family collection (4 ln.ft., 1775–1936), Gov. and U.S. Sen. Richard Yates (14 ln.ft., 1789–1873), and Illinois Secretary of State Ozias M. Hatch (3 ln.ft., 1818–91). The career of David Davis, who was a lawyer, circuit court judge, U.S. Supreme Court justice, and U.S. senator, is especially well documented (18.5 ln.ft., 1816–1953). See Robert L. Brubaker, *The David Davis Family*

*Papers, 1816–1943: A Descriptive Inventory* (Springfield, 1965). Among the Civil War generals represented by collections are John A. McClernand (15.5 ln.ft., 1823–1919), Benjamin H. Grierson (9 ln.ft., 1848–95), and two post-war governors who also served in the U.S. Senate, Richard J. Oglesby (13.5 ln.ft., 1845–1924) and John M. Palmer (5.5 ln.ft., 1811–1906). Also available are the papers of Lewis B. Parsons (18.5 ln.ft., 1799–1908), chief of rail and river transportation for the western armies.

The library contains thousands of Civil War letters, diaries, and reports. These collections describe not only military operations at the front but also daily life in camp and at home. They include, for example, the papers of Thomas Madison Reece (2 ln.ft., 1857–92), a doctor at Camp Butler, and the letters of Humphrey H. Hood (400 items, 1851–1903), a surgeon with the 3rd U.S. Colored Artillery. For information on collections obtained before 1963, see William L. Burton, *Descriptive Bibliography of Civil War Manuscripts in Illinois* (Evanston, 1966).

After the war, many veterans participated in the Grand Army of the Republic. Records of the G.A.R. Department of Illinois from about 1880 to 1930 include both quartermaster reports, giving membership data for eight hundred posts (30 ln.ft.), and minutes of more than one hundred posts (9 ln.ft.). General John C. Black's work as national commander of the G.A.R. and U.S. commissioner of pensions is documented in the Black family papers (9 ln.ft., 1829–1951). The Warren D. Crandall collection (4 ln.ft., 1860–1916) relates to the Mississippi Marine Brigade and its veterans society.

The Manuscripts Section also preserves the records of a number of organizations formed to commemorate Abraham Lincoln, ranging from the National Lincoln Monument Association (2 ln.ft., 1865–1920) to the Abraham Lincoln Association (45 ln.ft., 1908–81). The papers of Fern Nance Pond (1 ln.ft., 1933–45) and Gustaf Edward Nelson (2 ln.ft., 1914–39) relate to Old Salem State Park, the Old Salem Lincoln League, and the New Salem–Springfield Lincoln Trail Association. Other Lincoln sites were developed by the Lincoln Circuit Marking Association (1 ln.ft., 1915–32) and the Lincoln National Memorial Highway Committee (1.5 ln.ft., 1929–31).

In addition to the papers of previously cited political and military leaders of the Civil War, who were also frequently prominent in the late nineteenth century, the library holds the papers of U.S. Sen. Shelby M. Cullom (2 ln.ft., 1880–1914) and Robert Todd Lincoln (7 ln.ft., 1865–1912), the president's son, whose business and personal interests are illuminated in forty-six letterpress volumes. Legal history in the period can be studied in the correspondence, account books, and briefs of Clifton H. Moore and Vespasian Warner, law partners in Clinton (5 ln.ft., 1851–1901); Joseph Wright of Chicago (10.5 ln.ft., 1871–1912); and Thomas Worthington of Jacksonville, in the Worthington family collection (1 ln.ft., 1837–1957).

While some of these collections reflect the business interests of lawyers who invested in real estate, railroads, and other ventures, the economic history of

Illinois in the Gilded Age is documented more fully in records of businesses and banks. The account books of Phelps and Proctor of Lewistown (11 ln.ft., 1859–1921), McClaughry and Tyler of Hancock County (4 ln.ft., 1838–1915), and James Miller of Paris (2 ln.ft., 1853–86) reflect the operations of general merchandise stores. A Jacksonville firm, J. Capps and Sons (10 ln.ft., 1856–1974), manufactured woolen cloth and blankets and then men's suits. In Springfield, John Williams and Company (18 ln.ft., 1828–1905) was not only a general store but also a banking house. Williams also invested extensively in railroads and coal mines, as did Cassius M. Wicker, freight agent for several companies and commissioner of the Chicago Freight Bureau, whose papers are part of the recently enlarged French-Wicker family collection (9 ln.ft., 1836–1915). The archives of the First National Bank of Springfield (66 ln.ft., 1864–1923), the largest such collection in the period, includes the records of a number of area banks and businesses.

Aspects of agricultural development in the state are apparent in the records of A. Goodell and Sons (34 ln.ft., 1852–1920), a Loda loan and investment firm that funneled eastern funds into Illinois farm mortgages, and Duff and Cowan (2 ln.ft., 1853–90), Pontiac land dealers. Rural life, farming practices, and social interrelationships in agricultural communities can be examined in the diaries and papers of Clinton Campbell and his sons George and John Campbell of Hancock County (3 ln.ft., 1866–1964), the Henry A. Griswold family of White Hall (3 ln.ft., 1814–1937), Brown Munro of Peru (3 reels, 1851–1937), and Fred and H. Curtis Downer, brothers in DeKalb County (2.5 ln.ft., 1873–1939).

The library is the repository for a number of unusually fine collections of family papers, providing a microcosm of life in different periods. The family collections are all prime sources for the study of children's education, social values, the role of women, the effects of political and economic conditions on family life, the business and professional development of family members, family travels, and the quality of cultural and community life. Springfield families, especially from the mid-nineteenth to the early twentieth century, are portrayed in the papers of the Stuart-Hay family (500 items, 1817–92), the Bailhache-Brayman family (1.5 ln.ft., 1796–1905), the Matheny family (7 ln.ft., 1780–1940), the Condell family (7 ln.ft., 1855–1959), and the Wines family (1 ln.ft. and 3 reels, 1871–1940). Collections from other communities document the Wallace-Dickey family of Ottawa (9 ln.ft., 1816–1934); the Ingersoll family of Peoria (15 ln.ft., 1859–1935); the family of Theodore Bacmeister, a homeopathic physician in Toulon (7.5 ln.ft., 1848–1910); and the Herrick-Reasoner-Milnor-Sparks family of Alton, Litchfield, and Staunton (6 ln.ft., 1860–1967). Most of these collections depict prominent individuals in their own right such as Frederick H. Wines, an influential social reformer, and Robert G. Ingersoll, a lawyer and lecturer known for his anti-theological views.

The records of numerous churches and several colleges date from the early nineteenth to the late twentieth century. Typical collections are the minutes and membership records of two Springfield churches, First Presbyterian (13 ln.ft., 1828–1971) and First Methodist (1.5 ln.ft., 1836–1927). Records of Wilmington's First United Methodist Church (3 reels, 1866–1964) and Atwood's Lake Fork United Church of Christ (4 reels, 1877–1982) also include minutes of women's missionary, charitable, and fellowship groups. The largest accumulation of denominational sources pertains to the Baptists and includes the records of two related groups, the Illinois Baptist State Association (94 ln.ft., 1829–1986) and the American Baptist Churches of the Great Rivers Region (28.5 ln.ft., 1805–1987). These collections document doctrinal controversy, missionary fervor, the growth of local and regional church organizations, the role of women and young people, and the influence of the religious press. In addition, these collections include, respectively, the records of Ewing and Shurtleff colleges.

The history of education can also be studied in the records of Monticello College (87 ln.ft., 1794–1971), an early and long-lived women's school in Godfrey. Smaller lots include letters received by Newton Bateman (2 ln.ft., 1831–96), superintendent of public instruction, and Fred J. Armistead's papers (1.5 ln.ft., 1934–78) relating to the College in the Hills, a Depression-era educational experiment in Hardin County.

The medical profession in the Gilded Age is represented by the papers of John Francis Snyder (17 ln.ft., 1797–1921), whose interests in archaeology, history, and politics are also documented. The Carl E. Black collection (15 ln.ft., 1826–1944) reflects the increasing regulation of medicine at the turn of the century through medical legislation and organizations. The records of the Illinois State Medical Society (8 ln.ft., 1863–1950) include biographies of Illinois doctors, histories of Illinois hospitals, and proceedings of regional medical societies. The Frank Parsons Norbury collection (1 ln.ft., 1886–1954) contains his writings on mental and nervous disorders, while the voluminous files of the Keeley Institute in Dwight (275 ln.ft., 1866–1966) document a sanitarium based on Leslie E. Keeley's pioneering work in the treatment of alcoholism and drug abuse.

Other institutional efforts to improve the health and welfare of Illinoisans are represented in the records of the U.S. Marine Hospital Service in Cairo (23 ln.ft., 1877–1936), which began as a facility for the care of sick and disabled riverboat men and eventually became part of the U.S. Public Health Service, and the records of the Illinois Humane Society (67.5 ln.ft., 1873–1931), which early in its history endeavored to protect both children and animals. The changing nature of child care and family assistance is evident in the records of the Family Service Center of Sangamon County (96 ln.ft., 1865–1977), which had its origins in the Home for the Friendless (established 1863), the Lincoln Home for Colored Children (1898), the Springfield Day Nursery (1914), and the Family Welfare Association (1924).

Several important collections illustrate the role of Illinoisans in national as well as state politics in the early twentieth century. The papers of Joseph G. Cannon (7.5 ln.ft., 1879–1925) are fullest for 1906–10, at the end of his reign as

Speaker of the U.S. House. The papers of Sen. Lawrence Y. Sherman (75 ln.ft., 1871–1939) document especially his opposition to President Wilson's foreign policies. The papers of Lt. Gov. John G. Oglesby (17.5 ln.ft., 1892–1938) present a vivid picture of Republican party politics in the Progressive era and the workings of the State Council of Defense during World War I. Materials collected by the War Records Section of the Illinois State Historical Library (28 ln.ft., 1914–23) provide further details concerning the state's economic and social mobilization for war. The Len Small collection (197 ln.ft., 1908–36) fully covers his gubernatorial administration, particularly the state's highway program and its response to labor strife in the 1920s.

For the 1930s, the papers of Gov. Henry Horner (190.5 ln.ft., 1902–40), Congressman Kent Keller (154 ln.ft., 1828–1954), and City Commissioner Willis J. Spaulding of Springfield (23 ln.ft., 1889–1965) portray the efforts of government on different levels to cope with the Depression. The voluminous files of Sen. Scott W. Lucas (294 ln.ft., 1918–68) reflect national and international issues during the Roosevelt and Truman administrations as well as concerns of constituents in Illinois. The Horner and Lucas collections and the papers of Samuel Alschuler (5.5 ln.ft., 1883–1940) cover their legal careers, including Horner's years as Cook County probate judge and Alschuler's tenure as a federal circuit court judge.

A variety of collections illustrate business and agricultural life in Illinois during the early twentieth century. These holdings include the records of Jingling General Merchandise (13 ln.ft., 1891–1969), a Hopedale store owned and operated by a German immigrant; C. J. Jacoby and Company (5.5 ln.ft., 1895–1939), a furniture and undertaking business in Alton; and, in Springfield, the Illinois Tobacco Company (8 ln.ft., 1909–59), a tobacco, confection, and liquor wholesaler, and the Sangamo Electric Company (4 ln.ft., 1895–1972), a manufacturer of electrical equipment. The influence of businessmen in civic and economic matters is apparent in the minutes of the board of directors of the Illinois State Chamber of Commerce (4 reels, 1921–83) and the records of the Springfield Association of Commerce and Industry (28.5 ln.ft., 1908–67). Records of the Central Illinois State Bank in Mason City (5 ln.ft., 1922–44), the New Holland State Bank (6 ln.ft., 1899–1946), and the Greenview State Bank (1 ln.ft., 1932–40) demonstrate the impact of the Depression upon central Illinois farmers and financial institutions. Diverse agricultural endeavors are documented in the diaries of Frederick and Katie Blout (5 reels, 1882–1946), Fulton County farmers; the Hopkins–McVay family collection (8 ln.ft., 1836–1964), relating to stock farming in Granville; and the papers of Carl S. Vrooman (19 ln.ft., 1874–1970), a McLean County advocate of scientific farming methods.

The development of organized labor in the late nineteenth and twentieth centuries can be studied in numerous collections. Early aspects of the labor movement are apparent in papers of George A. Schilling (2.5 ln.ft., 1876–1943), who was active in the Knights of Labor, and Duncan McDonald (2 ln.ft., 1894–1960), an organizer for the United Mine Workers. Later collections include the records of local unions, statewide organizations, and regional offices. These collections typically contain minutes, financial records, and membership data, and sometimes document contract negotiations, grievance procedures, pension funds, and lobbying.

Local unions represented are the United Brotherhood of Carpenters and Joiners of America, Local 633 in Granite City (6 ln.ft., 1900–47) and Local 141 in Chicago (17.5 ln.ft., 1902–58); the American Bakery and Confectionery Workers' International Union, Local 147 of Springfield (10 ln.ft., 1915–69); the Brewery Workers' Local 77 of Peoria (1 ln.ft., 1945–76); and the Central Illinois Typographical Union 177 and its predecessor local unions in Danville, Decatur, Springfield, and Quincy (21 ln.ft., 1862–1978).

Organized labor in particular cities is documented in the collections of the Peoria Labor Temple Association (22 ln.ft., 1886–1971), which includes records of painters, bricklayers, and hotel workers unions; the Belleville Trades and Labor Assembly (1.5 ln.ft., 1891–1951); the Tri-City Trades and Labor Council (13.5 ln.ft., 1900–68), in the Granite City area; and the Springfield Trades and Labor Council (3 ln.ft., 1943–68).

Several collections relate to labor activities on state and regional levels. Labor's public policy interests can be traced in the files of the Illinois State Federation of Labor and Congress of Industrial Organizations (52 ln.ft., 1935–60), which reflect the work of its president, Reuben G. Soderstrom, and in the files of the United Transportation Union's legislative director for Illinois (20 ln.ft., 1958–76). Additional information on the development of railroad unions can be found in the records of the Brotherhood of Locomotive Firemen and Enginemen's general grievance committee (12 ln.ft., 1911–70), which operated in the Springfield and St. Louis areas. Records of the director of the AFL–CIO's Region 14 and Region 1 (3 ln.ft., 1952–81) include data on local unions in Illinois and nearby states.

A combination of personal papers and organizational records also document the history of women in modern times. The diaries of Jane Maria Ridgeley Jones paint a picture of Springfield social life (1 ln.ft., 1878–1920). The Jannotta family papers (21 ln.ft., 1809–1972) depict not only Alfredo Jannotta, an Italian-born composer and vocal instructor, and his son A. Vernon Jannotta, a World War II military officer, but also Stella Skiff Jannotta, a remarkable woman whose essays and correspondence reflect her interests in women's clubs, feminism, political equality, world peace, socialism, and other causes. The records of the Illinois Federation of Women's Clubs (26.5 ln.ft., 1894–1984) document the organization's community and legislative projects, often relating to education and social service. Its activities on the local level are illustrated by the records of the Woman's Club of Springfield (12 ln.ft., 1894–1988). The Illinois Woman's Christian Temperance Union collection (1.5 ln.ft., 1879–1960) includes records of the Bloomington and Normal chapters. Efforts to secure ratification of the Equal Rights Amendment are documented in the records of ERA Illinois (8 ln.ft., 1973–82).

A wide range of sources pertain to recent developments in health, welfare, religion, and education. The records of the Illinois Nurses' Association (433 ln.ft., 1901–84) illustrate its interest in nursing education, regulation of the nursing profession, and economic security. The Illinois Health Care Association (14 ln.ft., 1950–76) focused its attention on nursing homes, while the Illinois Society for Respiratory Therapy (9.5 ln.ft., 1972–86) addressed other health care concerns. The archives of the Illinois Emergency Relief Commission and the Illinois Public Aid Commission (44.5 ln.ft., 1932–63) contain field reports and statistical data not found in the published reports of these precursors of the Illinois Department of Public Aid. The rich but little-used John C. Weigel collection (21 ln.ft., 1901–56) relates in part to his work from 1926 to 1941 in the Illinois Department of Public Welfare.

Included in the records of the Illinois Commission on Human Relations (10 ln.ft., 1943–64) are assessments of housing, education, employment, health, and welfare resources in selected communities. Interconnections between social work and religion are illustrated by the papers of Richard Paul Graebel (22.5 ln.ft., 1947–75), pastor of the First Presbyterian Church of Springfield, who served on this commission and on the boards of local social service organizations. The records of the Illinois Conference of Churches, especially its Church Planning and Development Commission (17 ln.ft., 1949–76), reflect an ecumenical effort to address religious and social issues in the context of church relocations and congregational mergers. An important dimension of recent educational history is documented in the records of the Illinois Association of Community and Junior Colleges (16 ln.ft., 1935–70), while legislative and professional matters predominate in the Illinois Library Association collection (68 ln.ft., 1896–1988).

There is a wealth of information concerning the events, issues, and problems of the modern period in the Manuscripts Section's vast array of papers of public officials, including governors, U.S. senators and representatives, state legislators, and others in state government. The Adlai E. Stevenson II collection (256 ln.ft., 1948–53) and the papers of Walter V. Schaefer (6 ln.ft., 1949–51), chairman of the Commission to Study State Government, indicate that governmental organization and reform were priorities of Stevenson's administration as governor. The William G. Stratton collection (167.5 ln.ft., 1940–65) covers his years both as congressman-at-large and as governor. Part of Gov. Otto Kerner's papers (600 ln.ft., 1947–68) relate to his work as chairman of the National Advisory Commission on Civil Disorders, and his successor, Samuel H. Shapiro (70 ln.ft., 1961–69), kept some of his papers as chairman of the Mental Health Commission in the Kerner administration. The papers of Gov. Richard B. Ogilvie (130 ln.ft., 1969–73) are supplemented by the files of John W. McCarter, Jr. (2 ln.ft, 1969–72), the first director of the Illinois Bureau of the Budget. Governor Dan Walker's papers (371 ln.ft., 1968–77) complement the Walker collection in the Illinois State Archives. Recurring topics in these materials are education, public aid, civil rights, civil disorders, and revenue, while some of the collections relate to labor, civil service, constitutional reform, and economic development.

In addition, the library contains the senatorial papers of Ralph Tyler Smith (103 ln.ft., 1969–71) and Adlai E. Stevenson III (849 ln.ft., 1958–86), the latter collection including material on Stevenson's gubernatorial campaigns. The papers of Sen. Paul Simon (308 ln.ft., 1948–88) also relate to his years as state legislator, lieutenant governor, and U.S. representative.

Also available are the papers of a dozen members of Congress since World War II, including five representatives who served twenty years or more: John B. Anderson (439 ln.ft., 1960–80), Edward J. Derwinski (490 ln.ft., 1958–82), Paul Findley (596 ln.ft., 1960–82), Robert McClory (467 ln.ft., 1957–82), and William L. Springer (202.5 ln.ft., 1936–72). Research opportunities in these collections are enhanced because many congressmen were concerned with the same issues at the same time, such as the Taft-Hartley law, the Vietnam War, and Watergate. Their papers also document a spectrum of national and local matters, ranging from Anderson's campaign for President as an independent candidate to Springer's attention to the Oakley Dam project.

The work of the Illinois General Assembly is documented in the papers of over thirty recent legislators. Social welfare issues are prominent in the papers of two black leaders, Cecil A. Partee (17 ln.ft., 1961–75) and Corneal A. Davis (9 ln.ft., 1970–78). The papers of Goudyloch "Giddy" Dyer (12 ln.ft., 1968–80) and Eugenia S. Chapman (19 ln.ft., 1969–82) concern the status of women. Issues relating to education and health care are emphasized in the Arthur L. Berman collection (13 ln.ft., 1977–84). The problems of elementary and secondary nonpublic schools and of the Chicago Board of Education are highlighted, in turn, by the papers of Eugene F. Schlickman (13 ln.ft., 1969–73) and J. Glenn Schneider (3 ln.ft., 1970–81). Other collections illuminate policy issues in such areas as transportation, energy and the environment, labor, and insurance. Party politics and elections are also amply covered in the papers of most state legislators. Although these collections usually date from the late 1960s to the present, the papers of Noble W. Lee (85 ln.ft., 1900–78) relate to an earlier legislative career and to his tenure as dean of the John Marshall Law School. Several legislative collections, such as the papers of Abner J. Mikva (65 ln.ft., 1959–79), document careers in both the General Assembly and Congress.

The records of the Sixth Illinois Constitutional Convention (104 ln.ft., 1969–70) are deposited in the library and are frequently used to ascertain the intent of various provisions in the present constitution. The collection is supplemented by the papers of eighteen delegates, including Samuel W. Witwer (8 ln.ft., 1942–77), president of the convention, who had long been active in efforts to revise the 1870 Constitution. The implementation of one provision of the 1970 Constitution can be traced in the records of the Illinois Home Rule Clearinghouse and Policy Analysis Project (12 ln.ft., 1971–76).

In recent years, Illinois commemorated the anniversaries of a number of historical events, led by commissions created by the legislature. The records of the Civil War Centennial Commission of Illinois (11 ln.ft., 1959–65); the Illinois Bicentennial Commission, to celebrate the nation's two-hundredth birthday (101 ln.ft., 1972–77); and especially the Illinois Sesquicentennial Commission, to mark 150 years of statehood (105.5 ln.ft., 1965–69), not only document the programs that the commissions sponsored but also include research into different aspects of the state's past. Historical investigations of this kind are also preserved in the files of the Federal Writers' Project in Illinois (135 ln.ft., 1935–44), a collection of uneven quality, which includes some materials from the Historical Records Survey, another Depression-era project. The development of Illinois history as a field is further documented in the Illinois State Historical Library's own records (223 ln.ft., 1877–1988), which contain substantial information about the evolution of the library since 1889, the programs of the institution, and the growth, care, and use of its manuscript collections.

The library's Audio-Visual Section holds about 251,000 photographs of Illinois people and places in addition to audio and video tapes, films, oral history interviews, disc recordings, and broadsides. These materials, if drawn from manuscript collections, are maintained as distinct collections, accessible through a set of inventories and an unpublished guide. Large collections of photographs acquired apart from manuscripts, such as the Guy Mathis collection depicting early twentieth-century Springfield and the post–World War II *East St. Louis Journal* collection, are treated in the same manner. Small groups of photographs from various sources, however, are interfiled and arranged by topic. There is a card catalog for selected individual photographs, and part of the unit's holdings is also indexed by subject and by photographer.

The manuscripts, books, newspapers, and audio-visual materials of the Illinois State Historical Library have long supported considerable research in Illinois history. With the dramatic increase in holdings and the enhanced system of access in recent years, these collections should support much more research in the future.

# 16

# ILLINOIS STATE ARCHIVES

ROY C. TURNBAUGH, JR.

Archives Bldg.
Springfield, IL 62756
(217) 782–4682

THE ILLINOIS STATE Archives, a division of the office of the Illinois Secretary of State, collects and preserves the official records of Illinois state and local governmental agencies that have permanent legal, administrative, or historical value. The Archives was established in 1921 as part of the Illinois State Library but became a separate department in 1957. Margaret Cross Norton was appointed Superintendent of Archives in 1922, and it was through her efforts that the Archives Building was constructed. Located next to the State Capitol and completed in 1938, this stone and brick structure contains twelve levels of stacks and presently houses some 52,900 cubic feet of records. Margaret Norton was one of the pioneers of archives administration in the United States, and she left the Archives on a sound footing when she retired in 1957. Her accomplishments in acquisitions, the compilation of administrative histories, and the use of microfilm, and her success in securing basic public records legislation, underpin current Archives programs.

Several achievements have distinguished the Illinois State Archives since John Daly's appointment as director in 1974. Chief among these have been the publication of finding aids and the implementation of automated systems both for state and for local records. The basic guide to state records is Victoria

Irons (Walch) and Patricia C. Brennan, *Descriptive Inventory of the Archives of the State of Illinois*, a loose-leaf compilation, accompanied by a paperback *Index* (both Springfield, 1978). Robert E. Bailey edited a *Supplement to the Descriptive Inventory* . . . (Springfield, 1985), a packet of new and revised pages to interfile in the initial publication. Access to the *Descriptive Inventory* and the *Supplement* is provided by a revised *Index to the Descriptive Inventory* . . . by Bailey and Elaine Shemoney Evans, a bound volume combined with a set of thirty-four microfiche (Springfield, 1990). The comparable inventory of the largest body of local records is Roy C. Turnbaugh, Jr., *A Guide to County Records in the Illinois Regional Archives* (Springfield, 1983). This inventory is regularly expanded by microfiche, which list these holdings by subject and by county, township, city, and village.

The Archives uses automated databases both to maintain administrative control over its state and local records and to make these holdings known to researchers. While two systems, NEBO and OPAL, are used to update the inventory of local records, system PEARL provides on-line subject access to state records. In the latter system, the Archives staff has created a master record for each series that contains the inclusive dates of the series and also the subject descriptors for it. It is then possible, by specifying one or two descriptors and a particular decade, to retrieve all records that match such specifications.

Although the Archives in the first instance serves other agencies of state government by keeping permanently valuable records for their use, it also makes these records generally available to interested researchers, the largest group of whom are genealogists. The Archives contains census, land, and military records of considerable interest to family historians, and many of these resources have been indexed for their benefit.

State population censuses were taken every five years between 1820 and 1845 and also in 1855 and 1865, and the surviving records are listed in the *Descriptive Inventory* (pp. 33–39). The Archives also holds microfilm copies of all extant federal population censuses for Illinois from 1820 to 1910 (ibid., pp. 519–26, 921–22). The staff of the Archives prepared in past years a comprehensive card file index not only for all censuses through 1855 but also for many other early Illinois records, including election returns, legislative and executive journals, and certain French and territorial papers. This index to some 1.5 million names has been microfilmed (248 reels), and the Illinois State Library holds a set, any reel of which, for a specified part of the alphabet, may be obtained on interlibrary loan. The inclusiveness of this compilation often makes it more useful than the many publications that index a particular county or a single census. Indeed, no other single source provides so much information about Illinoisans before the Civil War.

The Archives recently completed a card index to the 1860 federal census of Illinois, insofar as the microfilm of the schedules can be deciphered, and it is now indexing the 1865 state census. The 1880, 1900, and 1910 censuses have been indexed by Soundex or Miracode, systems devised when Social Security began in the 1930s, and the Archives holds a microfilm copy of these indexes. Another set circulates on interlibrary loan from the Illinois State Library. Lesser known federal censuses, deposited in the Archives and available on microfilm, include Agricultural Schedules, Industrial Schedules, and Mortality Schedules for 1850–1880; Social Statistic Schedules for 1850–1870; and Schedules of Handicapped, Dependent, and Delinquent Inhabitants for 1880 (*Descriptive Inventory*, pp. 526–45).

Records of the sale of public lands in Illinois constitute a major collection of the Archives, but the information in these documents became accessible only recently through an innovative use of computer technology. By coding entries from over one hundred manuscript volumes into an automated database, the Archives not only created an index to the first buyers of the public domain but facilitated quantitative use of the information. Altogether the project documented 538,750 transactions whereby U.S. land office clerks, state and county officials, and even railroad agents parceled out the 54,740 square miles that comprise the State of Illinois. Each entry in this massive database includes the buyer's name, the date of purchase, a legal description of the land bought, the type of sale, the number of acres bought, the price per acre, the total price (unless a military bounty land warrant was substituted for cash), the gender of the purchaser (based on the buyer's given name), and, occasionally, the residence of the buyer at the time of purchase (usually a county in Illinois).

Having computerized its basic land records, the Archives is able to manipulate the data in a variety of ways for users. The most popular configuration is an alphabetical listing of buyers which is published on 144 microfiche with an explanatory booklet, *Illinois Public Domain Land Sales* (Springfield, 1985). The booklet is useful, for instance, in showing how to read the legal description of each tract of land and in listing the types of sale, which included federal lands from ten district land offices in Illinois; school, seminary, saline, canal, and railroad lands of the state; and swamplands of certain counties. The Archives has used the public domain database to prepare two additional microfiche sets, both county-by-county listings, one for buyers in alphabetical order and the other for land in legal order by meridian, range, township, and section. All these permutations are useful to genealogists, but the database stands ready to help other researchers as well. Historians, for example, might use it to discover how many buyers bought how much land for a certain price in a given period and, with such information, understand more fully the economic development and social structure of the state. Whatever the computerized listing, the data from the first land sales may be linked manually with subsequent documents such as deed and probate records.

Land transactions and related papers that survived from early Cahokia and Kaskaskia, and that document the transition from French to American society, are tabulated in the Raymond H. Hammes Collection of Illinois Records, 1678–1827 (2 reels). The Archives has indexed military records which list men who served in Illinois units from the War of 1812 to the Korean War. For the Civil War, for instance, both the muster rolls of regiments, arranged numerically by unit, and the regimental rosters in the *Report of the Adjutant General of the State of Illinois* (9 vols., Springfield, 1900–2), indexed by name, are available either at the Archives or from the State Library, having been microfilmed on 27 and 59 reels respectively. Volume 9 of the *Report of the Adjutant General* lists Illinois units in the Indian, Black Hawk, Mexican, and Spanish-American wars. The Archives has also alphabetized veteran bonus records for World War I, World War II, and the Korean War.

In 1985, the Archives in cooperation with the Illinois State Genealogical Society initiated a statewide marriage record index whereby marriage records, mainly in the counties, are used to build a computerized database from which to generate microfiche listings of Illinois marriages through 1900. In a project expected to document one million marriages, almost 257,000, in thirty-three countries, were indexed by 1990.

The *Descriptive Inventory of the Archives* and its *Supplement* point to voluminous records beyond those that have been minutely indexed. These materials are organized to reflect the governmental structures that created them. Thus, the records of the executive branch of state government are arranged by office, department, institution, or board, for each unit of which the Archives may hold a group of records. To explain the nature of each Record Group (RG), the *Descriptive Inventory* includes a brief administrative history of the unit, indicating its constitutional or statutory basis. These notes may be supplemented by Margaret C. Norton's massive compilation, *History of State Departments, Illinois Government, 1787–1943, including Bibliographies of Laws on Subjects Impinging upon Governmental Functions of Present State Departments* (37 microfiche, Springfield, 1984–85).

The earliest holdings of the Archives include the records of the territorial government, 1809–18 (RG 100), the most significant components of which have been published, as noted in the *Descriptive Inventory*. Each Illinois governor has deposited his official papers with the Secretary of State. In turn, these records have been acquired by the Archives. Collectively they constitute RG 101 and move from the administration of Shadrach Bond, who was Illinois' first governor, 1818–22, to the administration of Daniel Walker, who left office in 1977. The range of topics covered by these papers is great, from slavery to the public lands, and from wars to emergency relief programs. Again, the *Descriptive Inventory* notes the publication of records such as the letter books of the early governors.

Other records of the governor's office, including appointments, vetoes, proclamations, military commissions, grants of clemency, and extradition papers, 1818–1987, may be found in the Executive Section of the papers of the Secretary of State. The record-keeping responsibilities of the Secretary of State, especially in the office's Index, Corporations, and Securities departments, have led to a mass of records in RG 103, but the Archives holds as well the papers of other constitutional officials such as the State Treasurer, the Auditor of

Public Accounts, and the Superintendent of Public Instruction (RG 104–106). In addition to these basic records of state government, the Archives contains records of state departments, institutions, regulatory and non-regulatory boards, and internal improvement boards.

The records of major state agencies such as the Departments of Agriculture, Labor, Public Health, Public Welfare, Registration and Education, and Personnel are all held by the Archives. In recent years, the Archives has also accessioned records of other departments, including, for instance, Transportation, Corrections, and Conservation. These files, arranged in RG 201–247, mainly consist of administrative papers, minutes, reports, and correspondence.

The records of state institutions for the care of handicapped persons offer a fertile and virtually untapped field for research. It should be noted, however, that personal files of patients and inmates are restricted by law and may only be used by permission of a designated official. Illinois established facilities for the care of physically and mentally handicapped individuals at relatively early dates. The records of the Illinois School for the Deaf begin in 1839 and include minutes of board meetings, case files of admissions, and registers of pupils. Similarly, the records of state mental health institutions at Jacksonville, Elgin, Kankakee, Peoria, East Moline, Alton, Chicago, and Galesburg are replete with information about the care and treatment given to the mentally ill. The Archives also holds the records of Lincoln Developmental Center, formerly the Illinois Asylum for Feeble-Minded Children; Dixon Developmental Center, formerly the Illinois State Colony for Epileptics and also a school for the feeble-minded; and Herrick House Children's Center, a facility in Bartlett for the care of neglected and dependent children. The records of the Institute for Juvenile Research, which was located in Chicago, provide an essential counterpoint to the records of these institutions.

For students of military history, the records of the Adjutant General, who is appointed by the Governor and charged with administering and coordinating militia activities, offer promising material for research. Records of commissions and militia elections that date from the beginning of the state are included in this record group (RG 301), as are a wealth of records relating to the Civil War. The Adjutant General also kept detailed reports of militia and national guard units, down to each item of equipment issued.

The Archives holds the records of a number of regulatory boards, beginning with the bulky files of the Railroad and Warehouse Commission, now the Illinois Commerce Commission, 1872–1962 (RG 402). In addition, it holds the records of a host of temporary boards for particular purposes.

The records of the Illinois and Michigan Canal, completed in 1848, provide the researcher with a detailed picture of one of the state's most ambitious and, at the same time, most economically troubled projects, the construction of a canal from the Illinois River to Lake Michigan. Minutes of the canal commissioners, letter books, reports, land sale records, employee lists, construction records, tolls, boats cleared, plats, and engineering drawings make up the contents of this large and historically important record group (RG 491).

The responsibility of the Archives to retain all these records, while disposing of documents of only short-term value, is derived from the State Records Act of 1957, which created a commission to separate the wheat from the chaff. Its basis and procedures are set forth in a booklet, *State Records Act and State Records Commission Rules* (Springfield, 1986). Although the provisions of this act are mandatory only for the executive branch of state government, the General Assembly and the Supreme Court have voluntarily asked the Archives to provide retention and disposal schedules for their records. The Archives accordingly holds in RG 600 a mass of legislative bills, resolutions, reports, and indexes, 1819–1984, and in RG 900 an even larger quantity of judicial proceedings and opinions, 1820–1970. These records provide a rich and complex background for the published laws of the General Assembly and reports of the Supreme Court.

While the Archives houses all of its state records in its building in Springfield, it has decentralized its accessions of local records. In 1976, it established the Illinois Regional Archives Depository (IRAD) system in cooperation with six state universities: Northern Illinois (DeKalb), Western Illinois (Macomb), Illinois State (Normal), Sangamon State (Springfield), Eastern Illinois (Charleston), and Southern Illinois (Carbondale). The Archives opened a depository at Northeastern Illinois University (Chicago) in 1990. The capstone of the system, it contains governmental records of Cook County. Each downstate depository serves an area of from fourteen to twenty-three contiguous counties.

All of the local records acquired from a given region go to the depository for that region, thereby keeping them close to their place of origin. The Archives staff negotiates with local officials for the transfer of records to IRAD and coordinates the activities of the depositories, where the records are inventoried and opened for research. Each depository is staffed by two or three graduate student interns, who are compensated by the Archives and work under the direction of a university archivist or other on-campus supervisor.

As of 1989, IRAD contained about ten thousand cubic feet of records and nearly eight thousand reels of microfilm, almost all of which came from ninety-eight county governments. These records are listed in automated databases, and those accessioned before October 1983 are described in the *Guide to County Records*. Because the records of one county are quite like those of any other county, these finding aids simplify the IRAD inventories by listing the records of each county office as a single record group and by devising a common description for each kind of record, no matter how many counties have conveyed the series to IRAD.

Although the downstate depositories at first accessioned some rather bulky records, such as tax and court documents which space-conscious county officials were glad to transfer, the Archives staff, wanting additional sources for local and family history, has for many years sought out other records of research value. To find such materials, the staff often puts to good use the inventories of county records prepared by the Historical Records Survey, not only the published inventories for thirty-four counties (1937–42) but also the unpublished lists for sixty-seven additional counties in IRAD, lists that were stored in the Archives when the Survey was discontinued.

By placing local records in academic communities throughout the state, the Archives enhanced the opportunities for historical research in primary sources. County board and county commissioners' minutes and proceedings provide the user with a detailed picture of what actually occurred in a county. No item of business was too small or seemingly insignificant to be included in these records. Similarly, the minutes of local school boards document the process of public education as it really happened. Everything relevant to the operation of the schools appears in these records: finance, hiring (and firing) teachers, administration, curriculum, students, school construction. Court proceedings and case files offer equally rich opportunities for research into legal history.

Among the most interesting records are the pre-1848 election returns: because voting in Illinois at that time was *viva voce*, each voter's choices are recorded next to his name. This finely grained data, if combined with other records of the same locality such as census schedules and tax rolls, can illuminate patterns of political behavior. Studies of groups that fit poorly into the prevailing social environment can be based on almshouse and county home records and on different types of commitment papers, all of which assumed a more detailed format by the end of the nineteenth century. While the case files of state institutions are closed as a rule, county court proceedings to commit poor, incompetent, or delinquent persons to such institutions are open to research. Also of interest in this regard are jail registers.

As with state records, however, IRAD holdings have proven more attractive to genealogists than to historians. Wills and associated probate records are of greatest value to such researchers, as are birth, death, and marriage records; deeds; and naturalization papers. Moreover, this group of users has become increasingly aware of less traditional sources for family history. In consequence, tax lists, election records, and even land and chattel mortgages are being scrutinized by researchers who are anxious either to uncover missing ancestors or to develop a more detailed picture of the kind of life experienced by earlier generations.

The diversity of documents held by IRAD is apparent in Roy C. Turnbaugh, Jr., *Windows to the Past: A Selection of Illinois County Records from 1818 to 1880* (Springfield, 1982). This curriculum packet, designed for use in secondary schools, contains thirty-eight document facsimiles and an instructor's manual that explains each item.

Although the bulk of IRAD materials is county records, the Archives staff has begun to acquire city, village, and township records of historical significance. Again, the staff is partly guided in these accessions by the local inventories of the Historical Records Survey.

The authority of the Archives regarding local records is based on legislation passed in 1961 that created two commissions, one for Cook County and the other for all other counties in the state, each to establish retention and disposal schedules in its jurisdiction. The current statement of this responsibility, in pamphlet form, is *Local Records Act and Local Records Commission Regulations* (Springfield, 1984). For many years, the Cook County commission was inactive, but in 1983 it began to approve hundreds of schedules submitted by the Archives as its staff surveyed for the first time the governmental records of Chicago and Cook County. Records of permanent value, identified by this large and complex project, are earmarked for the IRAD facility at Northeastern Illinois University.

The proceedings of the Chicago City Council constitute the single most important series to have come to light as a result of the Archives survey in Cook County. Records predating the Fire of 1871 are accessible through Robert E. Bailey, ed., *Chicago City Council Proceedings Files, 1833–1871: An Inventory* (Springfield, 1987), a chronological listing, and a boxed set of ninety-three microfiche that provide subject access to the 35,650 documents. For sample papers in the series, see Bailey and Elaine Shemoney Evans, *Early Chicago, 1833–1871: A Selection of City Council Proceedings Files* (Springfield, 1986), a packet containing fifty facsimiles and an instructor's manual discussing the nature and context of the documents. A similar publication for the late nineteenth century is Bailey and Evans, *From the Ashes, 1872–1900: A Selection of Documents from the Proceedings Files of the Chicago City Council* (Springfield, 1990).

The fullest account of the programs and accessions of the Archives since 1975 may be found in its newsletter, *For the Record . . . .* Certain services of the Archives are summarized in *Genealogical Records and Mail Research Policy* and in another flyer regarding IRAD. Beyond the specific information of these publications, it should be evident that most of the records held by the Archives and its regional depositories lend themselves to certain types of research. Although genealogists may seek out particular holdings, other researchers, who focus on patterns and movements in the past rather than on individuals, may find other records of special value. Because the bulk of these sources contains information about large numbers of individuals, a quantitative approach may be especially effective in dealing with them. Even more important, however, is an approach that recognizes the utility of linking different records to produce a richer, more meaningful picture of the past.

# 17

# CHICAGO HISTORICAL SOCIETY

RALPH A. PUGH

Clark St. at North Ave.
Chicago, IL 60614
(312) 642–4600

THE CHICAGO HISTORICAL Society, the city's oldest cultural institution, was founded in 1856 by a group of prominent Chicagoans who recognized the role that such a society could play not only in documenting Chicago's past but also in securing its position as the new cultural mecca of the Northwest. The society at first enthusiastically collected materials broadly related to national history, creating not so much a historical society *of* Chicago as an American historical society *in* Chicago. The apogee of this approach to acquisitions was the society's purchase in 1920 of the Charles F. Gunther collection, an omnium-gatherum of Americana. Described in Clement M. Silvestro, "The Candy Man's Mixed Bag," *Chicago History*, 2 (Fall 1972), the Gunther collection included correspondence from conspicuous individuals and families of all regions of the nation and from all eras, from colonial times onwards.

Although the Chicago Historical Society will always be enriched by these expansive collecting efforts of earlier generations, it has concentrated in recent years on Chicago materials. This collecting scope, if ostensibly narrower, is also deeper. For the Archives and Manuscripts Department, it has meant the acquisition of sources representative of all phases of urban life in Chicago, providing a wealth of documentation for social as well as political historians and for demographers, sociologists, and other researchers, all conscious of the urban experience as a unique aspect of American life. The evolution of the manuscript collection and of related holdings in the society's Library, its Prints and Photographs Department, and its other units is summarized in Robert L. Brubaker, "The Development of an Urban History Research Center: The Chicago Historical Society's Library," *Chicago History*, 7 (Spring 1978).

Following the injunction of the society's first librarian, William Barry, to gather "the broad and teeming harvest of the present," the Manuscripts Department has grown enormously since the mid-1960s. Acquisitions under Archie Motley as curator not only have expanded the collection from about 350 to nearly 12,500 linear feet but have shifted its vital center well into the twentieth century. The holdings, old and new, are accessible through a large card catalog and an eighteen-volume Manuscript Handbook. The catalog contains subject tracings for processed materials and detailed entries for small collections, while the Handbook includes full-scale inventories or container lists for many collections.

The earliest sources for Illinois history at the Chicago Historical Society, collected mainly by Edward G. Mason and Otto L. Schmidt but now in three lots, the French America, Kaskaskia, and Louisiana papers (530 items, 1635–1848), illustrate the continuities in local life as the region passed from French to British and then to American control. Much of this material is summarized in the "Calendar of Manuscripts in the Archives of the Chicago Historical Society," Public Archives of Canada, *Report Concerning Canadian Archives for the Year 1905*, 1 (3 vols., Ottawa, 1906–7). The first Chicago-related item is La Salle's letter of September 1, 1683, sent from "Chicagou," and the collection includes early church registers and other documents from Cahokia, Kaskaskia, Fort de Chartres, and Prairie du Rocher. Business records and papers of Pierre Menard (1.5 ln.ft., 1778–1845) enrich studies of a leading French American on the Illinois frontier.

Materials relating to Fort Dearborn, established at the mouth of the Chicago River in 1803, and to the development of the fur trade in the region are discussed in Archie Motley, "Manuscript Sources on Frontier Chicago," *Chicago History*, 9 (Summer 1980). The society's holdings include letters from the fort before the massacre of 1812, in the Jacob Kingsbury collection (490 items, 1800–14); a group of muster rolls and medical records of the garrison, cataloged under "Fort Dearborn"; a transcript of John Kinzie's fur trade account books, 1803–22; American Fur Company papers, both originals and photostats (1 ln. ft., 1816–27); and the Gurdon S. Hubbard collection (6 ln.ft., 1818–1907), documenting his remarkable career as a fur trader, pioneer merchant, and meat packer.

The papers of Ninian Edwards (650 items, 1797–1833) and Elias Kent Kane (235 items, 1808–35), although acquired a century ago, continue to yield insights into early Illinois politics. The Whig party is pictured in the papers of John J. Hardin, in the Hardin family collection (8 ln.ft., 1733–1943), a major source for political, legal, and military history in the period. Other collections concern notable episodes of the frontier period, ranging from the papers of the George Flower family (1 ln.ft., 1812–1974), which pertain to the English Settlement in Edwards County, to the gathering of letters, broadsides, and newspapers that relate to the Mormon troubles in Hancock County. The vicissitudes of the Bank of Illinois at Shawneetown are represented in the minutes of its directors (1 vol., 1837–45).

The rise of Chicago is documented by the papers of early leaders who made fortunes in real estate speculation. The William D. Ogden papers (1 ln.ft., 1835–81) illustrate the business transactions of Chicago's first mayor, especially his dealings with Arthur Bronson of New York City. The Bronson collection itself (2 ln.ft., 1828–71) is a rich source on real estate ventures, fluctuating land values, and surveys in Chicago. The papers of John Wentworth (1 ln.ft., 1836–83), who was widely believed to own more land in Chicago than anyone else, touch on his activities as a publisher, politician, and real estate investor. Fernando Jones, the subject of another collection (3 ln.ft., 1834–1910), was known as the preeminent Chicago land title expert from the 1830s to the end of the century. The records of Charles L. Harmon's dry goods, grocery, and hardware business (30 vols., 1832–67) indicate that the city's growth also brought prosperity to retailers.

Several collections relate to the expansion of water and rail transportation outward from Chicago in the mid-nineteenth century. The construction and operation of the Illinois and Michigan Canal is documented in the papers of the president of its board, William Henry Swift (8 ln.ft., 1839–71). The Mason Brayman collection (3.5 ln.ft., 1820–95) includes his files as solicitor of the Illinois Central Railroad in the early 1850s. The formation of railroads to the west is covered in the papers of other lawyers, Charles S. Hempstead (400 items, 1840–62) and Madison Y. Johnson, in the Johnson family collection (2 ln.ft., 1822–1906).

These and other holdings illustrate the diverse activities of nineteenth-century lawyers. The James A. Mulligan collection (2 ln.ft., 1849–1900) includes not only his legal accounts but his papers as editor of the *Western Tablet*, the state's first Catholic newspaper, while the papers of Isaac N. Arnold (1 ln.ft., 1860–85) and Ezra B. McCagg (200 items, 1835–82) reflect their political and cultural interests. Diaries of some duration offer insights into other occupations. For example, Jeremiah Porter's journal (18 vols., 1831–48) concerns his experiences as pastor of Chicago's First Presbyterian Church, while the daybook of Augustus N. Conant (2 vols., 1836–53), a Unitarian minister, depicts rural life on the Des Plaines River.

The Manuscripts Department holds a variety of sources for the Civil War era. The papers of Logan U. Reavis (70 items, 1844–80), editor of the Beardstown-based *Central Illinoisan*, and the correspondence and account books of Zebina Eastman (3 ln.ft., 1841–85), editor of the Chicago papers, *Western Citizen* and *Free West*, focus on the slavery issue. The Civil War itself is captured in letters, diaries, and documents contained in over six hundred collections, an extraordinarily rich legacy for historians of the conflict.

The major events of Chicago's late nineteenth-century history are amply documented in the society's collections. The Fire of 1871 is recounted and analyzed in evidence taken by the Chicago Fire Department, narratives by survivors, and research notes compiled from personal and newspaper accounts by Robert Cromie (4 ln.ft.). The Haymarket Riot collection (6 ln.ft.) contains handbills and posters before the bombing of 1886 and a complete transcript of the ensuing trial. The World's Columbian Exposition of 1893 is covered by the records of the fair's Board of Directors and Board of Lady Managers (13 ln.ft., 1890–1905).

Business records of the period, in which real estate ventures are prominent, include the papers of Samuel H. Kerfoot (725 items, 1870–1910), Potter Palmer (15 ln.ft., 1849–1920), and Levi Z. Leiter (95.5 ln.ft., 1852–1969). The changing fortunes of George S. Bowen, a wool merchant, railroad entrepreneur, and mayor of Elgin, Illinois, are documented in the Bowen family collection (32 ln.ft., 1862–1928). The legal profession is represented by the diaries of Thomas Dent (39 vols., 1861–1924), who was president of the Chicago and Illinois State bar associations; the letter books of Rosenthal & Hamill, and related firms (126 vols., 1871–1925); and the papers of Henry S. Robbins (7 ln.ft., 1868–1943), who was counsel for the Chicago Board of Trade.

Women left a number of contemporary as well as retrospective accounts of nineteenth- and early twentieth-century Chicago. The journals of Jane Stowell Haven (65 vols., 1869–1905) and Frances Macbeth Glessner (52 vols., 1879–1921) contain notes on the social activities of their upper-class families. In the 1920s, Jeanette Hinchliff Root wrote a charming reminiscence of her family's life in Chicago, 1850–80; Francelia Colby described in more detail Chicago's Near South Side in the 1850s and 1860s; and Harriet A. Rosa, a former resident of the Old Town area, remembered Chicago places and events from 1844 to 1893. These recollections complement the sketches of pioneer Chicagoans, mostly men, in the papers of John Wentworth and Fernando Jones and in the records of two old settlers' societies (5 vols., 1855–1928). Letters to Alfred T. Andreas (400 items, 1872–84) contain biographical data not used in his published compilations. The Bessie Louise Pierce collection (35 ln.ft.) includes research notes and reports for her *History of Chicago* to 1893 and the unpublished continuation of that study.

The history of numerous twentieth-century businesses may be traced in the department's holdings. The records of the Bowman Diary Company (125 ln.ft., 1870–1972) chronicle a family-owned business which grew from the sale of milk from its own farm to a mammoth producing and distributing network throughout the Midwest. The Crane-Lillie family collection (11 ln.ft., 1877–1974) includes records of the Crane Company, which began as a bell foundry in Chicago but within a generation marketed plumbing supplies the world over. The Wieboldt collections (37 ln.ft., 1892–1963), containing business records of Mandel Brothers and papers of the Wieboldt Foundation, relate to the department store and the philanthropic history of the city. The Ernest J. Stevens family papers (45 ln.ft., 1872–1974) document the rise of a Chicago hotel dynasty. The Chicago Surface Lines collection (13 ln.ft., 1857–1951) contains the records of its component street railroad companies. Litigation affecting Chicago transit companies bulks large in the legal files of Gottlieb & Schwartz (40 ln.ft., 1930–49).

As Chicago's economy developed, its businessmen formed organizations to win public confidence and to exercise political influence. The records of the Commercial Club of Chicago (14 ln.ft., 1877–1927) reflect its interest in civic affairs. The Illinois Manufacturers' Association collection (85 ln.ft., 1893–1985) illustrates a concerted effort over the years to secure legislation favorable to business. The files of the Better Business Bureau of Metropolitan Chicago (106 ln.ft., 1940–80) contain information on individual businesses that it gathered in response to consumer complaints.

Chicago pioneered in the development of social settlements by which Progressive reformers helped less fortunate groups to cope with modern industrial society. The activities of two such settlement houses on the Near Northwest Side are delineated in the archives of Chicago Commons (23 ln.ft., 1894–1966); the papers of its head resident, Lea Taylor (10 ln.ft., 1901–67); and the records of Association House of Chicago (10 ln.ft., 1899–1972). The papers of Mary McDowell (25 ln.ft., 1894–1957) document the programs of the University of Chicago Settlement in the stockyards area. The records of Gads Hill Center (11 ln.ft., 1937–68) illuminate a Lower West Side community.

Other facets of urban social work are mirrored in the scrapbooks of Louise DeKoven Bowen, treasurer of Hull House Association from 1893 to 1953 (4 vols., 1864–1953), and the papers of Raymond M. Hilliard, an administrator of the Cook County Department of Public Aid from the Depression to the Great Society (63 ln.ft., 1922–67). The records of the Chicago Woman's Club (23 ln.ft., 1876–1962) and the Chicago Area Chapter of the National Association of Social Workers (10 ln.ft., 1921–53) also suggest different approaches to social reform. Two related collections, the papers of the Chicago Area Project (81 ln.ft., 1910–72) and the Institute for Juvenile Research (15 ln.ft., 1910–45), document efforts of social workers to understand and prevent juvenile delinquency. The records of the Young Men's Christian Association of Metropolitan Chicago (109 ln.ft., 1853–1980) and the Chicago Boys Clubs (86 ln.ft., 1901–69) describe programs to meet recreational and vocational needs in many neighborhoods.

Several organizations dating from the Progressive period endeavored to improve levels of health care in the city. These efforts may be studied in the records of the Visiting Nurse Association of Chicago (6 ln.ft., 1890–1968); the Infant Welfare Society of Chicago (10 ln.ft., 1903–74); the Chicago Tuberculosis Institute, now the Chicago Lung Association (5 ln.ft., 1906–77); and the Chicago Hearing Society (5 ln.ft., 1916–76). At the same time, Chicago's churches created nondenominational organizations to address urban issues, as the papers of the Church Federation of Greater Chicago (85 ln.ft., 1908–74) and the Chicago Sunday Evening Club (12.5 ln.ft., 1908–75) attest.

The society also holds the records of a group of umbrella organizations that have coordinated and supported social programs over the years. United Charities of Chicago and its predecessors, the Chicago Relief and Aid Society and the Chicago Bureau of Charities (30 ln.ft., 1867–1971), provided relief assistance, legal aid, and other services to people in need. The Chicago Community Trust (13 ln.ft., 1889–1975) distributed funds to various charitable groups. Jewish Community Centers of Chicago (37 ln.ft., 1904–77) sponsored educational and social programs at seventeen branches. The Welfare Council of Metropolitan Chicago coordinated a multitude of services in settlement houses, neighborhood centers, hospitals, and other institutions; its files (383 ln.ft., 1914–78) not only cover many topics but provide data on member agencies.

Other collections relate to efforts since the late nineteenth century to promote civic responsibility and good government. Concerned at first with such issues as fire protection, the water supply, and civil service reform, the Citizens' Association of Chicago (12 ln.ft., 1874–1964), after its merger with the Municipal Voters' League, concentrated on the need for honest elections and an honest City Council. The City Club of Chicago (23.5 ln.ft., 1903–78) advanced a full agenda of urban reforms, based on studies of the courts, transportation, racial discrimination, and similar matters. The Better Government Association of Chicago (210 ln.ft., 1923–82) became a clearinghouse of political information for good government advocates. Questions regarding prohibition, the police department, and the board of education occupied William E. Dever (5 ln.ft., 1884–1929), mayor of Chicago from 1923 to 1927.

For educational history, the Manuscripts Department holds personal, school, and union materials. The Flora J. Cooke collection (80 ln.ft., 1884–1960) contains both her papers as principal of the Francis W. Parker School, 1901–34, and the subsequent records of the school, an experiment in progressive education. The Citizens School Committee collection (30 ln.ft., 1911–72) documents its efforts to monitor the Chicago public school system as well as Mary J. Herrick's work as a teacher and union activist. The papers of Cyrus Hall Adams (16 ln.ft., 1958–68), a member of the Chicago Board of Education, relate to school desegregation and other educational questions. Also available are the records of the Chicago Teachers' Federation (39 ln.ft., 1864–1968), organized in 1897 to secure better salaries, pensions, and tenure protection for teachers, and the records of the Chicago Teachers Union (45 ln.ft., 1870–1972), founded in 1937 and soon engaged in negotiations with the Chicago school board.

Other labor organizations are also represented in the society's collections. The papers of John Fitzpatrick, president of the Chicago Federation of Labor (10 ln.ft., 1890–1965), supplemented by microfilm of the federation's minutes (6 reels, 1903–22), are fullest for the first decades of the century but also concern jurisdictional disputes of the late 1930s. The papers of William A. Lee (9 ln.ft., 1926–85), a later president of the federation, reflect the position of organized labor in the days of Mayor Richard J. Daley. The papers of Victor A. Olander (38 ln.ft., 1898–1948), secretary-treasurer of the Illinois State Federation of Labor, are rich in union data and also relate to relief and welfare programs during the Depression.

Additional material pertains to particular unions. The records of the Chicago Typographical Union No. 16 (47 ln.ft., 1871–1975) indicate that the city's oldest trade union served its members not only by negotiations and strikes but also through educational programs and social activities. The papers of Agnes Nestor (3 ln.ft., 1896–1954), president of the Women's Trade Union League of Chicago and a tireless worker for legislation beneficial to labor, are available on microfilm (7 reels) in a series with a printed guide, Edward T. James, ed., *Papers of the Women's Trade Union League and Its Principal Leaders* (Woodbridge, Conn., 1981). The records of the Chicago Newspaper Guild (3 ln.ft., 1934–71) deal with its strikes against the Hearst newspapers. Numerous administrative and operational issues are covered in the papers of District 31 (Illinois and northern Indiana) of the United Steelworkers of America (114 ln.ft., 1934–79), while the George A. Patterson collection (5.5 ln.ft., 1927–80) provides the perspective of a steel union organizer. The papers of Ernest DeMaio, president of District 11 of the United Electrical, Radio, and Machine Workers of America (14 ln.ft., 1936–74), include his correspondence with other progressive unionists. The files of Irving Meyers and David Rothstein (54 ln.ft., 1939–68) relate to their work as lawyers for the Newspaper Guild, the United Electrical Workers, and other unions in Chicago. Tapes of the interviews that Studs Terkel gathered for *Hard Times* (1970) and *Working* (1974) preserve the experiences of ordinary people.

Chicago became the home of thousands of immigrants, especially in the late nineteenth century. Although evidence of the city's foreign-born population can be found in most of the society's holdings, only a few collections may serve to illustrate this dimension of Chicago's history. The Mutual Benefit and Aid Society of Chicago (16 ln.ft., 1871–1973) endeavored to meet the insurance and social needs of the German community. The German-American Historical Society of Illinois (650 items, 1900–3) attempted to preserve records of the German contribution to the Union cause in the Civil War. Otto L. Schmidt (8 ln.ft., 1869–1940), who was president of the Illinois State and Chicago historical societies, also gave vital support to cultural and commemorative activities among his fellow German-Americans. The papers of Ivan Molek (8 ln.ft., 1905–68) reflect the career of a Slovenian language newspaper editor. The records of the Polish-American Political Organization (17 ln.ft., 1930–59), mostly in Polish, not only document its role in Northwest Side social and charitable functions but also illustrate the ethnic character of local politics in Chicago.

The Oral History Archives of Chicago Polonia includes a series of taped interviews with 138 Polish–American immigrants or children of immigrants who came to the United States between 1880 and 1930. Most of these tapes are transcribed, and all are analyzed in the project's *Master Index*. In addition, Ronald Zaraza prepared a *Teacher's Guide* to a set of tapes that combines segments of many interviews related to particular topics. The Chicago Polonia project, completed in 1977, was directed by Mary Cygan, and duplicate copies of the interviews and tapes are available at Loyola University and the Polish Museum of America as well as in the Manuscripts Department of the Chicago Historical Society.

Other sources record the experiences of blacks in Chicago. An outstanding collection in this field, useful for its topical files on many facets of black life, is available in large part on microfilm, with printed guides by Linda J. Evans, in *The Claude A. Barnett Papers: The Associated Negro Press, 1918–1967* (198 reels, Frederick, Md., 1985–86). Barnett founded and directed the Associated Negro Press, a Chicago-based news service for black newspapers. Collections documenting black fraternal action include the records of the Chicago Division of the Brotherhood of Sleeping Car Porters (75 ln.ft., 1925–76) and the papers of the Afro-American Patrolmen's League of Chicago (90 ln.ft., 1967–85). The Irene McCoy Gaines collection (3 ln.ft., 1893–1968) contains her correspondence as president of the Chicago Council of Negro Organizations. From the Black Women in the Middle West Project, the society acquired the papers of Louise Overall Weaver (4 ln.ft., 1945–84), church organist and accompanist to Mahalia Jackson, and Clementine Skinner (4 ln.ft., 1965–80), teacher and administrator in the Chicago public schools. Among the black political leaders represented in the collections are Arthur W. Mitchell (30 ln.ft., 1898–1968), a lawyer and Democratic member of Congress, 1935–43, and Archibald J. Carey (20 ln.ft., 1909–66), an African Methodist Episcopal minister and alderman from the South Side, 1947–55.

The papers of elected officials in the period since World War II include the department's two largest collections, deposited by Paul H. Douglas (700 ln.ft., 1932–71) and Charles H. Percy (1,800 ln.ft., 1939–85), each of whom served three terms in the U.S. Senate. Their files are a virtual cornucopia of information on the issues of the day. The papers of Joseph T. Meek (3 ln.ft., 1947–71) and William H. Rentschler (8 ln.ft., 1949–75) relate in part to their unsuccessful senatorial campaigns in 1954 and 1970, respectively. The Robert E. Merriam (7 ln.ft., 1947–55) and Leon M. Despres (103 ln.ft., 1945–82) collections reflect the work of liberal Democratic aldermen of Chicago's Fifth Ward, which encompasses the Hyde Park neighborhood of the University of Chicago.

The vibrant politics of Chicago have made the city an ideal location for political commentators. Since 1975, some ninety-seven Chicago journalists have been included in interviews taped by students of Northwestern University's Medill School of Journalism. The Len O'Connor collection (23.5 ln.ft., 1935–80) contains tapes and transcripts of his broadcast interviews with political leaders. Modern American conservatism is documented in the papers of Sterling Morton (22.5 ln.ft., 1891–1961), a businessman and philanthropist; Clarence Manion (48 ln.ft., 1922–79), a lawyer who broadcast the influential "Manion Forum"; and Ira Latimer (35 ln.ft., 1927–74), a disillusioned socialist who embraced a wide range of right-wing causes. Sharply different opinions are manifest in the papers of Sidney Lens (70 ln.ft., 1910–86), a Chicago labor union official who became active for world peace. Also available are the records of the Independent Voters of Illinois (15 ln.ft., 1944–66).

Several collections reflect the interests and concerns of modern feminist groups. The Chicago Women's Liberation Union (7 ln.ft., 1968–73) established itself as a radical, anti-capitalist, multi-issue organization. By contrast, E.R.A. Central (9.5 ln.ft., 1970–76), a Chicago-based group, concentrated on the Equal Rights Amendment. The papers of the Jane Addams Bookstore (14 ln.ft., 1977–84) not only document a feminist business but contain information regarding feminist organizations throughout Chicago.

Other sources also relate to recent agendas for reform. Harry R. Booth (19 ln.ft., 1930–74) was an advocate for consumers and taxpayers in gas, electric, and telephone rate appeals. Luis Kutner (31.5 ln.ft., 1916–81), another attorney, worked to improve the rights of indigents in criminal cases. The Midwest Academy (80 ln.ft., 1973–85) was founded to train leaders of community, church, senior citizen, minority, and women's groups. Business and Professional People for the Public Interest (55 ln.ft., 1966–85) litigated issues as diverse as the location of public housing and the safety of nuclear power plants.

Efforts to promote better race relations and housing opportunities emerge in a number of collections, including the papers of Daniel M. Cantwell, a Catholic priest (16.5 ln.ft., 1931–80); the Catholic Interracial Council of Chicago (50 ln.ft., 1932–68); and the Leadership Council for Metropolitan Open Communities (146 ln.ft., 1966–86). Other groups attempted to stabilize neighborhoods affected by rapid social and racial change. The Greater Lawndale Conservation Commission (11 ln.ft., 1950–67) was active during the years when Lawndale, a Jewish community, became predominantly black. The Uptown Chicago Commission (15 ln.ft., 1955–77) focused on economic and living conditions in that neighborhood. The Northwest Community Organization (14 ln.ft., 1964–86) coordinated grass-roots groups in the Logan Square and West Town areas and formulated legislative initiatives to maintain urban neighborhoods. The Jewish Council on Urban Affairs (19 ln.ft., 1965–83) provided technical assistance to organizations striving to upgrade middle-class communities. Issues related to race and poverty commanded the attention of the *Chicago Reporter* (19 ln.ft., 1972–89), published by the Community Renewal Society.

The Manuscripts Department also holds the records of organizations concerned with the development of the entire region. The Northeastern Illinois Planning Commission (56 ln.ft., 1923–72), working with local governmental units in Cook, DuPage, Kane, Lake, McHenry, and Will counties, attempted to coordinate the use of land and water resources. The Open Lands Project (29.5 ln.ft., 1961–76) sought not only to set aside undeveloped areas near Chicago but also to keep the public aware of issues affecting the lakeshore, parks, and preserves of the region. Another environmental organization, the Illinois Chapter of the Nature Conservancy (10.5 ln.ft., 1954–77), endeavored to preserve prairies, swamps, and other natural areas throughout the state. By arrangement with the Illinois State Archives, the Chicago Historical Society acquired the records of the Chicago World's Fair 1992 Authority (145 ln.ft., 1981–85), which was canceled for lack of government funding.

The resources of the Manuscripts Department are complemented by other research collections, especially the holdings of the Library. Containing books and pamphlets, newspapers and periodicals, maps, atlases, and ephemera, the printed collection is unmatched for Chicago history and not inconsiderable for Illinois history as well. Scarce but well-used sources include "Chicago Street Nomenclature," a typed index to street names, and *New and Old House-Numbers, City of Chicago*, a mimeographed key to street renumbering, 1909–11. The library also maintains a large newspaper clipping file, begun in the 1930s and organized by subject. The main card catalog is supplemented by special indexes, including a subject index to Charles S.Winslow's chronology, *Historical Events of Chicago* (Chicago, 1937).

The Prints and Photographs Department contains over one million images, concentrated on Chicago but also depicting other Illinois cities. The collection includes broadsides, posters, cartoons, postcards, slides, films, and video tapes, as well as prints and photographs, and is arranged both by subject and by archival lot. In addition to biography files and street files, there are separate collections such as the *Chicago Daily News* photomorgue negatives, 1902–65; drawings by John T. McCutcheon and Carey Orr, *Chicago Tribune* cartoonists; Raymond Trowbridge negatives of commercial and residential architecture in Chicago, 1923–32; Charles R. Childs images of Illinois cities and towns, made for his postcard business from the 1920s to the 1940s; kinescopes of "Kukla, Fran, and Ollie" programs of the 1950s; and news-film of WGN–TV (Chicago), 1948–73. The print collection includes an extensive and varied selection of nineteenth-century engravings and lithographs. The department also contains visual materials transferred from the Infant Welfare Society, Visiting Nurse Association, and other collections held by the Manuscripts Department.

Yet another research unit extending the society's sources for Illinois history is the Architectural Collection. Established in 1976 in collaboration with the Chicago chapter of the American Institute of Architects, this collection includes a wealth of architectural renderings, sketches, and drawings as well as correspondence, models, and other records of Chicago-based architects. The first major accession, the papers of Harry Weese and Associates (1954–75), was followed by the immense archives of Holabird & Roche and Holabird & Root (1880–1940). The collection also includes the records of the Illinois Society of Architects (1872–1974), Chicago Women in Architecture (1970s–80s), and the Fuller Construction Company (1900–70s), as well as materials representing the work of Arthur Hercz (1890s–1930), Alfred S. Alschuler and Friedman, Alschuler, Sincere (1900s–60s), John Lloyd Wright (1912–70), Barry Byrne (1914–67), and Rapp & Rapp (1920–65). The Graham, Anderson, Probst & White collection (1895–1975) contains some records of D. H. Burnham & Co., while church designs predominate in the Tallmadge and Watson collection (1910–40).

Documentation for two firms is of special interest to the Chicago Historical Society itself: Graham, Anderson, Probst & White designed the society's first building in Lincoln Park, the stately Georgian edifice completed in 1932, while Holabird & Root executed not only the most recent addition on Clark Street, opened in 1988, but also the subterranean storage areas which extend into the park and contain, in large part, the research collections that lie at the core of Chicago history.

# 18

# UNIVERSITY OF ILLINOIS AT CHICAGO

MARY ANN BAMBERGER

Main Library, MC-234
Box 8198
Chicago, IL 60680
(312) 996–2742

THE SPECIAL COLLECTIONS Department of the University of Illinois at Chicago holds a rich array of materials for Illinois and especially Chicago history. Established in 1965, the department preserves close to four hundred manuscript collections dealing with the Chicago metropolitan area. Containing also the university archives and special and rare book collections, much of which relate to Chicago, the department provides the resources for countless studies of the city.

The holdings of the University Archives document not only the present institution but also its predecessor, the Chicago Undergraduate Division of the University of Illinois, which began on Navy Pier in 1946. The University of Illinois at Chicago Circle opened in 1965 at Harrison and Halsted streets, and in 1982 Chicago Circle and the Health Sciences Center combined to form the University of Illinois at Chicago. With this merger, the archival programs of the two campuses became one.

Holdings are partly accessible through a mimeographed "Guide to the Manuscript Collections." This compendium, describing processed collections and listing unprocessed ones, is supplemented by in-house guides and inventories. For an overview, see Gretchen Lagana, "Special Collections in the University Library: Part I, Chicago," *UIC Library Reporter*, 1 (Spring 1983). The largest and most important collections deal with trade and commerce, design, fairs and expositions, social welfare, women, politics, and the literature of Chicago from the late nineteenth century to the present.

The records of the Chicago Board of Trade (1,535 ln.ft., 1858–1980) pertain to the development of commercial trading in Chicago and the Midwest. The collection documents the board's policies and its members' attitudes concerning such matters as trading in contracts for future delivery, the marketing of surplus agricultural commodities, and the regulation of exchanges by the federal government. It touches on many other topics, from military operations in the Civil War to illegal speculation in futures, and from the transportation and warehousing of grain to the architectural development of the Loop, including the construction of the Board of Trade buildings at the foot of LaSalle Street. Sketched in Owen Gregory, comp., *The Archives of the Chicago Board of Trade, 1859–1925* (Chicago, 1977), the collection is accessible through entries in an automated database.

The history of artistic concepts in Chicago is illuminated by numerous collections. The John Walley papers (25 ln.ft., 1937–74) include designs for murals, furniture, and toys conceived by artists who participated in the Illinois Arts and Crafts projects of the Works Progress Administration. The Rose Alschuler papers (14 ln.ft., 1916–73) point to the artwork of children as a key to their mental health. The Art Resources in Teaching records (32 ln.ft., 1894–1986) show an organization introducing the study of art to children in Chicago's public schools and establishing scholarships for them at the Art Institute of Chicago.

The Institute of Design collection (3.5 ln.ft., 1927–70) documents how a group of European artists brought to Chicago the revolutionary design concepts of the German Bauhaus—a synthesis of art and technology. The collection consists of correspondence, lectures, and other papers of faculty members and individuals associated with the school, including László Moholy-Nagy, Walter Gropius, Ludwig Mies van der Rohe, and Walter Paepcke. The Robert Vogele records (63 ln.ft., 1958–80) contain the design projects that his firm developed for many Chicago businesses. The collection not only illustrates the efforts of companies to enhance or change their corporate identities but also reflects the swiftly changing attitudes of consumers toward their products.

The R. Hunter Middleton Design Print Collection documents the role played by Chicago designers in the fields of graphic, industrial, and commercial design. Robert Middleton, for many years director of type design at Ludlow Typograph Company, personified the cohesiveness and sense of community that distinguished Chicago designers over a forty-year period. The collection includes the work of Middleton (40 ln.ft., 1930–79), Norman Forgue of the Black Cat Press (12 ln.ft., 1933–85), and John Massey of Container Corporation of America

(75 ln.ft., 1960–77). Also represented are Mary Gehr and Bert Ray (4 ln.ft., 1938–86), Herbert Pinzke (9 ln.ft., 1948–72), Bruce Beck (15 ln.ft., 1961–75), David Root (30.5 ln.ft., 1956–78), and Gordon Monsen (10 ln.ft., 1950–64). In addition, there are the records of the International Design Conference at Aspen (22.5 ln.ft., 1954–82), the 27 Chicago Designers (112 ln.ft., 1937–86), and the Chicago Book Clinic (151 ln.ft., 1936–86). The Middleton Collection lends itself to the study of typographic design, corporate and signage identity, book design, consumer advertising and packaging, and design theory and its applications, as well as a wide range of graphic concepts. For an introduction to these materials, see Gretchen Lagana, "Collecting Design Resources at the University of Illinois at Chicago," *Design Issues*, 3 (Fall 1986).

Voluminous records support the study of fairs and expositions in Chicago. Records of A Century of Progress International Exposition, the world's fair of 1933–34 (550 ln.ft., 1928–40), include data on previous fairs, especially the World's Columbian Exposition of 1893. These materials cover many topics, from the choice of a lakefront site for the earlier fair to the building plans, the Art Deco style, the special building code, the labor practices, and the successful management of the fair that marked the one-hundredth year since Chicago's incorporation. The collection also includes graphic materials—photographs, posters, set and costume designs—that depict the pavilions, exhibits, theater productions, and other events of the fair. Similar records are available for the Chicago Railroad Fair of 1948–49 (25 ln.ft., 1948–52), which celebrated the centennial of railroading from Chicago westward. The Lenox Riley Lohr papers (66 ln.ft., 1911–68) relate to his activities as general manager of A Century of Progress and as president of the Railroad Fair and of the Museum of Science and Industry. The Helen Tieken Garaghty collection (6 ln.ft., 1931–69) records the work of the theatrical producer who staged historical pageants for both fairs.

Chicago's social welfare history is well documented. Numerous collections reflect the efforts of social settlement houses, social welfare agencies, and social workers to address the problems created by the rapid growth and industrialization of the city, the needs of a large immigrant population, increased unemployment, child labor and neglect, and widespread vice and prostitution.

The Jane Addams Memorial Collection encompasses many of these sources, specifically the collections pertaining to Jane Addams and the residents of Hull House, and the social welfare agencies long associated with Hull House. Materials for Jane Addams's own life and career are also available on microfilm (82 reels, 1860–1960), with a printed guide, in Mary Lynn McCree Bryan, ed., *The Jane Addams Papers* (Ann Arbor, 1985). The Hull House Association records (100 ln.ft., 1889–1982) are important for Chicago's first social settlement, founded by Jane Addams and Ellen Gates Starr in 1889. Prominent Hull House residents are represented in the papers of Esther Loeb Kohn (15.5 ln.ft., 1896–1965), who supported protective social legislation for women and children in Illinois; Alma Birmingham (4 ln.ft., 1907–70), who taught music at Hull House and supported the Women's City Orchestra of Chicago; Adena Miller

Rich (7 ln.ft., 1890–1966), who in 1935 succeeded Jane Addams as head resident; and Russell Ward Ballard (21 ln.ft., 1875–1980), the fourth and last head resident of Hull House. The Jane Addams Memorial Collection also includes the records of the Juvenile Protective Association of Chicago (12 ln.ft., 1904–55), which evolved from the effort to establish the first juvenile court of Cook County in 1899, and the Immigrants' Protective League (19 ln.ft., 1909–70), which assisted newcomers to Chicago. The league merged in 1967 with a related organization, creating the Travelers Aid Society and Immigrant Service of Metropolitan Chicago (51 ln.ft., 1908–74).

These materials relate both to broad research topics such as the role of women and the peace movement in the early twentieth century and to local issues such as Nineteenth Ward politics and sanitary and housing conditions on the Near West Side. Hull House was a center for naturalization, cooking, and reading classes, theatrical productions, and arts and crafts, and its records, supplemented by samples of pottery, textiles, and paintings, reflect an appreciation of ethnic culture.

Other collections contribute to an understanding of the state's social welfare history, including the records of the Children's Home and Aid Society of Illinois (41 ln.ft., 1883–1970), an organization involved in adoptive and foster home placement; the Illinois Humane Society (273 ln.ft., 1879–1961), which provided protective services to women and children as well as abused animals; and the Institute for Sex Education (15.5 ln.ft., 1916–71), which combated venereal disease. Among the sources for the history of ethnic groups are the records of the German Aid Society of Chicago (18 ln.ft., 1878–1970); the papers of Jack Jatis (24 ln.ft., 1934–68), which relate to the experiences of Lithuanian immigrants in southwest Chicago; and the Italian American collection (42 ln.ft., 1920–83), which includes interviews, transcriptions, and other materials from the Italians in Chicago project of 1979–81.

Religiously oriented efforts are manifest in the records of the Ethical Humanist Society of Chicago (8 ln.ft., 1882–1956), the Marcy–Newberry social settlement (57 ln.ft., 1897–1968), and the Bethlehem-Howell Neighborhood Service Organization (21 ln.ft., 1891–1960). The papers of Preston Bradley (45 ln.ft., 1905–60), founder of the Peoples Church of Chicago, and of Irwin St. John Tucker (6 ln.ft., 1903–69), a clergyman and religious editor, offer other perspectives.

Evolving from a core of social welfare history materials is the Midwest Women's Historical Collection, a large concentration of resources documenting the lives of individual women, businesses and organizations founded and directed by women, and women's issues and concerns. Among the sources in this collection are more than five hundred letters from the anarchist Emma Goldman to her business manager, Ben Reitman, in his papers (21 ln.ft., 1905–51); the papers of Marcet Haldeman-Julius (14 ln.ft., 1833–1961), author and publisher of rationalist and socialist literature; and the papers of Neva Leona Boyd (7 ln.ft., 1911–71), a sociologist who wrote on play and game theory. The Young

Women's Christian Association of Metropolitan Chicago archives (33 ln.ft., 1876–1960) reflects its efforts to end child labor, improve working conditions for women, and promote integration. Also represented are the Women's Advertising Club of Chicago (25 ln.ft., 1917–82), Women in Communications (11 ln.ft., 1919–75), the Chicago Woman's Aid (40 ln.ft., 1882–1988), the League of Women Voters of Chicago (20 ln.ft., 1909–70), and Chicago Women in Publishing (15 ln.ft., 1971–86), all engaged in educational and career projects.

Other components of the Midwest Women's Historical Collection document more recent issues. The papers of Lonny Myers (4 ln.ft., 1955–75) relate to the founding of the Midwest Population Center, and the records of the National Abortion Rights Action League (16.5 ln.ft, 1961–78) pertain to the liberalization of abortion laws. Women Mobilized for Change (2.5 ln.ft., 1966–71) worked for civil rights. Another grass-roots activist organization, led by women, is the Committee for Handgun Control (10 ln.ft., 1968–79). The state's participation in the 1977 National Women's Conference is reflected in the records of the Illinois International Women's Year Coordinating Committee (8 ln.ft., 1977–78) and the papers of Marie Fese (6 ln.ft., 1960–77).

Many leaders in these and similar groups adopted the organizing tactics of Saul Alinsky, and the records of his Industrial Areas Foundation (15 ln.ft., 1940–72) provide information on the development of neighborhood organizations such as the Woodlawn Organization. The records of the Greater Lawndale Conservation Commission (5 ln.ft., 1953–68) and the papers of Stephen S. Bubacz (12.5 ln.ft., 1931–68), who, with others, led the Russell Square Community Committee, throw additional light on community action groups. Lengthy careers in social work are documented in the papers of Martin H. Bickham (130 ln.ft., 1905–76) and Harvey L. Long (22 ln.ft., 1919–68).

Efforts to coordinate and finance social programs throughout the city may be traced in the records of the Chicago Federation of Settlements and Neighborhood Centers (15 ln.ft., 1894–1983) and the Community Fund of Chicago (241 ln.ft., 1930–75). The papers of the Chicago regional office of the American Friends Service Committee (86 ln.ft., 1918–68) concern its work with youth and its efforts to minimize racial strife. The Chicago Urban League collection (300 ln.ft., 1916–84), fullest for the years since 1938, is the department's most notable resource for black history. Also available are the records of the Illinois Commission on the Employment of Youth (11 ln.ft., 1934–62), the Metropolitan Planning Council (100 ln.ft., 1934–80), and, finally, Business and Professional People for the Public Interest (300 ln.ft., 1949–83), a social issue law firm.

The study of politics in modern-day Chicago may be enriched by reference to many collections. These include the papers of Mayor Martin H. Kennelly (28 ln.ft., 1945–59), of Congressmen Barratt O'Hara (62 ln.ft., 1948–62) and Edgar A. Jonas (6.5 ln.ft., 1909–59), and of such state legislators as Esther Saperstein (60 ln.ft., 1949–88), Charles F. Armstrong (2.5 ln.ft., 1959–68), and W. Russell Arrington (3 ln.ft., 1965–76). Edmund K. Jarecki (41 ln.ft.,

1853–1966), judge of the Cook County Court, 1922–54, was also an important figure in the Polish–American community. Walker Butler (19 ln.ft., 1921–69) served in the Illinois Senate and on the Superior Court of Cook County.

Other sources pertain to Chicago as a literary place. There are the records of the Society of Midland Authors (4 ln.ft., 1915–71), whose members included George Ade, Harriet Monroe, and Vachel Lindsay, and the papers of Mary Hastings Bradley (150 ln.ft., 1882–1976), one of the society's presidents. Mary Bradley's career as the author of many novels and short stories, a war correspondent during World War II, and a prominent social figure in Chicago is well documented. As a world explorer, with her husband Herbert, daughter Alice, and naturalist Carl Akeley, she traveled to Africa to collect animal specimens and artifacts for natural history museums in Chicago and New York. The role of an independent press and the relationship between the publisher and many contemporary authors may be examined in the archives of the Swallow Press during its Chicago years (175 ln.ft., 1967–77).

The Lawrence J. Gutter Collection of Chicagoana, acquired in 1982, contains some nine thousand volumes about the city which not only provide a basis for innumerable studies of Chicago but also link together the department's Chicago-related research holdings. Distinguished by a selection of nearly four hundred pre-Fire imprints, by long runs of Chicago-based railroad reports, and by a full representation of the city's authors, the collection includes a manuscript section that ranges from a journal kept by the publisher A. S. Barnes of a book-selling journey through the Midwest in 1839 to items by Henry B. Fuller and Edgar Lee Masters of the Chicago Renaissance. The Gutter Collection together with the manuscript collections outlined in this chapter and many other holdings in Special Collections combine to serve scholars as they construct a profile of Chicago.

# 19

# UNIVERSITY OF CHICAGO

DANIEL MEYER

Joseph Regenstein Library
1100 E. 57th St.
Chicago, IL 60637
(312) 702–8705

THE DEPARTMENT OF Special Collections of the University of Chicago Library was formed in 1953 from the consolidation of existing book and manuscript collections. The department holds the university's rare book collections, manuscript collections ranging in date from the second century to the present, and the university archives. Sources in Special Collections related to Illinois history can be identified by reference to the inventories of individual collections and through a listing of manuscript holdings, "A Short Title Catalog of Manuscripts in the University of Chicago Library" (1986).

The department's earliest sources for Illinois history are found in the Ethno-History collection, which consists of microfilmed and photostated documents from numerous American and foreign repositories. Assembled and indexed by the Anthropology Department between 1936 and 1947, this collection includes letters, reports, maps, and other papers (altogether some fifty thousand pages) pertaining to Indian-white relations in the Mississippi Valley before about 1840. Another concentration of research materials is the Church History Documents collection (6.5 ln.ft.), containing photostats and typescripts of early nineteenth-century records from which William Warren Sweet of the Divinity School selected manuscripts for his series, *Religion on the American Frontier* (1931–46). The department also holds early records of the Illinois Baptist Convention (1 vol., 1830–45).

Two collections concern the leading political figures of the state's Civil War era. The Stephen A. Douglas papers (19.5 ln.ft., 1845–61) consist of letters that Douglas received from his Illinois constituents, especially in his last years as a U.S. senator. The William E. Barton Collection of Lincolniana contains originals and photostats of law cases argued by Abraham Lincoln; books from Lincoln's law office; a group of documents from the estate of his father-in-law, Robert S. Todd; Civil War era sheet music, broadsides, and prints; and the Osborn H. Oldroyd collection of contemporary autographs and portraits. An early description of these diverse sources, M. Llewellyn Raney, "Famous Lincoln Collections: The University of Chicago," *Abraham Lincoln Quarterly*, 1 (Mar. 1941), may be supplemented by an exhibition catalog, Christopher W. Kimball, *In Lincoln's Time: Sources on Nineteenth Century America in the William E. Barton Collection* (Chicago, 1986).

Other nineteenth-century holdings document an array of topics in social and cultural history. The papers of the Chicago Mechanics' Institute (3 ln.ft., 1875–1941) demonstrate the persistence of a pre–Civil War organization. A volume of Joliet Penitentiary testimony (1878) contains evidence of prison brutality collected by three commissioners. The Jenkin Lloyd Jones collection (6.5 ln.ft., 1861–1920) pertains to Jones's career as a Unitarian minister, editor of *Unity* magazine, and liberal reformer. The documentary richness of the period is particularly evident in the research reports of the History of Chicago Project, which are located within the papers of Bessie Louise Pierce (17 ln.ft., 1839–1974), author of *A History of Chicago* (1937–57).

The Progressive period is well represented in the department's collections. The papers of Gov. Frank O. Lowden (132 ln.ft., 1885–1943) include a vast range of materials on nearly every aspect of his political career. State colleges and universities, agricultural economics, public administration, Republican national politics, congressional and gubernatorial campaigns, and the business affairs of the Chicago, Rock Island, and Pacific Railroad and the Pullman Company (Lowden was the son-in-law of George M. Pullman) are only a few of the topics treated. No less substantial are the papers of Charles E. Merriam (156.5 ln.ft., 1890–1953), alderman, Republican reform candidate for mayor of Chicago in 1911, and professor of political science at the University of Chicago. Besides information on Merriam's political campaigns, the collection contains City Council reports; data on the Chicago charter conventions, the Commission on City Expenditures, and the Chicago Crime Commission; and correspondence with many prominent Illinoisans. The collection also preserves Merriam's scholarly studies of Chicago politics and Harold F. Gosnell's manuscripts dealing with Chicago precincts, voting behavior, and black politics.

University of Chicago faculty in social work and sociology were especially active in the effort to study and reshape the character of urban life. The Edith and

Grace Abbott collection (63 ln.ft., 1897–1958) includes material on Hull House and other Chicago settlements, the Immigrants' Protective League, the National Conference of Social Work, studies of child welfare and the role of women, programs for social work education in an urban context, and correspondence with many significant Illinois progressives. The manuscript autobiography of the Abbotts' colleague, Sophonisba P. Breckinridge (0.5 ln.ft., 1940–45), and the papers of Mary Bolton Wirth (2.5 ln.ft., 1922–75), a Chicago social worker, add important details to the record of social concern and activism. The papers of George Herbert Mead (10 ln.ft., 1899–1931) and James H. Tufts (2 ln.ft., 1900–26), both members of the Philosophy Department, also relate to civic reform. Mead was involved in the development of elementary education, vocational training, social settlements and agencies, and the Hart, Schaffner, and Marx labor agreement of 1911, while Tufts was chairman of the Chicago Arbitration Board established by that agreement when the board exercised its emergency powers to adjust wages upward in 1919.

The impulse toward private philanthropic social reform is nowhere better exemplified than in the papers of Julius Rosenwald (32 ln.ft., 1895–1932), president and chairman of the board of Sears, Roebuck and Company. Rosenwald headed the Bureau of Public Efficiency, the Chicago Vice Commission, and the Committee on Race Relations; he helped organize the National Association for the Advancement of Colored People; and he supported the National Urban League, the Tuskegee Institute and black education in general, the Young Men's Christian Association, various Jewish philanthropies, and the activities of Hull House and other Chicago settlements. A related collection, the papers of Ida B. Wells (2.5 ln.ft., 1884–1974), the black social activist, deals with civil rights and the anti-lynching movement.

Other aspects of Progressive reform are also apparent in the department's holdings. The Chicago Civil Service League (1 ln.ft., 1901–13) and the Illinois Joint Committee for the Merit System in the Civil Service (1 ln.ft., 1921–39) fought to secure observance of civil service laws and to strengthen requirements for appointments to government positions. The Chicago Committee of Fifteen (3 ln.ft., 1909–27), a specially constituted citizens' committee to investigate prostitution, collected vivid descriptions of stores, saloons, dance halls, and other locations within Chicago's red–light districts. But a succession of urban sociologists left the largest aggregation of research data. Ernest W. Burgess and his assistants studied local Chicago communities, delinquency, parole, marriage, family, churches, and old age, among other subjects. The Burgess collection (300 ln.ft., 1916–50) also includes material on the Chicago Area Project, the Chicago Relief Administration, the Illinois Association for Criminal Justice, and similar groups. Louis Wirth's papers (29 ln.ft., 1931–52) include his files on the Chicago Crime Commission, the Chicago Plan Commission, the Chicago Urban League, and the Illinois State Housing Board. The papers of Philip M. Hauser (26 ln.ft., 1925–77) contain material on Chicago school and housing desegregation controversies and data compiled by the Chicago Community Inventory.

Several collections reflect more recent political and social concerns. The papers of Thomas V. Smith (6 ln.ft., 1934–41), professor of philosophy, state senator, and congressman-at-large for Illinois, deal with the Democratic party in Illinois, public education, economic reform, and loyalty oaths. Robert E. Merriam's papers (20 ln.ft., 1947–55), like those of his father, relate to aldermanic campaigns in the Hyde Park neighborhood and to an unsuccessful campaign for mayor of Chicago in 1955. The records of the Hyde Park–Kenwood Community Conference (77 ln.ft., 1949–72) touch on many aspects of urban life: tenants' unions, park and playground development, air pollution, public education, housing rehabilitation, and urban renewal. The files of the Hyde Park Historical Society (13.5 ln.ft., 1878–1982) provide additional information on the university neighborhood and its reshaping by urban renewal in the 1950s and 1960s.

The Department of Special Collections also contains a number of important collections of literary manuscripts from the turn of the century to the present. The editorial files of *Poetry* (83.5 ln.ft., 1912–61) are among the most impressive, containing manuscripts and correspondence of hundreds of poets who submitted work to the magazine, including Sherwood Anderson, Vachel Lindsay, Edgar Lee Masters, and Carl Sandburg. The scope of the collection is suggested by an exhibition catalog by Kathleen Farley, *Poetry Magazine: A Gallery of Voices* (Chicago, 1980). The personal papers of *Poetry*'s founding editor, Harriet Monroe (10.5 ln.ft., 1873–1944), provide further details about Chicago's literary milieu. The William Vaughn Moody collection (3 ln.ft., 1889–1930) includes correspondence and manuscripts of his poetry and plays and is supplemented by the papers of his wife, Harriet Brainard Moody, who was later the center of a literary circle. Robert Herrick's papers (13 ln.ft., 1893–1939) contain letters, notebooks, and manuscripts of his novels. Robert Morss Lovett, an English Department colleague of both Moody and Herrick, is represented by a collection (1.5 ln.ft., 1876–1950) including material on the congressional loyalty investigation of Lovett in 1943. The papers of Saul Bellow (54.5 ln.ft., 1940–80) contain correspondence together with the manuscripts of many of his novels, short stories, essays, and other works. Richard Stern's papers (14 ln.ft., 1953–87) constitute another contemporary literary collection.

In addition, the department holds materials for the history of theater in Chicago. A rich but relatively unused source is the comprehensive record of theatrical performances from the mid-nineteenth to the mid-twentieth century which Napier Wilt and his English Department staff compiled (27.5 ln.ft., 1839–1955). This survey encompasses theater of all types, from minstrel shows and Shakespearean tragedy to melodramas and farce, and is organized into series by author, title, and date of performance. The Chicago Repertory Group collection (5 ln.ft., 1933–47) contains copies of the plays, songs, and sketches of a local theatrical organization.

The history of science and medicine in Illinois is documented by another concentration of manuscript materials in Special Collections. Many of these collections were part of the John Crerar Library before its merger with the university in 1984. Among the most important are those assembled by the Society of Medical History of Chicago, including some records of Cook County Hospital, Rush Medical College, and the Chicago Homeopathic Medical College, as well as prescriptions, lectures, and manuscripts of Chicago physicians. Other associations in the Crerar collections are the Chicago Laryngological and Otological Society, the Chicago Heart Association, the Chicago Neurological Society, the Chicago Pediatric Society, and the Chicago Psychological Association. Among the Chicago doctors represented by separate collections are Ludvig Hektoen, James B. Herrick, Julius Hess, Ralph S. Lillie, Arno Luckhardt, and Nicholas Senn. Holdings acquired before the acquisition of the Crerar collections include the records of the Illinois Society for Medical Research (6 ln.ft., 1890–1979) and papers of bacteriologist Edwin O. Jordan (2.5 ln.ft., 1895–1936) focusing on the building of the Chicago drainage canal, investigations of the influenza epidemic of 1919, and the work of the McCormick Institute for Infectious Diseases.

The department also holds the non-medical manuscript collections of the Crerar, including the archival records of the institution from its founding in 1889 to the merger of 1984, as well as a diverse group of small lots concerned with the Chicago Library Club, the Chicago Municipal Museum, the Illinois State Charities Commission, the United Mine Workers of Illinois, and several Illinois railroads. These and other Crerar collections, while not yet fully organized or described, are open for research use.

Finally, the Department of Special Collections contains the administrative records of the University of Chicago itself, part of which pertains to the history of Illinois and the history of Chicago in particular. The Presidents' papers (92.5 ln.ft., 1889–1945), the official files of the university's presidents from William Rainey Harper to Robert Maynard Hutchins, reflect the wide base of support for the institution among Chicago's business and cultural elites. Several Chicago institutions are documented in a group of smaller administrative series: the records of the Old University of Chicago (3.5 ln.ft., 1856–86), predecessor of the present university; the papers of Francis W. Parker (2 ln.ft., 1873–1904) and Henry H. Belfield (1 ln.ft., 1844–1967), both notable Chicago educational administrators; and the records of three institutions that merged to form the university's School of Education: the South Side Academy (1 ln.ft., 1897–1903), the Chicago Institute (1 ln.ft., 1900–1), and the Chicago Manual Training School (5.5 ln.ft., 1882–1913).

Also of interest are the papers of certain university trustees who were active in Chicago institutions, including Edward L. Ryerson, in the Ryerson family collection (4.5 ln.ft., 1803–1971); John Nuveen (40 ln.ft., 1922–65); and Emory Filbey (2 ln.ft., 1930–51). Fairfax Cone, Harold H. Swift, Laird Bell, and William Benton are among the other university trustees whose Chicago careers are documented by collections in the department.

# 20

---

# NEWBERRY LIBRARY

---

## DIANA HASKELL

60 W. Walton St.
Chicago, IL 60610
(312) 943–9090

THE NEWBERRY LIBRARY is an independent research center located on Chicago's Near North Side. Founded on a generous endowment provided for in the will of Walter Loomis Newberry, a Chicago businessman, the library marked its centennial in 1987. Its collections support the study of the humanities in Western Europe and the Americas. Although the history of Illinois is not a subject specialty per se, a surprising amount of pertinent material can be found within the larger collecting interests of the library.

The Newberry's present building, first occupied in 1893, was entirely re-modeled after the construction of an adjoining bookstack building in 1982. The Department of Special Collections, now located on the fourth floor, is responsible for the library's manuscript holdings, inventories and card catalogs for which are kept in the Reference and Bibliographical Center on the third floor. Many of the collections are described in the *Newberry Library Bulletin* (1944–79) and in *A Newberry Newsletter* (since 1973).

The massive subject-oriented collections of the Newberry contain certain manuscripts relating to Illinois history, some of which are described in Ruth Lapham Butler, comp., *A Check List of Manuscripts in the Edward E. Ayer*

*Collection* (Chicago, 1937) and Colton Storm, comp., *A Catalogue of the Everett D. Graff Collection of Western Americana* (Chicago, 1968). For example, the Ayer Collection includes six letters of Gov. Ninian Edwards regarding Indians of Illinois Territory, especially the Miami (1813–14); three letters of George Davenport pertaining to the Fox (1824–34); and a newly identified memorandum by Col. George W. Ewing concerning the Potawatomi (1846).

The John M. Wing Collection features sources for the history of printing and related arts in Chicago, including letters of Nathan C. Geer (17 items, 1846–59), a pioneer printer; records of the Blue Sky Press (1 ln.ft., 1900–21); and papers of Will Ransom (80 ln.ft., 1899–1945), a book designer and bibliographer; of Laurence Woodworth (2.5 ln.ft., 1896–1922), founder of the Brothers of the Book; and of several influential designers: William A. Kittredge (21 ln.ft., 1912–45), Ernst F. Detterer (15 ln.ft., 1913–47), Oswald Cooper (9.5 ln.ft., 1913–36), and R. Hunter Middleton (60 ln.ft., 1923–86).

The Newberry's collection of Midwest or Modern Manuscripts, an aggregate of some 180 individual collections, contains most of the library's sources for Illinois historians. It was Stanley Pargellis, the Newberry's fifth librarian (1942–62), who initiated the acquisition of these manuscripts as part of a program to make the library an active center of scholarly research, a program greatly expanded by his successor, Lawrence W. Towner (1962–86). Most of the collections relate to prominent Midwesterners of the late nineteenth and early twentieth centuries.

The greatest concentration within Midwest Manuscripts concerns the city's literary community, illuminating in particular the period of the Chicago Renaissance. Among the precursors of this school are several writers who are represented by small but useful collections: Joseph Kirkland (1 ln.ft., 1843–94), Henry Blake Fuller (14 ln.ft., 1874–1940), Mary Catherwood (1 ln.ft., 1860–1902), and Alice French, who wrote under the pseudonym Octave Thanet (4 ln.ft., 1871–1934). Of all the literary manuscripts, however, the centerpiece is the Sherwood Anderson collection (60 ln.ft., 1904–86). Anderson's papers are described in two issues of the *Newberry Library Bulletin*, 2 (Dec. 1948) and 6 (July 1971). Others who contributed to the cultural flowering of early twentieth-century Chicago include Floyd Dell (16 ln.ft., 1908–69); Eunice Tietjens (14 ln.ft., 1910–43); newspapermen such as Ring Lardner (9 ln.ft., 1907–72), George Ade (6 ln.ft., 1886–1949), and John T. McCutcheon (22 ln.ft., 1890–1951); and two literary critics, Harry Hansen (3 ln.ft., 1919–70) and Fanny Butcher (37 ln.ft., 1897–1987).

The Newberry also holds the papers of important playwrights in the period: Ben Hecht (64 ln.ft., 1915–78), Alice Gerstenberg (6 ln.ft., 1913–71), and Kenneth Sawyer Goodman (12 ln.ft., 1907–18). Two compilations relate to these collections: Faith D. Fleming, "Ben Hecht: Chronology and List of Works" (typescript, 1980) and Dennis Batory Kitsz, comp., *Kenneth Sawyer Goodman: A Chronology and Annotated Bibliography* (Chicago, 1983). In 1982, the library began to document the history of dance in Chicago. Sources now include the papers of Ann Barzel (207 ln.ft., 1915–89), a dance critic and historian, and

Edna McRae (22 ln.ft., 1912–87), a choreographer and teacher of dance; and the archives of the Walter Camryn–Bentley Stone studio (57 ln.ft., 1930–83), Chicago City Ballet (123 ln.ft., 1980–88), and Hubbard Street Dance Company (9 ln.ft., 1978–89).

For students of music, the resources of the Newberry are particularly rich. They include the papers of the founder of the Chicago Symphony Orchestra, Theodore Thomas (3 ln.ft., 1850–1972), and of his successor, Frederick Stock (60 items, 1904–42), plus the latter's manuscript compositions and scrapbooks; the papers, scrapbooks, and manuscript scores of Frederick Grant Gleason (9 ln.ft., 1875–1903), a Chicago music critic; and the scrapbooks of his colleagues, George P. Upton (1 ln.ft., 1860–76) and W. S. B. Mathews (1 ln.ft., 1872–1908). Two more important scrapbook series are those of the Auditorium Theatre (7 ln.ft., 1889–1939) and the American Opera Society of Chicago (6 ln.ft., 1924–89). Other collections include the papers of John Alden Carpenter (2 ln.ft., 1876–1951), composer of *Krazy Kat* in 1921; Rudolph Ganz (10 ln.ft., 1877–1989), concert pianist and president of Chicago Musical College; and Eric DeLamarter (151 items, 1904–71), assistant conductor of the Chicago Symphony Orchestra; as well as the archives of the Chicago Children's Choir (66 ln.ft., 1958–89), founded by Christopher Moore.

Among the holograph compositions in the Newberry's collections are George F. Bristow's *The Great Republic* (1880), Rossetter G. Cole's *The Rock of Liberty* (1920), and Hamilton Forrest's *Camille*, an opera written for Mary Garden (1930). Of an earlier historical interest are the volumes of dance tunes, part songs, hymns, and marches assembled in the 1830s and 1840s by Samuel Willard of Upper Alton and Jacksonville, Illinois. These manuscripts as well as other musical sources are fully itemized in D[onald] W. Krummel, ed., *Bibliographical Inventory to the Early Music in the Newberry Library, Chicago, Illinois* (Boston, 1977).

The Little Room manuscripts (1 ln.ft., 1898–1929) relate to an informal group of writers, musicians, and artists during the Chicago Renaissance. The city's cultural life may also be studied in the records of other, more institutionalized clubs: the Fortnightly Club of Chicago (30 ln.ft., 1869–1989), the Chicago Literary Club (26 ln.ft., 1874–1989), the Friday Club (24 ln.ft., 1887–1989), the Cliff Dwellers (15 ln.ft., 1906–89), and the Arts Club of Chicago (90 ln.ft., 1916–89). The papers of several civic leaders reflect their involvement in the arts: Charles Hutchinson (3.5 ln.ft., 1866–1934), a banker and the first president of the Art Institute of Chicago; Horace Oakley (6 ln.ft., 1880–1929), a lawyer and patron of the Chicago Symphony Orchestra; and Augustine Bowe (21 ln.ft., 1903–66), a judge and supporter of *Poetry*.

In the field of publishing, the Newberry holds the records of Stone and Kimball (24 ln.ft., 1889–1965) and A. C. McClurg (9 ln.ft., 1878–1967), and it also preserves the voluminous Kerr collection, which is inventoried in *The Charles H. Kerr Company Archives, 1885–1985: A Century of Socialist and Labor Publishing* (Chicago, 1985). In addition, the library holds the papers of Hermann

Raster (4 ln.ft., 1859–1940) and Wilhelm Rapp (3 ln.ft., 1846–61), editors of
the *Illinois Staats-Zeitung*, and of Francis Fisher Browne (6 ln.ft., 1890–1943)
and William Morton Payne (16 ln.ft., 1866–1919), editors of the *Dial*. The
course of Chicago journalism is especially well documented; the *Daily News*,
for example, is represented by the papers of its founder, Victor F. Lawson (72
ln.ft., 1873–1925); its editor, Charles H. Dennis (2 ln.ft., 1868–1942); and one
of its leading reporters, Edward Price Bell (33 ln.ft., 1890–1943). The archives
of the *Daily News* and the *Sun-Times* and predecessor newspapers (327 ln.ft.,
1925–84) are now at the Newberry.

Another important part of the Midwest Manuscripts collection comprises the
papers of certain men and women of social conscience: the founder of Chicago
Commons, Graham Taylor (40 ln.ft., 1862–1938); socialist and women's rights
advocate May Walden Kerr (5 ln.ft., 1890–1958); and lawyer and social reformer
Clarence Darrow (1 ln.ft., 1909–75), including especially his letters to Mary
Field Parton, a labor reporter. Also deposited at the Newberry are the papers of
the younger Carter Harrison (14 ln.ft., 1769–1953), five-term mayor of Chicago.

Large collections relating to Illinois railroads are accessible through Carolyn
Curtis Mohr, comp., *Guide to the Illinois Central Archives in the Newberry
Library, 1851–1906* (Chicago, 1951) and Elizabeth Coleman Jackson and
Carolyn Curtis, comps., *Guide to the Burlington Archives in the Newberry
Library, 1851–1901* (Chicago, 1949). Although steadily in use since the publi-
cation of these guides, both collections provide endless opportunities for the
study of the economic and social history of the region. The early years of the
Illinois Central are also documented by letters of company officials regarding
Kankakee and Bourbonnais (5 items in the Ayer Collection, 1853–55) and letters
between Charles Rich, a railroad engineer in DuQuoin, and his wife (103 items,
1853–54). The records of the Pullman Company are still uninventoried, but
some correspondence, a group of eighty–four scrapbooks, and over one thousand
ledgers and journals (1865–1949) are available to researchers at this time.

Other aspects of Illinois history are reflected in a variety of collections, such
as the correspondence of Christopher Pearce (1 ln.ft., 1839–51), an Ohio and
Mississippi river boat captain; the papers of Ephraim Cutler Dawes (4.5 ln.ft.,
1853–95), a Union Army officer and industrialist; and the correspondence of
Charles L. Hammond (213 items, 1891–95), which concerns the National Lincoln
Monument Association in Springfield.

The Newberry's manuscripts exemplify and elucidate the library's special
strengths for midwestern studies, the history of printing, music, and the settlement of North America. Together these published and unpublished materials
offer students of Illinois history a multiplicity of resources.

# 21

# OTHER CHICAGO-AREA REPOSITORIES

## KEVIN B. LEONARD

ALTHOUGH A FULL review of archival and manuscript collections in metropolitan Chicago is beyond the scope of this book, this chapter surveys to some extent the variety of repositories of interest to Illinois historians. In the following pages, it is possible to highlight a few of these repositories separately, but most of the archival scene can only be charted in general terms: their collections are largely tailored to the host institution, denomination, ethnic group, cultural institution, health care agency, or business corporation.

College and university archives in the Chicago area not infrequently contain important material for state and local history. For example, the Lake Forest College Library holds two collections of papers of Joseph Medill Patterson (66 ln.ft., 1874–1963), who was active in reform and socialist politics in Illinois, co-editor of the *Chicago Tribune* with his cousin Robert R. McCormick, and a playwright and novelist before 1919, when he founded the *New York Daily News*. Among the Chicago-related collections preserved at the DePaul University Archives are the papers of the Lincoln Park Conservation Association (82 ln.ft., 1954–89), documenting its commitment to community redevelopment, and the records of the Latino Institute (45 ln.ft., 1974–82), a research organization for the study of Hispanic life in metropolitan Chicago.

Theological seminary libraries also contribute to the reservoir of research materials in the Chicago area. Two of the University of Chicago's neighbors illustrate this point. Hammond Library of the Chicago Theological Seminary (United Church of Christ) contains the records of the Community Renewal

Society (20 ln.ft., 1882–1964), an organization engaged for more than a century in social welfare programs, while a collection in the Meadville Theological School of Lombard College Library documents the career of Jenkin Lloyd Jones (23 ln.ft., 1868–1918), an important figure in the evolution of Unitarianism.

In Evanston, next to Northwestern University, the library of Garrett-Evangelical Theological Seminary (United Methodist) contains the papers of Alvaro D. Field (2 ln.ft., 1850–1900), a pioneer historian of Methodism in northern Illinois, and Kimball Young (19 ln.ft., 1830–1962), a Northwestern sociologist who studied Mormonism, especially Mormon polygamy. The cornerstone of Garrett's holdings is the Ernest Fremont Tittle collection (105 ln.ft., 1918–65), reflecting the career of a noted clergyman, pastor of Evanston's First Methodist Church, and advocate for racial and economic justice. The Archives of the Northern Illinois Conference of the United Methodist Church, located in the Garrett–Evangelical library, exemplifies the denominational repository responsible for the records of defunct churches in a specified area. Its holdings document congregations of several antecedent denominations, both Methodist and Evangelical, especially Scandinavian churches, and include papers of ministers such as Nils O. Westergreen (5 ln.ft., 1822–1919), a Swedish Methodist, and John J. Wang (10 ln.ft., 1890–1959), representing the traditions of Norwegian-Danish Methodism.

Although the archives of the Billy Graham Center at Wheaton College document evangelical Protestantism in North America without regard to state boundaries, many of its collections pertain to Illinois history. When the Center opened in 1980, it had already accessioned the voluminous records of the Billy Graham Evangelistic Association and had microfilmed the papers of Billy and Helen Sunday, collected at the Grace Schools in Winona Lake, Indiana (29 reels, 1882–1974). In addition to these sources for evangelical campaigns in many cities, including Chicago, the Center now holds the archives of the Moody Memorial Church in Chicago (44 ln.ft., 1890–1980); collections regarding the Chicago Gospel Tabernacle and its founder, Paul Rader (6 ln.ft., 1922–79); the papers of Consuella Batchelor York, a chaplain at the Cook County jail (1 ln.ft., 1953–89); and the records of the Washington Street Mission in Springfield (2 ln.ft., 1914–82).

Materials for state and local history may also be found in other Chicago-area repositories with national or international interests such as the Brethren Historical Library and Archives, in Elgin; the National Bahá'í Archives, in Wilmette; and the archives of the Evangelical Lutheran Church in America, in Rosemont, with administrative headquarters nearby in Chicago. The Lutheran archives, formed in 1988, holds the records of earlier churches, including the collections described in Joel W. Lundeen, *Preserving Yesterday for Tomorrow: A Guide to the Archives of the Lutheran Church in America* (Chicago, 1977). The holdings of the Frances E. Willard Memorial Library, next to the Evanston home of the late nineteenth-century Illinoisan who led the Woman's Christian Temperance Union, supplement the microfilmed sources (45 reels, 1853–1934) that comprise Series I–III of the project described in Randall C. Jimerson et al., ed., *Guide to the Microfilm Edition of Temperance and Prohibition Papers* (Ann Arbor, 1977).

Archival resources at North Park College in Chicago document the college itself, the Evangelical Covenant Church in America, and the Swedish-American community of Chicago and the Midwest. Among the collections are the papers of David Nyvall (8 ln.ft., 1863–1923) and Clarence Nelson (17 ln.ft., 1959–67), presidents of the college and leaders of the Covenant church. Other sources—held by the Swedish-American Archives of Greater Chicago—include the papers of Henry Bengsten (5 ln.ft., 1904–70) and Carl Hjalmer Lundquist (4 ln.ft., 1923–64), both active in many Swedish-American organizations, and the records of such social and benevolent societies as the Independent Order of Svithiod (50 ln.ft., 1880–1985).

Several broadly defined ethnic, racial, and religious archives are located in metropolitan Chicago, including the Polish Museum of America, the DuSable Museum of African-American History, and the Chicago Jewish Archives at Spertus College of Judaica.

## Northwestern University

Deering Library
1935 Sheridan Rd.
Evanston, IL 60208

*University Archives*
(708) 491–3354

*Special Collections*
(708) 491–3635

After Northwestern University opened a modern, three-towered library in 1970, both the University Archives and the Special Collections Department expanded on the first and third floors of the Charles Deering Library, an older building in the Gothic style. Deering is now connected at ground level with the main library and accessible through it, and its units contain numerous collections of interest to Illinois historians.

The University Archives, while documenting in detail the institution's history since 1850, holds records such as the trustees' minutes and land books which illuminate the early development of the city of Evanston. It also preserves the letter books of Chicago Mayor Augustus Garrett (2 vols., 1843–45), which concern his business dealings in the nascent metropolis as an agent for a New York insurance company. The diaries of Abraham D. Graves (55 vols., 1847–1907), kept in Special Collections, provide a DeKalb County farmer's view of rural Illinois life. The Archives recently accessioned the records of Northwestern's Dearborn Observatory (18 ln.ft., 1863–1967), together with the records of the Chicago Astronomical Society (1 ln.ft., 1863–89), a useful source regarding patronage of early scientific work.

The voluminous papers of Charles G. Dawes (120 ln.ft., 1887–1951), in Special Collections, relate to his political and business interests in Chicago as well as his national career, and the papers of Rufus C. Dawes and his wife, Helen Palmer Dawes (4.5 ln.ft., 1870–1940), document in part A Century of Progress, the Chicago fair of 1933–34. Archival holdings for the early twentieth century include the records of the School of Domestic Arts and Science of Chicago (2 ln.ft., 1871–1978), which attempted to make home and family life objects of systematic study and prescribed activity, and the papers of Isaac A. Abt (3 ln.ft., 1888–1966), a leading pediatrician in Chicago and, in 1903, a founder of the Milk Commission, which later became the Infant Welfare Society. The papers of Earl Dean Howard (1 ln.ft., 1887–1978) and Frederick Deibler (2 ln.ft., 1910–42) relate to local and regional economic conditions, and especially to their efforts to arbitrate labor disputes during World War I. The Foster G. McGaw collection (150 ln.ft., 1928–86) includes personal papers and selected business records of the American Hospital Supply Corporation of Chicago, which McGaw founded.

Several collections pertain to twentieth-century legal and political history. The papers of John Henry Wigmore (150 ln.ft., 1863–1943), augmented by files unknown to his biographer, William R. Roalfe, range topically from the League of Nations to the Chicago Bar Association. The collection is administered by the Archives but kept at Northwestern's Law Library in Chicago. Newly available materials regarding the notorious Nathan Leopold and Richard Loeb case include, at the Archives, files of Harold S. Hulbert (850 items, 1920–56), a psychiatrist involved in the trial of 1924, and, in Special Collections, Elmer Gertz's papers (20 ln.ft., 1924–85), relating in part to Leopold's parole in 1958. In addition, the Archives holds the case files, correspondence, and other legal papers of Robert A. Sprecher (30 ln.ft., 1971–84), who served on the U.S. Court of Appeals for the Seventh Circuit. Widely separated points on the political spectrum are represented by Kenneth W. Colegrove, a political scientist at Northwestern, whose papers in the Archives (29.5 ln.ft., 1912–54) constitute a rich source for the study of McCarthyism in America, and Aleta Styers, a president of the Chicago chapter of the National Organization for Women, whose papers are held in Special Collections (5 ln.ft., 1966–72).

Numerous faculty collections at Northwestern document the cultural history of the state. The papers of Baker Brownell (26 ln.ft., 1904–65), a journalist, philosopher, and social critic of wide-ranging interests, include not only his extensive correspondence but also studies of communities in southern Illinois. The Lew R. Sarett collection (5 ln.ft., 1910–56) reflects the career of a noted poet and public lecturer who celebrated nature and the American Indian. The Archives also contains the editorial files of *TriQuarterly* (40 ln.ft., 1967–84), Northwestern's well-known literary magazine. The papers of James Alton James (1.5 ln.ft., 1888–1965), who led in the formation of the Archives in 1935, extend to his service on the Illinois State Park Commission, while the Carl W. Condit collection (2 ln.ft., 1942–87) centers on his studies of Chicago architecture. The papers of Eric Oldberg (2 ln.ft., 1941–64), president of the Chicago Symphony Orchestra, relate mainly to its administrative concerns, including scheduling, the engagement of personnel, and labor negotiations. Northwestern's Music Library, located on the second floor of Deering Library, holds the papers and marked scores of Fritz Reiner (70 ln.ft., 1919–64), musical director of the symphony, 1953–63.

## Loyola University

> Cudahy Memorial Library
> 6525 N. Sheridan Rd.
> Chicago, IL 60626
> (312) 508–2661

Established as St. Ignatius College in 1870 and so named until 1909, Loyola University of Chicago has evolved in recent years into one of the largest private institutions of higher education in Illinois. Its history is particularly well documented since the late 1920s, due to a series of part-time archivists and, since 1978, a full-time professional staff.

Among the holdings of the Loyola University Archives of interest to Illinois historians are the records of the Institute of Jesuit History (8 ln.ft., 1936–42), including photostats and microfilm of documents pertaining to early Jesuit work in the Illinois Country, as well as the research files of Gilbert J. Garraghan and Jean Delanglez, leading scholars in the field. These materials are supplemented by the files of the Illinois Catholic Historical Society (2.5 ln.ft., 1918–68).

The largest manuscript collection at Loyola, apart from its concentration of institutional records, is the Catholic Church Extension Society archive (250 ln.ft., 1905–63). Although worldwide in its efforts, the society is based in Chicago, and its correspondence includes several Illinois files. Collections in the field of Chicago history include the records of Chicago Inter-Student Catholic Action (5 ln.ft., 1932–57) and the correspondence and photographs of Leon T. Walkowicz (5 ln.ft., 1932–58), a Polish-American newspaperman, active in literary and dramatic organizations. A second Walkowicz collection is preserved in the archives of the Polish Museum of America. The papers of Samuel Insull (70 ln.ft., 1799–1962), perhaps the best-known of Loyola's collections, document the career of Chicago's leading utilities magnate of the early twentieth century.

## Archdiocese of Chicago

> Archives and Records Center
> 5150 Northwest Highway
> Chicago, IL 60630
> (312) 736–5150

The Archives of the Archdiocese of Chicago maintains an extensive collection of chancery records, correspondence, parish reports, and related sources documenting the most populous Roman Catholic jurisdiction in Illinois. Established at St. Mary of the Lake Seminary in Mundelein in the mid-1920s, the archives was relocated to Chicago in 1986, and most of its holdings are now fully open for historical research.

Some half million entries in a card catalog provide access by name, place, subject, and date to the early manuscripts of the archdiocese. Listed in William O. Achtermeier, "A Calendar of the Archive of the Archdiocese of Chicago . . . 1675–1918" (6 vols., M.A. thesis, Loyola Univ., Chicago, 1968), the catalog was continued through 1928 by Menceslaus J. Madaj, the archdiocesan archivist, 1968–84, and the archive itself is now known as the Madaj Collection (36 ln.ft.).

Documentation since 1928 is organized by series. The chancery correspondence files, for example, include the correspondence for the latter half of George Cardinal Mundelein's episcopate (16 ln.ft., 1929–39) and all of Samuel Cardinal Stritch's episcopate (76 ln.ft., 1939–58). The papers of their immediate successor, Albert Cardinal Meyer (58 ln.ft., 1922–65), document his entire career.

Aspects of Illinois social history are illuminated by the records of several agencies and institutions of the church. The St. Vincent de Paul Society collection (58 ln.ft., 1900–30) relates to Catholic charities, as do the records of Maryville Academy in Des Plaines (13 ln.ft., 1863–1958) and the Angel Guardian Orphan Society of Chicago (70 ln.ft., 1877–1968), each including training or industrial schools incorporated into those orphanages. The papers of Bishop Bernard J. Sheil (14 ln.ft., 1931–62), founder of the Catholic Youth Organization, contain his numerous speeches to unions in the Chicago area.

Parish church life is fully documented in annual reports of the parishes, dating from 1869, and in the parish-chancery correspondence files. The diocesan archives also holds a microfilm copy of many parish sacramental records, as well as a collection of parish histories.


## Chicago Public Library

*Cultural Center*
78 E. Washington St.
Chicago, IL 60602
(312) 269–2926

*Sulzer Regional Library*
4455 N. Lincoln Ave.
Chicago, IL 60625
(312) 728–8652

*Woodson Regional Library*
9525 S. Halstead St.
Chicago, IL 60628
(312) 881–6910

The Special Collections Department of the Chicago Public Library was formed in the early 1970s, a century after the library itself had been organized in the wake of the Great Chicago Fire. When the main library, built on Michigan Avenue between Randolph and Washington streets and opened in 1897, was renovated and reopened in 1977 as the Cultural Center, Special Collections obtained modern quarters adjacent to the Grand Army of the Republic Memorial Museum. The original G.A.R. collection is now greatly expanded by new acquisitions of books and manuscripts of the Civil War era. This and other collections in the unit, often used in exhibitions, are introduced in *Remarkable Chapters: 115 Years of Collecting by the Chicago Public Library* (Chicago, 1987).

The Chicago Theatre Collection is a rich and varied gathering of scrapbooks, broadsides, playbills, prompt books, scripts, set designs, correspondence, and other records of theatrical companies and theatrical productions in the city from the mid-nineteenth century to the present. Some of the major theaters represented in the collection are the Goodman Theatre (120 ln.ft., 1925–88), Steppenwolf Theatre (30 ln.ft., 1975–87), St. Nicholas Theater (64 ln.ft., 1975–81), and Body Politic Theatre (14 ln.ft., 1964–84). Supplementing these holdings are video tapes of theatrical productions and interviews with playwrights.

The Neighborhood History Research Collection (187 ln.ft., 1849–1989) is a combination of more than seventy separate collections representing fifteen Chicago neighborhoods. Containing the records of local historical societies, women's clubs, and improvement associations as well as scrapbooks and ephemera relating to neighborhood politics, businesses, churches, and schools, the collection opens windows to Chicago's development beyond the Loop, especially in the early twentieth century. The collection is particularly rich in photographic documentation, including over six thousand images. Most of the materials, accumulated at branch libraries, often in cooperation with neighborhood historical societies which began in the 1930s, were recently transferred to the Special Collections Department.

While the West Side, Chicago Lawn, Englewood, South Shore, and Calumet historical societies, and also several Woodlawn organizations, account for the bulk of the Neighborhood History Research Collection, materials relating to many North and Northwest Side communities are kept at the Conrad Sulzer Regional Library. The Sulzer, which opened in 1985 in place of the Frederick H. Hild Regional Library, holds, for example, the Ravenswood-Lake View community collection (16 ln.ft., 1844–1989), an assortment of materials donated in part by members of the Ravenswood-Lake View Historical Association.

The Carter G. Woodson Regional Library, located on Chicago's South Side, contains a group of manuscript collections of interest to Illinois historians. Most notably, it preserves the files regarding "The Negro in Illinois" compiled by the Federal Writers' Project of the Works Progress Administration. Intended for a historical study that was never written, the collection includes clippings, transcripts of interviews, research notes, and papers on black churches, black organizations, and similar topics. The collection was at first kept at the George Cleveland Hall Branch of the Chicago Public Library, but it was moved to the Woodson when that library opened in 1975. It is part of the larger collection of books and manuscripts named for the Hall's first librarian and accessible through *The Dictionary Catalog of the Vivian G. Harsh Collection of Afro-American History and Literature, The Chicago Public Library* (4 vols., Boston, 1978).

The Harsh Collection at the Woodson Library also holds the papers of the sociologist Horace R. Cayton, one of the directors of the Negro in Illinois project. In addition, it contains important materials for the history of black publishing in Illinois, including the papers of Ben Burns, who was managing editor of both *Negro Digest* and *Ebony*.

## Art Institute of Chicago

> Burnham Library
> Michigan Ave. at Adams St.
> Chicago, IL 60603
> (312) 443–3666

The Burnham Library of Architecture of the Art Institute of Chicago contains manuscripts, photographs, and selected architectural drawings of basic importance to the study of architecture, especially in the Chicago area. Among its collections are the papers of Daniel H. Burnham (19 ln.ft., 1890–1912), whose bequest created the library; the records of two of Burnham's associates, Peter J. Weber and Charles Herrick Hammond; and diverse lots documenting such leading architects as Louis H. Sullivan and Howard Van Doren Shaw. Sources for the history of city planning include Burnham's correspondence and reports relating to the *Plan of Chicago* (1909); the papers of Edward H. Bennett (12 ln.ft., 1900–54), selections from which appear in Joan E. Draper, *Edward H. Bennett, Architect and City Planner, 1874–1954* (Chicago, 1982); and the papers of Ludwig K. Hilberseimer (39 ln.ft., 1906–67), who taught at the Bauhaus and the Armour (Illinois) Institute of Technology. The Hilberseimer collection is described in Richard Pommer et al., *In the Shadow of Mies: Ludwig Hilberseimer, Architect, Educator, and Urban Planner* (Chicago, 1988).

An early and still useful effort to document the work of midwestern architects in the early twentieth century was the "Burnham Library–University of Illinois Architectural Microfilming Project" of 1950–53 (30 reels). Continued by the Burnham (10 reels), the project borrowed materials from architectural firms and private owners, to make accessible nearly eighty-seven hundred drawings, many of which are not available in public collections or have been lost since filming.

The microfilm also illustrates the work of architects such as Walter Burley Griffin and Marion Mahony Griffin who are represented in widely scattered collections. The reels are indexed by architect, building, and location in *The Burnham Index to Architectural Literature* (10 vols., New York, 1989).

While the Burnham Library holds the Art Institute's collection of books and manuscripts in the field of architecture, most of the Institute's architectural drawings as well as the architectural models and fragments collection are now the responsibility of its Department of Architecture. Another unit, the Archives of the Art Institute, was established in 1985 to organize and open for research the corporate and administrative records of the Institute, the records of the School of the Art Institute, and related materials such as exhibition records.

# 22

# UNIVERSITY OF ILLINOIS AT URBANA-CHAMPAIGN

MAYNARD J. BRICHFORD

*University Archives*
Library, Rm. 19
1408 W. Gregory Dr.
Urbana, IL 61801
(217) 333–0798

*Illinois Historical Survey*
Library, Rm. 346
1408 W. Gregory Dr.
Urbana, IL 61801
(217) 333–1777

BOTH THE UNIVERSITY Archives and the Illinois Historical Survey, two units of the University of Illinois Library at Urbana-Champaign, hold manuscript sources relating to Illinois history. Many of these materials are described in Maynard J. Brichford et al., *Manuscripts Guide to Collections at the University of Illinois at Urbana-Champaign* (Urbana, 1976). For the Archives, a more complete listing is Brichford and William J. Maher, *Guide to the University of Illinois Archives* (Urbana, 1986), which contains a printed introduction and three sets of microfiche, including a classification guide, a description of record series, and a subject index to record series.

Although the University Archives was not established on a professional basis until 1963, it holds today some 850 collections. Due to the university's long and close identification with the state, the Archives is rich in sources for Illinois history as a whole. Containing faculty papers that document research on Illinois topics and files of extension services that pertain to counties and communities throughout the state, the Archives has also accessioned the records of several professional organizations with some connection to Illinois, including, for example, the American Library Association and the National Association of State Universities and Land Grant Colleges. The audio-visual holdings of the Archives, including nearly a million photographs, are important for local and state as well as university history.

The Illinois Historical Survey, organized in 1910 as a unit of the Graduate College and traditionally associated with the History Department, served as an editorial office of the Illinois State Historical Library until 1939. In this role, it was responsible for two series published in Springfield, the Centennial History of Illinois and the Collections of the Illinois State Historical Library. At first, the Survey accumulated books, manuscripts, maps, and other sources to support those publications, but in time it developed relatively comprehensive holdings for research in Illinois history. In 1966, the unit moved from Lincoln Hall to the Library, occupying a room next to the University Archives until 1985, when it was allotted space in the Rare Book and Special Collections Library. Like the Archives, the Survey benefits from the vast holdings of the University Library as a whole.

The Survey's manuscript collections relating to early Illinois are in large part copies of documents in other repositories or in private hands. Sources for the colonial period, for instance, were drawn mainly from French, British, and Canadian archives. These materials—first transcripts and photostats, then microfilm and photocopies—created a derivative yet more complete basis for research than a collection limited to originals could have provided. Furthermore, certain sources, especially privately held manuscripts, have become unavailable, adding to the value of the Survey's reproductions. In recent years, this legacy of copies has been supplemented, for example, by materials assembled by Richard M. Phillips on Fort Crèvecoeur, the first French outpost in the Illinois Country, and by Kathrine W. Seineke on George Rogers Clark's role in the region during the American Revolution. Among the Survey's original manuscripts of the eighteenth century are the papers of George Morgan (257 items, 1757–1835), a frontier merchant and land speculator.

The Survey contains numerous collections for the years from statehood to the Civil War. Governors Ninian Edwards and Joseph Duncan are represented by two letter books (1802–32) and a volume of records (1834–41). Thomas Joyes's diary (1816–17) and John Messinger's notebook (1822) reflect the work of early surveyors. Business and politics mix in the papers of Lt. Gov. Pierre Menard (26 vols., 1808–40) and Amos Williams of Danville, in the Williams-Woodbury collection (4.5 cu.ft., 1820–1936). Political questions are also conspicuous in the correspondence of Edward B. Warner, treasurer of Whiteside County (238 items, 1858–69), and William W. Orme of Bloomington (0.5 cu.ft., 1855–94).

Among the Survey's recent accessions for Civil War history are the papers of George S. Durfee of the 8th Illinois Infantry (182 items, 1861–1901), Henry Van Sellar of the 12th (156 items, 1860–92), George W. Thumb of the 36th (1 vol., 1862–64), Edward McGlynn of the 42nd and 124th (14 items, 1861–65), and Albert P. Cunningham of the 76th, in the Cunningham-Creamer-Miller-Housh family collection (24 cu.ft., 1855–1974).

Several collections document different aspects of nineteenth-century agricultural history. The Survey contains the papers of Jonathan Baldwin Turner, a leading agriculturalist (1 cu.ft., 1834–1910); the records of the Flagg (2 cu.ft., 1819–1948) and Bodman (2 cu.ft., 1855–1903) family farms in Madison and Piatt counties, respectively; the journals of J. W. Phillips, a Peoria nurseryman (9 vols., 1863–76); and the records of the Champaign County Grange (3 vols., 1873–77). Similar collections in the Archives include the papers of Matthias L. Dunlap (1 cu.ft., 1839–77), a Champaign County horticulturist; the papers of the Allen family of Tazewell County (4.5 cu.ft., 1774–1975); the records of the H. C. Coles Milling Company of Chester (12 cu.ft., 1838–99), relative to grain shipments on the Mississippi River; and a letter book of the Illinois Farmers' Institute (1 vol., 1898–99).

Diverse sources in the Survey pertain to professional careers in nineteenth-century Illinois. Materials for legal history include the papers of Almeron Wheat of Quincy (113 items, 1830–71) and Henry Clay Whitney of Urbana (60 items, 1854–60); the diaries from 1856 to 1876 of Joseph I. Taylor of Princeton, in the Taylor–Langworthy collection (2 cu.ft., 1817–95); the notebooks of Judge Pinckney H. Walker of the Illinois Supreme Court (2 vols., 1860–61); and the papers of William E. Lodge of Monticello (5.5 cu.ft., 1865–1901) relating to his many activities as a lawyer, newspaper publisher, and real estate dealer. Also available are the medical records of Orin S. Campbell of Pittsfield (3 vols., 1836–57) and Cyrus Rutherford of Newman (2 cu.ft., 1880–1909).

The Survey's most substantial body of denominational records documents the Religious Society of Friends from the frontier period to the present, including materials from Illinois Yearly, Blue River Quarterly, Clear Creek Monthly, and other meetings (22 cu.ft., 1828–1989). Complementing this collection are the papers of individual Quakers such as Abel Mills (1.5 cu.ft., 1836–1919). The records of the McLean County Cooperation Society (2 vols., 1864–87) point to missionary work of the Church of Christ. The papers of Benjamin Applebee in western Illinois (0.5 cu.ft., 1845–95) and Jacob Sheets in eastern Illinois (1 cu.ft., 1849–1912) reflect, in turn, the endeavors of Methodist and United Brethren ministers.

Other collections evince a denominational orientation. A board of Methodist women was vested with responsibility for the Cunningham Children's Home in Urbana. Its papers (10 cu.ft., 1895–1989) are in the Survey, as are the records of the Roseville Temperance Union, in Warren County (1 vol., 1867–70); the Woman's Christian Temperance Union of Putnam County (1 cu.ft., 1889–1949); and the Tenth Congressional District WCTU, based in Peoria (1 vol., 1883–

1902), all organizations shaped by the Protestant ethos. Temperance reform is a persistent theme in the papers of Duncan Chambers Milner (3.5 cu.ft., 1861–1959), who headed the Armour Mission in Chicago. The Archives contains the architectural files of George P. Stauduhar (74 cu.ft., 1886–1928), who designed churches for sixty-four Catholic congregations in downstate Illinois.

The institutional records of the Archives are important for the history of higher education in Illinois. Files of the Board of Trustees and the President's Office date from the university's founding in 1867, and the correspondence of such late nineteenth-century heads as Selim H. Peabody (0.5 cu.ft., 1881–94) and Andrew S. Draper (8 cu.ft., 1894–1904) reflects their interest in elementary and secondary education throughout the state. Local sources in the Survey include the papers of James W. Hays, superintendent in Urbana (8 vols., 1865–1900), as well as administrative records and exercise books of the Champaign County schools (8 cu.ft., 1877–1941). In addition, the Archives holds the papers of early faculty with statewide interests, including Thomas J. Burrill in botany (0.5 cu.ft., 1854–1931), Stephen A. Forbes in entomology (48.5 cu.ft., 1871–1931), Nathan C. Ricker in architecture (6 cu.ft., 1873–1925), and Eugene Davenport in agriculture (9.5 cu.ft., 1857–1954).

Bridging the nineteenth and twentieth centuries is a collection of business records, assembled in the late 1930s by the College of Commerce but now administered by the Archives. These materials, drawn from twenty-one Illinois communities, document clothing stores such as Kaufman's in Champaign (62.5 cu.ft., 1879–1950), drugstores such as Knowlton and Bennett's in Urbana (10.5 cu.ft., 1884–1923), and banks including a group of ten establishments in Bloomington (80 cu.ft., 1857–1937). Coal mine operations may be traced in the business and labor accounts of George H. Haskins of Danville, a collection in the Survey (3 cu.ft., 1881–1933), and in the Archives' records of William T. Morris, a mine inspector and labor organizer in DuQuoin (0.5 cu.ft., 1897–1937).

Other sources in the Survey relate to important leaders of the labor movement, Thomas J. and Elizabeth Chambers Morgan of Chicago (6 cu.ft., 1880–1910) and John H. Walker, president of the Illinois Federation of Labor and of District 12 (Illinois) of the United Mine Workers of America. The latter collection (35 cu.ft., 1910–55) is accessible through Douglas W. Carlson et al., *Guide to the Papers in the John Hunter Walker Collection, 1911–1953* (Urbana, 1980). Among the Archives' holdings for labor history in modern-day Illinois, received from the university's Institute of Labor and Industrial Relations, are studies of labor-management relations in several downstate communities (13.5 cu.ft., 1947–59) and the papers of Milton Derber on public employee bargaining (19 cu.ft., 1938–87).

Sources for Illinois agriculture in the twentieth century are richly detailed and interconnected. For example, the Archives contains printed farm business reports that are based on farm account summary sheets (27 cu.ft., 1917–47), farm cost accounting records for six counties (17 cu.ft., 1912–65), and records kept by individual farmers in fifteen counties that document in comparable form their activities over many years (13 cu.ft., 1924–86). The Amos Burr (2 cu.ft., 1880–1961) and Meharry family (13.5 cu.ft., 1867–1941) collections in the Survey also illustrate agriculture at the operational level, while a network of grain elevators across central Illinois is fully documented in the Valley Grain Company collection (14.5 cu.ft., 1914–44). Files of the College of Agriculture (167.5 cu.ft., 1895–1964) include reports and field notes from every county of the state. Farm mechanization can be studied in the papers of Karl J. T. Ekblaw (4 cu.ft., 1917–29), Emil W. Lehmann (17.5 cu.ft., 1906–72), and James F. Evans (4 cu.ft., 1924–67) of the faculty and in the correspondence of the Joliet Manufacturing Company (31 cu.ft., 1903–39). Illinois is well represented in Martin L. Mosher's slides of American farmsteads and his data on their income in 1950 (3 cu.ft., 1916–78). The Archives also holds the papers of Charles L. Stewart (4 cu.ft., 1914–73) and David E. Lindstrom (3.5 cu.ft., 1930–75), useful for rural sociology, and the files of Herbert W. Mumford (1 cu.ft., 1919–38) and Harold W. Hannah (10 cu.ft., 1937–84), important for agricultural policy.

Aspects of environmental history in Illinois are documented in an array of faculty papers and cognate sources. The Karl B. Lohmann collection (13.5 cu.ft., 1914–63) is concerned with city, regional, and rural planning. James J. Doland (4.5 cu.ft., 1926–58) addressed questions of highway and airport design and construction. Louis B. Wetmore (10 cu.ft., 1931–88) focused on the preservation of the Chicago waterfront, while the Committee on Allerton Park (8 cu.ft., 1961–76) examined the environmental impact of a proposed dam on the Sangamon River. This question is also covered in the papers of S. Charles Kendeigh (33.5 cu.ft., 1919–85). In the Survey, the Riehl family collection (1.5 cu.ft., 1853–1946) relates to fruit-tree planting and a nursery business near Alton, while the papers of James S. Ayars (22 cu.ft., 1911–85) reflect a range of environmental concerns as well as attention to numerous social and political issues.

Several collections document problems of Illinois government in the twentieth century. The Edward F. Dunne collection in the Survey (2 cu.ft., 1873–1937) is weighted with materials on Progressive reforms, especially during his term as mayor of Chicago, 1905–7. In the Archives, John A. Fairlie's papers (32 cu.ft., 1885–1947) include files on the Illinois Efficiency and Economy Committee, 1913–15, while the papers of Henry M. Dunlap (2.5 cu.ft., 1874–1931), a state senator, relate to highways, police, and prohibition in the 1920s. Dunlap and Charles M. Thompson prepared a legislative history of the university to 1939 (3 vols., 1939–43), which supplements the legislative campaign files of Presidents David Kinley, Harry W. Chase, and Arthur C. Willard (6.5 cu.ft., 1921–45). Faculty papers in the Archives include the Ernest L. Bogart (3 cu.ft., 1910–35) and Whitney C. Huntington (0.5 cu.ft., 1926–54) collections, parts of which relate to the Illinois Emergency Relief Commission and the Civil Works Administration in the state during the Depression. The Survey holds a set of the CWA's final reports (1.5 cu.ft., 1934).

For the modern period, the Archives contains the papers of several elected officials, including John A. Wieland (1 cu.ft., 1935–41) and Vernon L. Nickell (6.5 cu.ft., 1910–59), superintendents of public instruction; Lloyd Morey (12 cu.ft., 1908–66), who was auditor of public accounts after serving as comptroller and president of the university; and two university trustees, Wayne A. Johnston (9.5 cu.ft., 1945–67), president of the Illinois Central Railroad, and Earl M. Hughes (2.5 cu.ft., 1948–86), a seed corn producer. Files of a state legislator comprise the Survey's Charles W. Clabaugh collection (12.5 cu.ft., 1946–87). Additional materials relate to the work of legislative panels. In the Survey, the Albert Tuxhorn collection (0.5 cu.ft., 1946–50) concerns the School Finance and Public Assistance commissions. In the Archives, Thomas Page's papers (6 cu.ft., 1952–76) pertain in part to the Civil Service Commission, while Samuel K. Gove's files (6.5 cu.ft., 1948–78) include the studies of state government and the General Assembly undertaken by the Schaefer and Katz commissions. Illinois elections and political parties are documented in the papers of Clarence Berdahl (40 cu.ft., 1919–88). Insights into Paul H. Douglas's senatorial career may be gleaned from the papers of his administrative assistant, Howard E. Shuman (10 cu.ft., 1936–90).

Collections regarding the judicial system of the state, in the Survey and the Archives, respectively, include the papers of Justice Robert C. Underwood of the Illinois Supreme Court (64 cu.ft., 1937–84) and Edward W. Cleary of the university's Law School (2 cu.ft., 1952–65). The Constitutional Convention of 1969–70 is documented in the Archives' series for David C. Baum (6 cu.ft., 1959–73), a lawyer for the convention, and by the Survey's records of the event, including the papers of Richard Murphy (0.5 cu.ft.), the convention's parliamentarian, and Henry I. Green (3.5 cu. ft.), a delegate from Urbana.

Additional sources pertain to the Chicago area and to downstate communities. The Survey holds the papers of Leverett S. Lyon and Gilbert Y. Steiner (3.5 cu.ft., 1955–63) relative to their work for the Northeastern Illinois Metropolitan Area Local Governmental Services Commission and also the files of James G. Coke (4 cu.ft., 1961–64), director of the university's Office of Community Development, which studied Peoria, Rockford, and Springfield in detail. Materials on these communities as well as on Belleville, Champaign–Urbana, Decatur, Joliet, and the Quad Cities comprise Daniel J. Elazar's Metropolitan Areas Study series in the Archives (12 cu.ft., 1959–63).

State and local political questions have been addressed not only by official commissions but by voluntary organizations. In this regard, useful sources in the Survey include the records of the League of Women Voters of Champaign County (7 cu.ft., 1922–71) and Charleston (1 cu.ft., 1962–80), as well as the papers of the Illinois State Division (36 cu.ft., 1924–90) and the Champaign-Urbana Branch (22 cu.ft., 1902–89) of the American Association of University Women. Other collections contain material on particular issues. Efforts in Champaign-Urbana to end racial discrimination, for example, can be studied in the Archives in the papers of W. Ellison Chalmers (2.5 cu.ft., 1948–64), Harry M. Tiebout (10 cu.ft., 1941–82), and John J. DeBoer (6 cu.ft., 1927–74).

Sources in different units of the University Library illuminate facets of the state's cultural history. The correspondence, notes, and manuscripts of Carl Sandburg (180 cu.ft., 1898–1968) are housed in the Rare Book and Special Collections Library, together with collections of Sandburgiana accumulated by Helga Sandburg (12 cu.ft.), William A. Sutton (17 cu.ft.), and Perry Miller Adato (52 cu.ft.). The Archives contains the literary estate of Stuart Pratt Sherman (4.5 cu.ft., 1903–26); the Homer E. Woodbridge collection, related to Sherman (1.5 cu.ft., 1900–45); and the editorial files of *Accent*, kept by J. Kerker Quinn and three colleagues in the English Department (37.5 cu.ft., 1926–89). The Survey holds the records of Illinois Writers, Inc. (4 cu.ft., 1976–86).

The fields of art and architecture are documented by the papers of Lorado Taft (17 cu.ft., 1857–1953) and Rexford G. Newcomb (7.5 cu.ft., 1915–82) in the Archives and by the records of the Central Illinois Chapter of the American Institute of Architects (7 cu.ft., 1917–72) in the Survey. Illinois artists, art education, and art extension are represented in the archival series for Robert E. Hieronymus (2 cu.ft., 1912–40), John W. Rauschenberger (3 cu.ft., 1932–72), and Walter M. Johnson (9 cu.ft., 1944–77).

Additional materials in the Archives pertain to education in the twentieth century. Sources for the secondary level include the North Central Association's file of high school reports (137.5 cu.ft., 1907–80), Charles Sanford's material on the Illinois Association of Secondary School Principals (2.5 cu.ft., 1943–67), and Van Miller's records of the Illinois Association of School Administrators (4.5 cu.ft., 1931–74). Collections relating to vocational education include the papers of the Mississippi Valley Industrial Arts Conference (3.5 cu.ft., 1909–80). Several official and personal files supplement the records of the Illinois Board of Higher Education (8 cu.ft., 1963–74). Also available are the papers of the University of Illinois chapter (7.5 cu.ft., 1934–77) and the Illinois Conference (6.5 cu.ft., 1958–80) of the American Association of University Professors.

The papers of individual historians constitute a final category of research materials. The Burt E. Powell (3 cu.ft., 1914–18), Carl Stephens (8.5 cu.ft., 1912–51), and Charles A. Kiler (2 cu.ft., 1868–1945) collections in the Archives pertain to the history of the university and the surrounding community. The Lincoln Room, a unit of the History and Philosophy Library, contains the papers of Harlan H. and Henrietta C. Horner (6 cu.ft., 1936–60), Lincoln collectors, and also certain files of William E. Barton (11 cu. ft., 1890–1954), a Lincoln scholar. The Survey's own archives (23 cu.ft., 1903–79) includes the papers of Clarence W. Alvord and Theodore C. Pease, substantial collections for the history of Illinois history.

# 23

---

# SOUTHERN ILLINOIS UNIVERSITY

---

## LOUISA BOWEN

THE ECONOMIC AND cultural diversity of southern and southwestern Illinois is readily apparent in the range of archival and manuscript resources available at the libraries of Southern Illinois University. Not only the proliferation of academic programs at SIU since the 1960s but also important aspects of the region's history are well documented in collections at Carbondale and Edwardsville.

### Southern Illinois University at Carbondale

Morris Library
Carbondale, IL 62901
(618) 453–2516

The Special Collections unit of Southern Illinois University at Carbondale was formed in 1970 when Morris Library's Rare Book and Manuscript Collection was combined with the University Archives. The rare book collection dated from 1956, the year that the library opened, while the University Archives had been established in 1963. Kenneth W. Duckett, appointed to the staff in 1965, was succeeded as curator of special collections and university archivist by David V. Koch in 1979.

The unit's collections are concentrated in several subject areas, including the Irish literary renaissance, the literature of American and British expatriates in Europe between World Wars I and II, and modern American philosophy, theater, printing and presses, freedom of speech, and freedom of the press. The bulk of sources pertaining to Illinois history, however, is in a group of regional collections, in the University Archives, and in the Illinois Regional Archives Depository, which contains government records from twenty-three southern Illinois counties. These records are open to researchers at the library's storage facility on McLafferty Road, on the west edge of the campus.

The history of the region is most fully canvassed in the papers of John W. Allen (21.5 cu.ft., 1940–69), who systematically collected information on the folklore, architecture, politics, and economics of each county in southern Illinois. A similar collection was left by George W. Smith (3.5 cu.ft., 1912–41), who published histories of Illinois and southern Illinois.

The Civil War era is depicted in numerous sources that have been acquired since the publication of William L. Burton, *Descriptive Bibliography of Civil War Manuscripts in Illinois* (Evanston, 1966). The Ulysses S. Grant collection (90 items, 1839–1911) contains papers written by, to, or about Grant, obtained in connection with the Ulysses S. Grant Association's editorial project, which is located in Morris Library. The papers of Benjamin L. Wiley of Jonesboro and Makanda (2 cu.ft., 1817–1911), who served as lieutenant colonel of the 5th Illinois Cavalry, include political and family correspondence as well as business and legal records. A similar combination of business and personal papers (1.5 cu.ft., 1831–1942) documents the career of a Rockwood resident, Lt. John P. Mann, of the same regiment. The letters of Pvt. Joseph Skipworth of Fredonia (99 items, 1861–65), 31st Illinois Infantry, and of Capt. John P. Reese of Cobden (0.5 cu.ft., 1862–65) and Pvt. Edwin A. Loosley of DuQuoin (113 items, 1862–65), both of the 81st Illinois, reflect the experiences of their units. The papers of Lt. Col. Monroe C. Crawford (180 items, 1835–1919), 110th Illinois, later a lawyer and circuit court judge of Jonesboro, contain an account of the war in 1862.

Southern Illinois religious history is documented in the records on microfilm of nine early Baptist and Presbyterian churches (1820–1974). The papers of the Presbyterian Church of Carbondale (3 cu.ft., 1850–1970) pertain not only to the congregation but to the town and one of its promoters, Daniel Harmon Brush. The Robert G. Ingersoll collection (4 cu.ft., 1868–1921), gathered by Gordon Stein, includes correspondence and photographs of the prominent agnostic.

Various sources relate to family and local history. The diaries of Isabella Maud Rittenhouse (6 vols., 1881–95), abridged in Richard Lee Strout, ed., *Maud* (New York, 1939), chronicle life in late nineteenth–century Cairo. The papers of the Joseph W. Rickert family of Waterloo (20 cu.ft., 1869–1971) reflect Rickert's law practice and also the cultural interests of three generations of a Swiss-American family. The papers of George Hazen French (3 cu.ft., 1859–1931), Southern Illinois University's earliest faculty collection, include his diaries from 1890 to 1931 as well as records of his work as an entomologist and museum curator. The Trovillion Press archives (24 cu.ft., 1908-58), one of the unit's private press collections, is supplemented by materials documenting southern Illinois history, including Ku Klux Klan activity and labor disputes in Herrin. The papers of Hugh Dalziel Duncan (32 cu.ft., 1903–70), a professor of English and sociology, relate in part to his studies of Chicago architecture and to the formation of the Chicago Landmarks Commission.

Information regarding communities throughout southern Illinois is available in three University Archives collections. The records of the Division of Area Services (48 cu.ft., 1947–65) and one of its units, Community Development Services (69 cu.ft., 1954–74), include data on local government, education, health and health planning, and economic resources of East St. Louis and selected small towns in the area. The Southern Illinois Folk Arts Research Project (4.5 cu.ft., 1978–81) yielded oral history interviews with members of church choirs and musicals, coal miners, storytellers, and folk artists in many rural communities. The archives of Comprehensive Health Planning in Southern Illinois (70 cu.ft., 1974–86) documents the operations of that umbrella organization and its members and the level of health care delivery throughout the area in recent years.

Special Collections also holds sources for labor history. The papers of John E. Jones (7 cu.ft., 1922–48), an authority on coal mine safety, include speeches, agreements, notes on safety inspections, and data about the United Mine Workers in southern Illinois. The Clyde Anderson collection (1.5 cu.ft., 1915–20) relates to reclamation farming as well as coal mining. Milton Edelman's files (16 cu.ft., 1956–74) document his work as a labor arbitrator in many fields in Illinois and nearby states. The records of the Education Department of the International Ladies' Garment Workers' Union, Southwestern Regional Office, in St. Louis (6 cu.ft., 1935–64), reflect the professional activities of working women. Other collections illustrate the projects of women in southern Illinois, including the records of the Carbondale Federated Women's Clubs (1 cu.ft., 1896–1968); the Carbondale League of Women Voters (4 cu.ft., 1967–81); Southern Illinois Citizens for Peace (100 items, 1962–65); and Honor Our Men's Efforts (1.5 cu.ft., 1967–72), an organization that sought through letter writing to raise the morale of American soldiers in Vietnam.

Several collections in the field of modern American philosophy contain an Illinois dimension. The John Dewey collection (24 cu.ft., 1858–1970), acquired to support the project at Southern Illinois University to edit and publish *The Collected Works of John Dewey*, relates in part to his career at the University of Chicago, where he first applied his philosophical theories to education in a lab school. The papers of James Hayden Tufts (3.5 cu.ft., 1782–1942) and Edward Scribner Ames (1 cu.ft., 1894–1958), two of Dewey's colleagues in Chicago's philosophy department, shed light on the development of the "Chicago School" of philosophy. The archives of the Open Court Publishing Company (66.5 cu.ft., 1886–1953), founded in LaSalle by Edward C. Hegeler, a wealthy zinc manufacturer, contains the correspondence of Paul Carus, its editor from 1887 to 1919, with many important philosophers and scientists of his day. The records of two liberal religious journals, *Christian Century* and *Christian Ministry* (65 cu.ft., 1939–73), document the vicissitudes of a Chicago publisher. These and related accessions are described in Louisa Bowen, ed., *The Philosophy Collections: Special Collections, Morris Library . . .* (Carbondale, 1984).

Other holdings relate to the cultural contributions of recent Illinoisans. The papers of Katherine Dunham (50 cu.ft., 1919–68) document her career as an anthropologist, dancer, and choreographer and as an educator in East St. Louis. The letters of Mark Turbyfill (0.5 cu.ft., 1907–68), her ballet teacher and colleague in Chicago, extend to his work as a dance critic, poet, and painter. The papers of H. Allen Smith (28 cu.ft., 1930–67), a popular American humorist, include correspondence, manuscripts, and such items as notes for *Lo, the Former Egyptian!* (Garden City, N.Y., 1947), an autobiographical account of southern Illinois. Robert Lewis Taylor, a novelist, biographer, and Carbondale native, is also represented (1.5 cu.ft., 1947–68) in Morris Library's collections.

### Southern Illinois University at Edwardsville

> Lovejoy Library
> Edwardsville, IL 62026
> (618) 692–2665

The formation of a research collection focused on Illinois and the Mississippi Valley was an early priority of Southern Illinois University at Edwardsville. Lovejoy Library opened in 1965, and its program for acquisitions in the fields of music as well as regional history soon prompted a handbook, Linda McKee, comp., *Guide to Research Collections . . .* (Edwardsville, 1971). The regional holdings include the University Archives, formally established in 1979, and the pre-1900 circuit court, chancery, and naturalization records of Madison County. Most of these collections were acquired and developed during John C. Abbott's tenure as the library's first director and as head of Research and Special Collections from 1982 to 1986.

A major accession, especially useful for the study of Mississippi Valley history and culture in the eighteenth and early nineteenth centuries, is the John Francis McDermott collection (76 cu.ft.). McDermott, who taught at Washington University, 1924–61, and at Southern Illinois University, Edwardsville, 1961–71, assembled copious materials related to the French and Spanish in the Illinois Country and to travelers, writers, and artists on the American frontier. The papers of Carl S. Baldwin (7 cu.ft.) also concern early Illinois, including a group of documents reflecting Isaac N. Piggott's business interests in Cahokia and Nauvoo. In addition, the collection reflects Baldwin's career as a journalist in East St. Louis in the 1940s and 1950s.

Lovejoy Library contains several collections regarding Illinois localities before the Civil War. Legal records of Highland and Marine (1 cu.ft., 1820–66), Madison County settlements, and the Raymond J. Spahn collection (10 cu.ft.) supplement the published accounts of the founders of New Switzerland, the largest Swiss community in nineteenth-century America. Madison County is also represented by a rich family collection (4 cu.ft., 1816–1916) containing letters, diaries, and business records of Gershom, Willard, and Sarah Smith Flagg.

The singular history of Nauvoo is documented in a collection of copied materials (103 reels) and a group of original manuscripts (433 items, 1824–63). The former is accessible through Stanley B. Kimball, comp., *Sources of Mormon History in Illinois, 1839–48: An Annotated Catalog of the Microfilm Collection at Southern Illinois University* (Carbondale, 1964; revised ed., Carbondale, 1966). The latter includes the correspondence in French of Étienne Cabet, the leader of the Icarian community in Nauvoo after the departure of the Mormons.

Labor and coal mining figure prominently in more recent regional collections. The library holds the records of six local unions of the United Mine Workers and the Progressive Mine Workers of America (8 cu.ft., 1908–62) and the papers of Clarence V. Beck, Sr., and his Gillespie Coal Mining Company (12 cu.ft., 1941–71). The papers of Frank W. Fries (11 cu.ft., 1922–68), elected to Congress in 1936 and 1938, document his later work as an arbitrator in the coal industry. The Harold J. Gibbons collection (75 cu.ft., 1919–83) extends to Metro-East locals of the International Brotherhood of Teamsters.

Another group of collections reflects a diversity of educational purposes, broadly defined. The papers of Edward Koch of Germantown (6 cu.ft., 1925–67) include his correspondence as editor of the *Guildsman*, a monthly journal identified with right-wing causes. The files of the Edwardsville League of Women Voters (9 cu.ft., 1952–77) concern public issues of the day. The papers of George T. Wilkins (11 cu.ft., 1920–70) trace his career in education, culminating as Illinois superintendent of public instruction, 1959–63. The records of Beverly Farm (20 cu.ft., 1897–1985) reflect the development in Godfrey of one of the nation's oldest private institutions for the developmentally disabled. The collection also contains the papers of its founder, William H. C. Smith, and his son, Groves B. Smith, both of whom were active in the Illinois section of the National Conference on Charities and Correction.

The ethnic and racial complexity of the region is apparent in a variety of sources. The Slavic-American collection, an extensive gathering of foreign-language imprints, includes over one hundred manuscript volumes containing the minutes, membership lists, and financial records of Czech, Polish, and other East European groups in the area. Most of these documents date from the early twentieth century and are cataloged in Stanley B. Kimball, ed., *Slavic-American Imprints* . . . (Edwardsville, 1972; *Supplement*, Edwardsville, 1979). Numerous topics, including the changing racial composition of the area, are documented in the clipping files since 1930 of the *East St. Louis Journal*, known as the *Metro-East Journal* between 1964 and 1979. This period is also covered by the papers of the mayors of East St. Louis between 1951 and 1979—Alvin G. Fields (10 cu.ft., 1949–71), James E. Williams (39 cu.ft., 1971–75), and William G. Mason (78 cu.ft., 1962–79)—and by the papers of Melvin Price (450 cu.ft., 1944–77), a Belleville Democrat who represented the Metro-East region in Congress from 1945 to 1988.

# 24

# NORTHERN ILLINOIS UNIVERSITY

GLEN A. GILDEMEISTER

Swen Parson Hall
DeKalb, IL 60115
(815) 753–1779

NORTHERN ILLINOIS UNIVERSITY'S Earl W. Hayter Regional History Center serves as the university's archives, as the Illinois Regional Archives Depository for northern Illinois, and as a center for manuscript collections documenting the region's history. Established in 1964, the unit was headed for fifteen years by J. Joseph Bauxar as university archivist. In 1976, it became part of the Illinois State Archives' network for preserving local government records, and in 1978, it was expanded into the Regional History Center, collecting not only official records but also manuscript sources for northern Illinois history.

The University Archives contains the institution's records since 1895. An important source for the history of higher education in Illinois, this collection is described in the Center's "Archives Guide for Northern Illinois University" (1985). The faculty series includes the papers of Earl W. Hayter (18 ln.ft., 1924–74), an agricultural historian who came to the university in 1936 and was instrumental in creating its archives. The Center was named in his honor in 1984.

It is the Center's regional collections that hold the greatest promise for research in Illinois history. The in-house "Guide to Sources: Northern Illinois History" (1988) summarizes the scope—and the lacunae—of nearly two hundred collections, each of which is accessible through a detailed inventory. This guide also lists both single items in a series of vertical file manuscripts and the theses and dissertations written at the university that relate to regional history. The index points to many collections beyond those that can be cited here for different topics in Illinois history.

Among these collections, two that document railroads have generated the highest volume of research activity and publication. The Waite W. Embree collection (72 ln.ft., 1900–50) contains over ten thousand photographs of rolling stock, thousands of timetables, and hundreds of blueprints of yards and stations of midwestern railroads as well as many pictures of people, buildings, and events in DeKalb in the early twentieth century. The Chicago and North Western Railroad Historical Society collection (32 ln.ft.) includes the correspondence, photographs, drawings, and memorabilia that the corporation regarded as its archives, and covers most fully the period from 1935 to 1950. Another dimension of transportation history is documented in the Samuel E. Bradt series of the Bertha G. Bradt collection (4 ln.ft., 1839–1954), reflecting his leadership in the development of Illinois highways. The records of the Smith Oil and Refining Company of Rockford (2.5 ln.ft., 1918–70) suggest the changing opportunities of a family-owned business.

Both large and small businesses have preserved their corporate archives in the Center. The records of the Wurlitzer Company of DeKalb (53 ln.ft., 1860–1960) document fully the history of a major manufacturer of theater organs, pianos, and jukeboxes, including, for instance, the impact of World War II, when the company changed over to the production of glider airplanes for the U.S. Army. The Center also contains the records of two industries in LaSalle, the Matthiessen-Hegeler Zinc Company (73 ln.ft., 1858–1978) and the Westclox Corporation, a watch and clock maker (21.5 ln.ft., 1885–1970). Vicissitudes of industrial development in the state's second largest city can be traced in the records of the Rockford Chair and Furniture Company (30 ln.ft., 1882–1973), the Rockford Mitten and Hosiery Company (3 ln.ft., 1881–1957), and the W. F. and John Barnes Company, a machine tool corporation (3.5 ln.ft., 1878–1963). The Rockford Small Business Collection (3 ln.ft., 1910–60) includes minutes, annual reports, financial statements, and publications of eleven firms. The records of the Joliet Region Chamber of Commerce and Industry (27.5 ln.ft., 1917–79) and the Sterling Chamber of Commerce (8 ln.ft., 1910–78) provide another perspective on local businesses.

About a third of the Center's regional collections document some aspect of the area's agricultural history. Isaac Ellwood (15 ln.ft., 1866–1920) and Joseph F. Glidden (4 ln.ft., 1882–1954) were early leaders in agribusiness in DeKalb, both associated with the invention and manufacture of barbed wire. The Starline Company in Harvard (7 ln.ft., 1902–73) made streamlined farm equipment. The

Gurler family of DeKalb (1.5 ln.ft., 1879–1905) and the John P. Case family of Naperville (3 ln.ft., 1922–65) were interested in milk processing and marketing. The Pure Milk Association (13 ln.ft., 1924–69) and the Mid-West Dairymen's Company (8 ln.ft., 1924–80) were milk cooperatives in northern Illinois.

The Center also holds the records of the Farmers Elevator Company of Yorkville (25 ln.ft., 1908–75). The farm bureaus of Carroll, DeKalb, DuPage, Grundy, Kane, and Kendall counties (58 ln.ft., 1913–80) are represented in the collections. The records of some fourteen local Grange chapters (12 ln.ft., 1874–1980) are available. Rural social life can also be studied in such diverse holdings as the records of the Wheatland Plow Match Association, in Will County (1 ln.ft., 1922–78), and the Princeton Game and Fish Club (3 ln.ft., 1877–1972).

Among the Center's political collections are the papers of Latham Castle (9 ln.ft., 1953–70). Although Castle held many public offices, from state's attorney of DeKalb County to judge of the U.S. Court of Appeals for the Seventh Circuit, the collection relates mainly to his years as Illinois attorney general, 1953–61, especially his prosecution of state auditor Orville E. Hodge for embezzling state funds. The Dennis J. Collins papers (17 ln.ft., 1931–74), the largest of several legislative collections in the Center, concern his forty-two years in the Illinois General Assembly, the longest consecutive legislative tenure in the history of the state.

The records of certain women's organizations relate to political and business affairs. The files of the League of Women Voters in Aurora, DeKalb, Elgin, Geneva–St. Charles, and the Joliet region (12.5 ln.ft., 1924–85) preserve the debate over many controversial issues. In addition, the Center contains the papers of the Business and Professional Women's Club in Belvidere, DeKalb, Mendota, Rochelle, Sycamore, and Woodstock (13.5 ln.ft., 1927–80). Aspects of small town life can be traced in the diaries of Frances Forsythe and Nellie (Forsythe) Woodbury of Sandwich (2 ln.ft., 1876–1921) and Laura Cooper of Byron (1.5 ln.ft., 1892–1965). The records of Shimer College (22 ln.ft., 1837–1978), a pioneer in women's education, document the institution's history in Mt. Carroll.

Several religious denominations, including Congregationalists, Methodists, and Lutherans, are represented in the collections. Some of these churches served immigrant communities; for instance, Swedes established the First Lutheran Church of Rockford (32 ln.ft., 1854–1970), while Germans founded Trinity Lutheran Church in Mt. Morris (14 ln.ft., 1857–1977). Ethnic traditions can also be traced in the records of the Order of Good Templars (11.5 ln.ft., 1888–1979), a Swedish temperance society in Rockford, and the Rockford Harmony Singing Society (1 ln.ft., 1923–66), a Norwegian group.

Organized labor accounts for a final group of materials. The largest collections in this series are the records of the Rockford Building and Construction Trades Council (14 ln.ft., 1937–68) and the Central Labor Union of Freeport (7 ln.ft., 1901–83).

Although some six or seven collections have been closely studied, most of the Regional History Center's holdings have not yet been well researched. In the University Archives, in records of local government, and especially in the regional collections, the Center offers students of Illinois history a wealth of untapped sources.

# 25

# OTHER DOWNSTATE REPOSITORIES

FRANK H. MACKAMAN

THE DIRECTORIES LISTED in the Introduction to these archival reports point to an array of historical societies, museums, public libraries, and other institutions in Illinois with printed and manuscript holdings of special importance for the history of particular localities. These repositories preserve unique sources relating to specific counties and communities. Furthermore, numerous academic, denominational, and corporate archives contain "Illinois" documentation for organizations not defined by state lines. An adequate survey of all these collections would require another book. The following pages merely introduce a few repositories with holdings of statewide or regional as well as institutional or local interest.

The line between local and regional collections is somewhat artificial, if not arbitrary. Consequently, the coverage here is not an index to the relative importance of dozens of repositories in downstate Illinois. In Bloomington, for example, the manuscript collections of the McLean County Historical Society are no less impressive than the nearby holdings of Illinois State University, and the library of the Central Illinois Conference of the United Methodist Church is in many ways comparable to other centers with denominational ties, such as Augustana College, a Lutheran foundation in Rock Island. Similarly, Eastern Illinois University, at Charleston, is the Illinois Regional Archives Depository for sixteen surrounding counties and thus participates with five other downstate universities in an archival network for local government records.

Moreover, a few special congressional collections in Illinois help to document state and district history. The Everett McKinley Dirksen Congressional Leadership Research Center, in Pekin, holds the largest archives of this kind. The Dirksen collection (1,160 ln.ft., 1900–77) is a copious source not only for his own career in the U.S. House and Senate but also for Illinois politics, the nature of constituent concerns, and the flow of federal dollars to the state in the form of public works from the 1930s to the 1960s. Other materials supplement the Dirksen collection, including the papers of Harold H. Velde (10.5 ln.ft., 1901–65), his successor in the House. Another downstate congressional archives, weighted with constituent correspondence, is the Leslie C. Arends collection (65.5 ln.ft., 1930–75), located at Illinois Wesleyan University in Bloomington.

## Knox College

Seymour Library
Galesburg, IL 61401
(309) 343–0112

The Knox College library contains numerous manuscript collections relating to Illinois history, especially the settlement of Galesburg and the development of west central Illinois. These materials, collected since 1890, were fully organized and made accessible during Jacqueline Haring's tenure as curator, 1965–83. The holdings of the College Archives and Manuscript Collections Department formed a substantial documentary legacy for Knox and Galesburg as they marked their sesquicentennials in 1987.

The papers of early settlers contain vivid descriptions of the difficult journey west, the virgin prairie, and the hardships and opportunities of pioneer life. The diaries of Sarah Fenn Burton, Jerusha Loomis Farnham, and Margaret Gale Hitchcock, the last in the Hitchcock family papers (2.5 ln.ft., 1835–98), trace their trips from Connecticut or New York to Illinois in 1835 and 1837–38. The papers of the Shaw and Calkins families (3 ln.ft., 1836–1916) and the Isaac M. Wetmore family (1.5 ln.ft., 1820–81) and the diaries of Samuel Hezekiah Brink (1 ln.ft., 1855–63) describe farming, teaching, and Civil War experiences. Perspectives on the religious life of frontier Illinois are provided by the journal of Horace Spalding (2 vols., 1837–43), a representative of the American Bible Society; the diaries of Samuel Guild Wright (1840–90), who settled in Toulon; and the Duffield family papers (1.5 ln.ft., 1816–78), including a six-hundred-page manuscript by George Duffield, Jr., regarding the differences between Old and New School Presbyterians.

Collections at Knox also reflect the activities of late nineteenth-century leaders. The papers of Newton D. Bateman (5 ln.ft., 1859–97) include his addresses and sermons as president of Knox and Illinois superintendent of public instruction. The Philip Sidney Post collection (52 ln.ft., 1857–95) documents his career as a lawyer, diplomat, and member of Congress, 1887–95. The papers of his daughter-in-law, Janet Greig Post (28.5 ln.ft., 1871–1964), relate to her work on the boards of Knox and the national Young Women's Christian Association and contain her extensive correspondence, including an interesting exchange with Jane Addams. Other important Illinoisans are represented in the papers of Edgar A. Bancroft (5 ln.ft., 1869–1950), a railroad lawyer and ambassador to Japan.

Certain collections contain research materials of considerable interest to Illinois historians. The papers of Philip J. Stoneberg (8 ln.ft., 1867–1919) concern the cooperative Swedish community of Bishop Hill. The William Mackintire Salter collection (1 ln.ft., 1884–1913) includes his notes on the Haymarket case and his correspondence with August Spies, one of the accused anarchists. The papers of J. Howell Atwood (6 ln.ft., 1930–60) reflect his sociological studies of race relations in Galesburg and across the nation.

Knox's cache of literary manuscripts of such figures as Eugene Field, Carl Sandburg, Edgar Lee Masters, Ernest Hemingway, and Don Marquis illustrates that the college holds many collections that are not primarily related to state history. In addition, of course, the Knox Archives preserves the records of the college. It also holds the records of Lombard College, another Galesburg institution, which closed in 1930. Elsewhere in the Knox library are several book collections pertaining to Illinois history, including the John Huston Finley collection on the Old Northwest, the Ray D. Smith collection on the Civil War, and the Eliott Pearlman collection on Chicago, while the Preston Player collection contains both printed and iconographic sources relating to the Mississippi River.

## Western Illinois University

University Library
Macomb, IL 61455
(309) 298–2717

The Archives and Special Collections Department of Western Illinois University, organized in 1970 to manage the institution's records, soon began to collect sources for regional history. Leading the effort to establish the unit was Victor Hicken, a long-time member of the university's History Department. Robert P. Sutton of the same department became director of regional collections in 1976, while John E. Hallwas of the English Department held this position from 1979 to 1989. The unit's interest in regional materials was expanded in 1976 when the library was designated the Illinois Regional Archives Depository for the records of sixteen western Illinois counties.

Archives and Special Collections contains a wealth of printed, audio-visual, and manuscript materials for local historical research. These holdings are particularly rich for Hancock County, especially the city of Nauvoo in the Mormon and Icarian periods. The Thomas Gregg papers (0.5 ln.ft., 1806–1950) and several retrospective collections—the Gordon-Vestal papers (10 ln.ft.) and scrapbooks compiled by Mary Siegfried (6 vols.), Ida Blum (5 vols.), and David C. Martin (13 vols.)—pertain to the Mormon years, while the Center for Icarian Studies has acquired for the department an array of relevant sources, including copies of the major collections held by other repositories and individuals. Since 1979, the Center has been a focal point of Icarian scholarship through its *Newsletter*. Archives and Special Collections also holds materials for the city of Quincy, especially photographs, including the J. S. Schott collection (4,250 prints, 1896–1940) and the H. J. "Junie" Berghofer collection (24,000 negatives, 1945–55).

The department preserves ten collections of correspondence and four diaries relating to the Civil War experiences of Illinois soldiers. Other early manuscripts include the Doris Sellars collection, containing letters from the Andrus, Miner, and Carrison families of Fulton, Mason, and McDonough counties (0.5 ln.ft., 1818–1907), and the diaries, letters, and milling and real estate records of John Whitehead of Liverpool, in Fulton County (1 ln.ft., 1845–80). Among the church records, business ledgers, and papers of civic groups dating from the late nineteenth century to the present are the archives of several local organizations, including the Child Welfare Club of Macomb (1.5 ln.ft., 1905–87), the Macomb Rotary Club (4 ln.ft., 1919–89), and Macomb Business and Professional Women (20 vols., 1930–78).

Two large collections document the activities of contemporary Illinoisans. The Tom Railsback collection (300 ln.ft., 1967–82) relates primarily to his career as a member of Congress. Railsback served on the House Judiciary Committee during the Watergate hearings and was interested in numerous social programs and construction projects affecting west central Illinois. The collection is described in Sheila H. Nollen, "Thomas F. Railsback and His Congressional Papers," *Western Illinois Regional Studies*, 9 (Spring 1986). The papers of Ray Page (40 ln.ft., 1963–70) include speeches, correspondence, and photographs from his tenure as Illinois superintendent of public instruction. Educational interests in the state are also reflected in the records of the Illinois Association for Counseling and Development (5.5 ln.ft., 1953–86).

The books and papers of the Center for Regional Authors constitute another group of collections in the unit. Organized in 1972, the Center holds both first editions of many literary figures from the region and a number of letters and manuscripts of such prominent writers as John Hay, Carl Sandburg, Edgar Lee Masters, and Don Marquis. Research into the state's natural history is preserved in the papers of Virginia S. Eifert (12 ln.ft., 1906–81), a nature writer, especially for children; Elton Fawks (15 ln.ft., 1900–89), a specialist on birds of prey; and John Madson (1 ln.ft., 1970–85), an authority on wildlife and the environment. Finally, the department contains the collection of reminiscences of early twentieth-century life in the region, selections from which have appeared in

*Tales from Two Rivers*, including three volumes edited by Jerrilee Cain (Tyson) et al. and a fourth volume edited by John E. Hallwas and David R. Pichaske (Macomb, 1981–87).


## Sangamon State University

> Brookens Library
> Shepherd Rd.
> Springfield, IL 62794
> (217) 786–6520


The Sangamon State University Archives was formed in 1972, two years after the institution opened. It now holds over one thousand cubic feet of university records, faculty papers, audio-visual materials, and manuscript collections. It also serves as the Illinois Regional Archives Depository for local government records from fourteen central Illinois counties.

Although these governmental records date from the nineteenth century, Sangamon State's holdings for local and regional history are concentrated in recent years, contemporaneous with the university and often related to the civic interests of its faculty. This emphasis is apparent in Nancy Hunt, *Guide to Manuscript Collections at the Sangamon State University Archives* (Springfield, 1986), which contains 135 entries for materials other than university and government records.

Among the holdings of the University Archives are the records of the Clayville Rural Life Center (19 cu.ft., 1819–1982), a living history museum of the 1850s, located at an old stagecoach stop northwest of Springfield. Its files include documents of the period as well as research papers and program records. Another notable series preserves the findings of the Center for the Study of Middle-Size Cities (28.5 cu.ft., 1972–81). Aspects of Illinois labor history are covered in the papers of John H. Keiser (2.5 cu.ft., 1920–77), a Sangamon State historian and administrator in the 1970s. A related manuscript collection, the Henry Weinhoeft accession (1.5 cu.ft., 1909–25), includes the records of Local 46 (Springfield) of the International Association of Bridge, Structural, and Ornamental Iron Workers.

Sangamon State's manuscript holdings encompass several local, grass-roots, and public interest organizations. The records of Streetside Boosters (6.5 cu.ft., 1976–85), based in Springfield's eastside neighborhood, relate to crime and delinquency, the campaign against the Madison Street corridor, and such educational and cultural activities as its Blues-in-the-Schools program. The Ernest Nielsen collection (9 cu.ft., 1976–83) pertains to the area's interest in fair housing, energy conservation, and community development block grants. Certain records of the Central Illinois Public Service Company (1.5 cu.ft., 1928–41) reflect its opposition to municipally owned utilities. Materials relating to the

Springfield voting rights lawsuit (1 cu.ft., 1984–87) document the case that overturned the city's commission form of government.

Other sources relate to recent developments in education. The papers of G. Ernst Giesecke (9 cu.ft., 1937–79) concern campus unrest, academic standards, and similar issues for higher education in Illinois. The records of the Center for Alternative Education (3 cu.ft., 1970–82) pertain to the Learning Community, an experimental secondary school in Springfield in the 1970s. The Cullom Davis collection (4 cu.ft., 1959–81) includes records of the Citizens United for Responsible Education, which initiated a desegregation suit against the Springfield school district in 1974.

Several women's organizations are represented in Sangamon State's collections, including Planned Parenthood, Springfield Area, and its predecessors (0.5 cu.ft., 1938–81); the Springfield chapter of the National Organization for Women (3 cu.ft., 1971–83); and Women's Alliance, a community resource and referral center (4.5 cu.ft., 1978–83). Another group of records relates to peace organizations: the Springfield World Federalist Association (4 cu.ft., 1948–73), the Springfield branch of the Women's International League for Peace and Freedom (3.5 cu.ft., 1954–86), and Springfield Mobilization for Peace and Freedom (4 cu.ft., 1982–84).

The records of the Handy Colony (33 cu.ft., 1933–64) document an important literary community in Marshall, Illinois in the 1950s. Established by Lowney Handy; her husband, Harry Handy; and James Jones, who wrote *From Here to Eternity* (1951) and other novels, the colony supported many aspiring writers. Manuscripts, correspondence, photographs, diaries, and other papers of the participants are inventoried in Thomas J. Wood and Meredith Keating, *James Jones in Illinois: A Guide to the Handy Writers' Colony Collection . . .* (Springfield, 1989). A literary experiment of a different kind is reflected in the records of the Spoon River Cooperative Association (7.5 cu.ft., 1968–79), a consumer book cooperative which specialized in small press, radical, and underground titles.

Several audio-visual collections round out the holdings of the Sangamon State Archives. Springfield's Booth-Grunendike family left an eclectic assortment of photographs, ranging across four generations (5 cu.ft., 1856–1956). William DiMarco, a Sangamon State alumnus, assembled images of electric, steam, and diesel railroading in central Illinois (1.5 cu.ft., 1901–81). And Richard M. Phillips of East Peoria photographed historical sites and vernacular architecture throughout the state (6 cu.ft., 1963–76). In the late 1950s, a group of captains, deck hands, and others recalled life along the Ohio, Illinois, and Mississippi rivers, in interviews recorded by the poet John Knoepfle (2 cu.ft., 1956–59).

A separate and major effort to document the recent past is centered in the Oral History Office of Sangamon State University. Since the early 1970s, this office has interviewed a host of central Illinoisans, some regarding their experiences in farming, coal mining, education, and other careers and professions; others as representatives of different ethnic, religious, and racial groups; and still others for their knowledge of political and cultural affairs. Information regarding these interviews, arranged topically, is reported in the *National Union Catalog of Manuscript Collections* for 1976 and 1984, and many transcripts are available on microfiche.

## Augustana College

*Special Collections*
Augustana College Library
3435 9 1/2 Ave.
Rock Island, IL 61201
(309) 794-7317

*Swenson Swedish Immigration Research Center*
Denkmann Memorial Library
3520 7th Ave.
Rock Island, IL 61201
(309) 794-7204

Topics in denominational, ethnic, and regional history are documented by a combination of collections at Augustana College. Founded as Augustana College and Theological Seminary in 1860, and located in Rock Island in 1875, the college kept most of the institution's archives when the seminary separated from the college and, in 1967, moved to Chicago. Thus, the college library, which formed a Special Collections unit in 1969, now contains, for example, the papers of Augustana's presidents: Lars Paul Esbjörn (1 ln.ft., 1846–70), Tufve Nilsson Hasselquist (6 ln.ft., 1852–91), Olof Olsson (4 ln.ft., 1868–1900), Gustav A. Andreen (45 ln.ft., 1872–1935), and Conrad Bergendoff (53 ln.ft., 1915–89). A substantial number of nineteenth-century manuscripts, written in Swedish, have been translated and published, and these collections as a whole have supported many studies, especially publications of the Augustana Historical Society.

The college also acquired materials that are broadly related to Swedish-American history, including books, newspapers, and manuscripts gathered in the early twentieth century by Oliver A. Linder, Gustaf N. Swan, and Ernest W. Olson, each a journalist and author. Olson, for example, compiled the *History of the Swedes of Illinois* (2 vols., Chicago, 1908) and *The Swedish Element in Illinois* . . . (Chicago, 1917). When the Swenson Swedish Immigration Research Center was established in 1981, the administration of these and related collections was transferred to the new unit. In recent years, the Swenson Center has expanded its holdings in part by microfilming records in private hands and in part by acquiring original sources, such as the diaries of Peter S. Nelson (33 vols., 1860–1916), a Knox County lumber and flour merchant. *Swenson Center News*, issued annually since 1986, and *A Guide to Resources and Holdings*, prepared in 1984 and updated in 1989, provide an introduction to the Center.

The Augustana library is rich in printed and manuscript sources for northwest Illinois and the Upper Mississippi Valley. John Henry Hauberg, a Rock Island lawyer, businessman, and historian, donated some of these materials, including not only his own papers and family records (30 ln.ft., 1811–1955), but also ledgers documenting George Davenport's trading with the Indians (8 vols., 1824–35). The library also holds the records of the Rock Island Millwork Company (60 ln.ft., 1897–1978) and the Moline Water Power Company (7 ln.ft., 1855–1960).

## Illinois State University

> Milner Library
> Normal, IL 61761
> (309) 438–7450

The University Archives and Special Collections unit of Illinois State University contains mainly the records of the institution since its founding in 1857 and printed holdings such as the Harold K. Sage collection of Lincolniana and the interrelated collections of circus materials. Yet it also serves as the Illinois Regional Archives Depository for fourteen counties in central and east central Illinois, and it preserves a number of manuscript collections pertaining to local and state history. While the book collections are maintained in Milner Library, the regional depository, the institution's archives, and some of its manuscript collections are located in Williams Hall.

The University Archives holds the papers of several presidents of Illinois State, including Richard Edwards (9 ln.ft., 1840–1908), David Felmley (2 ln.ft., 1900–30), and Raymond W. Fairchild (10 ln.ft., 1933–54). These collections are more than college archives in that they document the activities of prominent educators in the state. Edwards, for example, served as superintendent of public instruction, 1887–91, after his presidency at Normal.

George P. Ela's diaries and correspondence (1.5 ln.ft., 1850–81) provide insights into the early history of Bloomington. The papers of John E. McClun (1 ln.ft., 1836–88), a McLean County judge and state legislator, are weighted with business records, as are the papers of Archie M. Augustine of Bloomington (1.5 ln.ft., 1884–1957), a leading nurseryman of his day, known for the Augustine ascending elm.

More than a dozen Bloomington-Normal civic and literary clubs, many dating from the late nineteenth century, have deposited their records at Illinois State. The collection also contains the papers of Harold Sinclair of Bloomington (2 ln.ft., 1947–66), whose novels include *American Years* (1938) and *The Horse Soldiers* (1956). Aspects of social welfare history are documented in the papers of Elmer W. Powers (17 ln.ft., 1936–53), a district supervisor of the Illinois Public Aid Commission, and the records, largely since World War II, of the Morgan-Washington Home, chartered in 1889 as the Girls' Industrial Home of

McLean County (1.5 ln.ft., 1889–1976). Various civic concerns are apparent in the records of the Bloomington-Normal chapter of the League of Women Voters (1.5 ln.ft., 1933–68).

Sources for twentieth-century political history include the papers of Louis FitzHenry (11 ln.ft., 1863–1959), a member of Congress and a federal judge, and Florence Fifer Bohrer (1 ln.ft., 1924–51), in 1925 the first woman senator in the Illinois legislature. Milner Library also holds the collection of photocopies (52 ln.ft.) used in the preparation of Walter Johnson, ed., *The Papers of Adlai E. Stevenson* (1972–79).

# 26

# LIBRARY OF CONGRESS AND NATIONAL ARCHIVES

TIMOTHY WALCH AND
VICTORIA IRONS WALCH

SOURCES FOR ILLINOIS history are located not only within the state but across the nation. Indeed, voluminous documentation of the state's past is held by two national repositories, the Library of Congress and the National Archives and Records Administration. In a sense, these repositories complement each other by documenting the services of Illinoisans in the national experience and the contributions of the federal government to the state.

Research in the holdings of the Library of Congress and the National Archives need not require a trip to Washington, D.C. Many of the most valuable collections are available on microfilm, and finding aids to these and many other collections are also available. With the assistance of archivists and curators in Washington and at the Chicago repository of the National Archives, students of Illinois history will find the relevant sources of these national repositories surprisingly accessible.

## Library of Congress

Washington, DC 20540
Information: (202) 707–5000

*Manuscript Division*
Madison Bldg., Rm. 101
(202) 707–5387

*Prints and Photographs Division*
Madison Bldg., Rm. 339
(202) 707–6394

*Photoduplication Service*
(202) 707–5640

Of the many divisions of the Library of Congress, it is the Manuscript Division that holds most of the unpublished documentation of interest to Illinois historians. The basic in-house guide to the division's holdings is the Master Record of Manuscript Collections. This finding aid consists of two parts. Master Record I lists in a single volume the name, dates, and size of more than ten thousand collections. Master Record II contains in eight volumes a summary description of each of these collections and an index to the names and key terms found in these descriptions. Terms such as "Illinois" and "Chicago" are well represented. The library's internal online system is used for current information on the division's holdings.

Collections in the Manuscript Division range in size from one item to several thousand boxes. Most of the larger collections are reported in the *National Union Catalog of Manuscript Collections*, the entries for which are similar to the summary descriptions of Master Record II. These collections contain about twenty-six million of the forty million items held by the division. It is therefore important to look beyond *NUCMC* for information as to Illinois sources in the Library of Congress.

For some fifteen hundred collections, the summary description in the Master Record may be supplemented by a more detailed finding aid or register on file in the Manuscript Division's reading room. The typical register includes a scope and content note, a biographical sketch or chronology, a description of the different series in the collection, and a container list. Researchers may buy photocopies of individual guides, most of which are typescripts, but about half of these registers, 762 in all, are available on microfiche in the *National Inventory of Documentary Sources in the United States: Manuscript Division, Library of Congress*, a Chadwyck-Healey publication accompanied by a bound *Index 1983*, compiled by Victoria Agee (Teaneck, N.J., 1983).

The division's collections are listed by subject in several guides, and these publications index entries by state or city. Twenty-one Illinoisans are represented in John J. McDonough, comp., *Members of Congress: A Checklist of Their Papers in the Manuscript Division, Library of Congress* (Washington, D.C., 1980), a publication based on Master Record I. Chicago is indexed in Gary J. Kohn, comp., *The Jewish Experience: A Guide to Manuscript Sources in the Library of Congress* (Cincinnati, 1986), a publication that not only lists certain collections by title but identifies relevant series in other collections. A subject of perennial interest is inventoried in John R. Sellers, comp., *Civil War Manuscripts: A Guide to Collections in the Manuscript Division of the Library of Congress* (Washington, D.C., 1986).

Sources for Illinois history, although scattered throughout the Manuscript Division's holdings, are conspicuous in certain collections. Many of these collections are available on microfilm, reels of which may be borrowed through interlibrary loan or bought from the library's Photoduplication Service.

The Charles Butler collection (4 reels, 1819–1905) includes his diaries of a trip from New York to Illinois in 1833. Data regarding law and politics in Chicago before the Civil War may be found in the papers of John Dean Caton (14 ln.ft., 1826–95), who served on the Illinois Supreme Court, and Robert R. Hitt (16 ln.ft., 1830–1905), later a member of Congress. State politics and patronage are especially well illuminated in the letters received by Sen. Lyman Trumbull, in his papers (22 reels, 1843–94).

Other nineteenth-century Illinois holdings include the papers of Melville W. Fuller, Chief Justice of the United States (6.5 ln.ft., 1794–1949), and the papers of Elihu B. Washburne (31 ln.ft., 1829–82) and Henry P. H. Bromwell (2 ln.ft., 1794–1929), both members of Congress. The development of Bloomington and Normal is documented in the papers of Jesse W. Fell (2.5 ln.ft., 1806–1957). The Logan family collection (61 ln.ft., 1847–1923) is useful for Sen. John A. Logan and especially his wife Mary. Railroad construction in Illinois is important in the papers of Octave Chanute (24 reels, 1850–1910).

The Manuscript Division holds several collections related to the Progressive period in Chicago. Ray Stannard Baker's papers (97 reels, 1836–1947) document his years with the *Chicago Record*. The Walter L. Fisher collection (19 ln.ft., 1879–1936) pertains to his career as a municipal reformer. The papers of Harold L. Ickes (225 ln.ft., 1815–1969) extend to Chicago politics and the Illinois Progressive party. Congressman James R. Mann's papers (20 ln.ft., 1887–1922) reflect several important issues of his day. The voluminous records of the landscape architects, Frederick Law Olmsted (29 ln.ft., 1822–1924) and the Olmsted Associates (255 ln.ft., 1868–1950), much on microfilm, document their work in Chicago, particularly in planning and building parks.

Among the division's sources for Illinois politics after World War I is the Hanna-McCormick family collection (53 ln.ft., 1792–1951), including constituency mail received by Sen. Joseph Medill McCormick and the more extensive papers of his wife, Rep. Ruth Hanna McCormick. Her campaign for the Senate in 1929–30 is also documented in the papers of Mary Church Terrell (34 reels, 1851–1962), who was an advocate of black women's rights. Smaller collections include the congressional papers of J. Hamilton Lewis (2 ln.ft., 1907–39), Henry T. Rainey (8 ln.ft., 1904–34), and James M. Barnes (19 ln.ft., 1924–58). Illinois materials may be found in the archives of such organizations as the National Urban League, the National Association for the Advancement of Colored People, the National Council of Jewish Women, and the League of Women Voters of the United States.

Social and cultural history is exemplified in other collections. The correspondence of Sophonisba P. Breckinridge (37 reels, 1873–1949), in the Breckinridge family collection, reflects her many activities in the field of social work. Certain files of the Federal Writers' Project and the Historical Records Survey (630 ln.ft., 1935–42) relate to Illinois. Ludwig Mies van der Rohe's papers (27 ln.ft., 1921–69) are in the Manuscript Division, while his architectural drawings and job files are at the Museum of Modern Art, New York.

The Library of Congress contains not only manuscripts but visual sources for Illinois history. These materials are maintained by the Prints and Photographs Division, which is responsible for more than twelve million pictorial items. Perhaps the most accessible collections in this division are the files of the Historic American Buildings Survey and the Historic American Engineering Record, which together constitute the most comprehensive architectural archives in the United States. A checklist of these records, including over four hundred entries for Illinois, is in C. Ford Peatross, ed., *Historic America: Buildings, Structures, and Sites* . . . (Washington, D.C., 1983). The measured drawings of the Historic American Buildings Survey were microfilmed by the Library of Congress in 1974, and a microfiche edition of the related photographs and text, published in 1980, is available from Chadwyck-Healey.

Another collection of exceptional interest, also reproduced on microfiche by Chadwyck-Healey, is the photographic record of America during the Depression and World War II produced by the Farm Security Administration and the Office of War Information. Grouped by region, the collection includes thirty-eight file drawers for scenes in the Midwest. Robert L. Reid and Larry A. Viskochil, *Chicago and Downstate* . . . (Urbana, 1989) and Herbert K. Russell, *A Southern Illinois Album* . . . (Carbondale, 1990) provide a sampling of these photographs. The Prints and Photographs Division contains other files of particular value to Illinois history: the Stereographic File, including several hundred images of Illinois in the late nineteenth century, most of which document city parks around the state; the Geographic File, including approximately one drawer of pictures of Illinois cities, especially Chicago, in the twentieth century; and the Graphics File, including about one hundred prints, etchings, and engravings of Illinois places.

Documentation of Illinois subjects may be found not only in the Manuscript Division and the Prints and Photographs Division but also in other units of the Library of Congress, such as the Music Division and the American Folklife Center. Those who prepared *Illinois: The Sesquicentennial of Statehood* . . . (Washington, D.C., 1968), an exhibition catalog which provides a rich and representative selection of the library's sources for Illinois history, drew more materials from the Rare Book and Special Collections Division than from the Manuscript and the Prints and Photographs divisions, and also included items from the Geography and Map Division, the Law Library, and the general collections.

This catalog is instructive on another point, the value of full citations, including if available the library's photographic negative numbers. To obtain a reproduction of a previously printed photograph owned by the library, the researcher should provide a photocopy of the picture, an exact reference to its publication, and as much information as possible regarding the subject, place, date, original medium, and photographer. It is usually necessary to study visual materials directly; picture research is difficult, if not impossible, by phone or mail. More generally, any kind of collection must be personally examined when items of interest cannot be located from a distance. For this reason, the different units of the Library of Congress, like many other repositories, will provide lists of free-lance researchers who may be engaged by those unable to study the collections themselves.

## National Archives and Records Administration

Washington, DC 20408

*Reference Services Branch (NNRS)*
Archives Bldg., Rm. 205
(202) 501–5400

*Publications Services (NEPS)*
(202) 501–5240

The National Archives holds over three billion documents, five million photographs, and two million cartographic items. It is an awesome volume of historical records even for the most seasoned researcher. Yet most of these materials are simply the papers of the federal government, records of permanent value which are maintained by the Archives in their original order and which can therefore be located by knowing the agencies that created them. The Archives has assigned a Record Group (RG) number to each body of papers, according to its origin, and has prepared numerous finding aids to make these records accessible. Materials related to Illinois history are stored not only in the National Archives building in Washington and in other nearby facilities but also at the regional archives in Chicago, and many series are available on microfilm.

The starting point for research in these governmental records is the *Guide to the National Archives of the United States* (Washington, D.C., 1974), a hefty volume which describes more than four hundred record groups. Some twenty additional record groups are recorded in an expanded edition of this work (Washington, D.C., 1988), while *Prologue*, since 1969 the journal of the National Archives, carries announcements of new accessions. See also the latest *List of Record Groups of the National Archives and Records Administration* (1985).

The Archives has also published many guides to specific holdings, both inventories for particular record groups and special lists for series of records within a record group or for an activity of an agency. Guides still in print are shown in the current *Select List of Publications of the National Archives and Records Administration* (1986), a brochure distributed without cost by Publications Services. Many of these guides are also available at no charge, while out-of-print items may be obtained on microfilm. Many research libraries contain copies of the inventories and lists of the Archives. Furthermore,

Chadwyck-Healey's *National Inventory of Documentary Sources in the United States: Federal Records* reproduces on microfiche some 429 guides, about half of which are otherwise unpublished. This series, which also includes finding aids for collections in seven presidential libraries and the Smithsonian Institution, is accessible through Victoria Agee et al., comps., *Index 1985* (Teaneck, N.J., 1985).

The National Archives has prepared not only guides to its holdings but also microfilm of many records. These publications are listed in *National Archives Microfilm Resources for Research: A Comprehensive Catalog* (1986), supplemented by *National Archives Microfilm Update*, issued by Scholarly Resources (Wilmington, Del., 1989). Many of these microfilm publications may be found at the Chicago and other regional units of the Archives. Although some libraries have selectively acquired reels of interest and may make them available on interlibrary loan, individual researchers may rent certain widely used publications from the National Archives Microfilm Rental Program, Box 30, Annapolis Junction, MD 20701. Alternatively, microfilm reels may be purchased from the National Archives Trust Fund, Box 100793, Atlanta, GA 30384.

Most of these microfilm publications are identified by M or T numbers. In the past, each M publication reproduced an entire series of records, while each T publication contained only segments, by date or subject, of a larger series. More recent publications are assigned M numbers without regard to content. Some M publications include a description of the origin and content of the microfilmed records and a reel-by-reel listing of their arrangement. In most cases, this information is also available in a descriptive pamphlet that accompanies the microfilm but which can be obtained separately and without charge so as to anticipate whether a particular reel or an entire publication will meet a researcher's needs. In addition, the Archives has issued several descriptive catalogs which bring together by subject the information contained in numerous descriptive pamphlets. *Immigrant and Passenger Arrivals* (1983) and *Genealogical and Biographical Research* (1983), each subtitled *A Select Catalog of National Archives Microfilm Publications*, are among the titles in this series.

The Illinois holdings of the National Archives date from the earliest days of the nation. Among the *Papers of the Continental Congress, 1774–1789* (M247, 204 reels), records arranged in RG 360, are 10 items concerning the Illinois Company, 15 items concerning the Illinois River, and more than 140 items concerning the entire Illinois Country. Each of these items is described and located in the microfilm by John P. Butler, comp., *Index: The Papers of the Continental Congress, 1774–1789* (5 vols., Washington, D.C., 1978). The territorial period of Illinois is also well documented, mainly in the General Records of the Department of State (RG 59). Although many pertinent series have been microfilmed, these records are more widely available in the Illinois volumes (16 and 17) of Clarence Edwin Carter, ed., *The Territorial Papers of the United States* (Washington, D.C., 1948–50).

The federal government's relations with the Indians at Chicago may be traced in the Records of the Bureau of Indian Affairs (RG 75). These files include *Letters Sent by the Superintendent of Indian Trade, 1807–1823* (M16, 6 reels); *Letters Received by the Superintendent of Indian Trade, 1806–1824* (T58, 1 reel); and *Letters Received by the Office of Indian Affairs, 1824–1881* (M234, 962 reels), reels 132–134 of which concern the Chicago Agency, 1824–47. For further information, see Edward E. Hill, comp., *Guide to Records in the National Archives of the United States Relating to American Indians* (Washington, D.C., 1981).

The Records of the Bureau of Land Management (RG 49) include sources for the history of public lands in Illinois. Three series are arranged chronologically: *Letters Received by the Secretary of the Treasury and the Commissioner of the General Land Office from the Surveyor General of the Territory Northwest of the River Ohio, 1797–1849* (M478, 10 reels); other *Letters Sent by the Surveyor General of the Territory Northwest of the River Ohio, 1797–1854* (M477, 10 reels); and *Letters Received by the Surveyor General of the Territory Northwest of the River Ohio, 1797–1856* (M479, 43 reels). Additional records pertain to the transfer of land from the public domain to private ownership and are described in Harry P. Yoshpe and Philip P. Brower, comps., *Preliminary Inventory of the Land-Entry Papers of the General Land Office* (1949). Illinois materials in this series came from eleven district land offices (435 cu.ft., 1809–76). See also Laura E. Kelsay, comp., *List of Cartographic Records of the General Land Office . . .* (1964).

Papers relating to political appointments are located in the files of several departments. *Letters of Application and Recommendation to Federal Offices . . .*, published for successive administrations from 1797 to 1877 and arranged alphabetically by individual, draw on records of the State Department (RG 59), which in the nineteenth century was responsible for many aspects of domestic administration as well as the conduct of foreign affairs. Appointment Files for Judicial Districts, 1853–1905, is a series in the General Records of the Department of Justice (RG 60), while Records Relating to Customhouse Nominations, 1849–1910; Applications for Appointment as Customs Service Officers, 1833–1910; and Applications for Positions as Internal Revenue Collectors and Assessors, 1863–1910, may be found in the General Records of the Department of the Treasury (RG 56). All of these series are arranged by state, district, or port and then by applicant, allowing researchers to document specific locales or individuals during those years.

Papers concerning law enforcement also extend to Illinois. Justice Department records (RG 60) include two series, Letters Received by the Attorney General, 1809–70, and Source-Chronological Files, 1871–84, that contain correspondence from marshals, judges, lawyers, and citizens in the state. Similarly, the Records of the Solicitor of the Treasury (RG 206) include a series of letters received from district attorneys, marshals, and clerks of the court that contains Illinois letters from 1823 to 1898.

Undoubtedly the most popular records for researchers in Illinois, as elsewhere, are the population schedules of the Bureau of the Census (RG 29). These records are listed in *Federal Population Censuses, 1790–1890* (1971); *1900 Federal Population Census* (1978); and *The 1910 Federal Population Census* (1982), each of which is subtitled *A Catalog of Microfilm Copies of the Schedules*. Many libraries have acquired selected reels of this microfilm, often for the state in which they are located, and the National Archives makes available a microfiche tabulation of these holdings, *Federal Population and Mortality Schedules, 1790–1910, in the National Archives and the States* (1986). These census records and many other types of records of particular interest to genealogists are discussed in the revised *Guide to Genealogical Research in the National Archives* (Washington, D.C., 1985).

Turning briefly from the Civil Archives Division to the Military Archives Division, the researcher may find many series relating to volunteer military service in the nineteenth century, especially in the Records of the Adjutant General's Office (RG 94). Illinoisans first appear in reel 23 of the *Compiled Service Records of Volunteer Soldiers Who Served from 1784 to 1811* (M905, 32 reels). The Archives also has microfilmed the alphabetical indexes to similar records for the War of 1812, the Mexican War, and the Civil War. Illinois units are documented in reels 11–33 of the *Compiled Records Showing Service of Military Units in Volunteer Union Organizations* (M594, 225 reels) and in reels 26–85 of the *Organization Index to Pension Files of Veterans Who Served between 1861 and 1900* (T289, 765 reels). These and similar sources are described in *Military Service Records: A Select Catalog of National Archives Microfilm Publications* (1985).

Several record groups document aspects of Illinois history in the twentieth century. In RG 33, the *Extension Service Annual Reports, 1914–1944* (T858, 82 reels) include details of farm operation and rural life in the state. Patrick G. Garabedian, comp., *Preliminary Inventory of the Records of the Rural Electrification Administration* (1977) points to files in RG 221 for REA projects in some twenty-two Illinois counties, 1934–57.

Other records relate to tragic incidents in the state's history. The Records of the Bureau of Mines (RG 70) contain film and news reports of the mine disaster at Royalton in 1914. The Records of the U.S. House of Representatives (RG 233) include *Transcripts of the Hearings of the House Select Committee That Investigated the Race Riots in East St. Louis, 1917* (M1167, 7 reels). University Publications of America has duplicated these transcripts; added the trial record of LeRoy Bundy, who was charged with inciting the riot; and provided a brief outline of this material (8 reels) in Mike Acquaviva, comp., *A Guide to the East St. Louis Race Riot of 1917* (Frederick, Md., 1985). Finally, the Records of the National Commission on the Causes and Prevention of Violence (RG 220) include the papers of the study team that investigated the violence in Chicago during the 1968 Democratic national convention. These records are located at the Lyndon B. Johnson Library, Austin, TX 78705.

Two collections relating to recent Illinois politics are held by the Harry S. Truman Library, Independence, MO 64050. The papers of Sidney R. Yates (44 ln.ft., 1949–62) document his first seven terms in Congress, while the papers of Stephen A. Mitchell (43 ln.ft., 1947–60), chairman of the Democratic National Committee, are weighted with Illinois files.

## National Archives—Great Lakes Region

7358 S. Pulaski Rd.
Chicago, IL 60629
(312) 581–7816

The largest accumulation of federal records concerning the state is preserved not in Washington but at the Chicago repository of the National Archives. Located in southwest Chicago, this facility serves the states of Illinois, Indiana, Michigan, Minnesota, Ohio, and Wisconsin. It contains many microfilm publications of the National Archives and nearly fifty-four thousand cubic feet of records from federal courts and the offices of federal agencies within the region. Information regarding these materials is available in two booklets, *Microfilm List No. 3* (1978; addenda for recent accessions) and *Guide to Records in the National Archives—Great Lakes Region* (1989).

Records of the U.S. District Courts (RG 21) comprise the most voluminous holdings of the Chicago repository. This group contains case files and court records from federal circuit and district courts in Illinois (17,000 cu.ft., 1819–1964). The cases concern the settlement of land claims, bankruptcies, and other civil actions; the prosecution of criminal charges; and petitions for citizenship. Both the notorious and the anonymous appear in these files. John Dillinger and Al Capone, among others, faced criminal charges. The Pullman strike, the Ferris wheel, and the original Dixieland Jazz Band were subjects of civil litigation. But these cases are not typical; most of the files document the routine contacts between Illinois citizens and the federal courts.

The Chicago repository also holds certain Records of the U.S. Courts of Appeals (RG 276), including the files of the Seventh Circuit which embraces Illinois, Indiana, and Wisconsin (1,880 cu.ft., 1891–1964). Access to particular items in this series, as in the records of the district courts, often depends upon case citations that must be secured from indexes in the appropriate jurisdiction. The Records of U.S. Attorneys and Marshals (RG 118) for Illinois (25 cu.ft., 1936–63) contain precedent case files for espionage, income tax evasion, embezzlement, and other criminal proceedings in the state. The Gift Collection includes the papers of two federal judges, William J. Campbell of the District Court for the Northern District of Illinois (67 cu.ft., 1927–71) and John S. Hastings of the Court of Appeals for the Seventh Circuit (36 cu.ft., 1964–77).

The records most in demand at the Chicago repository pertain to naturalization proceedings in county and federal courts. The Records of the Immigration and

Naturalization Service (RG 85) include not only copies of Cook County naturalization papers, 1871–1906, but also an index to all naturalizations elsewhere in northern Illinois, 1840–1950. In addition, federal court records (RG 21) contain naturalizaton indexes for Peoria, 1905–54, and Springfield, 1906–56. Another series in RG 85 documents the Chicago District's enforcement of Chinese immigration laws, 1893–1939.

A variety of sources relate to transportation in Illinois. Topographical surveys of the state and projects on the Chicago lakefront, Illinois Waterway, and Mississippi River are documented in the pertinent district and division files (1832–1944) of the U.S. Army Corps of Engineers (RG 77). Ship traffic in and out of the ports of Chicago, Peoria, Rock Island, and Galena may be traced in the Records of the Bureau of Marine Inspection and Navigation (42 cu.ft., 1865–1952), the Bureau of Customs (4 cu.ft., 1914–44), and the U.S. Coast Guard (3 cu.ft., 1959–67), RG 41, RG 36, and RG 26, respectively. The Records of the Bureau of Public Roads (RG 30) and the Federal Highway Administration (RG 406) contain files for federal highway projects in the state (120 cu.ft., 1918–67). The Records of the Federal Aviation Administration (RG 237) include studies of airport airspace in the Great Lakes region (21 cu.ft., 1970–77).

Materials on other aspects of Illinois history in the twentieth century are often conspicuous in the records of regional offices of federal agencies. The U.S. Food Administration (RG 4) regulated the supply and distribution of foods during World War I (252 cu.ft., 1917–19). The Farmers Home Administration (RG 96), continuing the Depression-era programs of the Resettlement Administration and the Farm Security Administration, extended credit and other assistance to small farmers (175 cu.ft., 1935–47). The Chicago repository also holds the central office records (186 cu.ft., 1937–78) of the Railroad Retirement Board (RG 184).

Finally, many sources date from World War II and subsequent years. Records of the regional branch of the Office of Price Administration (RG 188) include files from selected city ration boards in Illinois, 1942–47. The Bureau of Naval Personnel (RG 24) operated the Naval Reserve Midshipmen's School at Northwestern University (44 cu.ft., 1941–45). The War Manpower Commission (RG 211) concerned itself with industrial, labor, and housing surveys in the state (30 cu.ft., 1942–45). After the war, the Farm Credit Administration (RG 103) disposed of sites used for air bases, ordnance plants, and housing projects (69 cu.ft., 1944–51), while the War Assets Administration (RG 270) liquidated Illinois companies engaged in war production, such as the engine plant taken over by the much-publicized failure, the Tucker Automobile Company (50 cu.ft., 1945–51). Among the Records of the U.S. Naval Districts and Shore Establishments (RG 181) are series from the Great Lakes and Glenview training stations (1,298 cu.ft., 1914–57). The National Archives facility in Chicago also retains the files (276 cu.ft., 1946–70) of the Argonne National Laboratory of the Atomic Energy Commission (RG 326).

# CONTRIBUTORS

**Mary Ann Bamberger** is assistant special collections librarian of the University of Illinois at Chicago.

**Laurel G. Bowen**, now university archivist, Georgia State University, was curator of manuscripts of the Illinois State Historical Library from 1977 to 1987.

**Louisa Bowen**, formerly curator of manuscripts, Southern Illinois University at Carbondale, is head of research and special collections of Southern Illinois University at Edwardsville.

**Maynard J. Brichford** is university archivist of the University of Illinois at Urbana-Champaign.

**Margaret Kimball Brown** is site manager, Cahokia Mounds State Historic Site, Illinois Historic Preservation Agency.

**John D. Buenker** is professor of history, University of Wisconsin–Parkside.

**Rand Burnette** is professor of history, MacMurray College.

**Cullom Davis** is professor of history, Sangamon State University.

**Rodney O. Davis** is professor of history, Knox College.

**Perry R. Duis** is associate professor of history, University of Illinois at Chicago.

**Glen A. Gildemeister** is director of the Regional History Center, Northern Illinois University.

**Diana Haskell** is the Lloyd Lewis Curator of Midwest Manuscripts at the Newberry Library.

**John Hoffmann** is librarian of the Illinois Historical Survey, University of Illinois at Urbana-Champaign.

**James Hurt** is professor of English, University of Illinois at Urbana-Champaign.

**Robert W. Johannsen** is the James G. Randall Distinguished Professor of History, University of Illinois at Urbana-Champaign.

**Titus M. Karlowicz** is professor of art, and **Sarah Hanks Karlowicz** is associate professor of music, at Western Illinois University.

**Kevin B. Leonard** is associate university archivist of Northwestern University.

**Frank H. Mackaman**, director of the Gerald R. Ford Library and Museum, was executive director of the Everett McKinley Dirksen Congressional Leadership Research Center from 1978 to 1987.

**Daniel Meyer** is acting curator, Special Collections, University of Chicago.

**Mark A. Plummer** is professor of history, Illinois State University.

**Ralph A. Pugh** is associate curator of manuscripts of the Chicago Historical Society.

**John Y. Simon** is professor of history, Southern Illinois University at Carbondale.

**Ralph A. Stone** is professor of history, emeritus, Sangamon State University.

**Richard S. Taylor** is chief of technical services, Division of Historic Sites, Illinois Historic Preservation Agency.

**Roy C. Turnbaugh, Jr.**, formerly head of Information Services of the Illinois State Archives, is now state archivist of Oregon.

**Timothy Walch**, who served as editor of *Prologue*, 1982–88, is assistant director of the Herbert Hoover Presidential Library. **Victoria Irons Walch**, formerly on the staff of the Illinois State Archives, is an archival consultant.

**Mark Wyman** is professor of history, Illinois State University.

# INDEX

314                                                      Index

Berchtold, Theodore A., 15
Berdahl, Clarence, 274
Bergen, John V., 20
Bergendoff, Conrad, 115, 155, 293
Berghofer, H. J. "Junie," 290
Berglund, Donald Herbert, 186
Bergquist, James M., 64–65
Berkhofer, Robert F., Jr., 44
Berman, Arthur L., 220
Bernardi, Adria, 100
Bernhard, Edgar, 91, 100
Berry, Brian J. L., 121, 139
Berwanger, Eugene H., 69
Bethlehem-Howell Neighborhood Service Or-
    ganization, 246
Better Business Bureau of Metropolitan Chi-
    cago, 235
Better Government Association of Chicago,
    236
Beuckman, Frederick, 157
Beveridge, Albert J., 54, 193
Beveridge, John L., 76
Beverly Farm, 281
Bevier, Isabel, 167
Beyer, Richard L., 4
Bibliographies, 4, 11–12, 29
Bickerdyke, Mary Ann, 70
Bickham, Martin H., 247
Biles, Roger, 99, 104, 138
Billington, Ray A., 44, 50
Billy Graham Center, Wheaton College, 260
Billy Graham Evangelistic Association, 260
Biographical works, 9–10, 29
Birch, B. P., 19
Bird, Harrison, 46
Bird's eye views, 21
Birkbeck, Morris, 50–51, 60–61
Birmingham, Alma, 245
Bishop Hill, 61, 115, 154, 289
Black, Arthur Davenport, 16
Black, Bessie McLaughlin, 16
Black, Carl Ellsworth, 16, 216
Black, Greene Vardiman, 16
Black, John C., 214
Black, Paul V., 80
Black Hawk, 54, 174
Black Hawk War, 50, 54, 212
Black Muslims, 162
Blackburn, Gideon, 146
Blackburn College, 146
Blacks, 17, 25, 27, 69–70, 80, 90, 110, 134,
    139, 162, 166; collections, 207, 208, 238,

299; at fairs, 126, 137. *See also* Slavery.
Blaine, Anita McCormick, 165
Blair, George S., 108
Blair, Harry C., 64
Blair, Virginia K., 187
Blair, William Irvine, 151
Blakemore, William Barnett, 159
Blanchard, Jonathan, 156–57
Blasingham, Emily J., 32
Bloom, Jo Tice, 45
Bloom, Mariesta Dodge Howland, 187
Bloomington, 100, 161, 213, 272, 294
Bloomington Law School, 17
*Bloomington Pantagraph*, 26
Bloomington Public Library, 26
Blout, Frederick, 217
Blout, Katie, 217
*Blue Book of the State of Illinois*, 5, 109
Blue Island, 80
Blue Sky Press, 256
Bluestone, Daniel M., 130
Bluestone, Donald Martin, 60
Blum, Ida, 290
Blumenfeld, Edward Marvin, 150
Bodman family, 271
Body Politic Theatre, 265
Boewe, Charles E., 60
Bogart, Ernest Ludlow, 5, 74, 83, 113, 116,
    273
Boggess, Arthur Clinton, 45, 59
Bogue, Allen G., 57, 78
Bogue, Margaret Beattie, 12, 78
Bohemians, 133, 160
Bohrer, Florence Fifer, 295
Bolles, Blair, 84
Bond, Beverley W., Jr., 45
Bond, Shadrach, 47
Bone, Robert Gehlmann, 144
Bonner, Thomas Neville, 14, 121
Booth, Harry R., 239
Booth, Stephane Elise, 110, 116
Booth-Grunendike family, 292
Bordin, Ruth, 80
Bordman, Gerald, 188
Boris, Eileen, 180
Boritt, Gabor S., 196, 198
Born, Richard A., 181
Bosch, Allan Whitworth, 160
Bossu, Jean-Bernard, 33
Bourbonnais, 114, 258
Bourgmont, Étienne Venyard, Sieur de, 33
Bowe, Augustine, 257